Grassroots Expectations of Democracy and Economy

PITT LATIN AMERICAN STUDIES

Billie R. DeWalt, *General Editor*

G. Reid Andrews, Catherine M. Conaghan, and
Jorge I. Domínguez, *Associate Editors*

GRASSROOTS EXPECTATIONS *of* DEMOCRACY AND ECONOMY

Argentina

in Comparative

Perspective

Nancy R. Powers

University of Pittsburgh Press

Powers, Nancy R. (Nancy Regina)
    Grassroots expectations of democracy and economy: Argentina in
comparative perspective / Nancy R. Powers.
        p. cm.—(Pitt Latin American series)
Includes bibliographical references (p.   ) and index.
    ISBN 0-8229-5745-0 (pbk. : alk. paper)
    1. Democracy—Argentina. 2. Argentina—Politics and government—1983–
3. Argentina—Economic conditions—1983- I. Title.   II. Series.
    JL2081 .P69 2001
    323.3'22'0982—dc21
                                                            00–012589

Contents

List of Tables		vii
List of Figures		ix
List of Abbreviations and Glossary		xi
Acknowledgments		xii
Introduction		1
Chapter 1	Political Views at the Grassroots	13
Chapter 2	The Political and Economic Context	34
Chapter 3	Housing Interests	50
Chapter 4	Material Interests	87
Chapter 5	Coping Materially, Focusing Politically	110
Chapter 6	Political Interests in Context	142
Chapter 7	Perspectives on Democracy	180
Chapter 8	Conclusions	210
Appendix 1	Methodology	241
Appendix 2	Demographic Profile of Persons Interviewed	249
Appendix 3	Political Profile of Persons Interviewed	250
Notes		251
References Cited		271
Index		287

List of Tables

Table 2.1 Poverty in Greater Buenos Aires during the 1970s
and 1980s   40

Table 2.2 Growth, Wages, Inflation, and Unemployment
in Argentina, 1983–1992   42

Table 3.1 Opinions about Home Ownership as Form of
Economic Security   52

Table 4.1 Respondents' Ideas about "Need" by Their Objective
Physical Needs   92

Table 4.2 Sources of Flux and Insecurity   95

Table 4.3 Incidence of Sources of Flux and Insecurity   95

Table 5.1 Coping Strategies Used   130

Table 5.2 Reliance on Coping Strategies   131

Table 5.3 Perceived Coping Capacity by Average Number of Coping
Mechanisms Used   132

Table 5.4 Focus and Perception of Capacity to Cope   134

Table 6.1 Attitudes toward Military, Democracy and Economic
Model by Attitudes toward Aldo Rico   169

Table 7.1 Legitimation Pattern Used by Education Level Attained   190

Table 7.2 View of Military Efficiency by Retrospective View of
Pocketbook, mid-1992   200

Table 7.3 View of Military Efficiency by Retrospective
Sociotropism, mid-1992   201

Table 8.1 Economic and Social Conditions in Argentina,
1991–1999   222

List of Figures

Figure 1.1 The Formation of Political Interests in Relation to
Material Conditions   21

Figure 5.1 Impact of Own Material Interests on Political Interests   135

Figure 5.2 Development of Perceptions about Material Interests   139

Figure 6.1 Median Opinion of Political Leaders among People
Dissatisfied with Menem's Economic Model   171

Figure 6.2 Median Opinion of Corruption Level in Institutions
among People Dissatisfied with Menem's
Economic Model   173

Figure 8.1 Forming a Picture of One's Political Interest   214

Abbreviations and Glossary

ajustes—from ajustar meaning both adjust and fit tightly; the word refers to structural adjustment policies, but has the added connotation of belt-tightening.

ATE—Asociación de Trabajadores del Estado (Association of State Workers), an anti-Menemist trade union

autogolpe—self-coup; describes Peruvian President Alberto Fujimori's closure of the Congress in 1992

Barrio Norte—an elegant and affluent section of the city of Buenos Aires

casa tomada—a building taken over by squatters; also called *casa ocupada* (lit., occupied building)

caudillo—political boss or strongman

changas—odd jobs, such as performed by a handyman

comité—in the Radical Party, the neighborhood-level organizing unit

Conurbano—the urbanized area, encompassing the nineteen counties in the province of Buenos Aires that surround the Federal Capital

conventillo—colloquial term for *inquilinato*, connoting an old, crumbling, noisy tenement building

Federal Capital *(Capital Federal)*—the city of Buenos Aires, which is also the country's capital; it has full representation in Congress and is autonomous from the province of Buenos Aires that surrounds it

FONAVI—Fondo Nacional de Vivienda (Housing Fund of the national government)

FREPASO—Frente del País Solidario (Front for a Solidaristic Country)

hotel—as used in this book, the word refers not to tourist lodgings, but to long-term one-room rentals, known in the United States as SROs (single-room-occupancies).

inquilinato—tenement building (rooming house)

inquilino—tenement renter

IPA—Investigación Sobre Pobreza en Argentina (Study of Argentine Poverty), carried out at end of the Alfonsín government

MAS—Movimiento al Socialismo (Movement toward Socialism)

MODIN—Movimiento de Dignidad e Independencia (Movement for Dignity and Independence)

MOI—Movimiento de Ocupantes e Inquilinos (Squatters and Tenants Movement)

ñoqui—slang for an employee with political connections who is put on the public payroll but not expected to work

Padelai—Patronato de la Infancia; an abandoned state orphanage in the San Telmo neighborhood

PAMBA—Programa Alimentario de la Municipalidad de Buenos Aires (Buenos Aires Municipal Nutrition Program)

la Patria—the Fatherland

PJ—Partido Justicialista; the Justicialist Party, informally known as the Peronist Party

salariazo—a huge payraise, promised in Menem's 1989 campaign

UCeDé—Unión de Centro Democrático (Union of the Democratic Center)

UCR—Unión Cívica Radical (the Radical Party)

Unidad Básica (U.B.)—in the Justicialist Party, the neighborhood-level organizing unit

villa miseria or *villa*—shantytown

villero—a shantytown resident

voting *en blanco*—to submit a blank ballot; meant to demonstrate participation in the process but disapproval of all choices

Acknowledgments

No researcher is self-sufficient—least of all, a foreigner doing field work. I relied on the generosity and the insights of many, many people in order to try to understand Argentine politics and society, to carry out a grassroots-level research design, and to turn the work into a book. It was a privilege to be able to know and work with the people named below, and many others I cannot name here, and I am grateful for their assistance.

Foremost, I thank the Argentines whose interviews form the core of the book for being willing to tell a stranger about their interests and their lives—and to do so at length, despite their many family and work obligations. Unfortunately, I cannot thank any of these people by name because of professional ethics on protecting people who are subjects of research. As the appendix explains in more detail, I use pseudonyms for each one. (Some friends may be curious about my choice of aliases for people who were interviewed. To paraphrase the movies: any resemblance between the person interviewed and real persons of the same name is purely a coincidence—one born, no doubt, of my limited imagination.)

My first visit to Argentina was in 1978. As a student on an exchange program that needed to shelter its charges from troubles, I had little awareness of the country's political situation. Nevertheless, I became fascinated by Argentina, thanks to the kindness of the Saya family, with whom I lived in the beautiful city of Córdoba.

When I next returned to Argentina, it was to begin the doctoral work that became the starting point for this book. I was fortunate to have Scott Mainwaring, Guillermo O'Donnell, the Reverend Timothy Scully, and Roberto DaMatta as intellectual mentors and supportive dissertation committee members. Mainwaring's seminars first inspired my focus on democracy; later as dissertation director, he had a knack for making the right suggestions without damaging either a student's confidence or her independence of thought. O'Donnell's challenging seminar on collective action sparked my curiosity about how material and political interests go together. Of course, the book's attention to citizenship and the quality of democracy further attests to his influence.

To my good fortune, Atilio Boron was the first person I knew in Buenos Aires. He opened numerous doors for me, starting with the one to an office at his research institute, where I found a collegial and intellectually rich place to work. I thank Atilio, as well as Silvia Canela, Eduardo Grüner, Clelia Guiñazú, María Alicia Gutiérrez, Diego Raus, and Tom Sheetz for their many insights, ideas, and leads, and the enjoyable lunches. Lidia Kotas and Merchy Puga provided assistance with the daily problems of research, but most importantly, gave me their friendship. Rut Diamint somehow always found time to make an introduction, answer a question, or have a *cafecito*. I also appreciate Mariel Lucero's efficient research assistance.

For innumerable great conversations about Argentina, for being women of abundant depth and warmth, and for each at one time or another putting a roof over my head, I am grateful to Lindsay DuBois and Ester Kaufman. For their special efforts to welcome me in Buenos Aires and help me move my project forward, I thank Nena Delpino and Luis Pásara. Particular thanks are also owed to Ed Gibson for early help setting up my field work, to Oscar Grillo and José Nun for lending an ear and valuable advice on key decisions, and to Marisa Solari for helping me get my interviews started. I also learned much from Elena Arengo, Angel Barraca, Chris Blake, Ernesto Cabrera, Gregorio Caro Figueroa, Paul Cooney, César Docampo, Vicky Murillo, Norberto Mendez, Lucia Solis, and Andy Tow.

The extensive knowledge of Silvia Agostinis, Enrique Amadasi, Laura Golbert, Gabriela Ippolito, Gabriel Kessler, Judy Lawton, Nestor López, Alberto Minujin, Lucas Rubinich, and Alejandra Oberti taught me a great deal about the sociology of poverty in Argentina.

Sara Gonzalez and Patricio Barbato gave me a warm welcome in their home and great opportunities to listen to their neighbors talk about politics. Patricia Gómez, María José Lubartino, Silvia Natali, and Eduardo Rosenfeld provided valuable introductions to residents of southern Buenos Aires. Edgardo D. Rodriguez took an interest in the questions of a total stranger and helped her arrange several crucial interviews. Nazareno Adami, Eduardo Reese, and Cristina Reynals took time to share their professional expertise. The members of the Movimiento de Ocupantes e Inquilinos opened their meetings to me. Nestor Jeifetz and Daniel Rossi graciously facilitated my work in many ways and shared their knowledge and experience in housing and grassroots politics. The Reverend Arturo de la Cuesta Avila, Juan Carlos Leva, Nélida de Naveiro, and Aldo de Paula and his colleagues at Madre Tierras took an interest in my research and provided opportunities to learn and to meet others. So too did Livio Fort and Américo García, whose contacts and knowledge of neighborhood politics were valuable. The Asociación de Fomento de

Montserrat, including Federico Díaz Barreda and María Julia Marín, were kind enough to include me as a guest at their meetings.

In the course of my field work in Argentina, I was privileged to meet a number of scholars who generously shared their time and insights, influencing my thinking in countless ways. I thank Carlos Altamirano, Florencio Arnaudo, the late Edgardo Catterberg, Marcelo Cavarozzi, Marcela Cerrutti, Maria del Carmen Feijoó, Joaquín Fischerman, Carlos Floria, Florial Forni, the late Emilio Mignone, Beatriz Sarlo, Kathryn Sikkink, María Nieves Tapia, Oscar Terán, Aldo Vacs, and Silvio Waisbord. Special thanks to Manuel Mora y Araujo, for being so forthcoming with his data and his time.

Ana Catalano, Mónica LaMadrid, and Mónica Markwald of the IPSA Audits and Surveys company, Marcelo Rosenberg and Adriana Semorile at INDEC, Nélida Archenti, María Braun, Horacio Fuentes, the late Congressman Simón Lázara, Ricardo Nícora, José Alberto Pietropaolo, Alicia Pose, Rolando Jorge Schneider, María Schwelm, Adolfo Torno, and Eduardo Valenzuela each in different ways took time to answer questions, provide leads, or talk to me about their work.

In planning the book, I benefitted from Evelyne Huber's detailed comments. John Guidry commented on the entire first draft, which was supremely helpful as I began to reframe the argument. Lee Metcalf, Phil Oxhorn, and Denise Powers each gave valuable critique on substantial portions of the work in progress, and warm encouragement too. Kurt Weyland helped me hone my argument through our many debates and he was always available for advice and comments. I was fortunate to have Bill Smith's critique on several occasions. Extensive comments from him and from Aldo Vacs sharpened the final version. I appreciate too the thoughtful input along the way from Carlos Gervasoni, HeeMin Kim, Jeff Mondak, Will Moore, Gerardo Munck, Monte Palmer, and Marco Steenbergen.

Petya Kostadinova provided helpful comments on chapter 8. I thank her and Juan Copa for their reliable research assistance. Steve Shellman was creative and energetic in designing the figures for the book. Jenni Lai tackled, with care and good humor, some tedious word processing tasks. Eileen Kiley, Marlene Allen, and Ann Walston at the University of Pittsburgh Press were knowledgeable, professional, and easy to work with. In short, with all of this brilliance behind me, I am surely responsible for all remaining errors.

I gratefully acknowledge the financial support of the Institute for the Study of World Politics, the College of Social Sciences and the Department of Political Science at Florida State University, and a number of supporters at the University of Notre Dame: the Helen Kellogg Institute for International Studies Seed Money and Dissertation Fellowship programs, a MacArthur Grant from the Institute for Peace Studies, the Zahm Travel fund, and the Department of Government and International Studies. The Department of Government and Law at Lafayette College provided research assistance.

Certain portions of the text have previously appeared in "Coping with Economic Hardship in Argentina: How Material Interests Affect Individuals' Political Interests," *Canadian Journal of Political Science* 32, no. 3: 521–49, and are here used with permission.

Anne Becker, Jean Graham-Jones, Wendy Hunter, Tim Power, and the "CRHP sisters" gave me the encouragement and wise advice of trusted friends. My late cousin, Francesca Sinopoli, and her family made me feel at home during weekends in Ezeiza.

The photography metaphors in this book most likely occurred to me because of my brother Tony. Time and again when we both aim cameras at the same scene, he proves that the quality of a picture depends on much more than the beauty of the object in the viewfinder. I thank my brother Jerry for the encouragement to do this work, and especially my parents, Tom and Jerry Powers, who despite their trepidations allowed me to go to Argentina at age seventeen and have lovingly supported my work, in every possible way, ever since.

I dedicate this book to my husband, John Duffey, for the optimism, amazing meals, humor, and the countless other signs of indefatigable support, and to the memory of my grandmother, Maria LaScala Jannazo—the source of my fascination with languages and cultures—who taught me the value, and who mastered the art, of listening.

Grassroots Expectations of Democracy and Economy

Introduction

Con la democracia, se come.
RAÚL ALFONSÍN, 1983

In late 1983, following a brutal military regime, Raúl Alfonsín of the Radical Party was elected president of Argentina with 52 percent of the vote, in a free and competitive election. An experienced politician and human rights lawyer, Alfonsín faced the challenge of building democratic institutions while revitalizing an economic system in ruins. He was an inspirational orator who argued that the democratic political system provided both freedom and the best means to assure economic progress. "With democracy, people eat," he promised.

By 1989, as the next presidential election took place, the country's debt-ridden economy was in hyperinflation. People were eating less, not more. Food riots broke out in several cities and soup kitchens were set up around the country. Democracy was not providing very well for the population's material needs, and yet the electoral process continued and was supported. Alfonsín's party was thrown out of power, but the democratic regime was not.

The new president was Carlos Menem, a Peronist who had promised a *salariazo* (a huge wage increase), a sound economy, and a "productive revolution" premised on "our absolute priority that every Argentine has a dignified job" (Menem and Duhalde 1989, 19). Six years later, Menem had indeed resolved the inflation problem, but had not delivered the wages, which remained, on average, lower than they had been during the first five years of the Alfonsín administration. While food prices were now stable, jobs had become scarce. The productive revolution had increased productivity, but joblessness reached levels unknown in modern Argentine history. Polls during the 1995 campaign showed 70 percent of the voters considered unemployment the principal issue for the campaign,[1] and yet Menem won reelection even as unemployment soared. Afterward, analysts widely attributed the win to Menem's defeat of inflation four years before.

Why would past achievements against inflation override the apparent failure to solve unemployment problems citizens considered critical in the present? Why would inflation be a decisive issue, but inequality, poverty, and low paychecks not be? To pose answers to these questions requires asking more general ones: What considerations do citizens use in judging their economic goals and the government's performance? How do they balance their economic expectations of government with their nonmaterial ones? If people did not expect democracy to feed them, what *did* they expect of it? To what extent did materialist concerns affect their evaluation of the regime? And when they did not, why not?

Answering those questions for the Argentine case, or similar questions for other societies undergoing rapid economic and political change, requires a finely tuned understanding of citizens' perceived interests, both political and economic. We need to know how those political and economic interests are interrelated, and how political and economic contexts affect the perception of interests. This book examines the material concerns of those who objectively have considerable material hardships—the less affluent members of society—and analyzes the relationship between those material concerns and their political views. I argue that to understand how people's material interests affect their political views, we first need to understand how they think about their material interests. Perceptions about material interests are shaped by objective material conditions, access to mechanisms for coping with those conditions, and expectations about what conditions and coping mechanisms are normal in their society and their lives. Only once we understand these perceptions about material conditions can we begin to understand how those conditions influence people's ideas about what they want from the political system.

Research Method

This study uses inductive methods and qualitative data to examine the relationship between perceived material and political interests. This relationship is explored through interviews with people of low to modest means in Argentina. Argentina had experienced dramatic transformations in the years just before this research. Both the political and economic systems continued to evolve rapidly, providing a case in which politics *and* economics could be ex-

pected to be highly salient to nonelites. The country has a long history of populism and redistributive conflicts that incapacitated and then destroyed its
democratic regimes. This history of materially based grassroots politics, combined with the dynamic policy and political environment of the early 1990s,
provided an ideal situation for observing the interaction between material and
political interests at the grassroots level.

The heart of the data is a set of lengthy informal interviews with forty-one
people, primarily during the first half of 1992.[2] (In further fieldwork in 1995, I
was able to follow up with about one-quarter of those originally interviewed.)
In order to understand fully the living conditions of those interviewed and the
political and economic contexts of their lives, I included in the fieldwork observations of meetings of grassroots organizations, church groups, political
parties, a public employees' labor union, and neighborhood groups, as well as
eighteen brief preliminary interviews in two lower–middle class neighborhoods of Buenos Aires. In addition, I interviewed over seventy political elites
during fieldwork in 1990 and again in 1991–1992 and 1995. These included
scholars, social workers, journalists, community organizers, elected officials,
neighborhood party leaders, and social policy makers, among others. These
interviews provided essential political, social, and cultural background, and a
comparative perspective through which to consider the views heard at the
grassroots. The appendices provide substantial details on the interview
methodology, background information about those interviewed, and discussion of the specific goals of a qualitative research design.

Qualitative methods and fieldwork are powerful means to discover unan-
ticipated relationships and to reframe basic questions. As an example, I should
say that I did not start out to write a book on interests. The initial research
proposal presupposed that people would be either materialistic, opposing politics that failed to serve their material interests, or idealistic, ignoring their material interests. Only in the field—by listening, observing, questioning, and
then by reformulating my listening, observation, and questions in light of new
insights—did I gradually realize that the question was not whether people
thought materialistically or idealistically. Rather, the questions are: How do
people think about material problems in their lives? How do they think about
politics? And how, if at all, do they connect those two things?

Grassroots-level fieldwork was an inextricable part of the process of finetuning questions as well as finding answers. The concepts emphasized in this
book—coping, subsidiarity, identities, contexts—differ from the concepts emphasized in works based on studying electoral outcomes or opinion surveys.
The concepts here are those that arose in citizens' own discourse rather than
those that citizens chose under conditions structured by others, such as voting

or polling. The concepts derive directly from hearing how people explained their lives and their political views. Fieldwork, and in particular, qualitative interviewing, is not merely a method of data collection but a process of discovering what the right questions are. The frequent and lengthy excerpts from qualitative interviews, which appear throughout this book, are intended to enable readers to hear and understand the complexities of the interests of the governed.

Why Study Nonelites?

The last twenty years have been a period of vast economic and political change in the world, with democracies emerging, or reemerging, throughout Latin America; in southern, eastern, and central Europe; and parts of Africa and Asia. The change in political regime often took place amidst significant economic turmoil caused by foreign debts, inflation, and stagnant production. Consequently, democratization was accompanied by dramatic economic changes. Concurrent with the establishment of electoral processes and political rights, economies shifted away from state-led development and inward-focused industrialization toward market economies based on export-oriented production and a diminished role for the state.

The democracy literature is replete with analysis of the relationships between these economic and political changes, but primarily at the national and elite levels.[3] Research has focused on the economy and elections at national levels, as well as on the political parties, domestic and international financial communities, and bureaucrats who affect the state's economic and social policies (Baloyra 1987; Diamond, Linz, and Lipset 1989; Haggard and Kaufman 1995; Mainwaring and Scully 1995; Nun and Portantiero 1987; O'Donnell, Schmitter, and Whitehead 1986; Remmer 1991, 1996; Sabato and Cavarozzi 1984). Not coincidentally, the focus on elites and institutions complements the procedural conceptions of democracy generally employed in these works. Democracies are understood as legally instituted processes that protect citizens' civil and political rights while assuring free and fair competition for leadership (Dahl 1989; Schmitter and Karl 1991). Starting from that definition, researchers naturally focused on elites, since they were the ones who engaged in competition for leadership or who had the potential to undermine citizens' rights.

If democracies emerge and survive due to competitions and decisions among elites, then why research nonelites? In particular, why bother to understand the ideas of the politically weak, the economically less affluent, and the less-organized members of society?

The first reason for studying nonelites is that the political and electoral

rights inherent in democratic processes are founded on assumptions of equality of citizenship (O'Donnell 1998). That means that weak citizens in a
democracy have a claim on the political system equal to the claims of more politically powerful citizens and institutions. Therefore, the study of common
citizens' views about how politics affects them will reveal something about the
quality of the democracy. If we take democratic processes seriously, including
their foundations in universal citizenship, then we must take seriously the political ideas and reasoning of nonelite citizens. This is a normative concern,
but also an empirical one. Empirically, paying attention to the views of
nonelites expands the narrow academic purview of what is politically meaningful. As Daphne Patai puts it eloquently, "There are no pointless lives, and
there are no pointless life stories. There are only life stories we have not (yet)
bothered to consider" (1988, 1). Political life involves not merely the means to
power, but the consequences of the pursuit and use of power. Therefore, if political science is to provide a complete account of political life, it should
"bother to consider" the impact that political competitions and policy decisions have upon the governed. Recent literature has studied that impact in
terms of the objective effects of policies and the accountability of the powerful
to the electorate. Largely missing from the literature is research on how people
who are not in positions of power perceive and evaluate the effects of policies
and political practices.

A second reason for studying the views of nonelites is that, as James Scott
(1985) recognized with his pioneering work on the "weapons of the weak,"
those who are excluded from the institutions of power are nevertheless not
irrelevant to political life, at either the regime or government levels. Nonelites
are not the necessary and sufficient actors to either sustain or bring down
regimes (Remmer 1991, 615), but nonelites create numerous interaction
effects. They influence political life as consumers, as their plight captures the
attention of more powerful actors (such as journalists or the Catholic Church,
who advocate for the poor), and as part of the public support upon which
politicians stake their strategies and policy choices.[4] Recognizing these forms
of influence compels us to understand more about consumers, voters, and potential supporters of policies and politicians. For example, we need to understand whether the poor and the working class in Argentina share in the
criticisms made on their behalf by small parties of the left, intellectual critics,
and the progressive wing of the Catholic Church hierarchy.

The third reason to listen to how those without power understand and
evaluate the conditions in which they live is that such understanding is the
basis of future economic development. As Jorge Lawton (1995, 22–31) re-
minds us, the "people-centered" development called for by the United Nations
Development Program (UNDP) will only occur if the people "below" are full

participants in their own development. The only way to pursue development at the grassroots level is to take seriously the views of those at the grassroots.

A fourth reason to understand the views from the grassroots is that, while nonelites are relatively powerless compared to elites, the aggregate of their views *does* have political clout. In countries where voting is mandatory and turnout is high, such as Argentina, the lower classes have proportionately more electoral clout than they do in the United States, and politicians must seek their support actively. Understanding the methods by which individuals evaluate the political and economic conditions around them can help us understand the components of aggregated public opinion.

Why Study Individuals?

On the issue of aggregating individual views, a few clarifications are needed. One way, beyond voting, in which nonelites have political clout is through social movements. There is a rich literature on these movements. Portions of that literature are discussed throughout this book when they speak to the question of how participation in movements affects citizens' opinion formation. The focus of my research, however, was deliberately on individuals' thinking, not on their collective activities. The individual, not the collective, is the citizen—the building block of a democratic society—and so starting from a concern with democratic citizenship, for reasons explained above, I am interested in the views of individuals. This premise is somewhat at odds with that of some leading scholars of social movements, who insist that the individual participants' attitudes do not matter: "We are convinced that movements are not aggregations of discontented *individuals*. . . . Collective action is a profoundly *collective* phenomenon" (McAdam, McCarthy, and Zald 1988, 709). No doubt, collective movements involve organizational and social dynamics that make them *more* than the aggregation of dissatisfied individuals, but nevertheless, those movements must appeal to, as well as develop, the interests, reasoning, and identities of individuals, who are potential new participants and followers. This book examines those perceived interests, patterns of reasoning, and identities. Since one goal of the movements is to *change* citizens' perceived interests, patterns of reasoning, and identities, this book also pays attention to the sources of the individuals' thinking, their potential for developing collective identities, and, in chapter 3, to a potential obstacle to that goal.

In short, to assume that individual views have political relevance—both as motivators of various kinds of political activity, and as indicators of the quality of the democracy for its less privileged citizens—does not deny the separate importance of collective action. Most political behavior (beyond the erratic and ill-conceived) reflects thinking: about one's interests, about how those interests might be achieved, about how political processes work, and what politicians' actions mean, etc. This thinking is the focus of the book. Without denying the importance of collective action as a fundamental phenomenon of grassroots politics, this book examines a different fundamental phenomenon, the views of the individual who may or may not be connected to any organized political activity, but who is affected by public policy and regime behavior.

An individual has the opportunity to respond to public policy and regime behavior in a variety of ways. As Dietz (1998, 14–19) has emphasized, these can be formal, such as voting or joining a political party, or informal, such as debating with neighbors, speaking out in the press, joining in neighborhood organizations or social movements, participating in demonstrations, or rioting. The individual may also respond by abstaining from any and all of the above. Some of these political responses involve collective action and others do not, but all have political ramifications. These responses differ, and *qua* behaviors need to be studied separately to understand the structural and contextual factors that determine the levels and kinds of public actions or inactions toward governments; however, by understanding how individuals think about their political interests, as I seek to do with this book, we have the building block for understanding the behavior that follows.

Advancing Democratic Theory

The starting point for my study of nonelites was the rich literature on the poor of Latin America, which attempts to explain citizens' perspectives by identifying the ideologies, identities, rational choices, and socialization that shape attitudes and actions. Much of that literature was written before the democratic transitions period, at a time when very different political and economic ideas and structures prevailed.[5] Today, we need research that considers the views of citizens in the political and economic contexts of the "posttransitions" period.

Specifically, research on nonelites provides theoretical underpinnings for recent empirical observations. One of those observations has to do with the durability of posttransition democratic regimes in Latin America. Scholars widely expected that regime legitimation would suffer if the regime's economic performance were poor. During the regime consolidation phase, Karl (1990, 40) argued, democracies must "demonstrate that they are better than their predecessors at resolving fundamental social and economic problems" (also see Diamond 1992, 487). In a similar vein, Angell (1993, 566) warned that "in

Latin America, given the poverty and worsening income inequalities associated with the military regimes, it is important that the newly restored democracies demonstrate real concern with the needs of the poor, otherwise the
long-term legitimisation (*sic*) of democracy will suffer." Haggard and Kaufman
(1995, 334, 325) argued that over the long term, a democracy will not be able
to maintain support from elites or masses without growth, which "can reduce
the frustrations and conflicts resulting from inequality or other social cleav-
ages, and thus can mute the tendency to political alienation and destabilizing
social violence." Przeworski (1991, 189) wrote that "the durability of the new
democracies will depend . . . to a large extent on their economic performance."
Contrary to these expectations, democratic regimes have managed to survive
poor economic performances across Latin America.[6]

One way of explaining these democratic survivals is to emphasize the importance of elite support for democracy. Remmer (1991, 793–94) argued that in
the 1980s, an elite consensus in favor of democracy (and in favor of economic
change) prevented the emergence of viable antiregime alternatives in Latin
America, even in the face of poor economic performances. Others have
pointed out that organized labor—the most likely political opposition to the
austerity policies favored by other elites—did not pose a serious threat either
to the elite consensus or to democracy itself (Geddes 1995, 204–6). Following
years of military repression, labor was both politically weak and leery of any
nondemocratic "solutions" to their concerns. The "elite support" argument
makes sense. Given that intraelite conflicts led to the breakdowns of democracy in the 1970s (Linz 1978), policy consensus among elites would have facilitated democratic stability in the 1980s and 1990s.

Yet elite behavior is not the full story. Mass publics have also supported
democracy. For example, a 1996 survey found that even while Latin Americans have not been particularly pleased with the quality of the democracy in
practice, most preferred democracy to any alternatives.[7] In even greater numbers, survey respondents expressed willingness to defend democracy against
alternatives. Lagos (1997, 134–35) offers two possible explanations for the
preference for democracy being smaller than the willingness to defend it. One
is that the survey question about defending democracy was misinterpreted as
asking about willingness to defend the country. Another is that those who prefer some other regime may nevertheless be "benefitting from the current situation in their country and therefore, even if not altogether satisfied, might well
be willing to defend it." Part of my reason for writing this book was to dig
more deeply into this relationship between satisfaction with a regime, benefits
from the regime, and support for the regime. In particular, I explore the extent
to which dissatisfactions with the regime are rooted in economic conditions

and I explain the thinking of citizens who support democracy even though they are not satisfied with its practices and appear not to have benefitted economically under its tutelage.

A second way to explain the survival of democracy during hard times is to question the underlying assumption that a regime—that is, a system for governing—would be judged by citizens on the basis of its economic performance (Tironi 1989). After examining electoral outcomes during periods of economic crisis, Remmer (1991) questioned the notion that newer democracies were uniquely fragile and concluded that they did not have to prove themselves by economic performance to any greater degree than long-established democracies. Linz and Stepan (1989, 55–56; 1996, 76–81 and 439–44) argued that citizens could distinguish government effectiveness from regime effectiveness. Because democracy allows citizens to hold an incumbent *government* responsible for its economic performance, they tend not, at least in the medium run, to reject an otherwise valued democratic *regime*, on the basis of poor economic conditions.

These explanations beg many questions about how citizens understand and evaluate regimes. How, precisely, do citizens balance their materialist goals with other expectations of government? If citizens do not expect democracies to provide them with better material lives, then what *do* they expect of them? Through the in-depth study of grassroots political thinking, this book answers these kinds of questions and so provides an underpinning for the explanations of democracy's survival that have been offered by scholars of elite-level behavior.

The second empirical finding that calls for more theoretical underpinning occurs at the level of government, rather than regime. The finding is that neoliberal economic policies did not engender as much grassroots opposition (either in the form of support for opposition parties or in public protests and demonstrations) as had been expected. Governments who made clear that their priorities were to satisfy foreign investors and creditors, while they restrained organized labor, eliminated consumer subsidies, laid off public employees, raised sales and services taxes, or ignored growing inequality nevertheless won support among the popular sectors. Summarizing the political economy literature, Geddes (1995) concluded that democratic governments can get away with imposing painful economic policies because they have faced relatively weak opposition from citizens hurt by the policies. Indeed, neoliberals such as Peruvian President Alberto Fujimori and Argentine President Menem received substantial and reiterated support from poorer and lower middle-class citizens, despite implementing policies at odds with the ones on which they had first campaigned.

How can we explain the weak opposition? Part of the explanation is that national economic policies affect the popular sectors in diverse ways, making concerted opposition less likely. Nelson (1992) described these differential impacts at a macroeconomic level. In chapters 3 and 4 of this book, I explore them at the microlevel of households.

A further explanation for weak opposition is that the popular sectors benefit more from neoliberalism (particularly from monetary stabilization plans) than its critics had anticipated (Rodrik 1994, 79–80). Nelson (1992) suggested that popular sectors want policy competence and will support governments that inspire confidence in a better economic future for them, even if those sectors have seen little improvement in the present. Weyland (1998b) used prospect theory to fine tune this explanation. He argued that citizens will "swallow the bitter pill" of neoliberal reform, when conditions are so bad that continuing with the status quo is more painful than taking the austerity "pill." These explanations focus on the contextual factors and elite behaviors that individuals at the mass level consider in determining their position toward their government.

Initial research at the mass level has also focused on the national context in which citizens evaluate their economic positions. Stokes (1996) pointed to psychological expectations, such as optimism or pessimism about future economic conditions, which are rooted in the public's reading of economic and political contexts. In a study of the 1993 Polish elections, Denise Powers and James Cox (1997) found that historical context explained why citizens did not prefer the communists, whose platform appealed to their personal economic concerns.

All of this literature highlights certain elite-created contexts in which citizens would evaluate elite-created economic policies. I too find elite-created contexts essential to understanding responses at the grassroots. So I examine a comprehensive spectrum of contextual factors that affect how people interpret their political interests. Yet I also show that contexts are only part of an explanation for citizens' views, because individual members of society are not simply objects reacting to elite-created circumstances. First of all, people bring to those contexts objective material conditions. Their capacity to cope with material hardships without help from the state will depend upon the type of hardships faced and the resources and assets available, both through their own household and through their local community. Secondly, social and partisan identities will affect how people interpret national contexts. Thirdly, people have differing ways of interpreting the world around them—that is, they read contexts in different ways. These different interpretations fall into identifiable patterns. In sum, by examining contexts in conjunction with individual-level factors, I am able to show *why* people respond to contextual circumstances as they do. The result is a comprehensive explanation of how nonelites with economic concerns respond to what political elites are offering.

Organization of the Book

The first two chapters provide the theoretical and empirical background needed to understand the substantive research examined in later chapters. Chapter 1 gives a more detailed introduction to the arguments of the book. It begins with findings from two in-depth interviews from the fieldwork, which illustrate contrasting ways that people with severe material needs might think about politics. In both cases, a politically-active citizen ignores the relationship between national policies and his own difficult living conditions. The interviews serve to illustrate the central question for the book—what causes people to perceive or not perceive a relationship between government actions and their own lives (what I call the micro-macro linkage)? The rest of the chapter stakes out my position within the diverse literatures that attempt to theorize micro-macro linkages and their absence. I set forth an argument for the subjective conceptualization of interests and for analyzing material interests prior to political interests.

Chapter 2 provides a brief economic and political history. It demonstrates that the economic hardships faced by Argentines in the 1990s had developed over a long period of time—an empirical point that later in the book will become important theoretically. For readers unfamiliar with recent Argentine affairs, this chapter also introduces the players, conditions, and contexts to which reference is made later.

The next three chapters develop the argument about material interests. In these chapters, I dissect the experience of economic hardship in the lives and conversations of those interviewed, in order to explore how people understand their material concerns and how those concerns are taken into account (or not) as they think about the larger world of politics. Chapter 3 is a case study of a particular type of material hardship—deficient housing. It shows the complexities of housing interests, the political and nonpolitical measures that people take to try to improve their shelter, and the reasons why an objective material hardship, such as deficient housing, does not tend to be perceived as a political interest. Chapter 4 builds on findings from the housing case in order to analyze the nature of material interests more generally. I argue that people perceive their material interests not in terms of needs or quantities of possessions, but in terms of eliminating the stress, the exclusion, the constraints on opportunities, and the constraints on choice, which result from their particular material conditions. Chapter 5 outlines a three-part typology of individuals' responses to the material conditions that constrain them. It then describes the measures that people take to cope with their material constraints, analyzes the political implications of a perceived "capacity to cope," and discusses the contextual factors that shape perceived coping capacity.

Chapters 6 and 7 are about political interests. Chapter 6 discusses perceived interests in terms of the government and its policies. It shows Argentines defining their political interests with the help of partisan and class identities and in the context of historical, economic, and political experiences. These identities and contexts shape their expectations and judgments about the past, present, and future. Chapter 7 explores how people think about their interests as they consider the democratic regime. It explains the extent to which, and the reasons why, democracy is valued in Argentina. Chapter 8 puts the findings of the earlier chapters into a comprehensive framework for understanding grassroots political thinking. It then examines the usefulness of this framework for explaining observations beyond the set of interviews and finds that the explanation holds up over time in Argentina, as well as in other cases of Latin America and Eastern Europe.

r

Chapter

1

Political Views at the Grassroots

This book analyzes how nonelites view their political interests. In particular, it explores whether and how they perceive their personal material interests to be "part of the picture" of their political interests. The method of analysis is inductive, meaning that the conclusions emerge from the process of seeking to make a coherent whole out of data collected through field interviews and observations. Through that inductive process I found, metaphorically speaking, that some Argentines looked at politics through a zoom lens, narrowing in on problems of personal interest, while others used a panoramic camera, examining the broad national picture with little regard for their place in it. Put differently, the former focus on that which is "micro," while the latter focus on the "macro." Still others link micro and macrolevels; that is, they put themselves in the picture, viewing their individual lives as part of, and affected by, the political and policy landscape.

A brief presentation of two of the people interviewed for this book will serve both to illustrate these concepts and to introduce the fieldwork from which they emerged. I'll call them Eduardo and Jorge. They lived about two miles apart in the central southern area of Buenos Aires, Argentina. Both middle-aged men were gracious and outgoing, with visible affection for their wives and children. Our dialogue was easy. In Eduardo's case, we had two long conversations at his home, totaling nearly five hours. In Jorge's case, we talked on a single evening, after having been introduced on an earlier occasion. Each had substantial experience as a political activist, Eduardo in the Peronist party and Jorge through a housing rights movement. The material conditions in which they lived were similar: each had been a squatter since the early days of the democratic transition, living in a dilapidated building, owned but abandoned by the state. Their one-room homes were crowded and the buildings were structurally unsafe. Jorge's income was more substantial and steady than Eduardo's. He was a skilled laborer and his wife was employed in hotel housekeeping, while Eduardo and his wife were unemployed and depended largely on his doing odd jobs and on some assistance from neighborhood party leaders.

Jorge's perspective on politics was "micro." Like a photographer with a zoom lens, when he thought about politics, he focused on his housing situation. He had once been embarrassed by his living conditions. Then he began to see them as an affront to his human right to a home, which he could fight, rather than as a burden to be borne. He and his neighbors engaged in a multiyear struggle to legalize their tenancy, eventually winning approval from the municipal government.[1] In the process, Jorge became a savvy political activist, meeting with politicians and helping to organize protest marches.

For many months, Jorge worked constantly on his community's housing struggle. In that sense, politics was part of his everyday life. Yet he said he was completely uninterested in any political issue other than housing. His declared lack of interest was corroborated by two hours of conversation, during which he mentioned no political opinions beyond concern for other people needing housing. His thinking about his own and others' housing interest was particular and narrowly focused; that is, he did not put his material interest in housing into a larger ideological or social context about the purpose of government, the goals of public policy, or the conditions of the working class. Jorge and his neighbors won their victory by arguing for a specific group of people needing housing in a particular piece of city property. Although he understood poverty as a problem experienced widely in society and he thought this an injustice, his approach to poverty was to beat it by focusing on microlevel possibilities, not macrosocial change. He did not see his family trapped by macrolevel social structures. Rather, he believed that with him as a hardworking role model and his children's diligence in studying, they could make their way in the world.

Eduardo's view of his own situation and of politics was quite different. He was not actively engaged in changing his material conditions. He expressed bitterness about the age discrimination he encountered in his job search and was too proud to have his wife do domestic work to support them. He and his wife María Elena were both self-conscious about where they lived, defending their single-room home in an abandoned school building as "being just the same as if we were in an apartment, just a little bit older" and volunteering that "we don't have any cholera here," thanks to adequate bathrooms. The objective reality, however, was that the deteriorated building was dangerous. Their own daughter had died in a fall through a broken balustrade in the hallway.

Eduardo's discourse about politics differed from Jorge's in every respect. He was conversant with national politics and largely discussed politics in the "macro" terms of national-level parties, leaders, and policies. Where Jorge focused on the microlevel lives of individuals and on efforts to improve their conditions, largely ignoring the wider social and political factors affecting individual lives, Eduardo directed his personal frustrations toward macrolevel social conditions that he found ugly and uncontrollable. He identified himself as "poor," but was clearly uncomfortable talking about his own needs. Even the tragic story of his young daughter's death—a death indirectly due to her poverty—came up only in the context of a diatribe against a society without sufficient opportunities and without solidarity among fellow citizens. Thinking about his problems in a wide social context, he was stymied by the odds against him and apparently could not admit the immediate and individual-level need for structurally safe housing so that tragic accidents would not recur. Eduardo perceived socioeconomic issues, *in general,* as public and political problems, but he understood his particular standard of living as a malaise for which he saw neither a public nor a private solution, and thus it was not a focus of his attention when he thought about political problems.[2]

Whereas Jorge expected that by studying hard and following his good example his children would succeed, Eduardo felt helpless about, rather than responsible for, his fate and his children's. In discussing social and economic conditions, he focused upon the macrolevel forces that affect individuals' lives. So, for example, he wanted Argentine industry to be protected from foreign competition and Argentine poor people to be saved from drugs, AIDS, and a life of crime. While he saw his partisan political activities as a means to win assistance for himself from neighborhood Peronist leaders, he was deeply discouraged that such help had not been constant and substantial enough to make any difference in his life prospects. Even so, he did not focus on these microlevel political ties when he discussed politics, nor did he abandon his lifelong partisan loyalties when they failed to improve his standard of living. His political loyalties were based on the party's overall performance and macrosocial identity, not the microlevel effects on his family.

In sum, neither man perceived Argentine politics as specifically relevant to his immediate personal experiences in poverty. For personal material needs (or any other individual-level concern) to affect political thinking, the micro and macro levels must be linked together—that is, the microlevel interests must be seen as affected by macrolevel decisions.[3] As long as people remain either microfocused or macrofocused, their personal material interests and their understanding of national politics remain independent. In contrast, when people link microlevel interests with macrolevel politics, then their perceived material interests become their perceived political ones.

Rethinking Interests

This point becomes clearer if we first rethink the underlying concept. "Interests" is a ubiquitous term in political science and public discourse, yet it is used inconsistently. Marxism viewed interests as observable *material* circumstances and presumed that *political* interests are simply material interests properly understood. In practice if not theory, the liberal view that politics is about "who gets what, when, and why" also implies a material basis for political interests. Throughout the discipline, as well as in everyday political discourse, "interest" is often used as a catch-all term to describe the desires of some actor or collective, usually with the implication that such desires are observable and known, even though often they are not. Such usage makes it difficult to distinguish nonpolitical interests from political ones or to think about the relationship *between* material interests and political ones.

In this book, *interests* are subjective and constitute an evaluation of what one wants. (As such, interests precede political behaviors, including demands, votes, expressions of opinion, or protests.) The term is used only to refer to wants that a person might feasibly pursue—thus, wanting to take a trip to the moon or wanting to become a billionaire do not, for most people, constitute *interests*, as understood here.[4] *Material interests* refers to subjective judgments about the material conditions one wants. The term *material* includes both money and the physical conditions (health, shelter, security, comfort) and consumption (clothing, food, appliances, vacations, luxuries, and conveniences) that money buys. Because this definition of interests is based on subjective wants, two people who squat in the same dilapidated building may have quite different material interests, since one might be eager to find a safer dwelling while another is preoccupied with finding a job and satisfied with a rent-free residence. *Political interests*, as used here, means subjective judgments or beliefs about what one wants (or does not want) from government or from the political process. If two people hold the same material interest in finding safe, inexpensive housing, but one hopes that the government will pass new laws to foment construction while the other perceives no connection between law or policy and the availability of affordable housing, then the former has a *political interest* in low-cost housing while the latter does not.[5]

My goal is to understand the process by which people think that the material things they want in life are ones that they want the political process to attempt to provide. By defining interests subjectively, I make no presumptions about what an informed or politically "conscious" person would seek from their government. For example, I do not presume that ameliorating poverty or bridging the inequality gap should be (or should not be) the chief political interest of a poor person.

The complexity of political interests can be better understood by first looking at an "easy" case, where it seems safe to presume political interests on the basis of objective conditions. Consider first an elite actor with a defined political role. This is a case where interests might seem objectively obvious. The goals and priorities of such actors—their interests—may be safely presumed on the basis of the roles in which they find themselves. It can be safely assumed, for example, that political campaign managers are interested in winning votes for their candidates or that military strategists are interested in winning battles while minimizing loss of personnel. They are hired to fulfill those goals, not to question them. In comparison, the interests that common citizens have vis à vis their governments are both more numerous and less clearly defined. Even where we can safely presume certain desires exist, we cannot presume how citizens will think about those desires as they develop their political views, nor how they will perceive those desires to have been met in the political arena.

Consider now the case of a working class woman in Buenos Aires. She engages in a variety of activities—listening to a television news program, reading a campaign poster, discussing politics with relatives, and voting—to which she brings her goals about public affairs. Yet her goals will be less specifically defined or tightly constrained than those of the campaign manager or military strategist. We might, of course, make some safe presumptions about things that she and citizens like her would find desirable for a government to produce: prosperity for the country and themselves; improved educational and housing opportunities for their families; less arbitrary use of force by the police, but more effective law enforcement to stop crime and drug trafficking; faster and better care at the public hospitals; stability in the democratic regime; a secure retirement; and peace in the streets and at the borders. These are all material desires; that is, they affect her physical well-being in one way or another. She will also have nonmaterial desires, such as for justice, privacy, identity, and other normative goals. One reason for not conceptualizing interests "objectively" is that interests include these normative and emotive concerns that cannot be safely presumed. Yet even if we put those aside and focused only on the safe-to-assume goals for physical well-being, our assumptions would run into problems when the interests conflict. Fiscal and political realities make it unlikely that a single political candidate or public policy path would attempt to address all of a person's material goals. Furthermore, the vast intertwined array of institutions and policies involved in reaching any of the goals means that, not infrequently, the policies designed to meet them might be mutually contradictory. For example, the goal of protecting borders might involve giving the military more resources and authority, while the goal of regime stability is threatened by military autonomy. Creating technologically advanced hospitals and schools might require spending levels that strain the state's capacity to meet its debt obligations, which must be met to reach the goal of overall prosperity, and so on. We cannot safely assume how people sort out their multiple and conflicting interests.

One way to find out about the subjective priorities among multiple interests is to ask. Public opinion polls frequently ask people to rank order a list of policy goals. This kind of questioning will reveal what is on people's minds but not why it is on their minds.[6] Some surveys also ask respondents to listen to two opinion statements (each exemplifying a different core value, such as equality versus liberty) and choose the one that is closest to their own beliefs. Questions that pose abstract choices are useful in mapping a country's "political culture"—the prevailing values of the people—but they do not get us very far in evaluating the concrete choices that people would make when confronted with competing values and conflicting goals during times of economic and political change.

In order to understand those choices, we need to know not merely *what* people think their various interests are but *why* they think as they do. *What* is on people's minds is a subjective matter, but *why* it is on their minds can, to a great extent, be explained—that is, it has observable causes.[7] So while I conceptualize interests subjectively, I seek to understand the objective conditions that would shape those subjective perceptions. Notice that I do not, therefore, perceive citizens' political views as relatively fixed but rather as dynamic responses to the many interests that they perceive to be at stake if the state acts or neglects to act in certain ways.

Individuals evaluate what is at stake politically in light of the feasibility that their concern might be addressed through state action, the feasibility of addressing it without state action, and the perceived urgency of the concern or interest. Thus, for example, urgency (or lack thereof) may cause a rearranging of priorities. People might, in the abstract, value democracy more highly than prosperity and yet, quite rationally, support a political party with a stronger record on prosperity than on democracy if prosperity seemed to be at stake in the election but democracy were not. At the same time, politics affects whether or not people are aware of the mutual incompatibility of their many interests. Adroit politicians work hard to keep citizens unaware of such incompatibility by promising all things to all people so that the ballot choices may not appear to encompass trade-offs among competing interests.

Likewise, feasibility is a consideration as people think about how their interests might be affected by politics or attainable through the public sphere. Feasibility is evaluated based on the historical records, political alliances, and ideological leanings of the available alternative contenders to power (e.g., the parties, the military), as well as on the particular international and economic *contexts* in which politicians compete and policies are made. As Eckstein (1989, 4) put it, "what individuals consider their self-interest can only be understood in the context of broader social and cultural forces" and, I would add, political ones.

Finally, the evaluation of feasibility and urgency derives from subjective and objective views about subsidiarity (that is, the best level at which a problem can be resolved) and about the objective capacity to cope with a problem sans assistance from the state. In other words, whether a personal (microlevel) interest is perceived as a priority when a person considers national politics depends in part on whether it can be met in nonpolitical and subnational ways. For example, a citizen might prefer that the government increase pensions, provide low-cost loans for housing, or spend more money on vocational schools but at the same time *expect* that the government would do none of these things. The citizen might expect the normal course of events would require that he or she find individual-level means to provide for a better pension, an affordable home, and skills-training. If indeed there are individual-level ways to cope with these interests (even if not to maximize them) and the person perceives this individual-level coping on these matters as normal, the person would not hold the government accountable for not providing the desired policies.

In sum, citizens desire a great many material and nonmaterial things but the desires do not constitute the *political* interests that would inform political behaviors such as voting, debate, or activism. The making and prioritizing of political interests out of multiple and often contradictory material and normative desires are complex processes. This book explores those complexities as it explains how nonelite members of society evaluate their political interests during periods of dramatic economic and political change and personal material hardship.

It should be emphasized that the focus of this research is the political thinking of people who may or may not understand their material conditions to be caused or improvable by political processes. The formation of their political interests, then, is a different process from that, say, of the affluent and politically-connected actor who lobbies for (or against) a tax law, regulatory change, or government concession that would directly affect personal or business profits. Those actors take for granted that there is a link between macrolevel decisions and their microlevel gain or loss. They also have feasible means of accessing the elites who make the decisions that could yield enormous material benefits (or threaten existing gains). This is not a study of those political interests. Instead, it is a study of the thinking of people for whom the link between national level political decisions and their lives is an open question. These are people whose feasible political activities—voting, expressing opinions to friends, co-workers, or the occasional pollster or journalist, working with grassroots organizations, joining a public demonstration, helping out at a local-level political party with campaign activities, and such—do not offer efficient means to get government to take direct action for their personal benefit. When these people look at national political competitions and the actions of their governments, it is not necessarily clear to them how or whether political decisions will have a meaningful impact on their personal material conditions. It is an open question whether and when these nonelites perceive their difficult material conditions as priorities to be ameliorated or improved through the world of politics.

A Picture of the Argument

Figure 1.1 sketches the major components of the argument that will be developed over the course of the book. To understand the sketch, it may be helpful to return to the camera analogy used at the start of this chapter.[8] Two photographers facing the same object will often produce completely different pictures because of differences in how the object strikes the photographer and how the photographer focuses the camera. Also, even photographers with the same perspective on the object and using the same camera focus will produce different pictures when lighting conditions or lens filters change the context in which the object is viewed. When individuals picture their political interests, a similar process occurs. Particular material conditions affect individuals in particular ways, which may or may not seem to call for political solutions. So they focus on those conditions and/or on something else within their view. The contexts of history, economics, and politics enlighten, color, and provide background to their perspective.

This process begins at the left side of figure 1.1, which shows that objective *material conditions* affect the possibilities for an individual to cope with those conditions without government action. *Expectations* about what level of living is normal and acceptable will shape the person's perceptions of coping capacity. When nonelites perceive particular material conditions as expected ones and see themselves as capable of coping with those conditions, then they tend to pursue those material interests without government help. That is, those material interests do not become political interests. Some people facing certain conditions take a *microfocus*, like Jorge, and seldom consider the meaning of national politics to their lives. Others use a *macrofocus*, like Eduardo, who was concerned about political affairs but focused only on social or national issues. On the other hand, if nonelites perceive certain material conditions as unusually onerous, or their capacity to cope as inadequate, then they will pursue those material interests through politics. That is, they will tend to focus on the *link between their microlevel material conditions and macrolevel politics.*

The focus of a person's political attention is merely the beginning of the process of forming a picture of political interests. Once a person is focused, he or she needs to determine which of the political interests under focus are priorities—and doing so will involve considerations of personal values as well as of the feasibility of the alternatives in the political arena. Feasibility will be assessed in the *contexts* of historical experience, the national economy, and the competition among political elites.

On Linking Material and Political Interests: Theoretical Approaches

The argument depicted in figure 1.1 and elaborated upon over the course of this book attempts a more comprehensive explanation of grassroots-level political interests than existing literatures. The impact of material conditions

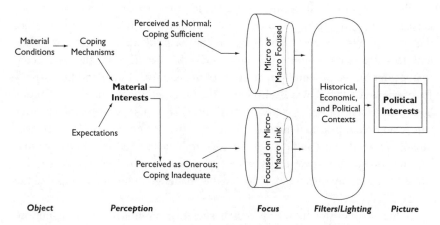

Figure 1.1. The Formation of Political Interests in Relation to Material Conditions

upon political views has been a subject of study in political science for some time, but unfortunately the divergent literatures have often talked past one another. Early research by Easton (1965, 70–116) and Dahl (1971, 95–104) examined the cultural and psychological conditions under which individuals' personal material interests would come to be perceived as matters of political interest (and then expressed as political demands). Over the next three decades, social science research began to emphasize, in addition, structural and political factors affecting the micro-to-macro linkage. The literature diverged in numerous ways so that today at least three distinct bodies of work—on public opinion and economic voting, on social movements, and on populism—all deal in some way with the questions of if, when, and how material interests are linked to political ones in grassroots-level political views.[9] These literatures do not, however, reach any consensus. On the contrary, each uses such different levels of analysis, methods, and normative assumptions that they exist side by side in social science, seemingly unaware of their sometimes contradictory approaches and conclusions on the question of how material and political interests are related.[10] Moreover, they leave important questions begging: about when individual-level grievances become matters of political interest and how nonmaterial political interests interplay with material ones in the development of political viewpoints. This book is designed to address those questions, even as it starts from the existing accounts of grassroots-level political thinking. To begin, I will examine those accounts and the problems they leave unresolved.

Does the Pocketbook Shape Political Views?

Public opinion and voting research finds that personal ideology (and/or partisanship) is the strongest predictor of political viewpoint, but to the extent that individuals evaluate politicians on the basis of material concerns they look less at personal conditions (their "pocketbooks") than at the overall economic conditions, past and prospective, of the country (Eulau and Lewis-Beck 1985; Kiewiet 1983; Lewis-Beck 1988). The latter, nonpocketbook perspective is termed "sociotropic." *Ceteris paribus* voters with a sociotropic perspective who experience personal material hardships while the country experiences prosperity would vote in favor of the government that had presided over that national prosperity. Sociotropes who experience personal economic success while the economy sags would vote for the challenger who might improve the national economy.[11]

Some work in this literature depicts sociotropism not merely as common, but logical and well-informed. This work starts from the assumption that the economic question facing a voter is the sociotrope's question: *How is the government managing the national economy?*[12] It concludes then that pocketbook voting results when a person lacks the information needed to make sociotropic judgments. For example, Weatherford (1983, 161–67) sees voters as "information processors" who fall back on their own pocketbooks as indicators of governing capacity when they lack, or are unable to make sense of, national-level information. Goren (1997) claims that more knowledgeable voters are better able to judge national economic conditions and therefore are most frequent users of sociotropic judgments as the basis for voting decisions. These researchers argue that sociotropic voting, at least in the countries where they have studied it, is salutary, because it is unlikely that the condition of one's pocketbook, if it differs from the condition of the nation overall, reflects the competence of a national leader (Goren 1997, 406; Kinder and Kiewiet 1979, 523, quoted in Weatherford 1983, 160; Weatherford 1983, 160–161). In other words, when survey respondents say their personal economic conditions are poor while the nation is doing well, they are assumed to be people whose pocketbooks are hurting from individual-level circumstances, such as a divorce, new dependents, illness, or personal failures. Working from cases of affluent liberal democracies, such research makes the classical liberal assumption that an individual's fortunes are independent of society or government policy. "The logical relationship between family finances and how the president is doing is . . . a leap," according to Mondak, Mutz, and Huckfeldt (1996, 253; also see 254–55).

If the only relevant question is how does the national government manage the country as a whole (or its economy), then it is a truism that an individual's personal circumstances (and pocketbook) are poor anecdotal sources of information upon which to evaluate national-level management. Yet democratic citizenship implies a broader question. From the perspective of a citizen seeking a representative government and not merely an economic manager, the overarching question may be: *Does the government govern on my behalf?*[13] That is, does it work for my interests?

Some research has argued that where individuals perceive a clear responsibility of government for their personal conditions, then pocketbook voting is more likely. This attribution of blame might occur where mediating institutions make the linkage clear, or where the microlevel impact of a policy shift is quite strong, such as perceived by a recipient of government benefits, when the benefits are changed (Feldman 1982, Feldman 1985, 154–59; Powell and Whitten 1993). In a recent book, Mutz (1998, 159–75) portrays pocketbook voting not as illogical but as the product of media interpretation of macrolevel conditions. Where microlevel conditions parallel macrolevel ones, she sees the

media as a means to intensify individuals' identification of their personal interests with political affairs. On the other hand, where microlevel experiences
differ from the media reports of macrolevel conditions, the media becomes an
obstacle to micro-macro linking, because it convinces people that their conditions are idiosyncratic. The literatures that look to the causes of linkage thinking are more persuasive than those that presume such linkages are irrelevant.
Rather than seeing pocketbook voters as people focused on microlevel affairs
because they are uninformed about macrolevel ones, this literature pays some
attention to identifying the contexts and the types of interests that might facilitate the perception of a micro-macro connection.

One reason that much of the literature on economic voting and public
opinion reduces the citizen's concern to choosing a good national manager,
rather than choosing a government to govern on one's behalf, is that it takes
citizens' interests for granted. Sociotropic or pocketbook voters are all presumed to be narrowly self-interested, merely using different sources of information to judge their self interests.[14] What precisely those interests *are* is not
explored. By focusing on the information sources people use to make judgments about how the government governs the nation, this literature tends to
conflate people's interests with their information about those interests.[15] Yet
while perceptions of personal interests are certainly influenced by information
(Mutz 1998, 147), they cannot be reduced to, nor fully explained by, information.[16] The literature that focuses on sources of information about government
performance (whether the pocketbook, neighborhood, class, or nation) and
on the quality of information that people receive begs the questions of what
people *want* from government (that is, what they judge to be beneficial economic performance or harmful performance), how relevant they expect government to be to their lives, and what experiences, assumptions, or identities
shape how they interpret the information they get. These questions have to do
with the formation of their interests.

Of course, it is clearly in most citizens' enlightened self-interest that the government manages the national economy well, as Kiewiet (1983, 132) pointed
out. Yet while successful macroeconomic management is generally a necessary
condition for a government that works on someone's behalf, it is certainly not a
sufficient one. The U.S. case, from which so much of the sociotropism literature derives, is a good example of this. The Clinton administration was widely
praised for managing the economy well, and even the poor benefitted to the extent that the unemployment rate reached record lows. Poverty levels dropped
during the 1990s. Yet low or middle income citizens seeking more affordable
housing or health insurance did not find that the administration succeeded on
behalf of those interests. Those interested in diminishing inequality likewise

found that the prosperity brought a growing gap between the most affluent citizens and the least.[17] So if the democratic citizen's question is, *Does government work on my behalf?* then we need to know what people consider to be "acting on their behalf." We need to know what their interests are, and *then* we need to know whether they see a link between those interests and politics.

Governing on one's behalf is not merely a matter of positively affecting *material* interests. Most citizens have multiple interests they wish to see the government address. These include managing the national economy well but might also consist of "pocketbook" concerns such as low taxes, affordable health care, or preventing a plant closure that would leave the person unemployed; altruistic social concerns, such as the welfare of children and the elderly; noneconomic, national-level concerns, such as national security or the environment; and noneconomic concerns affecting their personal security and welfare as well as that of other citizens, such as the human rights record of the police or the efficiency of the tax collection services. This means that a person's pocketbook is more than merely a (poor) source of *information* about how the government performs at the national level; it also constitutes *one* of several interests that the person might plausibly, and intelligently, wish for a representative government to serve.

In countries undergoing economic development and democratization, it is often painfully obvious that if the government mismanages the economy, it is not working on one's behalf. In situations where family finances are wiped out overnight by hyperinflation or devaluation, personal finances are directly and overtly affected by public leaders. In those cases, it could be argued that the sociotropic judgment overlapped with the pocketbook judgment, both leading the individual to judge the government as not performing well, for the country or for the individual.[18] Yet an individual's life may also be affected by the government in a way that is not universally experienced across the economy. Again, in the developing world these effects may be painfully apparent, as, for example, when a fiscal crisis of the state delays paychecks to public employees and pensioners for months at a time.

Often, however, connections between government policies and an individual's well-being are direct, yet not convergent with national-level macroeconomic indicators and not clearly apparent.[19] For example, a person having trouble finding a job may not understand that high unemployment levels were caused by government regulations designed to slow inflation by slowing growth. Or a young adult might see chances for upward mobility cut off by the out-of-pocket costs of public education yet unless mobilized by student organizers might not attribute those costs to the fiscal decisions of debt-strapped public officials. Or tax and lending policies might favor upscale development and discourage construction of affordable housing, yet the average consumer unable to find a home would not perceive the connection from tax and lending policy to housing scarcity unless the connection had been made into a political issue. In cases like these, the linear relationship between government policy and individual hardship may be strong but not obvious in the absence of some interpretive assistance from political actors. These actors are not limited to the media. Since the media's explanations are often both selective and superficial, the mere fact that they provide information about the nationwide extent of a problem does not mean that they have served to open citizens' eyes to the *linkage* between public policy and their lives, in the way that social movements (see below) and other political actors aspire to do.[20]

The Social Movements Perspective

In most developing countries, governments have historically worked on behalf of the few, not the many. Much of political conflict in the twentieth century involved populist parties, revolutionary groups, and social movements that arose in the name of the many to take on the few—and the opposition they faced. Given this context, it is perhaps not surprising that the research on formation of political interests found in the Latin American social movements literature differs strikingly from that in the sociotropism literatures just discussed.

Social movements frequently organize with the goal of bringing public attention to the connections between national policy and individual-level economic circumstances, so that people will learn to recognize when national-level policies are not working on their behalf. Scholarship on these movements seeks to understand the conditions under which citizens perceive those connections and act upon them. Studies of social movements among Latin America's poor find that successful grassroots mobilization occurs where political organizers, policies, or parties have led people to see those connections and to hold political leaders accountable for the material conditions in their own lives and neighborhoods (Cornelius 1974, 1131–134).[21] Only certain types of grassroots organizations draw those connections and hold leaders accountable (Castells 1983, 194; Stokes 1995). In the absence of such "consciousness raising," people are susceptible to clientelist means of politicizing their personal material needs. From the perspective of this literature, if the national economy thrives while some social sectors remain in poverty, then it is *not* salutary that the poor would be "sociotropes," ignoring their personal experience and rewarding an incumbent for successfully managing the national economy. Rather, through civic education and organization, individuals would learn to see the consequences that national-level policy decisions have upon individual lives and to assert themselves, as citizens, to demand that the government enact policies that better their lives and those of people like them (Freire 1974; Mainwaring 1987, 148–50; Stokes 1995).

Studies of new social movements look at information as a means by which people focus upon and define their interests. In contrast to those public opinion studies that see information and political awareness as means to depoliticize personal experience, social movement studies see political awareness and access to information as potentially creating a *greater* sense of connection between personal experience and the world of politics. Whether that potential is reached depends on a variety of factors that shape the information people receive and how they interpret it (see Eckstein 1989). In other words, whether people see connections between political issues and their personal lives depends not merely on whether they are knowledgeable about national news,[22] but on *how* the issues are portrayed in the news and by political actors. Grassroots organizations try to show citizens the connections that the news coverage of a national political debate or campaign might gloss over. By this reasoning, the expectation that government has an impact on individual lives is an ideological and political one, not an illogical one.[23] If citizens do not expect the government to improve their own lives it may be simply because no credible actors in the political arena—politicians, social movements, nor media—have suggested ways by which government *could* address their personal-level material conditions. From the social movement vantage point, a sociotropic perspective results not from political sophistication but from particular political contexts that fail to politicize personal-level interests. For example, in the U.S. context (in which much of the public opinion literature is written), the two major parties do not propose radical changes that would significantly improve the lives of individuals with substantial material needs. Within this narrow ideological context, it may *appear* that the president's policies do not affect an individual's material welfare simply because no alternative candidate proposes policies to affect the individual's welfare differently. If more radical alternatives existed in the party system, then voters could indeed hold a president accountable for failure to see his job as more expansive than simply managing the economic status quo. In multiparty contexts, with many small parties of the left and right, citizens more often have the option to vote their dissatisfaction with the economic system overall—that is, in effect, to hold the incumbent accountable for not spearheading radical change to improve life at the grassroots.

In sum, leaders of social movements deliberately set out to discourage sociotropic thinking and to encourage the linking of the personal and the political as a means to encourage an awareness that politics matters to daily life. The social movements literature tends to focus on organizers' capacities to educate citizens about micro-macro linkages. This is an important step forward from the economic voting literature, but it is insufficient. In this book, I show that whether a person links personal material interests with perceived interests in national political affairs has to do not simply with exposure to political agents who encourage such linking but also with the particularities of their microlevel interests and of the national political context. By focusing not on the behavior of social movements but on the interests around which they organize, I help explain why raising awareness of micro-macro linkages is so notoriously difficult. Furthermore, chapter 3 examines closely the assumptions in the social movements literature about how political participation might engender micro-macro linking. It shows how politicization may occur without real consciousness raising. That is, it describes the identities and strategies through which people might become politicized about some interests in their lives without ever becoming aware of the broad links between national politics and their material interests. More broadly, over the course of this book, I build a general framework for understanding all kinds of thinking about political interests, both that of people exposed to social movements and that of the majority who are not.

Populism

Studies of populism offer a third approach to examining grassroots-level politics, albeit one focused on a particular variant. The populism literature is largely concerned with analyzing the macrolevel contexts on the far right side of figure 1.1 rather than the entire process depicted there.[24] The political reasoning of individuals facing such contexts, which is examined in detail in this book (depicted in the "perception" and "focus" portions of the figure), is only indirectly considered in most of the populism literature.

Populist leadership is typically defined as personalistic, charismatic, top-down, antiestablishment, nationalistic, and supported by a socially heterogenous constituency.[25] The literature traces the emergence of populism to macrolevel economic and social changes. Classic populism was linked to the early- to mid-twentieth century switch from an economy controlled by agrarian exporters to an import substitution industrialization model that fomented urbanization (Ianni 1975; O'Donnell 1979; Weffort 1976). More recent appearances of populism have been traced to times of economic crisis, which enabled leaders to convince voters to try neoliberalism (Roberts 1995; Weyland 1996). By describing these as top-down phenomena, occurring in particular macrolevel contexts that allow a leader to mobilize support against other elites, the literature on populism largely ignores the populace. Its level of analysis is designed to talk about the populist's acquisition and use of power, not about citizens' reasons for supporting (or not supporting) a populist.[26]

For example, the influential literature on classical populism, rooted in the neomarxist analysis common in Latin American social science in the 1970s, discussed grassroots interests merely in terms of the assumed interests of social classes. According to that literature, because populism was based on an alliance of many classes, it caused confusion among subaltern sectors about their real class interests (Ianni 1975, 130–33; Weffort 1976). These scholars assumed that interests are objective things that can be inferred from social class—an unpersuasive position, for reasons outlined earlier.

Other populism scholarship has emphasized political rather than class structures. It finds that when traditional elites and civil society are weak or intensely divided, they leave space for a populist to establish unmediated links to followers (Hennessy 1969, 31; Oxhorn 1994, 60–61; Roberts 1995; Weyland 1996, 13–14, and 1999, 17–21; Worsley 1969, 246).[27] Put differently, the leader is able to obtain a mass following because of a particular political context (which the populist may well have helped to create).[28]

Because the populism literature is focused on the economic and political conditions in which populism arises, it is relatively silent about the thinking of populists' adherents. Nevertheless, some inferences are evident. The literature strongly implies that people's interests are primarily in material goods, including economic security and inclusion. Indeed Ianni (1980, 130) argued that most followers of populists were more interested in economic and social mobility than in democracy. The literature frequently describes populists garnering political support by distributing material benefits in a clientelistic fashion, while not ceding to the people real political influence (Castro Rea, Ducatenzeiler and Faucher 1992; Hennessy 1969, 35 and 53; Roberts 1995, 88–91). Classical populists won supporters through state-funded material payoffs (public sector jobs; higher wages; generous social policies; new schools, sewers, and health clinics). More recent populists faced fiscal and structural constraints on state spending, but nevertheless sought to create material benefits for their constituencies by lowering inflation, targeting social programs to the very poor, and stimulating demand (Palermo 1998; Roberts 1995, esp. 88–91; Weyland 1996, 19–21). Some literature has noted that populists win support by making people feel *included* or by gutsy policies that attempt to bring people out of conditions of great material loss and anxiety (Di Tella 1965; Madsen and Snow 1991; Weyland 1996, 10 and 20–21; and 1998b). In sum, although the literature on populism puts relatively little attention on the reasoning at the base, much of it has implied that people are attracted to the security of paternalistic relationships and that they favor leaders who provide them with material benefits or at least provide material goods to people *like* them (as opposed to benefitting traditionally powerful sectors). So, rather differently from the economic voting literature, the populism literature describes the popular sectors as strongly motivated by personal material interests rather than interest in the national-level economy. Furthermore, according to much of the work on populism, the followers of populists do not possess an informed view of the link between their pocketbooks and national policies. Despite scholars' observation that they are largely disempowered by the politician's tactics, the scholarship portrays followers of populism as simply happy to be included, at last, in some small way, in the political system.

In my fieldwork for this book I found that political attitudes and loyalties were seldom linked to material benefits in *quid pro quo* fashion, but they were indeed rooted in desires for inclusion and security. In chapters 4 and 5 I discuss at length how material inclusion and security affect the perception of interests. These chapters bring to political analysis the rich literature on poverty and inequality found in other areas of social science. This provides a theoretical grounding for the unexplored implication, found throughout the populism literature, that material inclusion is a significant political interest to nonelites. These chapters also examine closely the nature of material interests. Much of the populism literature treats all material benefits as equally desired, as if the popular sectors are undiscriminatingly acquisitive. No distinction is made between spending on schools, food programs, job training, or public housing, or policies to create higher wages, lower inflation, or more jobs. Any kind of materialist interest served by a public policy is used as evidence of a "populist" tactic, if the policies result from a top-down decision rather than a process of pluralist competition. While such decisions may well have "populist" intent on the elite actor's part, we cannot assume that they are indeed popular decisions capable of producing political support for that actor. For example, in 1999, the Republican majority in the U.S. Congress proposed nearly $800 billion in tax cuts but the proposal sparked little public support and was vetoed with apparently little fear of repercussions for the president's party. The Republican politicians seemed to have presumed voters would be intent on maximizing their disposable income while polls showed Americans put a priority on other interests. The politicians in Congress had failed to recognize that people have multiple interests and are not simply pocketbook maximizers.[29] In this book, I emphasize that the heterogeneity of material conditions that exists even among people of seemingly similar social status means there exists a great diversity of material *interests* among them, and thus a great diversity in the types of material benefits that they would consider to be matters of political interest.

On the specific case of Argentina, my research shows that the literature on populism, by analyzing recent Argentine politics from the perspective of national-level political and economic contexts, has partly misinterpreted the Menem period. Recent literature has described Argentine President Menem as following different policies from classical populists (such as Perón) yet employing populist tactics, such as undermining organizations of civil society (Roberts 1995, 111) and seeming to take on the business and political establishments and to foster the social inclusion of the poor (Weyland 1996, 15 and 19–20). Although Menem showed populist traits in his campaign style and in his efforts to subordinate labor and party organizations, many of his actions toward the popular sectors, and the reasons people supported him, cannot be well described as populist.[30] As I will argue in chapter 6, Menem's support among the lower classes relied heavily upon preexisting party identification.[31] Perón had employed a typical populist message—that is, one designed to include the common person, in opposition to the privileged, establishment enemy. Populists have been observed to retain their reputations long after ceasing to provide substantial benefits to the lower classes (Drake 1982, 236) and in Perón's case, he established his party's identification as antiestablishment. Those interviewed who supported Menem did so because they identified with Peronism and *in spite* of Menem's rather unpopulist behavior, which included neoliberal policies that were perceived as favoring business and political elites, a reputation for cozy relationships with the business establishment, and repeated public denials that poverty was a problem. As many scholars have pointed out, by fighting inflation, Menem clearly benefitted the lower classes; yet low inflation also benefitted the nation generally. When it came to policies specifically benefitting the popular sectors, he showed very little interest until midway through his first term, after more than three years of being criticized for his social policies. Then, and throughout his ten years in office, his approach to helping the unorganized poor was largely reactive, not proactive (Powers 1995, 111–12). So in a number of ways, Menem's behavior was not consistent with the behavior the literature expects of a populist. Indeed, by and large, the reaction to Menem among those interviewed was *not* a positive response to populist tactics. Among those interviewed were non-Peronists who associated Menem with the demagoguery of his predecessor Perón—but these did not approve of the populism they perceived. Also interviewed were disenchanted Peronists who perceived Menem as favoring the establishment over the poor—that is, of neglecting to follow Perón's populist path. Few of those interviewed perceived Menem behaving in ways scholars associate with populism *and* also approved of that behavior, and those few who did were people who had been attracted by Peronism's populist themes before they associated Menem with them.

A Comprehensive and Bottom-Up Alternative

In summary, most discussions of populism imply (without thoroughly examining the individual-level process) that personal economic interests strongly affect citizens' political positions. The sociotropism literature argues that personal economic conditions do not tend to affect political views (either because the connections between public policy and individual lives are irrelevant or because the media or the political context make it difficult for voters to attribute responsibility to the government for their conditions). By focusing on sociotropic judgments, and often proclaiming them to be the only sophisticated or relevant ones, this literature minimizes the kind of micro-macro linking that the social movements literature finds most significant for social progress and a quality democracy. Research on new social movements suggests that personal economic conditions do not affect political views *until* local organizers, parties, or politicians demonstrate for citizens the numerous connections between public policies and private conditions.

Given these divergent and incomplete theoretical perspectives, further research is warranted. The existing literatures do not employ a level and method of analysis that enable individuals to describe their economic concerns, their political interests, and any connections they indeed perceive between them. This book provides that analysis. It examines the grassroots through its component parts: the individuals who live and act in society. I do this not from a commitment to methodological individualism nor from a denial of the importance of collective organization to the empowerment of nonelites but rather because there is a need for research on the experience of those who live in societies undergoing democratic and economic change. This approach differs from studies of populism and of public opinion, which examine mass behavior but often analyze that behavior from the perspective of what it means for the political power of elites. Public opinion studies focus on the ways that the public receives or rejects messages from elites and studies of populism examine the rise of populist leaders in a political context of weak alternatives.[32] The new social movements literature uses a comparatively more "bottom-up" approach but it focuses on the collective organization of grassroots actors and the possibilities for collective action to make demands upon elites (cf. Cardoso 1989; Gay 1993; Jelin 1987).[33] (Here, I consider cases where political relationships and involvements shape citizens' views, but I also analyze the views of people without such relational ties.) In short, all three literatures are interested in the views of individuals primarily to the extent that those views indicate mass-level support or opposition to political elites. Those three literatures also seek to identify societal-level forces or conditions (e.g., the media, the leadership of grassroots organizations, direct clientelist ties to a populist, or changes in economic conditions) that would bring grassroots actors to perceive their interests in one way or another. In my argument, societal conditions limit the *options* individuals perceive as feasible and desirable, but individual-level conditions determine how the citizen grapples with those options. Thus, I show political interests to be a product of both contextual and individual-level conditions. The individual citizen is neither a lone agent of will and desire nor a mere product of structural or political conditioning.

The key to my argument is that in order to understand the connections or lack of connections that people make between their material conditions and their political views, we first need to examine the conditions themselves and how people live with them. The public opinion literature tries to explain pocketbook or sociotropic voting on the basis of citizens' knowledge of politics and perceptions of conditions in their group or community, the populist literature examines the strategies and tactics of populist leaders, and the social movements literature focuses on collective organization around existing "grievances."[34] All of these explanations focus only on the politicization side of the equation—they largely take the "grievances" as given. They discuss the political reasons why some grievances cause political reactions but other grievances do not, but they ignore the material reasons. I argue that to understand why some people would vote for a politician who ended inflation but oversaw the biggest increase in joblessness in history requires understanding something about how people live with inflation and how they live with joblessness. To make sense of the political views of people undergoing material hardships requires first understanding their views about the hardships they experience. So, while the contexts of political views are examined at some length (in chapters 6 and 7), this book begins (after discussing the political and economic contexts of the Argentine case, in chapter 2) by analyzing how people who objectively have material "grievances" perceive their material interests (chapters 3 through 5).

Chapter

2

The Political and Economic Context

> *The loss of the money isn't even the important thing. The important problem is that you can never recoup what was lost. If you have a car that you have to sell because it's too expensive to own, you won't be able to get to the point of being able to afford a car again.*
>
> MARÍA JOSÉ, clerical worker

As the wife of an officer in the armed forces, María José was, for most of her life, accustomed to a comfortable middle-class lifestyle. As she told her story, in 1986, she sold her second home, which had been purchased as a hedge against inflation. The financial markets crashed the following day and her just-liquidated life savings lost about 75 percent of their value overnight. From that point on, María José's economic condition steadily declined. Six years later, over seventy years old and widowed, she was working in a clerical job and sharing a home with her daughter and granddaughter. The daughter was educated and employed, so the family was not living in poverty, yet they lived without comforts they had taken for granted before the economic crisis hit their home.

María José's words quoted above underscore the consequence of years of economic crisis in Argentina: a lasting decrease in living standards for millions of citizens. This decline began under the military regime and can be blamed in part on the indebtedness that regime bequeathed to the country. Yet the experience of decline largely took place on democracy's "watch." The diminished possibility for upward mobility, both for those who had fallen into poverty and for the millions who were born into it, meant that the vast majority of Argentine citizens faced difficult and uncertain times as they approached the second consecutive decade of democratic rule in their country.

This chapter examines briefly the political and economic history of Argentina that brought María José and millions like her to conditions of loss, material insecurity, or poverty. It describes the Argentine economic policies, material conditions, and political actors and events with which readers need to be familiar in order to understand fully the interviews and analysis in later chapters. It should be noted that this chapter is about the conditions prior to and at the time of the field research because those conditions are the pertinent reference points for the interviews. Chapter 8 analyzes later changes in economic and political context through early 2000.

Regime Changes and Democratic Development

Argentina has not enjoyed a strong history of democracy. Although the country had a stable, constitutional regime from 1862 to 1916, the de facto electorate was so small and the elections so fraudulent that it could not be called democratic. Political power was controlled by the landowning, financial, and emerging manufacturing elites. In 1912, universal male suffrage and cleaner election rules were enacted, enabling the Radical Civic Union Party (known by its Spanish acronym, UCR) to win the presidency four years later. The Radicals won in a populist campaign that united the urban and rural middle classes with portions of the agrarian and business elites.[1] The new period of inclusive politics was short-lived, however. The Conservative Party, unaccustomed to sharing power and frightened by populism, retook power through a military coup in 1930. For the next fifty-three years, Argentine politics would fluctuate between civilian and military governments as various sectors of society played out a fierce competition for power. This competition was exacerbated by social and economic changes taking place as the economy was transformed, starting in the 1930s, by import substitution industrialization (ISI).[2]

Starting in the mid-1940s, the power struggle would revolve around Peronism. Juan Domingo Perón was a junior participant in a military coup that toppled the Conservatives in 1943. Appointed to the previously minor post of Secretary of Labor and Social Security, he recognized the political potential of the growing urban working class and feared their potential mobilization by socialists. He empowered the labor movement, by legalizing collective bargaining and the right to strike, and yet he manipulated the movement by limiting those rights to unions that received official government recognition.[3] Perón was elected president in 1946 and again in 1951, although the second competition was less free and fair than the first.[4]

Perón's policy legacy was substantial, including paid maternity leaves, annual bonuses and paid vacations for all workers, improved working conditions, compensation for injuries, severance pay, and labor courts.[5] These benefits and protections, together with the sense of dignity and empowerment that Perón and his wife Evita created by incorporating the working class into Argentine politics, built a loyalty base for Peronism among the working class and the poor.

Import substitution policies created Perón's base of support. The expansion of the public and manufacturing sectors meant growth in the working class. Controls on prices and exchange rates benefitted urban consumers. ISI was financed by the agricultural sector (which was required to sell its products, at below-market prices, to the state) creating disincentives to production in this critical export sector.

Perón's policies were not sustainable, politically or economically.[6] By 1949, the economy was in crisis for a number of external and internal reasons, including a severe downturn in the terms of trade and deleterious agricultural policies. By this time, Perón had not only alienated the agrarian elites who had been accustomed to ruling the country, but he also was losing support among industrialists who, despite benefitting from his ISI policies, resented the state's regulatory and prolabor stances. With the economy in severe crisis, Perón was forced to back away from the high-wage, low-prices policies that favored his urban base. As political opposition grew, it was repressed with censorship, harassment, and imprisonment.

In 1955, the military responded by a coup that was supported across a wide spectrum of Argentine society, including the Radical Party and the Catholic Church. Soon after the coup, General Pedro Aramburu emerged as president and instituted policies to repress Peronism.[7] Constitutional government was restored by 1958, but the eighteen-year period between Perón's overthrow and his third election in 1973 was politically turbulent. Electoral participation by Perón's Justicialist Party (PJ) was proscribed or restricted, and the Radicals, who were permitted to win elections, were twice deposed by military coups.[8] The political and economic conflicts that had led to Perón's ouster remained unresolved.[9] The quest for economic development and social progress was stymied by chronic inflation and, increasingly, foreign debt. Politically, tensions grew among traditional Peronists, who sought to regain the political and economic status enjoyed in the mid-1940s, the left-wing Peronists, who sought to radicalize Perón's social agenda in line with the revolutionary tenor across the globe in the 1960s, and others of the center and right, who not only wanted to avoid the agendas of the left and of the labor movement but also wanted to move away from the ISI model of development.[10]

The 1960s and 1970s were periods of substantial political violence in Argentina. Guerrilla organizations, inspired by the Cuban Revolution, had emerged in the early 1960s but were largely suppressed. By the end of the decade, however, several new groups had organized. Some identified themselves as Peronists; others eschewed Peronism's populist and reformist past and sought to follow the revolutionary path of Che Guevara. The groups announced themselves with dramatic and violent actions that shocked the public, including an attack on a military base in 1969; the kidnapping and execution of a former authoritarian president, General Aramburu, in 1970; and, also in that year, the military occupation of a small city (Hodges 1988, 49–68). Tactical and retaliatory violence continued into the 1970s. Guerrilla groups killed military and business leaders as well as labor union leaders and also robbed banks and kidnapped for ransom. In response, right-wing death squads emerged, with apparent links to the federal police. The most notorious death squad, the Argentine Anti-Communist Alliance (Triple-A), announced in 1974 lists of "subversives" and "sympathizers," who were subsequently targeted for death—including academics, artists, politicians, and journalists (Rock 1987, 360; Hodges 1988, 77 and 121–23). By late 1974, the government declared a state of siege to authorize the military to suppress the armed left (Rock 1987, 364).

Previous to these last developments, Perón had returned from exile in 1973 and been elected president. When he died a few months later, his third wife, Isabel, became president. Completely unprepared for governance, Isabel Perón was unable to control an economy suffering from hyperinflation, a nation torn by political violence, or a Peronist movement deeply divided into ideologically-distant factions. In March 1976 she was deposed by a junta of the three armed services.

The bureaucratic-authoritarian regime that took power in 1976 extended the military's repression in a "dirty war"—actually, a systematic attempt to destroy not only the armed guerrillas, but all of the political left as well as Peronism's organizational base in the labor movement (Pion-Berlin and Lopez 1991; McSherry 1997, 86–90; and Munck 1998, esp. 65–69). Estimates of the number of people "disappeared" by the state (i.e., kidnapped and murdered) range from 9,000 to 30,000. Additionally, some 30,000 were imprisoned and 500,000 went into exile.[11]

The repression of organized labor and other political opponents was part of what the new regime called a "Process of National Reorganization," or *El*

Proceso. Repression facilitated implementation of the regime's economic strategy, which was designed to stabilize prices and restructure the economy, while destroying the ISI model under which organized labor had achieved political power. The new liberal policies included tariff reductions, lower wages, higher taxes and public sector prices, reduced state subsidies to manufacturers, and the elimination of taxes on agricultural exports. The result was dramatic deindustrialization, a permanent deterioration of real wages compared to the Peronist years, and an upward redistribution of wealth.[12] Public protests in 1982 daringly demanded economic relief for workers hard-pressed by inflation and plant closings. The government responded by diverting the public's attention through a military attack on the British-controlled Falkland (Malvinas) Islands.

In light of its economic performance and embarrassing defeat in the Falklands/Malvinas war, the military called elections in 1983. The Peronists had never lost a presidential election in which they had been allowed to present a candidate, so many observers were surprised when the Radical Party's Raúl Alfonsín won the election with a 12 percent margin of victory over his primary competitor from the PJ.[13] Alfonsín promised to improve the economy, but his first project, clearest objective, and greatest success were in making the transition to democracy last. A powerful orator, he called for a new commitment to democratic principles. He also pursued a campaign promise to hold the military accountable for human rights abuses under the previous regime. The National Commission on Disappeared Persons, which he appointed, documented the circumstances under which 8,961 people had disappeared (CONADEP 1986). In 1984–85, civilian courts tried the nine officers who had comprised the ruling juntas during the authoritarian regime, finding five guilty of various charges from rape and torture to murder. Lower ranking officers were not punished. In the wake of two barracks uprisings, Congress had enacted laws to put a time limit on the initiation of new prosecutions and to prevent prosecution of officers below the rank of colonel, on the grounds that they had merely followed orders.[14] The media covered CONADEP's lengthy hearings, its report called *Nunca Más* (Never Again), and the trials of the junta leaders, thereby documenting for the public the scope and brutality of the repression.

The democratic regime took another step forward in 1989, when an election was held on schedule and presidential power was transferred from the Radical Party to the Justicialist Party. The new president, Carlos Menem, implemented dramatic changes in the economy and improved civil-military relations. Despite polls showing overwhelming public opposition, Menem pardoned the five military officers imprisoned for human rights abuses, saying pardons were needed for national reconciliation. While using the pardons to reduce military antagonism toward civilian leaders, Menem was able to further the project of professionalization Alfonsín had started. He sold military real estate and industries, ended conscription, cut force size and consolidated units, and changed the recruitment, education, and promotion conditions of officers with the goal of promoting a military culture that would be less detached from civilian life and more supportive of democracy (Zagorski 1994).

The democratic regime had lasted nearly a decade by the time of the interviews analyzed in this book. Fears of a military coup had subsided and politics based on inter- and intraparty competition was becoming the norm. The democratic institutions were not, however, all functioning to check and balance each other as intended by law, nor were civil rights well protected (see O'Donnell 1994; 1996). High-level corruption scandals had become commonplace, and abuse of authority by the police was widespread. Under President Menem, the courts, particularly the Supreme Court, became subservient to the executive branch (Larkins 1998). Moreover, despite laws that make voting obligatory, electoral participation was falling, from a mean of about 85 percent in the 1980s to 78 percent in 1991 (De Riz 1998, 135). Public confidence in state institutions dropped considerably following the optimistic first years after the democratic transition. By the time the grassroots interviews for this book had begun, surveys showed the Argentine public had little confidence in *any* state or civil society institutions.[15] On the other hand, elections remained competitive and basically fair, the military leadership was submissive to civilian rule, an active civil rights community vigilantly protested and publicized rights violations, and while there were incidents of journalists being harassed by both government officials and anonymous assailants (incidents which became more frequent and more severe in the mid- to late-1990s), the country enjoyed, overall, a free press, with myriad media outlets representing a vast ideological spectrum.

Democracy was very much alive, if not wholly well, in 1990s Argentina. This regime survival was not merely remarkable because of Argentina's checkered democratic history but because the regime had survived during years of severe economic crisis, periods of recovery and then relapse, and dramatic changes in the structure of the economy and the labor market. The next section outlines these economic fluctuations.

Economic Policy: Changes and Grassroots Impact

During the first half of the twentieth century, Argentina was widely perceived as a land of opportunity and economic progress—a country with substantial natural and human resources, fortunate not to be plagued by either the plantation cultures or the significant ethnic divisions that undermined development and democracy in some other Latin American countries. In social and economic terms, Argentina was among the first countries in Latin America to industrialize, urbanize, and develop a large middle class. Unfortunately, that material and social progress was based on an economic model that was not sustainable over the long term. Much of the politics of the past forty years has been a fight over whether and how to redirect the country's economic development.

The Military's Economic Policy

The authoritarian regime that took power in 1976 sought to liberalize Argentina's economy.[16] They succeeded in causing a rapid deindustrialization, particularly in the food processing and textile and clothing industries, which were opened up to foreign competition (Smith 1991, 251–55). Some 120 public companies were eliminated or privatized, and public employment declined by 42 percent from precoup levels (World Bank 1993b, 1). The labor market deteriorated as public sector and manufacturing jobs were lost to bankruptcies, foreign competition, and privatizations. The number of workers in manufacturing jobs in 1980 was just 88 percent of its level ten years before (CEPAL 1991a). Workers' share of the national wealth also declined precipitously: wages, which had constituted almost 50 percent of the GDP in 1974, were merely 29 percent of the GDP by 1980.[17] As more middle and working class people found themselves with lower wages and/or working in the informal

TABLE 2.1. POVERTY IN GREATER BUENOS AIRES DURING THE 1970S AND 1980S
(By percentage of population)

	Unmet Basic Needs [a]	Income Below PL[b]	Total Poor
1974	31.1	3.2	34.3
1980	21.2	10.1	31.3
1982	23.1	28.0	51.1
1985	17.2	20.6	37.8
1987	22.0	25.2	47.2

Source: INDEC (1990, 38). Data pertain to metropolitan Buenos Aires, excluding the capital city, for which data are not available.

[a] Households lacking at least one of five basic needs related to quality of housing, sanitary system, and the education of children and the chief wage earner. This category includes people with incomes above and below the poverty line that measures income sufficiency.

[b] Those with basic needs met but household incomes below the poverty line. INDEC (1990) defined these as pauperized.

sector, Argentina experienced an unaccustomed social condition: downward mobility (Torrado 1992, 327–30). Income became more concentrated and urban poverty grew (Altimir 1996, 49 and 51). As table 2.1 shows, structural poverty, measured by unmet basic needs, showed improvement (albeit not continuous) during the military period. This is attributable to amelioration of structural insufficiencies in schooling and sanitation systems in rural areas. On the other hand, impoverishment, as measured by inadequate income, grew dramatically during the military period.

In addition to deteriorated social and labor conditions, the regime burdened its democratic successors with a substantial challenge—an external debt of $46.5 billion, which was over five times what it had been when the military assumed power. The indebtedness had external as well as internal causes, yet the magnitude of Argentina's debt can be appropriately attributed to the military's mismanagement, weapons spending, and policies to encourage middle-class consumerism through borrowing (see Smith 1991, 249, 260–61).

Alfonsín's Economic Policy

The 1980s were a period of economic distress across most of Latin America, brought on by the dramatic outflow of resources to make debt payments. Many countries, including Argentina, suffered high inflation, while those that had already stabilized their monetary systems experienced recession (CEPAL 1989). Overall, as the head of the U.N. economic committee for the region put it, the decade "marked a tremendous step backwards in the material standard of living" across the region (Rosenthal 1989, 7). While progress continued on some indicators, such as mortality rates and access to sanitation, clean water, and education, by other measures, the standard of living deteriorated substantially. As wages fell and formal sector employment declined, inequality levels grew (Rosenthal 1989; CEPAL 1991b; IADB 1993, 116–17). Argentina was among the countries most dramatically affected by these trends.

When Raúl Alfonsín took office in December 1983, he initially resisted the neoliberal policies associated with the military regime and tried nonrecessionary heterodox approaches. The economy recovered somewhat, and with it, real wages improved and poverty declined (tables 2.1 and 2.2). By mid-1987, however, his economic team had shifted definitively toward monetarist stabilization policies that relied on shock treatments and wage suppression to curb inflation. Economic ministry officials also proposed more thorough economic restructuring, including tax reform, deregulation of financial markets, free trade, and privatization of state industries (Smith 1990, 17–25; see also Smith

1991, 267–97). Implementing the proposals proved difficult. The Peronist opposition in Congress, in league with organized labor but abetted by unhappy industrial interests, obstructed the government's new designs (Smith 1990, 21–28, 32–34). The General Labor Confederation (CGT) called thirteen general strikes during Alfonsín's presidency (McGuire 1997, 234). With a presidential election less than a year away, the Peronist-dominated Congress blocked the president's last major economic plan, the *Plan Primavera*, which Alfonsín ultimately tried to implement by decree (Smith 1990, 25–26).

As table 2.2 shows, by the end of Alfonsín's presidency in 1989, inflation was skyrocketing. Also, wage gains made in the beginning of the democratic period had eroded, particularly in manufacturing and public administration (Smith 1991, 289). Under these conditions, pensions lost their value, small retailers and self-employed people went bankrupt, and the economy was decimated by capital flight. As a result, the deindustrialization that began under the military regime continued. The number of workers in manufacturing jobs in 1990 was down to only 62.6 percent of its 1970 level (CEPAL 1991a). As more Argentines became self-employed or joined very small businesses, the number of workers without full health and social security benefits and legal protection doubled during the 1980s, reaching almost one-quarter of all workers (Gallart, Moreno, and Cerrutti 1991, 4; also see Galin and Novick 1990; Nun 1989).

Argentina had long enjoyed a majority middle class and relatively moderate income disparities, so the declining standard of living was striking. Thousands of Argentines who had never been poor had to manage on incomes below the poverty line. A 1988 government study of poverty found nearly 37 percent of the households and over 44 percent of the individuals in Greater Buenos Aires were living either with income below the poverty line or in con-

TABLE 2.2. GROWTH, WAGES, INFLATION, AND UNEMPLOYMENT IN ARGENTINA, 1983–1992

	1983	1984	1985	1986	1987	1988	1989	1990	1991	1992
Growth[a]	1.2	1.0	−5.7	6.2	1.3	−3.3	−7.4	−1.3	7.6	7.4
Wages[b]	100.5	127.1	107.8	109.5	103.0	97.3	83.3	78.7	81.8	81.4
Inflation	433.7	688.0	385.4	81.9	174.8	387.7	4923.8	1343.9	84.0	17.6
Unemployment[c]	4.6	4.6	6.1	5.2	5.9	6.3	7.6	7.5	6.5	7.0

Source: ECLAC (various years).
[a] Percentage change in GDP/capita.
[b] Index of average real wages in manufacturing, 1980=100.
[c] Nationwide urban unemployment (May–October average, except 1986).

ditions that did not meet the basic minimum needs of life. The study found over half of all households were poor in the smaller interior cities of Neuquen, Posadas, and Santiago del Estero. In all locations surveyed, the number of citizens who were thought to have fallen into poverty due to insufficient income was substantially greater than those whose structural conditions (housing, sanitation, education, etc.) indicated long-term poverty (INDEC 1990, 32; also see Minujin 1991; Murmis and Feldman 1992).

Inequality worsened as well. Those of middle as well as lower incomes saw their share of income fall throughout the 1980s (Beccaria 1993, 130–41). In Greater Buenos Aires, the income discrepancy between the wealthiest 10 percent and the poorest 40 percent increased from a ratio of 6.7 in 1980 to 9.3 at the end of the decade (ECLAC 1998b, 216).

In the weeks leading up to the May 1989 election, conditions continued to decline, and by the end of May, the economy had collapsed. Hyperinflation provoked looting and riots. The consumer price index peaked at a monthly rate of 196.6 percent for July 1989 (CEPAL 1991a). As the country faced increasing economic and social turmoil during a lengthy constitutional "lame duck" period, Menem chose to be uncooperative on economic policy, forcing Alfonsín to hand over the reins of government in a humiliating admission of inefficacy five months before the end of his term. Menem accurately calculated the long-term political benefit he would gain by public memory of the Radicals' failure to finish their term.

Menem's Economic Policy

Following the classic strategy of Perón, Menem had eschewed ideological labels and argued for creating a unique and "practical" Argentine path for economic development. His platform rejected a reliance on market mechanisms, instead calling for a Social Pact through which business, labor, and the state would agree on the rules of the game for creating a "productive revolution" (Menem and Duhalde 1989, 35–37). He said he would foment that revolution without the monetarist shocks that Alfonsín had used since 1987 in his unsuccessful attempt to curb inflation by curbing demand. Instead of austerity, Menem promised a consumption-friendly *salariazo* ("huge pay raise"). Anyone who bothered to read the self-published book promoting his campaign would discover that the "*salariazo* implies a *gradual* but inexorable increase in the people's purchasing power" (1989, 42, emphasis added). Menem already showed signs of accepting the logic of economic restructuring by calling for a more efficient, less regulatory state. Yet he rejected the laissez-faire idea that there was no role for the state in a market economy (1989, 86–87). On privatization, his platform was unspecific, mocking the idea that privatizing would miraculously solve economic problems yet arguing that the state should sell industries that were not "the essence of state activity" so that it could be free to "do the things it really has to do." He emphasized that privatizations that were "necessary" would be done with the approval of Congress and organized labor and would be "transparent, honest, and realistic" (Menem and Duhalde 1989, 83–85). He also called for a negotiated refusal to pay the foreign debt for five years in order to stop the drain of resources needed for investment and development and to avoid "intolerable adjustment policies" (Menem and Duhalde 1989, 64–66). The campaign was filled with appeals to the traditional Peronist concern for "social justice" and professions of concern for the poorest citizens. All fine print aside, the *salariazo* became the watchword of the campaign.

Once Menem took office, the *salariazo* was postponed, but the debt payments were not.[18] On the first anniversary of his inauguration, Menem issued a new book explaining his plan for reforming the state. While not directly contradicting his earlier proposals (and in fact, maintaining rhetoric about an effective state and "social justice"), subtle changes in wording documented the direction already revealed by actions. For example, his campaign platform had spoken of the "popular economy" built on a *salariazo* that would strengthen the "popular market," then defined as increased consumerism. In the new program, the phrasing was changed slightly, but meaningfully. Now, Menem called for a "popular and market economy."[19] The economy would be "popular" because it promised to promote the common good and protect working conditions, but at the same time it would be a market economy that rewarded private initiative, competition, and efficiency (Menem and Dromi 1990, especially 27).

Menem loyalists, including those interviewed in the course of this research, justified the new directions as necessary and enlightened, but dissidents within the party, and most political sectors to their left, were quick to highlight the contradictions between promises and policies.[20] Eventually, Peronist dissidents broke away and by 1993 had formed an alliance, called Frente Grande, with certain small parties of the center-left. By 1995, this Frente had evolved into a larger alliance, Frente del País Solidario (FREPASO), incorporating prominent former Peronists and Radicals.

The government's policy on paying the foreign debt was substantially different from Menem's position in the campaign. In April 1992, the Economic Ministry concluded months of negotiations with the U.S. government and private banks from the United States and Europe, permitting Argentina's participation in the Brady Plan. The plan called for restructuring the debt owed the foreign banks, combining a thirty-year commitment to payment with a reduction of either the principal or the interest rate (at the banks' options) on the outstanding debt. By putting an end to perpetual negotiation of short-term agreements, the Plan was designed to give Argentina the ability to make long-term decisions and to build confidence on the part of international financial markets.[21] Ultimately, reestablishing creditworthiness with the banks encouraged foreign investment in the Argentine economy, which fostered economic growth.

As for privatization, Menem's vague campaign statements soon became a commitment to privatize nearly every productive or service operation in which the state engaged in order to diminish public debt, obtain capital, and reduce fiscal deficits. Sales of the national telephone company (ENTEL) and national airline (Aerolineas Argentinas), which the Alfonsín government had sought without success, were completed quickly. Menem pushed forward with the ENTEL sale, despite a strike by the telephone workers' union, thereby sending a message to other unions who might hope to politicize their opposition to privatizations (McGuire 1996, 240). Menem then proceeded rapidly with a long list of privatizations, including toll roads, water, oil fields, the electric generation, transmission, and distribution systems, passenger and cargo railroads, ports, a national park hotel, petrochemical and steel companies, and the postal service. By 1993, the privatizations had netted a $12 billion reduction in foreign and domestic debt, $8.5 billion in cash, and an estimated savings of $1.5 billion in annual fiscal expenditures to public companies. Between 1990 and the end of 1993, 95,000 public workers were let go with severance pay and another 19,000 retired as part of the pre- and postsale downsizing of thirteen large public industries (World Bank 1993b, 13–15). Privatizations continued despite numerous improprieties in the processes and despite bids that were much lower than anticipated.[22] The speed of the privatizations meant that in sectors central to economic development, such as public utilities, for-profit monopolies gained access to Argentine markets without an adequate regulatory framework in place to protect consumers or assure long-term investment.[23]

As leader of the majority Justicialist Party, Menem was uniquely situated to undertake the dismantling of Perón's legacy of state-led development and labor union hegemony. Union leadership had been so tightly allied with Peronism over the years that alternative political affiliations or postures were inconceivable to many in the labor movement. Menem's policies worked to put the unions, particularly in his first term, in a weakened and defensive position in which they needed him more than he needed them. Labor leaders acquiesced to most of Menem's proposals, despite their members' depressed wage levels and job losses. In effect, Menem's policies were continuing the process of dis-empowering organized labor that had begun in the late 1970s under the military regime. James McGuire identified several ways in which Menem's policies diminished the unions' capacities and willingness to oppose his policies. First, labor's political muscle was undermined by depleted union membership rolls, due to privatizations and downsizing in the public sector. Second, Menem decreed limits on the rights of public sector unions to strike. Third, he decreed changes that facilitated collective bargaining at firm and subindustry levels, thus diminishing the influence of national-level labor leaders. Finally, he threatened legislation that would cut union leaders off from their source of enrichment—their control of the huge employee and employer contributions to the health insurance organizations known as *obras sociales* (1997, 223–38).

While keeping labor pressures in check, Menem built good relations with various business sectors. In naming his first two economics ministers, he chose executives from the firm Bunge y Born, a multinational conglomerate that epitomized the financial and commercial establishment. In November 1991 he decreed a massive market deregulation, abolishing corporatist regulatory bodies as well as longstanding subsidies for particular industries.[24] He also won the support of the economically liberal Union of the Democratic Center (UCeDé), whose leading members became policy advisors to the president. By 1993, with the party no longer serving in the role of opposition, it had lost its *raison d'être* and all but disappeared (Gibson 1996, 191–204).

In April 1991 Congress enacted a new stabilization plan designed by Menem's economics minister, Domingo Cavallo. The Ley de Convertibilidad (Convertibility Law) was designed to control inflation by effectively pegging the exchange rate to the U.S. dollar, backing that rate with Central Bank reserves, and prohibiting the practice of indexing wages to inflation.[25] The government's firm commitment to the policy helped engender private sector confidence, the absence of which, in the past, had spurred upwardly spiraling prices and currency speculation. A year after the Convertibility Law took effect, the annual inflation rate was down to 22.4 percent in May 1992, about the time when most of the interviews described in this book took place.[26] That official inflation rate was based on a "market basket" of consumer goods that did not include such things as apartment rents, restaurants, and professional services, all of whose prices increased well beyond the stated inflation rate.[27] Nevertheless, the general trend toward stability was politically crucial and earned Menem wide support from consumers of all social classes, as well as from the business community and international investors.

When the interviews for this book were conducted, memories were fresh of the harried and insecure days of hyperinflation, when any salary not spent on payday had to be converted into more secure dollars. Supermarket prices were listed on a chalkboard and menu prices were written in pencil so that they could be erased and changed on a weekly or even daily basis. A year into the convertibility plan, the people interviewed were enjoying the freedom of not having to do their shopping on payday and not checking the exchange rates daily. Although real estate mortgages were not available for the overwhelming majority of citizens, credit on smaller items, such as household appliances, had reappeared. Conversely, hefty surcharges for credit card purchases disappeared. Few of the people interviewed for this research used credit cards, but many enjoyed taking advantage of the new credit for consumer goods. Newspapers were filled with advertisements offering the chance to own a refrigerator, fan, or color television by making low monthly payments (at comparatively usurious levels).

As inflation declined from its 1989 peak, so did poverty levels.[28] By the time of my interviews, 19 percent of the population of Greater Buenos Aires had incomes below the poverty line. This was a substantial improvement from the high of 47 percent in October 1989 or even the May 1991 level of 29 percent recorded just after convertibility was instituted. Nevertheless, it was high by historical standards (CEPA 1993b, 12). Argentina was accustomed to low single-digit income poverty rates during noncrisis periods.[29]

By the early 1990s, not only were there more Argentines struggling to make ends meet than historically but there was also a larger gap between the living conditions of the most affluent Argentines and everyone else. Income inequality had increased through the period of debt crisis and high inflation of the 1980s. While poverty rates improved somewhat after convertibility, inequality did not. In 1980, Argentina and its neighbor, Uruguay, had approximately the same level of social inequality (Gini coefficients of .375 and .379, respectively). By 1994, Uruguay had become *more* equal (Gini =.300), while Argentina, with a Gini coefficient of .439, had achieved levels of inequality close to its much poorer neighbor, Bolivia (ECLAC 1998b, 216).[30] The economic growth spurt following the convertibility plan was enjoyed almost entirely by the upper half of the population, and by 1993, only the wealthiest 10 percent were enjoying the fruits of the economic boom (see World Bank 1995, 20).

While inflation brought down the poverty level, substantial material concerns remained. The *salariazo* Menem had promised in his 1989 campaign never materialized. Average wages during Menem's first term remained below the levels of the Alfonsín term or even the worst economic years of the military regime (see table 2.2). Salaries were held down by a weak job market. By late 1991 unemployment had surpassed inflation on the public's list of national problems.[31] With few job opportunities in the formal sector, the informal sector, with all of its insecurities, was the source of income for many Argentines. In 1993 nearly half the population of the country and more than half of the poor and nearly poor were informally employed (World Bank 1995, 13).

Grassroots Impact of Crisis and Policy Change

During the span of their lifetimes, most adult Argentines have experienced substantial losses in living standard—losses that began in the 1970s, increased sharply during the 1980s, and continued for many of them into the 1990s. The losses occurred in real income, employment opportunity, the quality of public and social infrastructures, social equity, and social and income security.[32] Although important economic indicators improved after the convertibility plan was instituted in 1991 (e.g., poverty declined, foreign investment increased), other indicators worsened (unemployment and underemployment levels). Despite the economic growth in the early 1990s, unemployment, poverty, inequality, and wages remained considerably worse than the levels Argentines had once taken for granted.

It is difficult to isolate the several factors that caused this long decline: the politically and economically unsustainable ISI policies; the mismanagement by military authorities, as well as external shocks (world commodity prices, lending practices, and interest rates), which created the debt crisis; or the concentration of wealth, deindustrialization, and labor disempowerment, which were fostered by neoliberalism (Green 1995, 93–94). From a policy standpoint, pinpointing causality in a scientifically defensible way would be useful, but from a political standpoint, the actual cause does not matter. It is the effects, not the causes, that constitute citizens' actual material interests. It is the attribution of blame to particular political actors or even regimes (regardless of whether that attribution is valid from a social scientific examination of causality) that could make those material effects politically potent.

As table 2.2 indicates, the Argentine economy showed robust growth in 1991 and 1992. Business periodicals in the U.S. and elsewhere talked of the Argentine "miracle." This, of course, was just the talk that the government actively encouraged as a means to attract and keep investment. The talk in the streets of Buenos Aires was rather different. The improvements that were taking place in Argentina at the time of the research—diminishing inflation and increasing investment and growth rates—were in their earliest months. Figures showing diminishing poverty levels were not yet available, for example. Rather, the major study of poverty that the government had done in 1988 and released in 1990 was just being analyzed by social scientists, so the media were reporting on the dramatic decline in incomes and living conditions that had occurred during the course of the 1980s. Although later studies revealed that poverty levels declined with the fall in inflation levels, no one interviewed believed that poverty was a diminishing problem in the country. The convertibility plan seemed to be working in 1992 but was just about a year old when most interviews were completed, so people were cautiously optimistic yet not really confident that it would last. While the government denied that it was neglecting social concerns, the media regularly carried reports of the unmet needs of the poor, flood victims, and pensioners, and the deteriorating lifestyle of the middle class. Frequently, leaders of the Catholic Church, as well as scholars and journalists from the center-left, questioned the inequitable distribution of benefits and costs in the new economic policies (Powers 1995a).

The people sought out for this project were those who were not doing well despite the overall upward trend in the country. Most lived at or near the poverty level or were suffering other material hardships such as a loss of employment, low pensions, informal sector jobs, or inadequate housing. Whatever the national indicators might show, their personal pocketbooks were not doing well. Because the people interviewed were generally worse off than the typical Argentine, my interviews and their timing provided a means to talk about politics with people whose objective pocketbook conditions were not improving as well as the macroeconomic conditions in the country.

The Argentine case provided a population who could be anticipated to have high expectations that their government should provide for their economic well-being. Politics had, for generations, been a distributive contest. Governments had, for decades, tried to shape prices, wages, and growth levels through direct intervention in the economy. Living standards had been higher and more equitable than in most of the rest of Latin America for generations. Given these precedents, how would less affluent Argentines link their material and political needs in the democratic period? That is the question pursued in the rest of this book.

Chapter

3

Housing Interests

> *Sometimes they show the poor in the U.S.A—*
> *but they aren't poor! They have houses. If I had*
> *a house I'd feel like a multimillionaire!*
>
> HILDA, homemaker

In urban areas of the developing world, one of the most severe and widespread material hardships is the lack of adequate housing. This chapter examines how people in Buenos Aires deal with this objectively severe hardship—how they think about this material burden, how they live with it or try to resolve it, whether those efforts involve making demands on the political system, and how interactions with the political system affect, and fail to affect, the person's perceptions of political life. This case study of housing will begin to reveal how objective material conditions come to be perceived as material interests and under what conditions material interests come to be perceived as political interests.

A Home Makes All the Difference

Perhaps the most visible sign of material hardship is unsatisfactory housing. Social scientists have seen adequate shelter as a fundamental need in and of itself, the absence of which would constitute poverty. Shelter has also been used as an indicator that money resources are insufficient. In the Study of

Argentine Poverty known as IPA (INDEC 1990) and the many subsequent studies based on IPA data, people who lived in crowded or precarious residences or who lacked indoor sanitation were identified as "structurally poor." The term has been used as a substitute for "chronically" poor (e.g., Beccaria and Vinocur 1991, 24). IPA distinguished the structurally poor from the "new poor," the latter status indicated by inadequate current income but adequate housing and educational resources (presumably attained under better times). This operational innovation was suggestive but obscured the fact that while good housing is indeed a reliable indicator that a person has not suffered a lifetime of resource deficiencies, the converse is not true. People with inadequate housing may or may not have been poor all their lives. Whether due to a lifetime of meager resources or a recent change in circumstances, they simply cannot accumulate the capital to afford satisfactory housing.

Among those interviewed who lacked satisfactory shelter were people who once enjoyed comfortable, legal housing. Their standard of living fell gradually, and eventually they ended up in terrible situations. In looking at their pasts one found that they were not chronically poor; but looking forward, one can see that their poverty had become great enough and their living circumstances troubled enough that their condition could indeed become chronic.[1]

Housing is an obstacle to a comfortable lifestyle independent of the obstacle of income.[2] People with skilled jobs and steady incomes but inadequate housing are likely to see their incomes rise above the poverty line before they can accumulate the capital to rise above the poor level of living created by their shelter. As a homeless, underemployed man put it after mentioning that his ex-wife was about to lose her job, "but she has a home, paid for, and that makes all the difference."[3] This attitude is typical. As table 3.1 shows, most Argentines believe home ownership is evidence of whether or not a person is economically secure. This view is consistent across all classes, although weaker among the wealthy and strongest among the lower class. In other words, the view that home ownership indicates security is strongest among those who most often have neither (IPSA 1985–86, 1988–90).

Overview of the Argument

To illustrate how and why housing makes a difference in the daily lives of lower-income people in Buenos Aires, this chapter begins with a portrait of the living conditions in nonshantytown, substandard urban housing in the capital city. It describes various housing types, each presenting residents with unique problems, each offering different options for resolving those problems, and each shaping the residents' identities. I argue that this diversity of substandard

TABLE 3.1. OPINIONS ABOUT HOME OWNERSHIP AS FORM OF ECONOMIC SECURITY
Percentage, of each SES level,[a] who strongly agree with the statement:
"People who don't have their own house are not economically secure."[b]

	1985	1986	1988	1989	1990
Upper-income	42	26	42	36	36
Middle-income	51	41	48	47	45
Working-class	56	42	55	55	52
Poor	61	43	62	55	56
Total Population	55	41	54	51	51

Source: IPSA Audits and Surveys, "Estudio RISC," (Buenos Aires). Data provided to author by IPSA staff. Data for 1987 were unavailable. IPSA uses a national sample that does not include residents of shantytowns, hotels, or rooming houses.
[a] IPSA uses four socioeconomic categories, abc1, c2, d1, and d2e, defined by a combination of education, occupation, and housing.
[b] Table depicts those who answered "completamente de acuerdo" to the statement: "Las personas que no tienen casa propia no están seguras económicamente."

dwellings separates the poorest people of the urban grassroots from each other, in both physical and identity terms.[4] That separation, in turn, makes it less likely that a poor person would see an individual interest in housing as a political concern and/or engage in collective action to address it.

Following a discussion of the heterogeneity of living conditions in sub-standard urban housing, the rest of the chapter examines the extent to which housing deficits affect the political attitudes of those who suffer them. Given that housing is one of the chief material concerns of the very poor and that through years of economic crisis and then adjustment Argentines' possibilities for improving their housing deteriorated, we could expect that those with insecure or inadequate housing might feel dissatisfied with their living conditions. We also could expect that such dissatisfaction might cause them to see political leaders as inadequate because they did little to address these conditions. A number of interviews are analyzed to see whether and how the interviewees related their material need for housing to their evaluations of political questions and their views of the government.

Low-Cost Housing in the Federal Capital

Through a close examination of differences in the housing situations in Buenos Aires, this section argues that the material conditions of a person's residence, in and of themselves, structure a person's choices and opportunities.[5] Housing structures eating habits, sleeping habits, and sexual relations. It can be a material source of daily stress and long-term anxiety. It can affect self-esteem as well as an employer's estimation of a job applicant. It determines the kind of impact that economic crisis and economic adjustments have on a particular family. By examining how and why particular kinds of housing have these consequences and other kinds do not, we begin to see the complexities in how people experience their material problems, how they define their material interests, and how they seek to redress those interests.

The Housing Shortage

The shortage of low-cost housing, due to market and state failures, is a severe problem throughout the developing world (e.g., Castells 1983, 175–90). Argentina's housing deficit began growing in the late 1960s, when the emerging financial crises made real estate investment less attractive for financiers and less affordable for consumers (Lumi 1990, 193–94). In Buenos Aires the shortage was exacerbated by policies of the military regime that took power in 1976. As Oszlak (1991, 29) demonstrated in his detailed analysis of the regime's urban policies, those policies represented a "new and coherent conception of the right to urban space"—a conception that did not include the right of poor people to live in the capital city. The supply of low-cost housing fell due to strict regulations for new construction, high interest rates, the elimination of rent controls, and lower demand for inexpensive housing (caused by lower real wages). New construction focused on luxury apartments and condominiums in the northern section of the city.

For those unable to buy, rental housing has been scarce. Only 21 percent of residences in the Federal Capital were rented, according to a study in the mid-1980s. In the sprawling Buenos Aires suburbs, where single-family homes predominate, that study found a mere 8 percent of residences were for rent. In fact, in the combined capital and its suburbs, squatting was nearly as common as renting (INDEC 1988, 12, 40–41).

Public housing has never come close to compensating for the void left by the market. A government housing fund (FONAVI) was established in 1972 to construct multiunit complexes, providing basic apartments that low-income people could purchase at affordable payments. For the lucky few, a FONAVI home provided an adequate, secure, long-term solution to housing, allowing them to focus their resources and worries in other directions. Unfortunately, few families ever emerged from the waiting lists and those that did might be offered the chance to buy a house in their native province, not in the capital, where they had come to live and work.[6] Moreover, years of mismanagement of FONAVI funds and a paltry 1 percent average collection rate on housing loans hampered the program's fiscal capacity to meet the housing deficit (World Bank 1993a, 214–15). Beginning in late 1991, FONAVI lost its designated funding source and status within the federal bureaucracy and therefore had to compete with various other social programs for federal revenue sharing (Lo Vuolo 1997).

When the market and state do not provide homes that people of modest income can afford to buy or rent, and when those people do not wish to leave the conveniences of urban life and the proximity to their places of employment, they accept alternatives that tend to be overcrowded, structurally unsafe, and legally insecure. In 1992, 10.6 percent of all Argentine households had irreparably precarious dwellings. Another 18.2 percent of residences were redeemable but needed maintenance or sanitation improvements, while 5.9 percent were overcrowded (averaging two or more persons per room).[7] Estimates of the number of people living in unsuitable conditions in the Federal Capital vary widely, but in the early 1990s, inquilinatos (rooming houses), residence hotels, casas tomadas (occupied buildings), and villas miserias (shantytowns) were homes for at least 3 percent of the municipal population and perhaps two or three times more.[8]

Poor people within the capital city live differently from those in the Conurbano, which surrounds the capital, or those in the provinces. Unlike in those other areas, the predominant option in low-cost housing in the capital is not the self-contained shantytown, known as a villa miseria, nor the more organized and planned squatter settlements, known as asentamientos.[9] Rather, those who cannot afford to rent or buy a traditional apartment are likely to end up in the old and dilapidated buildings scattered throughout the streets and avenues of the city. Each building houses multiple families in single-room households.[10] Eighteen of those interviewed for this research lived in these dwellings or were essentially homeless. Another four lived in shantytowns in or just outside the capital, able, therefore, to provide a comparative perspective on life in the hotels, tenements, and squats. The other half of those interviewed lived in more standard housing, which they rented or owned.

The rest of this section examines the various kinds of precarious housing found in the capital, aside from the quite visible (and more frequently studied) shantytowns. This will demonstrate that the type of shelter dramatically affects a person's level of living as well as influencing the possibilities for changing that level of living, individually or collectively.

Casas Tomadas

A government study released in 1992 found that 18.5 percent of Argentine households were juridically "irregular." Housing without proper title was most common in some rural areas, reaching nearly a third of the households in the provinces of Posadas and Tucumán but occurring in 20 percent of the homes in the Buenos Aires suburbs and 12 percent of those in the Federal Capital.[11]

In the Federal Capital, the growth in squatting began with the economic crisis of the 1980s, when rents in residence hotels and *inquilinatos* soared. At the same time, parts of the central city were rezoned for commercial use, engendering real estate speculation. Both processes resulted in tenant evictions and homelessness (Grillo 1995, 10; MOI 1992, 2). A new solution homeless people undertook, made safer by the reemergence of democracy, was to take up residence in ancient vacant buildings, which became known as *casas ocupadas* or *casas tomadas*.[12]

"Tomada" is the common—although not neutral—way to describe such residences. The term asserts the importance of acquiring a home and the right *to take over* a place to meet a basic need for shelter when nothing else is available.[13] People who disapprove of the presence of squatters in their neighborhood are more likely to focus on the affront to property rights that such occupations imply, calling the residences *casas usurpadas* (usurped) and their occupants *intrusos* (trespassers).

Typically "occupied" buildings are rundown rental properties or private homes abandoned by owners who no longer wish to maintain them. Sometimes they were public facilities such as schools or factories, or in certain parts of Buenos Aires properties vacated for highway projects that were never completed. The original squatters have been known to treat their shelters, once taken over, as sellable assets, charging newcomers for the right to live in a room in the house.[14] An extreme case of such "entrepreneurship" occurred at the Patronato de la Infancia (Padelai), a vacant, publicly-owned orphanage in the San Telmo neighborhood, into which one hundred families settled in a matter of days in 1984. The man who first broke into the building charged each family for admittance and "protection" provided by his gang. Some occupiers were charged a onetime entry fee of several hundred dollars, others were charged a daily rent, and others paid with valuables such as television sets. Until he was finally arrested, the man also charged residents for electricity, even though he had hooked it up illegally and was not paying the electric company.[15]

The central city neighborhoods of San Telmo and Montserrat, where the majority of my interviews were conducted, have an unusually high concentration of occupied buildings (MOI 1992, 3). This is partly due to the historic character of the neighborhoods. A city zoning ordinance established by the military authorities in 1979 created a historical protection zone known as U-24, which included the historic buildings of the Avenida de Mayo and the southeasternmost sections of San Telmo and Montserrat. This law was intended to preserve the historical architecture of the oldest part of Buenos Aires by prohibiting the modernization of colonial facades or the demolition of existing buildings. In practice the restrictions engendered severe neglect. Rather than comply with expensive but historically appropriate rehabilitation, property owners simply let their properties deteriorate.[16] Others, unable to repair and use their buildings, stopped paying property taxes and abandoned the property altogether.[17]

Not all occupied houses were forcibly "taken." In some cases, the property owners or their heirs simply left their buildings to existing tenants rather than try to maintain deteriorating real estate. The tenants were allowed to remain without paying rent but were sometimes asked to pay the utilities or property taxes. In my interview sample, Samuel and Carlos were in this situation. Samuel's family shared a formerly rented building with another family, Carlos and his family with nine other households. They perceived their housing arrangements as legitimate and distinct from the usurpation of property rights of those who take over vacant buildings. Their families treated the homes as their own and they refurbished the crumbling structures.

In some ancient residences in San Telmo, generations of families passed on their rooms to their children, the aged owners having long ago stopped collecting rent, paying taxes, or maintaining the property. Eventually ownership reverts to the municipality because of unpaid taxes or probate decisions. In these large residences with dozens of families, organizational problems often make it difficult to take collective action, either to make repairs to a deteriorating structure or to fight eviction by the municipality.[18]

"Occupying" a house is a very insecure way to live.[19] One insecurity of this situation is the possibility of arrest. Although the police ignore many of the occupations—a situation that convinced some neighborhood elites who were interviewed that the occupiers had strong political ties—arrests are not uncommon and were becoming more frequent at the time of my fieldwork.[20] For example, Cecilia reported to me that her husband had been arrested twice for trespassing, although he was only held briefly; however, she could no longer count on a quick release because in the previous year some occupiers had gotten three-to-four-year jail terms.[21] By the following year, newspapers were reporting prominently about police raids on occupied houses. Another uncertainty of occupation is the possibility one may be evicted through the civil courts. Squatters who do not have the means, knowledge, or collective organization to fight eviction proceedings may return home to find their belongings on the curb and the building locked. Building occupiers are more likely to be evicted than shantytown dwellers because of the smaller number of residents per property occupied as well as the political pressure from nearby apartment residents, who see squatters as a blight on their neighborhood.

Sometimes occupied houses do not meet building code standards for habitable property, so even if the property owners do not seek to evict the residents the city may do so for safety reasons. The municipality's safety codes may be used to harass or evict residents, but even if a building is not condemnable, the hazards of life in a neglected, century-old building are genuine. Illegal electrical hook-ups, missing stair steps, structural weaknesses, leaking roofs, and broken or overtaxed sanitary facilities greatly increase the chances of accidents or illness for people living in these houses. A particularly tragic example among the interviewees was that of Eduardo, mentioned in chapter 1, who lived with his wife and four daughters in a large upstairs room in an abandoned school with dark cavernous marble hallways and stairways and balustrades in disrepair. Their daughter, barely school-age, fell through the balustrade to the marble floor below. After a harried search for help, they managed to get her to the public hospital (they had neither a phone nor a car, and taxi drivers refused to stop), but nevertheless, she died from her injuries.

Hotels

Safety is no greater in the so-called hotels found in the Federal Capital.[22] In these overcrowded buildings, usually in disrepair, lodgers pay a daily rate for a room, sharing the bath and kitchen with a number of other residents. One study found that about half of these establishments have the legal status of tourist lodging (Labado, Ladillinsky, and Garmendia 1991, 46–48). Few provide any of the amenities of a genuine hotel other than some minimal furniture, such as a bed, table, and wardrobe. These rooming houses are registered as hotels merely to enjoy the juridical freedom to treat their residents as "lodgers" rather than accord them the rights of "tenants."[23]

Residence hotels serve two distinct clientele. The first group needs temporary housing because they are newlyweds, divorced, or young singles just out on their own. These people may find space in the better residence hotels that have a few amenities, such as linens and a private bathroom. The second group of hotel residents are workers who cannot afford any other legal housing. This group includes people who are chronic hotel residents (frequently moving from one to another seeking better conditions) and people who moved to the hotels upon migrating to Buenos Aires from the interior or from a neighboring country. Migrants find hotels more convenient than other rental situations because they can obtain shelter quickly, without having to commit to a two-year lease (Gazzoli, Agostinis, Jeifetz 1987, 21–22).

Newcomers to the capital often hope some day to move out and "up" to an apartment, but people on working class wages find that the expensive daily rates at the hotels are an obstacle to saving for the future. Typically, residents in 1992 paid $200–$400 per month for one room plus extra for cooking gas and for each clothes iron, television, refrigerator, or other electric appliance they owned.

Because of the difficulty of accumulating capital, many residents discover that hotels are the first in a series of miserable housing experiences rather than a temporary stop on the way to better housing. Besides the migrants from the interior, hotel tenants include people who once owned their apartments but were forced to move when condominium fees became too expensive. Typically, homeowners economize first by moving to a rented apartment, perhaps first with two bedrooms and later with one. As rents exceed their wages, the former homeowners next move down to a hotel but ultimately they may end up in a *casa tomada* or *villa miseria*.[24]

Residents perceive the hotels as a step above a *casa tomada* because of the legitimacy and dignity of paying for a legal room. Evictions from hotels are not uncommon, but at least lodgers (as opposed to squatters) have some prior knowledge of a brewing disagreement with management, and besides, they are unlikely to face arrest. Hotels are also seen as advantageous compared to shantytowns because they are integrated into the fabric of the city and have better access to bus lines, stores, and other conveniences.

Despite these perceived advantages, one can argue that the family hotels offer the *worst* urban living conditions in Argentina. Hotel residents not only suffer problems with safety, hygiene, and crowding similar to those in other substandard housing, but they also endure severe restrictions on personal freedom. Compared to most *inquilinatos*, *casas tomadas*, or shantytowns, the hotels are less likely to offer a patio or other communal space because the buildings have been remodeled to maximize rentable square meters (Gazzoli, Agostinis, Jeifetz 1987, 36). Essentially, residents are confined to their rooms. In the worst hotels I visited for this research, rooms were dark, stiflingly hot places with no windows to the outside and with just enough floor space for a bed, a small table, and a couple of dressers or bookcases filled with clothes, dishes, cookware, and all other possessions.

Hotels regulate residents' lives more than other housing arrangements. Rules are abundant. Petty, sometimes tyrannical hotel managers can easily evict "lodgers" who are behind in their rent or who complain about conditions. Many hotels do not permit children or only permit small families, and where children are allowed, they are often required to stay in their family's room, day and night. Parents keep their children quiet and controlled for fear of annoying the manager and being evicted. Managers set restrictions on use of the building's telephone, monitor and sometimes prohibit visitors, and otherwise mind their tenants' business.

In many hotels, the cooking facilities are insufficient for the number of families, resulting in rules for usage that effectively restrict residents' diets even beyond the restrictions of their budgets. For instance, Hilda and Sara lived in a hotel where everyone on their floor shared a kitchen that had one range and a sink with a cold water spigot. Each resident was allowed to use only one burner. These restraints assured monotony in diet: the women repeatedly prepared stew, spaghetti, and other meals that could be fixed in one pot. The alternative solution is to buy a toaster oven or electric burner for one's room, but if the hotel permits such appliances, it usually assesses an additional monthly surcharge (purportedly for the electricity used).

While managers regulated their lodgers' lives, they were not themselves regulated well. Statutes were vague, contradictory, and not enforced (Labado, Ladillinsky, and Garmendia 1991, 46–49). Municipal housing inspectors were notorious for their corrupt relationships with hotel managers, meaning that unsafe, unsanitary, and unfair conditions went unchecked.

Inquilinatos

Buenos Aires has an urban collective rental arrangement, known as the *inquilinato*, which dates from the last century. Originally the *inquilinatos*—also called *conventillos*—were constructed as profitable rooming houses providing cheap shelter for European immigrants. Many of the original *conventillos* still operate in the neighborhoods of La Boca, Barracas, and Dock Sur, but today, inquilinato describes any low-rent situation where four or more families reside, usually in single rooms of very old buildings, with some sharing of patios, bathrooms, and kitchens among households.[25] These arrangements exist throughout the city, particularly in the southern neighborhoods. San Telmo and parts of Montserrat were once dominated by these dwellings but in the 1950s the principal avenues of the central city were widened, and in the process, hundreds of old *conventillos* were razed and replaced by tall apartment buildings. Today the old *conventillos* remain on the dozens of side streets in the area.

Two of those interviewed lived with their families in an ancient *conventillo*. A three-story structure, with a spacious interior patio shadowed by three levels of crisscrossing clotheslines, the building's stairwells and the multilevel walkways circumventing the patio could have been the model for an Escher drawing. Shared sinks, washtubs, bathrooms, and latrines are situated throughout the building. Most families have their own cooking ranges and refrigerators, either in their rooms or located in the open-air walkways outside the doors to their rooms. Rents in 1992 were only $80–$100 per month per room—a fraction of the cost of a room in a residence hotel. Some families with children rented two rooms.

Generally, *inquilinatos* and residence hotels have similar living conditions but in the former the management tends to be less repressive and the juridical protection from eviction stronger. *Inquilinatos* permit families with children. They are less expensive than hotels and offer somewhat more private space since rooms are a bit larger than in hotels and kitchens may be private. Structurally, they tend to be in worse repair than hotels, but since the buildings have not been remodeled to maximize rental space, they are more likely to retain patios and adequate ventilation (Gazzoli, Agostinis, Jeifetz, 1987).

Inquilinatos are used as long-term housing, primarily by people who are chronically poor. A study by Gazzoli, Agostinis, and Jeifetz (1987, chap. 2) found that 75 percent of those living in *inquilinatos* had lived in the Federal Capital for more than ten years. Amanda fit that study's profile of a typical *inquilino* in many respects: chronically poor, with five children, a native of Buenos Aires, and employed in the private formal sector as a janitor. At her 1992 interview, her home consisted of one well-ventilated room that served as bedroom, family room, and kitchen for her adult son, four school and teenage children, and herself. Amanda had lived all but three years of her life in this room. Although she had left the city early in her marriage, she soon returned to the *conventillo*—and the same room within it—in which she had lived as a child with her mother. When reinterviewed in 1995, she had expanded their home to a second adjacent room.

Some of the capital city poor live in dwellings that do not quite fit into the category of house, apartment, hotel, *casa tomada*, *inquilinato*, or shanty. Atilio's living arrangement fit the census definition of an *inquilinato* but the quiet, bright, spacious building lacked the congestion and noise commonly associated with *conventillo* life. He and his nephew lived in one room and shared two baths, a kitchen, patio, and phone with three other families, who jointly held the lease to the ancient building. Adriana described her family as illegally subletting their room from someone who was renting the entire floor in an old walk-up. She lived with her husband and son in one large room but shared the bathroom and patio with other tenants. Indicative of the uncertainty of such arrangements, when I met her she was facing a six month deadline for finding a new home because the leaseholder had decided to move.

The Challenge of Collective Living

In any of these types of housing, living in close quarters with strangers is a challenge. For example, Julio said that the living environment contributed to his inability to develop himself in more productive ways: "Well, look, to enjoy literature you need to be in a good mood, you need to have time, and to have tranquility. You need an appropriate place to read. . . . In a *conventillo*, you won't have any of that." Living in a single room makes family life difficult. Parents have little chance for intimacy when their bedroom is created by a curtain around the bed. School-age children try to complete their homework in the same room where their mother is doing chores, younger siblings are playing, and others in the family are watching television. When one person in the family has a guest, everyone has a guest—or has to go outside.

Escaping the room to the common space in a *casa tomada* or *inquilinato* brings additional difficulties. As in the larger society, these microcommunities face governance problems that arise from competing interests and clashing rights, but they do not have legitimate authorities to resolve many of the conflicts. Jorge, who lived at a large *casa tomada* known as the Padelai, described the tensions of communal life in this way: Every child has a right to play in the center plaza of the building, and yet every resident also has a right to hang laundry there. The two rights collide when someone attempts to tell the children not to play near their laundry. With neither sufficient physical space nor any authority to implement a solution to this problem, Jorge found it to be a continuing source of tension among the one hundred families living there. Dozens of similar problems augment the stress of daily life in an inadequate housing situation. Jorge noticed that when a local church bussed residents to a private park for a picnic, both adults and children enjoyed themselves, shared their food, played games together, and did not argue. When residents were away from the strains of their living quarters, they got along well.

To resolve the tensions arising from their housing and to try to improve their living conditions, some occupiers try to set up practices of democratic self-governance. The best organized establish a housing cooperative, with elected leadership. Elected or volunteer leaders have tried various approaches to handle noncooperation among fellow residents in order to create a cleaner, safer, more secure living environment. Yet some of their neighbors refuse to join their efforts because of differing personal goals, free-riding, distrust, or disbelief in the efficacy of collective action. At the Padelai, they eliminated one of their collective action problems by, as Jorge put it (in ironic reference to the government's solution to public sector failures), "privatizing." That is, after failing repeatedly to induce residents to share in the cleaning of common areas, the leaders finally decided to hire one resident as janitor, paid from the collective fund of the housing cooperative.

Given the difficulties of this collective lifestyle, Jorge was indignant when some people criticized his housing cooperative's effort to get public financing

to improve their occupied building. Jorge's critics said, in effect, "Sure, you
have a right to a home, but why should the government subsidize your housing in the heart of historic San Telmo, where property is expensive?" Jorge
ignored the policy issue about appropriate types of government aid. Instead he
responded to the self-righteousness of those who recognized only one currency for the purchase of an asset, saying that he *had* paid a high price to live
in a *casa tomada*. In his view, living in one room with all his children, sharing a
bathroom with other families, and having no privacy constituted heavy costs
that people without housing alternatives paid for their shelter.

Identity: The Relationship to the Means of Shelter

Housing, as described so far, involves problems with shelter, security, freedom, and social relations. In this section, I argue that it also has ramifications
for personal identity, self-esteem, and opportunity. Getting a job is difficult
when one's address is in a shantytown or *casa tomada* because those housing
arrangements are perceived as illegal, and as home to "marginal" or criminal
sectors of society.[26] At a community meeting to discuss housing needs, one
woman told of twice being rejected for jobs doing piecework at home. Prospective workers had to provide some collateral or evidence of credit in order
to obtain the production materials. Two companies refused to give her the materials because she lived in a shantytown beneath the expressway.[27]
Apparently the reliability of prospective employees is evaluated by their relationship to their means of shelter.

Interviews revealed clear connections between housing, self-esteem, and
opportunity. Juan Antonio said he never tried to hide that he lives in a *villa
miseria*, but after being transferred to the maintenance section of the Ministry
of Economics and Public Works (as part of the state's reorganization), he
felt that his new coworkers at the high-prestige ministry looked down on him
because he was from a shantytown. Feeling stigmatized, Juan Antonio consciously worked to change his coworkers' image of the ignorant *villero* by
bringing his insights on news or cultural topics into his workday conversations.[28] Jorge, a pipefitter, had also struggled with the stigma of residence: "I
used to feel ashamed to be from Padelai. You'd leave the house in the morning
with head and eyes cast down as you walked out into the neighborhood. It was
degrading. If you went to get a job and they asked if you owned or rented your
house and you said 'neither,' you might not get the job. When the kids went to
school, they didn't have a home address [to use on official forms] because the
police wouldn't certify a *casa tomada* as a home address."

The stigma of address affected Jorge's entire family. For example, in planning a party for his daughter's fifteenth birthday—a traditional rite of passage for Latin American girls—he said he would try to find a place away from home to hold it. He feared that otherwise some of his daughter's classmates would not attend because the Padelai is rather dark at night and has a reputation as a sinister place.

This identity of place separates people with severe housing problems not only from the rest of society but also from each other. In my fieldwork, I observed a hierarchy of legitimacy in housing, which puts legal tenancy in hotels and *inquilinatos* above squatting in *casas tomadas*, and the latter above living apart from the rest of the city in the crowded *villas miserias*. All of those situations, in turn, would be considered better than living in a rural shack lacking modern plumbing and urban access. People living higher up the hierarchy perceive their housing problems as less desperate than those living further down the list. (The reverse is not necessarily the case. A resident of a *villa*, who owns her home, although not its land, may well feel advantaged compared to those in *casas tomadas* or hotels. She has more freedom to come and go without a manager overseeing her actions and she may well live in a larger space.) Although the poor who manage to avoid the stigma of shantytown living often feel relatively advantaged, they lack a strong identity of place—an identity through which shantytown dwellers may create political action.

Political and Non-Political Means to Shelter

The first sections of this chapter have described the objective burdens of life in nonstandard housing situations in central city Buenos Aires. Safety, privacy, space, and sanitation are concerns common to each of the housing types described, although each particular housing type also poses unique burdens. Generally, the people interviewed perceived improving these objective conditions as a strong personal interest. Did this material interest become a matter of political interest? The rest of the chapter examines how people sought to address their housing interests, whether they perceived their housing interests as matters of political interest, and whether or not their political perceptions overall were affected by their frustrated attempts to redress a material priority.

The Alternatives

Solving any problem requires an alternative to the status quo. When it comes to urban housing for the poor, few alternatives exist. People of limited means can only dream of purchasing an apartment in the city given an expensive real estate market and limited opportunities for long-term mortgages.

A more feasible option is to purchase an improved lot, typically far in the outskirts of Greater Buenos Aires, and then slowly to construct a dwelling, a room or two at a time as savings permit (Feijoó 1984, 33–62; Raggio 1995). Thousands of lower income Argentines have taken this option but it carries its own risks and disadvantages. Many people accustomed to the central city neighborhoods of San Telmo or Montserrat would see such a move as trading off one unacceptable level of living for another. Among those interviewed, Adriana had rejected a related option: a construction company offered her the barest skeleton of a house for about $1,040 down, plus monthly payments of $80. For this the new homeowner would finish the job of completing the house, including adding such basics as doors, window shutters, and plumbing fixtures. Adriana said she did not care if she got a used house or a new one but she wanted one that was finished.

The potential for upward housing mobility is low because of the formidable startup costs of renting an apartment in Buenos Aires. Apartment leases require cosignatures from at least two local property owners plus a deposit of up to five months' rent. Many of those interviewed dreamed of having a private apartment some day but few had any realistic possibilities for saving the required deposits.

Hilda and Ramón's story demonstrates why "moving up" is difficult, even for a household with income well above poverty level. Ramón supported their two children and his pregnant wife on about $600 per month with benefits. He was comfortable and secure in his job as a kitchen worker in another hotel, located nearby. After paying the monthly rent, however, they had less than $200 left, which was far less than the government estimate for the nonhousing costs of providing for a family of four at that time. In numerous interviews with poor people, social scientists, and neighborhood elites, I heard Ramón's assessment of the problem repeated: "You could pay two months' rent for an apartment with what you pay for a hotel. The problem is getting in. You need two cosigners and almost $1,000 down. Living in a hotel, you can't save that. In Argentina, you always spend more than you have. We can never save [for housing, because we're] always thinking about whether we'll have money for food later in the month."

Nonpolitical Action

Many people who were interviewed for this research responded to their difficult housing problems in individualistic and nonpolitical ways. Some who had legally secure but crowded shelters perceived their housing as normal for people of their socioeconomic level.[29] Not that they necessarily thought that their living conditions were just—they simply saw their housing as one of many disadvantages bound up with the difficult life of people with little income, assets, or education. They saw housing as a manifestation of their poverty and part of a composite, ill-defined need for "social justice"—not as a specific and resolvable interest. Thus their political discourse, to the extent it was based on their material interests, focused on wages and employment. (This is somewhat shortsighted, since a pay raise or a full-time job is unlikely to be sufficiently large to allow a move to better housing.)

The modest hopes of people in this category were to make their homes a bit more comfortable through individual effort, changes in wage and employment levels, and good luck. If they moved, they would do so in search of minor improvements, such as Leonardo's hope to rent a room in someone's private home rather than in a hotel, or Atilio's move from a congested *inquilinato* without hot water to a spacious one with sufficient bathrooms for the number of residents. Amanda is an example of these modest hopes. She could not afford to move from her *conventillo*, so she could not understand why her neighbor, who made a good income, did not do so. Yet she and her family were also emotionally comfortable where they were. While she said she dreamed of getting a modest apartment, her children did not want to move to a more comfortable home because their friends lived in or near the *conventillo*. For the more immediate future, her goals were not to find new housing but simply to pay off the television, get a new refrigerator, and buy a bunk bed so that her youngest son did not have to share her bed. Three years later, when I revisited her, she had indeed gotten a new refrigerator and expanded her family's sleeping quarters to two rooms—but her youngest son had died after falling through a shoddy railing at the dilapidated *conventillo*.

This set of people did not expect to be able to improve their housing dramatically through either personal, political, or government effort. For Amanda, her low expectations indicate resignation to the only lifestyle she has ever known or found affordable. For others, such as Carlos and Julio, low expectations signal their frustration and despair over their personal tragedies to be stuck in an unjust social system with neither individual opportunity nor any likelihood of social revolution. In Julio's case, he was deeply discouraged by his failed efforts to organize those in his *casa tomada*. Eventually the squatters were evicted and he landed back in an expensive and restrictive hotel. He attended a meeting or two of the Squatters and Tenants Movement (MOI) but his previous experience with freeriders left him deeply skeptical about the group's belief in collective action. In Carlos's case, his one-room home was overcrowded (by government standards) yet more comfortable and secure than a room in a hotel or *casa tomada*. Changing his housing was not his highest priority, although he spent many hours trying to make his home more comfortable. Carlos was repairing a plaster wall when we met for the fourth time on his day off. He said that if his sons studied hard they would never have to do such work because they would not be "marginal." He was frustrated by his own social exclusion, and he voted with parties of the left in order to try to change the social system, but he saw little prospect that he would improve his living conditions without either education or a political revolution.

Overall, the people described in this section did not see their *housing* conditions as problems to solve politically, nor did they blame the government for those particular conditions. As later chapters will show, they did tend to see the *general* material conditions of the working class as political issues, but the particular burdens that preoccupied them on a daily basis, such as housing, were handled privately and individually. Their burdensome daily material interest was not their specific political interest.

Individual Demands on Government: Hilda

Another way to respond to inadequate shelter would be to make housing a priority and evaluate political affairs accordingly. This response was uncommon—surprisingly so, given the severe impact of housing on the quality of daily life. Only a few interviewees volunteered that government should engage in more active housing construction or mortgage programs for the poor. Hilda (but not her husband, Ramón) was among the rare single-issue respondents. Hilda's views revealed an individualistic, instrumentalist understanding of the political process, in which she judged politicians on the basis of her greatest interest, housing. When the president or governor was on television, she remembered what he said about housing proposals. Otherwise, her curiosity about politics was limited to well-publicized scandals. She found her life too arduous to interest herself in a political process that seemed irrelevant to most of her daily concerns. Yet after spending most of a difficult pregnancy confined in a single hotel room with her two toddlers, she was particularly eager for a better living situation. Housing was an area in which she had found it impossible to be self-sufficient, so she turned to politics, specifically, to old patterns of clientelism.

Recognizing that hard work and a steady job would not be sufficient to get them out of their hotel room before their third child was born, she devised a strategy to obtain government vouchers to cover hotel rent for a couple of months, during which she and Ramón could then save money for a deposit on a better home. Hilda had learned through experience that much time and bus fare could be wasted talking with low-level bureaucrats so she went directly to the national Congress to speak with an aide to the congressman from her home province. Although the vouchers were a municipal program, not under congressional jurisdiction, she presumed that political clout mattered more than process. Starting at the top gave her a feeling of efficacy, although so far she had been unable to obtain the housing voucher. The day I accompanied her she was sent to three different offices but finally left with the assurance that she could retrieve the voucher the following day. Not surprisingly, the next day, no voucher materialized. She had spent many afternoons trekking between political offices without success but was optimistic by nature and did not perceive another solution. Hilda had multiple material concerns, but housing was her priority interest. As populist literature that emphasizes clientelism and material motivations would expect, she supported political actors on the basis of how they helped her meet that material interest.

Collective Demands on Government: Martín

Despite the substantial organizational hurdles, some people decide that collective action to legalize their present shelter is more feasible than any alternative, given the housing market in the capital. These collective actions are discussed at some length later in the chapter. Here I introduce Martín's eight-year saga of housing troubles in order to illustrate a decision to fight for the lesser of two evils in a market of restricted choice.

Martín had a secure, full-time job as a landscaper. He had once rented housing in the Federal Capital but at some point could no longer afford renting an apartment for his large family. He had applied for public housing eight years before but despite having the highest priority classification had never been awarded a home. Once put out of their rented home, Martín's family spent several months in one room in a relative's apartment, then a night on the streets, before learning about squatters in the former orphanage in San Telmo, known as the Padelai. They had expected to live there for a month but they gradually settled in. Eventually Martín devoted years to helping his fellow residents convince municipal authorities to grant them title to the building.

This was not their preferred housing. Martín's wife disliked the social ambience in the building and wanted to leave. Nevertheless, Martín's investment of time in the cooperative's struggle was bearing fruit. With $700 per month combined income, he and his wife were unlikely to find affordable rental housing within the capital for them and their six children. They did not want to live outside the capital because of the time and money involved in traveling an hour or more into the city to his job with the municipality. Moreover, in the outskirts, it is difficult to get odd jobs to supplement the family income, it is hard for women to find domestic work (which was his wife's source of employment), and it is less likely that schools offer the afternoon shifts and in-school meals that make it easier for students' mothers to work. If he could have accumulated the necessary deposits, renting an apartment in the capital would have cost over half his income—leaving far too little for food and other essentials. Moreover, even if he had adequate income, renting might never be an option for Martín because landlords routinely deny apartment leases or hotel rooms to large families.

Faced with these conditions, Martín had few choices. His decision to fight for legal tenancy in a *casa tomada* made financial sense. He paid 15 percent of his income to the housing cooperative, which used the money for legal and other community expenses. This payment would guarantee his place in the renovated Padelai, where—if the cooperative held together and the planned renovations were completed—one day he would have a new four-room apartment, purchased with a twenty-year mortgage capped at an affordable 25 percent of income. He could not rent four rooms anywhere else in the city for $175 per month.

Effect of Housing Type on Collective Action

Hilda and Martín both had partisan political affiliations, and both sought to engage political actors for individual gain—that is, to solve their housing problem. Unsurprisingly, Martín participated in (an initially successful) collective action to resolve his housing problem, while Hilda chose an individual route. Their different choices reflect their specific material conditions. That is, the type of housing structured the conditions for collective action. Hotel residents like Hilda have little opportunity for collective action to improve the conditions in their own hotels because of the corruption of city lodging inspectors and residents' fears of being evicted.[30] Additionally, hotel residents tend to be relatively new to the city and so maintain hope that their fortunes will change. Therefore, these conditions and expectations leave hotel residents isolated from each other.

Other types of housing offer more potential for politically effective self-help. Seven interviewees had joined organized efforts to improve their housing, working either to "privatize" the city-owned former orphanage called the Padelai or joining a grassroots organization known as the Squatters and Tenants Movement (MOI). The MOI sought to help residents of occupied houses and land to find realistic and legal solutions to their housing needs through political strategizing and in-house organizing. Conditions for organizing are more favorable in *casas tomadas* than in hotels. First of all, *casas* tomadas do not have building managers to disrupt meetings or evict "trouble-makers." Second, squatters, having already hit bottom in housing, are more likely to see themselves as long-term residents, whereas hotel residents are usually hoping to move on.

The housing movement sought to negotiate safer, more stable housing, either through legalizing and improving the occupied houses or, if those could not be rehabilitated, by negotiating with public officials for alternative affordable housing of the tenants' choice. The MOI met with some success, as city officials entered into negotiations with a few highly organized *casas tomadas*; yet those officials were unwilling to commit to comprehensive solutions for the housing needs of all building squatters. MOI organizers read this unwillingness as a preference to keep housing as a clientelist payoff. To them politicians seemed to negotiate only on specific buildings from which they expected political gain. MOI organizers believed that city and national government officials deliberately avoided both recognizing a large-scale squatter problem and legitimizing their housing movement. They concluded that their best hope for policy change over the long-term was to try in the short term to create successful demonstration projects (MOI 1992, 5–6).

Shantytown leaders in the city of Buenos Aires had been more successful in their housing pursuits. Since the democratic transition, shantytowns had reemerged and grown in the capital and its environs, yet rather than squash this growth, as the military had done, municipal authorities had made a public commitment to negotiate with *villa* leaders, enabling squatters to remain in their homes, legalize their tenancy, and make infrastructure improvements.[31] Most likely public officials tried to resolve the demands of shantytown residents because most of the shantytowns are not located on valuable real estate and legalizing their current status was easier than expanding public housing.

Since shantytown residents were *less* numerous than residents of hotels or *casas tomadas* in the Federal Capital, their successful collective action cannot be attributed merely to their voting power. Rather, shantytowns have a visibility, identity, and in some cases a history that facilitate collective action compared to other types of inadequate urban housing. Along the streets of the central city, dreadful living conditions are hidden behind unremarkable doorways. In contrast, shantytowns present sprawling, visible conglomerations of poverty. Still, they are segregated from the rest of the city (partly because, being irregularly constituted, they tend to lack city services, so that zoning, street lights, sewage, and pavement often end at the edge of the *villa*). The physical isolation of the shantytown creates a greater sense of common identity among its residents than in the lone hotels, *casas tomadas*, and *inquilinatos* scattered amidst the owner-occupied apartment buildings of San Telmo and Montserrat.[32] Poverty is more hidden in the central city, where there are a few shanties built beneath overpasses or on vacant lots but no conglomerations of them. The association of poverty with *villas* is so strong that "*villero*" is used interchangeably with "poor person" in the Argentine urban lexicon, implying that all poor people live in *villas*.

The shantytown leaders negotiated a coherent, unified project for the transfer of title and the initiation of infrastructure improvements in *villas* throughout the capital city. Organizing the shantytown movement was certainly not easy, yet by the early 1990s the neighborhood organizations and leadership in the *villas* had a decade of experience.[33] The development of those organizations and their leadership was facilitated by the physical characteristics of shantytowns. Because of their size and location, they have become self-contained communities where activities are organized in, by, and for the shantytown. Churches, schools, day care centers, soup kitchens, and political party offices exist within the shantytown, cementing the identity between residents, neighborhood, and their type of residence.[34]

In contrast, in central city neighborhoods like San Telmo and Montserrat, the political party offices, social services, park programs, and clinics are established by poor and middle class neighbors together. They are conceived as projects for the entire housing-diverse neighborhood. The Peronist, Radical, and Socialist local party offices—and the poor people who participate in them—identify with the larger neighborhood, not merely with its lower levelst. In the central city, poverty is not limited to any single housing type and neighborhood-based organizations do not limit themselves to the specific legal and comfort problems of particular housing types. When those with a material interest in better housing are scattered in various types of housing, and isolated from each other, organizing collective political action to address their housing interests becomes more difficult.

Building Micro-Macro Links with Social Movements?

Collective Action and Consciousness: Theory

Among non*villeros* in the Federal Capital, one of the more ambitious collective actions for housing occurred at the *casa tomada* where Martín, Jorge, and Francesca lived—the cavernous former orphanage known as the Padelai, which housed about one hundred families. Residents had engaged in a multiyear political struggle, which began in 1986 when some San Telmo neighbors first sought to evict the squatters.[35] The residents formed a cooperative, run by elected leaders, and eventually persuaded the Buenos Aires city council to give the cooperative legal title to the former orphanage, to authorize $1 million in municipal funds for renovating the building into modern apartments and shops, to give Padelai residents preference for the construction jobs involved in the renovation, and to establish an affordable payment plan for the new apartments. Mortgage payments would go into a municipal fund earmarked for housing projects for families in other *casas tomadas*.[36] The proposal offered permanent solutions to their individual needs by giving them not only access to housing but also to a capital asset. At the same time, it promised to improve their surrounding community and institutionalize funding to resolve the housing problems of others in similar situations.

The collective effort to obtain the city councilors' support and funding involved a long struggle with constant setbacks and organizational hurdles (such as the physical threats to organizers by a gang leader; freeriding by non-participatory residents; distrust and disagreements among residents; substantial time and resource constraints consistent with their poverty; and double-crossing by local politicians). The residents' decision to take political action to form a cooperative and legalize their tenancy was a decision encouraged by outsiders who had both a social agenda favoring grassroots participation and social eq-uity and who had the technical and political knowledge to promote it. The first outside supporters were university students. While volunteering in an after-school tutoring program, engineering students who belonged to a "social action" group came to know the residents' housing situation and the threats they faced from the gang who terrorized the building. Because they knew chil-dren from families throughout the expansive building, the students were able to help build links among people who, living in a climate of fear and distrust, were not well-acquainted. Students also provided space at the university where residents could hold meetings safely in the days before the gang leader was arrested. Over the next two to three years, the students accompanied the residents as they met with city and electric company officials, talked to the media, and formulated their political message and tactics. Francesca and Martín acknowledged the students' contributions and perceived them as sup-portive and helpful in the residents' own struggle.

Later, a nongovernmental organization (NGO) that employed architects to study housing issues and that was funded by international donors became the cooperative's main adviser. The principal architect eventually left the NGO and focused all of his energies on Padelai and the formation of the MOI. The cooperative's goals expanded as the technical assistants suggested bigger possi-bilities, which were rooted in their knowledge of property and housing codes and international models for solving urban housing problems. The residents' internal decisionmaking also became both more democratic and more complex. They implemented electoral rules to choose delegates from every geographic sector of the building and established decisionmaking committees.

Like the students before him, the architect-adviser perceived his role as raising "consciousness" and empowering people to believe in their own political efficacy. He believed that grassroots organizing requires professional help in order to provide the "social, material, and subjective space in which low-income sectors can learn to make decisions and recognize their leadership role" (MOI 1992, 3). He also pushed the residents to form a larger "movement," the MOI, in order to seek housing solutions for people in *casas tomadas* and *inquilinatos* generally, rather than limit themselves to resolving their individual problems.

As they decided to forgo individualistic solutions and to work collectively to demand government assistance, the residents learned from scratch about the politics of legislation and policymaking. Unfortunately, they made tactical errors and local politicians with personal agendas tried to exploit their cause. Ultimately they learned from their mistakes and acquired sophistication in collective democratic organization, media relations, legislative process, and influencing public debate. Although their technical advisers clearly influenced the scope and content of their demands and helped them shape their political message, the residents themselves worked out the policy and strategy decisions during frequent and lengthy meetings. The residents' elected leaders learned the art of public relations, learning to speak at city council meetings, media interviews, and meetings with other housing activists.

Did the campaign increase the residents' interest in political activities beyond the housing movement? Did it change their understanding of political phenomena and relationships? Did the intense experience of a protracted grassroots fight, based on a spirited defense of the dignity and rights of the poor and aided by ideologically-informed advisers, affect their thinking about social policies, their ideological understanding of state-society relations, and their view of the democratic process? Previous research on new social movements suggests that the answers would be "yes." Participation in grassroots movements has been seen as both a result of a person's ideas about political life and as a catalyst for changing political ideas (Mainwaring 1987, 48). Participation is a result when "new goals, beliefs, and identities" lead people to try to solve their problems through grassroots action (Stokes 1995, 124). The engineering students understood their work at Padelai in these terms. They saw themselves engaged in "raising the level of consciousness of those families who, as a consequence of the unjust social order, were obliged to suffer a situation of marginalization and violence. This raising of the level of consciousness would make it possible to form an organization, which in turn would be the vehicle for generating the transformations that would bring these families to live with dignity, and by a standard of social equality in which charity/welfare had no place" (Centro de estudiantes 1991, 86). Participation is a catalyst, because participants' political consciousness is further transformed through their activism. This might happen in two ways. First, the experience of participating in an effective organization against staunch political opponents empowers people, giving them a new sense of efficacy (Alvarez 1990, 39; Levine 1993; Neal and Seeman 1964, cited in McAdam, McCarthy, and Zald 1988, 708). Even when the organization does not live up to its promise of equal participation by its members, the experience of membership can lead people to demand larger roles in the organization and to develop a new consciousness of their identities (Alvarez 1990, 57–82). Second, participation in a social movement exposes a person to new ways of thinking about the causes of, and solutions to, their material conditions.[37] Oxhorn (1995, 135–39) observed this consciousness-raising in the shantytowns of Santiago, Chile. Stokes (1995, 68 and 116–17) found that Peruvian shantytown leaders with a "radical" approach to solving their neighborhood problems were often those who had learned a confrontational worldview through labor union activities (and in contrast, those with a "clientelist" worldview had acquired their understanding of the social and political world from the more traditional organizations in which they had participated).

Not only has the transformative, consciousness-raising power of participatory activities been described in empirical research but it has also become a matter of faith among grassroots organizers. In keeping with the ideas of Paulo Freire (1974) and liberation theology, grassroots organizers throughout Latin America have sought to educate people to reexamine the nature and causes of their material conditions and then act upon their analysis collectively. For example, in Peru Stokes found that more radical, less-clientelist neighborhood leaders "believed that participation should change the attitudes of people toward their social and political surroundings in addition to allowing the poor to acquire the material services their communities needed. Participation should 'create consciousness'" (1995, 73; also Oxhorn 1995, 135–39). The technical assistants at the Padelai had this vision. They hoped that the act of participation would be empowering so that members of the housing movement would "learn to make decisions and recognize their leadership role. In turn, this growing consciousness will strengthen the organization" (MOI 1992, 3).

If participation has the transformative effects that have been attributed to it by both empirical and normative sources, then collective political action to get housing for one's family should lead the actors to put their housing needs in a broader context of social justice claims and public policies to meet basic needs. The three Padelai activists who were interviewed (Francesca, Jorge, and Martín) are interesting in the extent to which they did *not* become more broadly politicized, did not put their personal housing need into a larger political context, and did not attribute their views on national politics to their grassroots participatory experience. Unfortunately, it was impossible to compare their political thinking before and after involvement in the Padelai, so we cannot determine whether current attitudes are new ones the three activists developed due to contact with other participants in the housing movement. Nor, of course, can any conclusions about the general impact of participation on political views be drawn from studying three people. Yet, by listening in some detail to *how* these activists explained their own political ideas in relation to their work at Padelai, the logical contradiction between the new social movements' tactics and their desire to raise consciousness will become apparent.

In Practice: Politicization without Consciousness?

The experience of working in the Padelai cooperative, as the social movements literature predicts, did nourish a greater sense of political efficacy on the part of Francesca, Jorge, and Martín. Over time, the members of the cooperative developed an ambitious vision of how to use the political process. They moved away from the clientelistic relationships and individualistic solutions each resident previously used to gain housing. Nevertheless, exposure to the political process and participation in a democratically-organized cooperative did not turn the residents who were interviewed into active participants at other levels of political activity. In Francesca's and Martín's cases they already had lifelong involvements in partisan campaigning. They found the Padelai effort a source of pride and hope but their successful self-help campaign at the municipal level did not translate into optimism about the chances for the poor at the level of national politics. In Jorge's case, although through the housing fight he had become a seasoned political strategist, he nevertheless remained thoroughly uninterested in any other political affairs. His ambitions were limited to obtaining good housing for his family and sharing with other poor people his acquired knowledge of how to obtain housing. Doing so required him to spend hundreds of hours away from his family and substantial time off from the pipefitter's job with which he supported them, and he did not wish to expand that time commitment to other issues. He said that the only news he had time to read was that relating to Padelai and that he had no interest in partisan politics.

While their campaign taught them about political process and increased their sense of efficacy, Francesca, Jorge, and Martín insisted that it did not affect their views on any other political subjects. This lack of effect seems to result from deliberate organizational choices. Following a common (although not universal) strategy of urban movements, they sought to prevent partisanship from interfering with their housing struggle. "Clearly everybody has their own political beliefs," Francesca acknowledged, explaining that the residents had learned early on that in order to trust each other to cooperate in the pursuit of housing they would have to put aside partisan and ideological preferences and make housing their common priority. As a complement to this internal pluralism, they adopted an externally pluralistic strategy. Early in their work, a neighborhood Peronist councilman had been their advocate but later reversed his loyalties, siding with a UCeDé councilman intent on evicting the residents. The Padelai leaders felt betrayed and learned from this betrayal to avoid partisan connections. As Martín stated, "So we said 'that's enough of politicians!' They can all come, sure, and do their advertising and talk with the people. But the cooperative isn't going to give its support to any of them. In spite of the fact that within the cooperative there are various parties. Among the leadership, there are Radicals, leftists, and Peronists. So we said 'no, enough, not any of them—politics out!' Our politics is housing." They avoided becoming a client of any party and instead built crossparty support as well as support in the neighborhood and in the media. Later, when the city council voted to grant them title to the building, members from all parties but the UCeDé supported the residents.

The residents' decision to remain independent of parties is a decision commonly reached by new social movements. The shantytown movement in the Federal Capital had likewise found it effective to avoid partisan entanglements (Zaffaroni and Armada 1991). Even Peronist loyalists (whose party was in charge of the municipal government and thus could have used the shantytown movement in clientelist fashion to win support for their party) were firmly committed to the movement's nonpartisan strategy. As Esperanza, one of the movement's activists told me, "The shantytown movement should be pluralist. It doesn't have any creed. It doesn't have any party." Oxhorn's (1995, 162–66) study of urban social movements in Chile showed activists choosing the nonpartisan strategy for the same reasons and using very similar language to the people I interviewed in Buenos Aires.[38] The strategy is so common that Castells (1983, 280, 299, and 322) has defined autonomy from a political party as the "*sine qua non* condition" for an urban social movement to bring about any substantial transformations in society. He argued that those urban movements that do not maintain that autonomy can only achieve limited goals.

The three Padelai activists interviewed used their commitment to autonomy from parties as a reason to avoid exposing themselves to new political
ideas or linking their immediate material interest, housing, to their interests in
national politics. Analyzing how each of them reasoned will show that the
nonpartisan commitment created mental obstacles to linking personal interests with political ones.

Francesca.— By adopting a nonpartisan strategy to obtain housing, the Padelai activists consciously divorced their urgent material concern, as well as their
political experiences in the housing movement, from their thinking about
other aspects of Argentine political life. For Francesca, it is certainly possible
that her experience fighting for Padelai had changed some of her political attitudes, leading to the opinions she expressed. She felt that politicians could
never be trusted, that public officials treat the wealthy well and discriminate
against the poor, and that social inequalities in Argentina are too great to consider it a "democracy." Through Padelai, she had experienced dishonest politicians, she had felt mistreated on the basis of her poverty when the Padelai
delegation went to register a complaint at the local commissary, and she had
experienced social inequality as more affluent citizens rejected the residents'
claim to a right to housing in San Telmo. On the other hand, having been
raised by a staunch Peronist, she also could easily have learned those same attitudes earlier. Nevertheless, while her attitudes might have developed or been
reinforced by her experiences in the housing movement, she did not perceive
them as a coherent and new set of attitudes reflecting new insights on political
life. On the contrary, she insisted that the housing fight had taught her about
the political process but had not changed her political ideas. Interpreting the
concept of "political ideas" as preferences about the arena of party competition, she said that their housing organization worked "without political ideas"
in order to avoid suspicions of each other's political motives. In short, if her
consciousness had changed, she was not aware of it because she denied any
changes took place. Rather than linking her own needs to the larger political
and social system in the way consciousness-raisers would hope, Francesca
thought more like the "sociotropes" found in the public opinion literature.
That is, she separated her own situation from the larger society and said that
her political views were based on what was good for the entire nation. She said
that "when one sees so many things in the streets," one realizes that people are
suffering and need help: "God helps me, and thanks to God and the Virgin
Mary, I have what I need for my kids. But I can't just think about me, but about
others."

Her claim to be interested in the larger society was backed up by her discourse on national politics, which focused on children and employment. She expressed particular concern about the difficult agrarian labor market, which had caused her to move her family to Buenos Aires from Corrientes, where she preferred to live. She did not discuss her more immediate material interest, housing, as a national problem that elected officials should resolve. Also, she did not make any connection between what she learned in the housing movement and what she thought about national politics. As she perceived them, the housing movement was an arena free of partisan politics, while national politics were defined by partisan struggles, and so there was no connection to be made between the two arenas.

Jorge.— Jorge too expressed no relationship between his political work and his view of larger political issues. He explained his housing struggle to me using the arguments the residents had found useful in convincing the local community and city council of Padelai's cause. When a politician tried to discredit the Padelai, suggesting it was a den of iniquity in beautiful San Telmo, Jorge said he had told the council member that to his knowledge the charge was a lie but he certainly would not want his family living among prostitutes, addicts, and thieves. Calling the councilman's bluff, Jorge asked him to supply names and facts about any thieves living in the Padelai since it was the politician's civic duty to report crimes so the thieves could be arrested. As for prostitutes and drug addicts, Jorge recognized these as social problems rather than crimes, suggesting that if such people were identified they should be given dignified jobs or addiction treatment. When critics objected to spending city funds to house trespassers, Jorge replied that no one wanted a handout, merely an opportunity to purchase the building where they already lived rather than having the city sell it to someone else. Jorge repeatedly ignored the fact that the residents lived illegally in order to focus on the fact that they needed a place to live. In Castells' (1983, 319–21) terms, he employed an argument typical in urban movements: he depicted "the city as a use value" against adversaries who saw the city for its "exchange-value." Jorge also argued that the entire neighborhood was safer now that there were tenants in the formerly dark, infested, and vacant building and that many San Telmians would benefit from the daycare center that was to be built as part of the building rehabilitation.

Analyzing these and other arguments that Jorge considered persuasive, we find he relied on four tactics: first, discrediting his opponents by making their arguments look either hypocritical, elitist, or greedy; secondly, reassuring other citizens that the Padelai residents shared mainstream values of honesty, family, and hard work; thirdly, pointing out how the neighborhood's interests

would be served by the conversion of Padelai; and fourth, insisting without
apology or compromise on their *rights* to decent housing in San Telmo. The
first two tactics are savvy and ad hominem. Their underlying ideology is consistent with the dominant society. These arguments ignore social and policy
questions relating to material needs in order to focus on the honorableness of
the opponents in the debate. The third claim seeks to change opponents' views
of their own interests by arguing that the orphanage rehabilitation would be
mutually beneficial—a public good of interest to all. Only the fourth tactic
makes a strong normative claim, but in a country where housing is a constitutional right, the controversial aspects of his claim are that he implies that
housing rights are stronger than property rights (and thus justify trespassing
on them) and that he insists that the right to housing includes the right of
poor people to housing in the desirable central city. Jorge asserted the dignity
of poor people and their right not to be moved out of their homes against their
wills. He attacked the snobbishness of those who thought the poor did not
belong in San Telmo. While the implicit claims of a right to trespass and a
right to *subsidized* housing *in* the city are highly contested in Argentina (as was
evidenced in my interviews with neighbors and community leaders in San
Telmo), the basic values Jorge explicitly emphasized were widely shared and un-
threatening to the status quo: human dignity, opportunity for the less-fortunate,
and a right to shelter. His pragmatic and emotionally-charged arguments were
no doubt more effective with his multipartisan audience than arguments
rooted in leftist conceptions of a just social structure would have been.

While the reasoning Jorge used to defend their struggle seemed well-
practiced and had likely developed through conversations with his political advisers, there was no evidence that the arguments were insincere, in the
sense of his actual reasoning and motivations being grounded in a different
ideology.[39] Everything in his discourse as he moved beyond the Padelai campaign to discuss his family life and employment was consistent with the pragmatic but righteously indignant arguments he used to advance Padelai's cause.
He never used the vocabulary of class that is common in Argentina among
sympathizers of both Peronism and the left. Although he recognized that social processes affect individuals (e.g., he saw prostitution as the result of
poverty rather than immorality) and he valued collective goods, nevertheless,
his concerns and focus were largely local and individual. He did not attribute
his material needs to larger national and international forces as others interviewed who were highly active in politics had done.[40]

Jorge's discourse revealed that the experiences of deeply felt material need
and successful political struggle had improved his sense of self-worth, confirmed for him the dignity and rights of the poor, widened his view of the

scope of the housing problem internationally, and taught him how to play political hardball. They had not, however, engendered interest in electoral politics beyond the local level where his housing decisions were made nor promoted a recognition of the structural and policy contexts at the national or international levels in which his material reality arose.

Martín.— In Martín's case, working in a movement with a nonpartisan strategy did have one effect on his political ideas: he learned to work side by side with, and to trust at a personal level, people whose partisan loyalties differed from his own. Active in the Peronist Youth at a young age, Martín said that he had learned in school and later in a labor union and in his partisan work to see the left as the enemy. The reason, he explained, was that the left was the most combative threat to the Peronists' monopoly of support among the working class. Yet in the Padelai housing campaign, he had seen support, as well as exploitation and betrayal, come from across the partisan spectrum. The technical advisers and the students who helped their housing fight were "leftist intellectuals" in his view, but he was impressed that they had worked untiringly and apparently without ulterior partisan motives for the good of the people of Padelai. So this made him think "a bit" differently about the left:

> I've changed my way of talking with people from the left. It's not that I have changed the idea, say, about being on the left myself, but now I try to understand more their way of working. As I was telling you, they are the ones who fight the hardest. The Radicals don't fight at all. . . .The majority of the left is intellectuals and students, so there's always been a bit of suspicion, you know? A lack of trust. In Peronism the majority are workers—the base, I mean, the activists, are workers. And on the left, here in Argentina, the majority are university or tertiary or master's students—another level. And so there's always a bit of distrust too. And we don't have the same level as them. We don't understand their struggle.

> Q: And maybe they don't understand your struggle?
> Martín: Sure, there are always differences. . . . There are problems too, they don't understand workers and we don't understand intellectuals. Although now, we—or myself at least—are a bit more in dialogue. One of the MOI leaders, Miguel, comes here. He's from the left, but one can converse with him, we see his work, and this is a bit of what's convincing me. Because he doesn't come to impose anything. He comes to help. He's not here to gain advantage for any leftist party—

he's of the left, as he's always said, but doesn't come here for political gain. . . . And there were people who came from leftist parties who were seeking political advantage—and folks from the Peronist party itself too—from the right, left, Peronists.

It took a particular experience in politics with individual political actors—an opportunity provided by the Padelai's nonpartisan strategy—to expose Martín for the first time, in a nonthreatening way, to a plurality of political views. Nevertheless, as he was quick to point out, his identity and loyalties remained thoroughly Peronist. He said that he perceived "social justice" to be inseparable from Peronism. Political participation had softened his blind distrust of people from the left but had not changed the categories by which he organized and evaluated the political world.

Martín's change in thinking about the left was completely dependent on their respecting the nonpartisan strategy of the housing movement. When reinterviewed in 1995, he no longer trusted the MOI organizers because he saw them as too closely tied to the dissident unionist movement, which was allied with the FREPASO party and in open opposition to Menem. While MOI organizers, as quoted above, saw their role as consciousness-raisers, Martín was threatened by what he perceived as partisan attempts at conversion. He believed that they had crossed the boundaries of nonpartisanship. In 1995, using the same terms he had used three years before to describe the traditional distrust between "intellectual leftists" and "workers," Martín described the gap that had arisen between himself and MOI: "The MOI was founded at Padelai and by Padelai people, but we don't like the direction it's taken. Padelai and MOI folks don't have much in common. Miguel is turning MOI more into a political party and has associated it with FREPASO and since Padelai folks aren't in FREPASO, and moreover, want to follow our own politics, we don't want to mix politics with our housing. We don't want to go to a MOI meeting that's held at the CTA headquarters [a labor federation that had broken with Menemism and supported FREPASO]."

Limitations of the Nonpartisan Strategy

These three Padelai activists perceived social movements and parties not as alternative means to achieve demands but as functionally distinct.[41] Housing was an issue for social movements, while other policy questions were matters for interparty competition. The Padelai residents were determined not to fall into the clientelist trap of allying with any single party in exchange for goods, but unlike the nonclientelists Stokes (1995) and Oxhorn (1995, 32) identified in residentially-based movements, the Padelai activists were not ideologically radical and their organization did not impute a transformative political vision. In the Padelai case, the political consciousness that the literature predicts would be enhanced by active participation in a social movement was undercut by the residents' nonpartisan strategy. By adopting that strategy, Martín effectively treated partisan politics as irrelevant to his housing struggle and in doing so cut himself off from those institutions—parties—with the capacity at the national level to put his material needs into a larger context of related policy concerns. Likewise Jorge, although learning a good deal about the political process via his experience as an organization leader, did not acquire a comprehensive worldview. His success as a spokesman for a controversial project had depended upon his narrow focus on housing. His political activities involved convincing elites, potential mass-level opponents (neighbors), and Padelai's own residents that the cooperative's work did not involve partisan aims or ideologically-threatening policies. Such a stance was not conducive to developing the broader political consciousness that the architect-adviser, quoted earlier, hoped would come from the social movement. The fear of being coopted by political parties kept the Padelai residents focused narrowly on local government housing policies, which was counterproductive to any potential consciousness-raising. If social movements have the potential to show people the connections between their personal material interests and the national government's weak social policies, that potential is undermined by the avoidance of national issues—an avoidance that arose as part of a commitment to avoid the divisiveness of partisan politics and the cooptation of partisan alliances.

Martín, Jorge, and Francesca perceived national-level political ideas as embedded in parties. Since they wanted to avoid partisan attachments in their work, any linkage between their housing struggle and the debates over social and economic opportunity at the national level was thwarted by their refusal to define their struggle in partisan terms. Thus, precisely *because* the social movement's strategy was designed to be nonpartisan, attract broad sympathies, and appeal to multiple points of view, it could *not* politicize Martín, Jorge, and Francesca in ways that would change their fundamental political values or loyalties. They were politically active but not politically transformed. They had not changed "consciousness" and not come to connect their chief "pocketbook" concern (housing) with a broader understanding that the housing shortage was but one example of a state unresponsive to material needs at the grassroots of society.

Castells (1983, 329–31) observed that urban social movements are usually locally focused because they "appear to have no other choice." He described them as "reactive" rather than proactive. They are weak, disillusioned, and defensive, unable to transform their larger society in the face of the distant and top-down powers of the state, the electronic media, the parties, and the global capitalist economy. The narrowly local goals and cautious self-defensiveness that Castells observed are evident in Jorge's singleminded focus on housing and his carefulness in presenting his demands as consistent with, rather than a challenge to, mainstream values. In Francesca and Martín's fear of linking their housing struggles to partisan politics we recognize a defensive posture against cooptation and clientelism by more powerful organizations.

Yet clearly their focus was local not merely because they lacked other choices. The local level also appeared from a short-term perspective to be the *best* choice. Local authorities owned the building they occupied and had the power to legalize their tenancy, therefore local action was the logical first step.

Jorge, Francesca, and Martín's failure to progress to the next step—that is, the failure of their politicization to result in increased consciousness despite the intentions of the outside advisers—seems partly rooted in their commitment to avoid partisanship. Autonomy became an article of faith. It prevented the movement's members from recognizing their material demands in the context of other citizens' similar interests (i.e., the national deficit in affordable housing). Autonomy also prevented them from seeing their housing interests as part of the larger context of national-level economic and social policy debates, which were carried out along partisan lines. Thus, the feature Castells saw as crucial to the movements' capacity to push for radical change—their autonomy from parties—may become a behavioral norm that prevents the movement from building independent relationships with parties, relationships which Castells (1983, 284) and others have argued are necessary in the long term if new social movements are to be effective (e.g., Mainwaring 1987, 154).

Martín, Francesca, and Jorge did not make the connection between their personal experiences (of material hardship and of petitioning their government) and the national-level conditions necessary for people like themselves to enjoy economic opportunity, decent housing, and access to their representatives. As discussed in chapter 1, some literature on sociotropic voting suggests that such a connection is usually not made because sophisticated people recognize that personal problems are not the government's fault. That argument does not hold here. As a matter of strategy and tactics, these highly politicized Padelai activists deliberately closed off opportunities to make a connection between their strong material interest in housing and their national-level political interests. Since the activists refused to be partisan and sought to avoid clientelist obligations, partisan political leaders had no reason to place the activists' material interest, housing, on the agenda for wider political debate.

Therefore, the consciousness raising that is supposed to occur in social move-ments—the linking of the local to the national and the personal to the politi-cal—did not take place.

Yet we might wonder why people did not on their own initiative blame the national government for its failure to guarantee the constitutional right to housing. Why did they not link their personal interest to their political ones? They expected to resolve their housing need at a local level and did not wish to risk that solution by complicating their housing demands with larger ones. Martín and Francesca thought sociotropically about national politics, but not because their personal material interests were not, empirically, relevant to na-tional politics. Housing is a right guaranteed by Article 14 of the national con-stitution. Furthermore, there was at the time a national-level public housing agency, and the housing deficit was a problem nationwide. Rather, the Padelai activists ignored the national-level ramifications of their interests because they perceived adequate means to address those interests at a lower level. As will be seen further in chapter 5, people think about their material interests first in terms of coping. If local means to cope are available, they do not think about those interests as supralocal ones.

The consequence, of course, is that the residents never put pressure upon national level politicians to address the housing issue comprehensively. Con-sequently, while their personal housing needs were, due to market realities and to the constitution, a national matter, they remained *de facto* local issues. Francesca and Martín discussed national politics as responsible for the things that they had *not* organized to demand locally: children's needs, job creation, health care, etc. These were issues for partisan competition and thus were the topics the two interviewees raised in their discourse on national politics. Their personal material interest in housing was a matter for political action, but only locally. Thus, their sociotropic attitudes were not due to any logical or "appro-priate" disconnection between personal interests and national politics but rather were due to political parties (which failed to draw connections between housing shortages and national policies) being treated as the primary framers of national political discourse.

The case of the Padelai activists shows how people with strong material interests, even when immersed in political action to resolve those interests, may divorce their individual action and personal interests from their larger political views. Several other interviewees, not at Padelai, had participated in collective action to obtain or retain housing.[42] In their discourse, their need for secure housing also was not used to define or justify their points of view on national politics. Their housing interest was a matter for political action but they did not base their political evaluations on their housing interests.

Conclusions

This chapter set forth three empirical findings about how people evaluate and deal with their housing concerns and examined the implications of each. First, to establish that shelter is a severe material concern that we could expect to be a political concern, I described the housing conditions in Buenos Aires. These conditions demonstrated how the quality of one's life is strongly affected by the qualities of one's housing. Certain housing conditions (overcrowding, noise, tensions, stigma) are a hindrance to studying, to personal relationships, and even to a job search. In these ways, poor housing conditions are more than mere discomforts or simple indicators of low income. The conditions themselves have consequences for a person's opportunities and relationships. This means that at a given income level, people who can avoid these hindrances because they own their homes, live in public housing, or have secure rental apartments are in a very different material position from those who live in hotels, *inquilinatos*, or *casas tomadas*. Furthermore, poor housing conditions are not merely objectively difficult; people who live with these conditions perceive them, subjectively, as significant material interests. The people I interviewed dreamed, schemed, and complained about housing. They recognized its control over their quality of life.

Second, through the case of housing, this chapter demonstrated the heterogeneity of material interests and, most important, why that heterogeneity is relevant to understanding how citizens respond to their material interests. The particular *type* of residence can affect a person's freedom, health, comfort, identity, capacity for collective action, and potential to make personal progress. This heterogeneity means that lower-income Argentines, in the periods of economic crisis and adjustment, suffered in varying ways. For example, renters facing a fixed monthly payment are in a different material circumstance from people of the same income level who own their homes (whether apartments or shanties) or who live rent-free in a *casa tomada*. On the other hand, poor people without rent obligations face their own different set of hardships due to their housing: in a *casa tomada*, this includes the fear of eviction or arrest for trespassing; in a shantytown, social and physical marginality.

In addition, this chapter examined closely the political reasoning of individuals who saw housing as a preoccupying material interest and it found that the material interests did not directly shape the political reasoning. The people interviewed who had pressing desires for better housing responded to those interests in very different ways. Some chose collective political action, others individual nonpolitical action, but only two (Hilda and Adriana) spoke of housing as an important state responsibility that might affect their evaluation of political actors.

Despite the significance of their housing conditions to their daily lives, those who needed better housing did not premise their political views on their most basic material need—not even those like Jorge, Francesca, and Martín, who understood politics as the arena in which their problem could be resolved. This is not a problem of public versus private spheres of action, for Argentines consider housing to be a public concern. A dignified residence is a constitutional right and for decades the state has taken some (albeit ineffective) role in housing through statutes and programs concerning mortgages, rent control, and housing construction. So how can a problem be so important to people's daily lives, be clearly understood as a public issue, and yet trigger so little response in the political views and preferences citizens express and the actions they take?

At the level of collective responses, the answer to this question lies in the diversity of the material problem. In central city Buenos Aires, the heterogeneity of housing hinders mobilization among those lacking adequate shelter; each housing type carries with it different advantages and disadvantages to its tenants and has several political effects. To begin with, the spacial arrangement of central city poverty housing separates the poor from each other and hides them from the larger community. Thus, this type of urban, nonshantytown poverty is prevented from becoming a bigger political issue simply because it is not as visible as other types of housing needs. Furthermore, the diversity of living arrangements means that urban residents may share the experience of crowding but not share other housing problems—such as restrictive hotel managers, fear of eviction, illegal electricity, collective organizing challenges, or the stigma of address—which are only associated with certain types of housing. Thus, the residents of hotels, *casas tomadas, inquilinatos,* and shantytowns do not acknowledge a common set of shelter problems nor do they seek similar solutions. In addition, the hope that individual effort will allow them to move up the housing ladder prevents some people from looking at their housing need as a political issue. Organizers have difficulty convincing people that collective action is feasible and effective. Finally, even where there was collective action seeking housing, the people interviewed saw their need in narrow terms, not related to macrolevel politics. In fact, they shunned any attempt to link their material (housing) interest to larger political or partisan issues.

At the individual level, the answer to the anomaly lies in the way people think about their material interests, about how politics works, and about their political priorities. These ways of thinking are explored at length through the rest of the book. Here, the case study of whether housing interests became political interests provided the first clues for a more general analysis to come. The housing study suggests that people's material interests lie not merely in the physical discomforts of their material conditions, but also in the stressful family relations, social stigma, isolation, and constrained opportunities that those conditions may produce. Further, it finds that the interviewees mostly relied on individual, nonpolitical means to try to improve their housing conditions. Some employed local-level political means, but they eschewed partisan entanglements. Almost no one interviewed expressed any expectation that their housing interests would be addressed in national-level political contests. Taking up these issues in a more general way in the next chapter, I examine how material hardships other than housing affect people's daily lives, self-perceptions, hopes for their future, and expectations of government.

Chapter

4

Material Interests

> A beggar sitting on the street and reading a newspaper account of President Menem's claims to have moved Argentina toward the First World: "This thing about being part of the First World is very good. Before, I used to feel like a poor person from Calcutta or Bombay. But now I feel like a poor person from New York or Paris."
>
> CRIST, Clarín (7 May 1992)

The case study of housing provided insights into the nature of material interests. They are not broadly categorical. People may speak in broad class terms about being "poor" but the material problems they identify are quite specific (Cornelius 1974). People do not see themselves as "not having adequate housing," but rather as "living with the insecurity of a *casa tomada*," "living in the crowded, expensive conditions of a *hotel*," or "not being able to save for a downpayment on an apartment." Moreover, the complaints that people voiced about their housing were not simply material—wanting cleaner bathrooms or more space—but rather were complaints about the particular *consequences* of their material conditions. That is, their material living conditions had consequences for their family relationships, their job opportunities, their social status and self-esteem, and for how they spent their free time. Furthermore, the strategies people undertook to address their housing interests varied and were sometimes highly political, yet those efforts largely did not lead people to link their severe material interest in housing to their evaluation of the policies of national-level politicians.

This chapter builds on the findings from the housing cases in order to analyze the nature of material interests more broadly. These interests are not merely a function of quantity of material goods (i.e., of poverty or wealth), since perceptions of material interests are only partially explained by the scarcity or abundance of goods. To conceptualize those interests in broader terms, I build on economic development and social policy literatures that have made substantial advances in conceptualizing poverty. Bringing these literatures into the political study of citizen interests, I argue that the political ramifications of material difficulties can be best understood if we recognize how people experience material hardships—stress, exclusion, constraints on opportunities, and restrictions of choice—and how they process or think about those experiences. To make the argument, this chapter highlights the discourse of people who face their material constraints in differing ways—by experiencing anger, acquiescence, or hope.

On the Quantity and Quality of Material Life

Material interests might seem to be simply a matter concerning people's material needs plus their material desires, with the former (applying Maslow's hierarchy of needs [1954]) having priority. Yet if our goal is to understand which material conditions become the basis for a person's political interests, focusing on the most severe conditions will not get us very far. As the previous chapter illustrated, people had quite diverse reactions to their lack of decent housing—something widely considered a basic need—and most did not demand or expect national-level action on housing problems. In this section, I explain why trying to define "needs" is fraught with problems and why material interests can be better understood as arising from insecurities and constraints rather than from objective "needs."

The attempt to define "needs" is widespread. In political, everyday, and academic discourses, material interests are commonly discussed in terms of needs versus luxuries. There are strong normative reasons for distinguishing the two, given the moral claim that minimal human needs deserve to be met before nonnecessary desires (Shue 1980). Operating on this norm, the World Bank urges targeted social spending in order to avoid wasting scarce public funds on the less needy. Certain philosophies about government also require distinguishing needs from comforts on the premise that, regardless of the state's resources, the state's proper role is not to spend public money for desires not essential to human existence. The dichotomy between need and comfort is not limited to moral and policy arguments but is also at the root of certain empirical measures commonly used in the social sciences. For example, poverty headcounts and measures of inadequacies in housing, education, or sanitation are premised on definitions of material "needs." Policy makers have relied on such distinctions in order to measure socioeconomic change as well as to define policy priorities.

An example of how this reasoning enters political discourse is found in the following quotation written at the time of my field research by an Argentine journalist disputing reports of growing poverty. Note that the argument rests on the widespread assumption that need can be defined in terms of lacking specific material possessions and on the view that public policies are adequate as long as they cover those basic possessions: "[The official poverty level reported in the newspapers] is not poverty and bears no relation to our [magazine's] minimum working class budget that costs about 230 pesos a month for a family of four. Even this, however, finances survival, gas, electricity and a limited amount of bus transport to and from a stable dwelling house. It is a dreary and unpleasant existence, but it is not poverty, anymore than the plight of a single pensioner struggling to live on, say, 200 pesos. The really poor live, or somehow survive, below this level, and there are certainly not nine million of them" (The Review of the River Plate, 17 September 1992, 142–43).[1]

In terms the indignant journalist would have found oxymoronic, many of those interviewed for this book defined themselves as poor even though they did not need basic necessities. Oscar, a janitor in a formal sector job and owner of a modest, legal, self-built home in the outskirts of the metropolitan area, exemplified this view: "*Somos pobres todos, pero tenemos para vivir.* (We are all poor, but we have enough to live.)"

For Oscar and others heard in this book, poverty is not a measure of where one's income falls compared to a poverty line that measures the costs of purchasing basic necessities. Material conditions occur on a continuum, and few people are aware of whether they have crossed the policy maker's line distinguishing "poverty" from sufficient resources or "necessity" from "comfort." Rather, for Oscar and others in similar situations, poverty implies both a social identity as well as a standard of living. That social identity is frequently the basis of political interest, as chapter 6 will show; however, the standard of living and the actual material needs are only occasionally of political interest, as this and the next chapter will explain.

It is not that citizens do not accept the needs/comforts dichotomy—they frequently do. In fact, like Oscar, many pointed out, in what was evidently a matter of self-esteem, that while they lacked comforts, they had everything humans need to live. Yet while the needs/comforts dichotomy is well accepted, the dividing line between needs and comforts is not. Survey research on subjective evaluations of poverty has found evidence that for every ten percent increase in average income, a person's judgment about what income level constitutes "poverty" increased about six percent (Kilpatrick 1973, 327–32, cited in Haveman 1987, 69).

Distinctions between necessity and luxury are not only subjective but are also highly malleable to self-interest. Consider the comments of Gabriela and her husband Raúl. Gabriela, a lifelong San Telmian of modest and deteriorated means, was proud of San Telmo's history of being a neighborhood for working class people in *conventillos*, like herself. At the same time, she and her husband had strongly opposed the squatters' project to remain in, and rehabilitate, the Padelai orphanage. "There's a difference between need and comfort," Raúl argued. "Those people want not just to meet their need for housing but to have the comforts of living in the city." Gabriela finished his thought by saying, "Because it is more comfortable living here in the capital. I, for example, am used to living in the capital, because I was born here! I would suffer if I had to move out. They weren't born here. Understand?" She felt the residents of Padelai would not "understand." They argued that even they who were not lifelong residents of San Telmo also "needed" the conveniences of the stores, parks, busses, and the shorter commute that they would lack if they had to move out to the poor neighborhoods in the outskirts of Buenos Aires.

In addition to the problem of subjective bias, a second problem with defining "necessity" is context. Norms of insufficiency versus luxury change over time and place (Altimir 1982, 13–15; Haveman 1987, 54; Townsend 1970, 18–19). As certain conveniences and advantages become widespread, from telephones and televisions to a high school education, a society begins to take their availability for granted. Job applicants find the application asks for a phone number and a diploma. The complexities of modern urban life, from privatized retirement systems to insurance, taxes, and rental contracts, require greater basic literacy than in the past. Public health and safety announcements are made on television, and children are asked in school to discuss a program televised the previous night. Those without the appliances or the education that have become commonplace are disadvantaged—needy—in a way that they would not have been a generation before or in a different society. Certainly the people interviewed defined their interests in the context of their particular society's norms. They dreamed of achieving goals reached by others in Argentine society.

Because "needs" change with context, Peter Townsend (1970, 42–45) argued that poverty is a relative concept, which should be defined by a low level of those resources which, in a particular society, affluent people take for granted as "customary." These resources would include not just income levels, but assets, social services, and job perquisites. Townsend's purpose was to define poverty in order to conduct social policy research. Extending his conceptualization, however, I consider below whether there are political ramifications from being left outside the social norm. Do those who are objectively excluded from society by virtue of their material conditions subjectively perceive themselves as excluded? If so, do they hold the state or the political system responsible for that exclusion? These questions are addressed later in this chapter.

A third problem with distinguishing "needs" from "luxuries" is that such distinctions tend to see human needs only in physical terms. Thus, even though social scientists have long recognized that people value love, security, personal development, and other goods beyond physical ones (e.g., Gurr 1970, 25–26), nevertheless, discussions of economic and social policies tend to focus on their impact in physical terms, such as effects upon nutrition, shelter, water, health care, sufficient education to be employable, and sanitation services.[2] Yet several people interviewed argued that human beings need culture and recreation as well as nutrition and shelter. Olivia, a recently laid-off bookkeeper accustomed to the benefits of public sector employment, described her summer vacation as a "necessity." María José, the widow of a career military officer and a person whose living standard had declined markedly over the years, said that the economic situation had forced her to postpone purchases of clothes and shoes, which she defended as "things that really aren't luxuries, but things you need." Her adult daughter, María, initially mentioned the books and movies the middle class could no longer afford as foregone luxuries; immediately she reconsidered her statement, saying that they were not luxuries, but rather, essential to "nourish the spirit." Carlos, a low-skilled factory worker who lived in much more meager circumstances than the three women just quoted, nevertheless shared their sense that a meaningful life *requires* more than mere biological necessities. Asked about current standards of living in Argentina, he volunteered the following analysis of needs:

It depends what you mean by living—living is one thing, surviving is another. Let's start there. So, what does a typical family need to live in a dignified way? Access to shelter, right? I believe that's a constitutional right, no, that a typical family has the right to housing? What other rights? Well, that you work and you make enough to eat. But the thing is that here in Argentina we are simply used to surviving, which is something different. That is, what do people do? They go from home to work and work to home. Right? Well, so what about recreation? Doesn't a guy need to go on vacation, for example? Here, say you say "I'm going to the theater." Many people here look at that as a luxury. Or for example, we have a friend who sells newspapers at a newsstand. He told me that in this country they sell 3 million copies

a day—in the whole country, right? But in a country with, say, taking
out the children suppose there are 20 million adults [i.e., who could
potentially buy a paper], and it's just a newspaper. That's an extremely
low number of papers. . . . Let's say I can tell you that, for example, it's
been about six months since I've bought myself a new pair of pants,
ok? Clothing isn't something of prime necessity. That is, a guy can live
without new clothes. Understand? I can also live without going to the
theater. I can live. But the thing is that I think it's a question of what it
[i.e., depriving oneself, in order merely to survive] does to the culture
of the people.

Across the entire set of interviews, I was able to identify clear statements
about whether persons thought of their needs only in terms of physical survival or in broader terms in twenty-five of the interviews. (This was not a
question one could ask directly and expect a valid response, so I categorized
interviews as expressing the view that survival was sufficient if the person
made statements such as "I have what I need to get by," or if the person used
the distinction between physical needs and "comforts.") Of those twenty-five,
ten expressed the "survival is sufficient" perspective, while fifteen suggested
that life in general (or their lives in particular) requires leisure, music, recreation, contemplation, etc.—not mere physical survival. As table 4.1 shows,
those who objectively had life's physical needs secured, by standard measures
of satisfied basic needs, were more likely to speak of nonphysical "necessities"
than those living without the basics.[3] What is most interesting is that about
half of the latter group also expressed the attitude that they needed more than
mere survival.

The "need" for culture, leisure, and beauty, which Carlos, Olivia, and the
others expressed, is not due solely to idiosyncratic preferences for spiritual
or emotional enrichment. The desire for these types of enrichments arises

TABLE 4.1 RESPONDENTS' IDEAS ABOUT "NEED" BY THEIR OBJECTIVE PHYSICAL NEEDS

| | Unsatisfied Basic Needs[a] | | Basic Needs Satisfied | |
	%	(n)	%	(n)
Need involves more than physical survival	47	(7)	80	(8)
Need means physical survival	53	(8)	20	(2)
Totals (n)	100	(15)	100	(10)

[a] Unsatisfied Basic Needs is a common poverty measure (See INDEC 1990, 27). Here I have used three "basic
needs" as indicators: quality of housing, overcrowding, and whether there is a bathroom in the home.

because low levels of *material* resources have created ignorance, stress, and ugly surroundings. Yet the perceived need for culture, leisure, and beauty is not a material concern that gets counted by standard binary categories such as poor or not-poor, needy or comfortable, which tend to focus only on identifying the point at which a certain low quantity of material resources or low degree of earning capacity would threaten *physical* well-being.

Recognizing the problems with conceptualizing material interests solely in physical terms, Amartya Sen has argued that physical needs such as stable housing or sanitation and the income needed to achieve them are merely instrumental to what really counts, which is "what life we lead and what we can or cannot do, can or cannot be" (1987, 16). For Sen, positive freedom provides people with the capacity to achieve an adequate level of living. Thus, to use his example, while someone who is malnourished because she cannot afford to buy food is poor, someone who is malnourished after choosing to fast for religious purposes is not, because the latter had the freedom to choose between malnourishment and nourishment (1987, 37–38). To be needy is to lack such freedom.

Julio Boltvinik, formerly of the United Nations Development Program (UNDP), provides further insight on how a person's level of material resources affects freedom of choice. For Boltvinik, a family is in poverty if they must choose between staying childless but above the poverty level or following their desire to have children while knowing that, with dependents, their standard of living would be lowered below poverty levels (due to overcrowding, diminished income, etc.) (1992c, 359). Regardless of the choice made, such a family's material condition is low if they face a choice between the basic human right to eat and the basic human right to reproduce. One can argue that everyone, or at least everyone short of billionaires, experiences some limitations on their material conditions and therefore must make choices, but Boltvinik suggests that poverty consists of being in a position where the choices are not between alternative diversions but between the basic items needed for full participation in society, such that a person cannot freely choose the kind of life he or she will lead. As Boltvinik sees it, when people are forced to leave school to support their families or to work such long hours that there is no time left to relax, then they are subsisting by depriving themselves of an education and recreation.

The most recent innovations in measuring severe poverty, proposed by the UNDP, rely strongly on Sen's conceptualization of deprivation as *constraint* on the freedom to live. They also rely, implicitly, on Townsend's recognition that to be deprived is to be relatively constrained from participating in the life a particular society offers—that is, to be excluded. As a UNDP document puts it, "*relative* deprivation in incomes and commodities can lead to an *absolute* deprivation in minimum capabilities [to be and do valued things]" (UNDP 1997, 16–18, emphasis added; also, Boltvinik 1992a; Boltvinik 1992b, 483).

"Needs," therefore, are not nearly so simple to identify as the Argentine journalist quoted earlier would believe. If material conditions have consequences not just for physical survival and comfort but for freedom, social inclusion, emotional and intellectual well-being, and life opportunities, then we should expect that the material interests citizens perceive would be shaped not merely by their incomes and the absolute physical level of their well-being but also by the freedoms, exclusions, emotional and intellectual deprivations, and diminished opportunities that their material conditions create for them relative to others in their society. It should be emphasized that although Sen and others sought to conceptualize the severest kinds of material constraints, their concepts can travel far beyond the study of poverty. They have much to offer political scientists trying to understand how people perceive their material interests regardless of whether those interests are based in conditions typically defined as "poor."

Do people see the strains and constraints in their lives and do they blame the state for either causing, or failing to remove, those impediments? If so, what are the consequences for the elected government and for the democratic regime? If people do not perceive impediments or do not blame the state, why not? And, again, what are the consequences for government and the regime? I devote the rest of this book to attempting to provide some answers to these questions.[4]

Perceptions of Objective Constraints

Objective Insecurity and Flux

Among the greatest strains perceived by people of low or falling incomes is not their material level of living per se but insecurity (Levine 1993, 195; Scott 1976, 1–55). Argentine sociologists often describe the "precariousness" of life for the poor, an apt term for the insecurity of both poor and middle-class people in the 1990s. Those employed informally were particularly vulnerable to small employers' closing shop or laying off employees. The flux in the lives of those interviewed was striking. They were constantly turning up new options, hopes, and possibilities for making a bit more money, as well as for dealing with unexpected job losses or other changes in fortune. Among those interviewed on more than one occasion, it was not uncommon for their strategy for making a living to have changed from one meeting to the next.

Tables 4.2 and 4.3 list the kinds of insecurity and change experienced by people in the two years previous to their interviews.[5] In most cases, these experiences were current and ongoing. People worked constantly just to maintain their standard of living, and they were always looking for ways to improve it, which resulted in substantial flux in their lives. More than two-thirds of those interviewed experienced significant instabilities or lifestyle changes owing to their economic status. In some cases, the insecurities were created by new family circumstances such as a major wage earner's serious illness, but even among these people their low incomes intensified the misfortune brought by poor health, by preventing them from getting first-rate medical care that would enable them to return to work more quickly. Of the twelve people interviewed who reported no incidents of change in the prior two years, five had lived through significant job insecurity during an earlier period of economic

TABLE 4.2. SOURCES OF FLUX AND INSECURITY

Sources of Flux and Insecurity	Number of interviewees
Job change	2
Residence change	3
Insecure employment[a]	15
Insecure housing	12
Health problems interfering with work	5
Wages perceived as below expenses[b]	7

[a] Includes those without work, those with only part-time and informal work, and those whose jobs were being restructured. Does not include all informal sector jobs, only those where the interview revealed evidence of insecurity.
[b] Not an objective measure of income sufficiency nor a count of those wishing to make more but rather a count of those who in the course of the interview described their earnings as inadequate.

TABLE 4.3. INCIDENCE OF SOURCES OF FLUX AND INSECURITY

Number of Table 4.2 sources known to apply	Number of Interviewees
0	12
1	18
2	6
3	2
4	2
Insufficient information on whether any apply	1
Total interviews	

turmoil in posttransition Argentina, when they lost jobs due to changes in company ownership, restructuring, or the vagaries of the informal sector. Therefore, at best, only one in six persons interviewed had lived free of the insecurity of flux in employment or housing.

Most of those interviewed, from the poorest to those in the lower middle class, found it challenging to make ends meet. With little or no margin for a rainy day, their standard of living was as precarious as their job situations. They could not afford to repair home appliances that broke or to pay unexpected bills. The lack of peace of mind—their inability to accumulate resources and save for the future—was one of the greatest problems for the falling middle class during 1991 and 1992, when wages were low and the endurance of the newly low inflation rate was in doubt.

Perceptions of Insecurity and Flux

We can observe objectively the ways that a person's material conditions limit choices and create uncertainty but whether the person perceives these material constraints as either unjust or intolerable varies. To examine this variance, I will consider the perspectives of two people, Amanda and Graciela. Although Graciela has a substantially higher per capita family income than Amanda, each experienced the constraints that Sen and Boltvinik highlighted in that their resources did not allow them the freedom to make basic life choices. The two women showed substantial differences in their tolerance for life under such circumstances. In each interview, a second person (Amanda's son and Graciela's older colleague, respectively) listened to at least part of the interview and occasionally interrupted, providing an additional perspective on the interviewee's point of view and further demonstrating the wide discrepancies in the ways people interpret the acceptability of material constraints. In each pair, we see the younger person more demanding and feeling more constrained. The older person, perhaps with fewer unmet goals ahead, is more accepting of constraints on opportunities.

Amanda.— Amanda was a middle-aged single mother of five children, one an adult. She had completed elementary school. She and her two oldest children constantly adjusted their employment and goals in order to try to improve their lives. Between our first two interviews, Amanda took on an additional four-hour daily shift at her job as a janitor in order to bring in extra cash. With a one-hour bus trip each way, she had to leave her home at dawn, returning at nine in the evening. The additional income from her job, together with her oldest children's jobs, most likely put her household income well over the government's poverty line, but her living conditions in a decrepit *conventillo* met most definitions of "structural poverty" or "unmet basic needs." She identified herself as "lower class" and a "worker."

Amanda did not resent the trade-off she made between higher earnings and less leisure and family time. In her view, the things she did to cope were not exceptional—simply necessary. She did not think of her decision to take on extra work in political terms. She supported President Menem for his Peronist identification with her social class, for his charisma, and for his success in fighting inflation. As she stated to me in our interview, "It seems that in every country, there are rich and poor. You have poor in your country too, don't you? I figure that there have been rich and poor since the time of Christ—or since the time of the Pharaohs, when the poor did all the work." Amanda said she wondered sometimes why such great disparities exist. When asked if it would be possible to have fewer poor people, perhaps through government policies, Amanda answered that some people are lazy and people need to work hard to try not to be poor. To my suggestion that she herself worked very hard and yet was, by her own description, poor, she replied, "Well, it does seem that the poor should earn a little more or the *ajustes*[6] could be a little less. For example, I'd like to be making $600 a month."[7]

Amanda's son Pepe saw economic opportunities a bit differently and was less willing to accept the trade-off between income and other valued goods (such as self-respect or time). In other words, he saw the costs of coping with low income as too high. He complained about the competition for jobs, saying that there was "discrimination" because job applicants were evaluated on the basis of military service, past experience, property ownership, marital status, education, grooming and clothing, and myriad other credentials. His mother, having supported the family for years through menial labor, insisted that there were plenty of jobs in janitorial or construction work, where education and the right appearance were not demanded, but her son was not interested in these. City-born youth like himself, he said, would not want to take the menial construction jobs that migrants from the poorer provinces would accept.

His mother, on the other hand, consistently showed in interviews that her self-respect was rooted in her labor, no matter how undesirable the work, and she figured that if she could do it, it was reasonable to expect others to do it too.[8]

For Amanda, political discourse, events, and alternatives in Argentina had not changed her way of understanding the relationship between her personal problems and her politics. She did not disconnect her poverty from her politics but rather she made the connection at the general, broad level of her social class instead of at the particular level of her daily bout with constraints on social participation. She objectively suffered poverty, knew that outside forces such as government could facilitate or burden her life, voted on the basis of the party (PJ) that historically seemed to represent less economic burden for her class, and yet still found it most helpful to think of her specific and personal economic circumstances in terms of individual effort, not in terms of government policy or national economic conditions.

Graciela.— Graciela, on the other hand, thought about her life and politics very differently from Amanda. At age twenty-six, and with two years of college education, she worked as an administrative employee in the Secretariat of Public Works. She had recently been laid off from an additional part-time job in the informal sector.

Graciela believed her individual efforts were stymied by national economic conditions and policies. Although public employees' wages were at that time rather low relative to the cost of living and she reported bringing home only $360 per month, she and her engineer husband enjoyed a household income of over $1000 monthly—well over the poverty line. Nevertheless, she was suffering materially and in a politically relevant way not demarcated by the poverty lines designed for use by economic and social policy makers. As a young person trying to plan for the future, she was consumed by frustration at her lack of control over her life: "If I kill myself working and my husband kills himself working, I still don't have peace of mind! I'm not talking about swimming in money, but not having that peace of mind! To not know that, well, within two years I'm going to be able to buy myself an apartment, if I make sacrifices and save so much. But one doesn't know this. Not when, nor how, nor why, nor where! You don't know!" Graciela interpreted her situation as Sen and Boltvinik might: as her lack of freedom to make choices. She understood this lack in relative terms, as an inequality in Argentine society between the rich who "get rich the same as always" and "the rest of the people" who don't have "the possibility of being better off": "I, for example, don't have the possibility of buying housing, except if I were earning four thousand or five thousand dollars a month. Because right now, a two-room apartment is thirty thousand dollars. And so, I don't have the possibility of buying a home! And it's not very easy to rent in Argentina either!" "No, it's expensive," I agreed. Continuing her point, Graciela explained that in a system where landlords frequently refuse to rent or renew leases to families with children, the rental market created constraints on the pursuit of fundamental human goals:

> It's expensive, and there aren't a great many rentals. And so, therefore, for me . . . and the whole world doesn't think the same as me, that's for sure—but for me, this stops me somewhat from having a child, be-

cause I don't know if they'll renew my lease or not renew it. [And] if I don't have money to look for another apartment at this point—because it takes [a down payment of] five months and it's at four hundred dollars. That's two thousand dollars that I'd have to put down to rent an apartment! And if I have a child, what do I do? And so, I'm twenty-six years old and I don't have the freedom to have a child! And I don't have the freedom to say, "I live here and I don't like it and they're doing such and such thing to me and so I'll move." Because I don't have that freedom!

As Graciela recognized, not everyone would perceive the economy as a constraint on reproductive liberties. Her colleague Rodrigo found her view unreasonable: "No, but you have the freedom! Who's deciding for you?! . . . This isn't a question of liberty, if you wish to wait for another time to have a child! It's not a question of not being able to have one. . . . But there's no reason that things have to be the way one would like them, instead of the way reality is." Rodrigo believed that unpleasant choices and risks are normal so he made an argument for negative freedom (freedom from legal or forcible constraints on action) rather than positive freedom (the affirmative capacity to act).

Like Graciela, Rodrigo worked for low pay and in the demoralizing and uncertain atmosphere in the public sector at a time of restructuring. Now a middle-aged public administrator, he had long ago formed a family and bought a house. At his point in life, he experienced the adjustment policies as discomfort—but not as a constraint on his ability to progress and to attain fundamental human goals, such as having offspring. He was more worried about his children's future than his own, and his opposition to Menem's policies was based on dispassionate intellectual arguments, not his own needs. In terms of income, Rodrigo and Graciela were in similar circumstances, but because of their different assets, ages, life possibilities, and subjective understandings of their own situations, Graciela felt the anxieties and pressures of the Argentine economy more personally and powerfully than Rodrigo did.

Objective Constraints on the Future

Current material conditions not only affect present choices, but also, particularly when material difficulties are experienced over a long period, future ones (Sherraden 1991). Severe financial circumstances interfere with the pursuit of career goals and the opportunity for mobility. As a World Bank (1995, 27) study of Argentina put it, based on research by Silvia Montoya and Oscar Mitnik (1994): "On the average, persons with the least education earned four times less than those with the highest educational attainment. Educational attainment determines an individual's ease and/or level of entry in the work force, as well as the type of employment obtained." Nearly every parent of young children told me that they wanted their children to get a good education so that they would have these options and opportunities, but many of them wondered if that would be possible, owing to personal or national economic conditions.[9]

In Argentina, public education is officially free; nevertheless, school supplies, materials fees, bus fare, and fees levied by parents associations seeking to upgrade the school are all expensive for lower-income budgets. For example, both Pepe and Martín mentioned a local technical high school, highly regarded for training electricians, which they said their families could not afford because of its $100 per month fees. Juan Antonio, a maintenance worker, had one child in elementary school and his oldest was in high school, but his middle son never started high school for lack of money. According to a 1988 study in Greater Buenos Aires, 19 percent of children who finished primary school from Juan Antonio's social and economic background (i.e., structurally poor) did not start high school, like his middle son. Children whose families had only recently encountered economic difficulties were less likely to forego high school (13 percent) than those structurally poor.[10] Among nonpoor children, only 8 percent failed to start high school after finishing primary school (INDEC 1990, 149).

School attendance reflects not only the limits of parental finances but also the parents' attitudes toward, and experiences with, education (Torrado 1992, 368–75). Nevertheless, independent of class-based socialization patterns, income shapes schooling decisions. Although primary school attendance in Argentina is high across all socioeconomic groups, when younger children do drop out of school, family finances have been a major cause, particularly in poorer families. A study of the reasons primary school–age children dropped out of school found that 45 percent of those from structurally poor families who left school did so for economic reasons, compared to 31 percent of those from newly impoverished families, and 25 percent of those from nonpoor families (INDEC 1990, 150). Families recently impoverished are more likely than those that are structurally poor to socialize their children toward staying in school. Data on reasons for leaving school at older ages are not available, but data on the differences in school attendance among three socioeconomic strata suggest that some combination of household finances and socialization is relevant. School attendance begins to drop at age fourteen, with substantially stronger tendencies to drop out among the structurally poor than the recently impoverished (which suggests a socialization effect), but also stronger tendencies to drop out among the impoverished than the nonpoor (which suggests an income effect) (INDEC 1990, 145).

Not only is schooling costly, but many find the need to make money for living expenses takes away the time and energy needed to study at the higher levels. For example, Betina, a twenty-eight-year-old domestic worker, and Pablo, a thirty-four-year-old bank clerk, had quit high school and university, respectively, in part because their families needed them to work. Another example is Samuel, twenty-one, who was working odd jobs and starting a six-year university program in electrical engineering when I met him. By our last meeting, he was taking classes at night and working full-time, splitting his days between electrical work at a construction site and teaching electronics at a high school. He said it was difficult to concentrate on studying at night because he was so tired. (That schedule also left him no time for teaching preparation. Somewhat sheepishly he said that his pedagogical style was to open the book and read to his students.)

Historically, almost no Argentine children of working class background attended university (see Torrado 1992, 369–70). Education rates across the population increased during the 1980s, yet almost three in four college-age students from structurally poor families were not in college in 1991.[11] One person I interviewed, Ignacio, was unusual in that he *did* attend university, but his chances of finishing remained uncertain. When I met Ignacio, twenty years old at the time, he was taking one university course and spending time on political campaigns and community work in the shantytown where his family lived. He said that after the elections he expected to seek a job, probably as a day laborer in construction, because "my family needs my help. Not because I want to, but because of my family's need." Neither of his parents had a steady or full-time job. When asked if he expected to be able to continue his studies while working, he claimed optimism: "I believe that I will, but, let's say, I'll do it slowly. Last year I was able to do it."

Perceptions of Constraints on the Future

The political implications of this variation in educational and occupational opportunities depend upon citizens' views of the restrictions on their futures, including whether people even perceive the constraints. If they do perceive them, they do not necessarily believe that the political system should offer remedies. Whether constraints on the future are perceived as political interests depends upon whether they are perceived as restraints that can be surpassed through individual effort; ones that should be remedied by government action (either for the individual's direct benefit or to change societal and economy-level conditions that affect the individual); ones to be remedied by some combination of individual and structural change; or ones that are fated and irremediable.

Listening to the interviews reveals that most respondents did indeed perceive material conditions as creating substantial constraints in their own or poorer people's lives. They took for granted that family resources would limit a child's possibilities for getting an education. Interviews included topics such as the causes of poverty and wealth, the occupations deserving pay raises, the role of government in alleviating poverty, and other subjects through which people revealed their views about material inequalities and constraints. Very often these topics were first raised by the person being interviewed. Some interviews included a question that was particularly helpful in detecting attitudes about life opportunities. Respondents were asked if two children born today, one in a *conventillo* in San Telmo and another in a place such as Barrio Norte (a fashionable, elite neighborhood), would have the same opportunities to be president, or to be a doctor or lawyer. The consensus on the hypothetical San Telmo newborn was that any future was possible with intelligence and extraordinary effort but that attaining the presidency or a profession was unlikely, because the child's parents would not have the income to provide the necessary education. One respondent, Vicente, a construction worker, reasoned about the barriers simply on the basis of the historical evidence: "No one born in a *conventillo* has become president. They've all had [more] opportunities. . . . In the last century and beginning of this century, they've all been people who were educated in Europe. For a kid who is born here in such needy circumstances, it's going to be very difficult for them to end up with advanced studies."

Overall, the respondents agreed that Argentine children are not born with equal opportunities.[12] Only occasionally, however, did a respondent describe this reality fatalistically.[13] For example, Eduardo, an unemployed construction worker, was repeatedly despondent over the hopelessness of individual effort in the face of structural factors: "Logically, the poor one, even if very intelligent, won't get as far as one from a rich family. At the point they are born, it's already known which one will end up stealing, or picking up garbage, and which one will sleep in silk sheets." Walter, a Bolivian immigrant and supermarket employee, suggested that barriers were not so much impenetrable from below, as reenforced from above: "I think that it's to certain people's advantage that the people continue being illiterate and ignorant."

Individual Solutions.— Most of those interviewed, however, believed that change, if not probable, was at least possible. Some of these tempered their views by seeing individual effort as the means to defeat socioeconomic disadvantages, at least partially. Their evidence was anecdotal and their hopes were highly personal. They tended to believe that they and their families were among those who would make progress at least a bit beyond that which their social background would predict. Jacobo, a young father and Uruguayan expatriate, was one of these. His initial response to the question about the San Telmo newborn was that family finances often force poor children to abandon their studies at a young age. After further consideration, he described himself as having been a product of those barriers and yet able to overcome them. His success in becoming a skilled auto mechanic, while his friends never learned a trade, had taught him that with a combination of persistence and luck, one could beat difficult family and national economic circumstances.

Another interview question people were asked was about their hopes and expectations for their children's futures.[14] Respondents were about evenly divided between those who said their children would live better than they and those who said the children's lives would be like theirs. It is difficult to know to what extent the former group believed their optimistic words to an interviewer, but their explanations for optimism indicate something of the way people reason about overcoming financial obstacles. They said that their children would prosper because the children were getting better educations or better parenting than they themselves had—in other words, not because societal constraints would change but because their children *as individuals* would be better poised to face the constraints.

For example, Adriana's reason for saying that her twelve-year-old son had a bright future was that he had set his sights on a good profession, electrical engineering. Carlos, whose political reasoning was thoroughly and consistently rooted in class analysis and structural explanations, believed that radical change was necessary to really change his children's lives, but he hoped that individual action could at least partly improve upon structural realities. His goal for his sons was that, by studying hard and learning from their parents' work ethic, they would have a better life and not be "lumpen, like me."

Individual effort was not perceived as a cure-all. The interviewees' hopes for self-advancement were not of the Horatio Alger type. Francesca and Jacobo, for example, each believed that they had achieved some success relative to others they knew by dint of their own initiative. They did not talk about financial obstacles blocking their children's futures. Nevertheless, their material goals for their children were quite modest. They did not express the expectation that their families could rise above poverty, merely that they might be less poor. Instead, they each focused on their hopes for their children's character and happiness, which they believed individual effort *could* affect. As Francesca, a domestic worker, stated, "I'll send my older kids out to do odd jobs, because if parents maintain their kids too long, that's when they get into drugs and learn to be lazy. I laugh at the intellectual folks who say that kids have to dedicate all their time to studying. Sure, they have to study and develop a vocation. These days, if you don't have a vocation, you're lost. But they also have to be taught to work as well as study. . . . The parents have to know how to raise their kids." Jacobo, an auto mechanic, expressed, "Whether it's a construction laborer or a street sweeper, if they can walk around with their head high and no one can point a finger at them, then they should do what they want to do. They'll choose when they [are old enough]. They will do elementary school, no matter what. After that, they'll be at an age to study what they like."

Betina.— Betina's perspective on her life chances reveals some of the complexities discussed earlier. Betina was twenty-eight, married, and had one school-age son. She described both herself and her husband as coming from very poor families (*familias humildes,* in her words). By age fifteen Betina had dropped out of high school to take a job in a perfume factory and she now worked as a housekeeper and nanny. Her mother, after a botched abortion, had died when Betina was an infant. Betina was later adopted by relatives and grew up in a one-room home in an *inquilinato* in the Federal Capital. She considered the adoption fortunate; her brother, who remained with her father, had grown up in squalid conditions in the far outskirts of Buenos Aires and was now indigent. He lived without electricity or indoor plumbing and had to beg and depend on charity to feed and clothe his family. In comparison, Betina and her husband lived comfortably in San Telmo in a small apartment they were provided in exchange for her husband's job as a building superintendent.

She spoke with great empathy for people who had to beg or trespass because they could not afford food or rent. Even her word choices implied that opportunities are limited: she spoke of people having more or fewer "possibilities" due to their background. Reflecting on her own upbringing, Betina said that children from her social class lacked the role models to help them conceive of individual effort as a means to beat the structural odds against them:

> I think that if a person can't pay for his studies, he's not going to be able to do what he wants, right? . . . Because if his father can't work anymore, or if I can't work anymore, who's going to help him?! Although I think that if he tries hard, that is, if he puts in a bit of effort to say my mom can't buy me this book, but I'm going to try to make photocopies or ask a friend to lend it to me so I can write a summary of it, then I can study it just the same. That is, putting out a bit of effort. That's something that I, I didn't have anybody to say to me if your mom can't buy you the book, how about if we make a summary or

something [to avoid the expense]? I didn't have the support of someone teaching me to have these opportunities and to reach the level of
studies I wanted.

Asked about the hypothetical child born in San Telmo (i.e., in circumstances
similar to her upbringing) versus the child from the wealthy Barrio Norte, she
replied: "Well, this question of one who has and one who doesn't, it's two different things. What happens is that as likely as not, the one who has the
money can [do what he wants] and doesn't know how to make the most of it;
and the one who doesn't have money has to put up with it because it can't be.
That's what I think. . . . But I think that if he would make an effort, he too
could succeed. Because why not? I think that, yes, the one who is born in a
conventillo would have his possibilities."

Unintentionally, Betina had revealed her assumptions about the vastness
of the distance between her economic position and a college education for her
son. The distance is not merely due to costly fees or years of foregoing wages
in order to study. Betina assumed that even books may not be within her
child's reach except through unusual effort. Nevertheless, as proof that barriers
are not unsurmountable, she recalled a neighbor in the *conventillo* where she
was raised who became a successful architect. Asked if this was an exceptional
case, she insisted it was merely a result of effort and determination.

Despite hoping that disadvantageous material conditions are not permanent barriers, she clearly perceived them as at least partial constraints. While
expressing hope that with hard work her son Francisco would become a pedi-
atrician or an engineer, she was still not confident that he would achieve such
goals: "But who knows? Maybe he'll become a mechanic or whatever. That is,
whatever he chooses for his future will be welcomed. The important thing is
that he come to be something more important than what we are, since I'm a
domestic employee and his father—well, he's an electrician, but to have a little
more, some more study with which he can stand out. And that he would have
opportunities to go out and know more things. This is what I'd like—for Francisco and [*chuckle*] for us too!"

Betina was well aware of the difficulties and constraints created by material conditions, but she and her husband had, through much hard work and
thrift, managed to begin to create a better standard of living than the severe
poverty in which she was raised. Betina had very little awareness of or interest
in political issues. She looked at the world from the perspective of her own
family, focusing each day on coping with their financial constraints and relying
on the hope that hard work would lessen those barriers.

Influences beyond Individual Control.— A few people acknowledged that the future would depend not just on individual accomplishment and resources but on national-level economic and labor market conditions. With youthful assurance, Pablo and Samuel perceived their own futures as bright because in their views the national economy seemed to be looking up. Some parents who had lived through Argentina's ups and downs were less confident. Soña said the future was absolutely unpredictable in her country. Andrés had decided to urge his sons to reverse the steps of his immigrant grandparents and seek a better life back in Spain. He had read news reports about research done by the Economic Commission on Latin American and the Caribbean (ECLAC) that found declining conditions across the region, and so he had little hope that his sons would find a bright future in Argentina. María was simply hoping that Argentina would "fix itself" sufficiently so that her daughter, a university student in a highly specialized subfield of engineering, would be able to pursue her chosen career without having to emigrate.

Some people attributed national-level economic conditions to the actions or inactions of governments. For example, Soña said that during Perón's time the public schools were very good. She said a person could not tell by looking at kids whether they went to private or public school the way one could today. Julio complained that during the current period the government was ignoring the schools, the arts, and other forms of culture, so these things were no longer affordable to all. "Can we get to the First World without culture?" he asked rhetorically. Esperanza, a Peronist activist but staunch critic of Menem's neoliberal policies, saw her living conditions as rooted in failed economic policies: "Perhaps according to them, according to the experts, we're better off. But I know that in my refrigerator there's no cheese and no eggs. I'm an economist too, because in my house I economize and I know how it is." María said that a child born in a San Telmo *conventillo* would be able to reach her dreams "if and when this is a real country." Andrés (a homeless former computer programmer) worried that upward mobility would be stymied by Menem's policies: "For now, something like this [a child from the *conventillo* becoming a professional] can occur. But now they're talking about charging tuition at the university, whereas it was free. So I don't know up to what point this will permit the children from *conventillos* to get to college." Although he was the third generation of his family to live in his shantytown, Juan Antonio blamed his children's poor future not on his disadvantaged upbringing nor on long-term inequalities in Argentine society but on current government policy. "I didn't go to school because I didn't want to, but my kids can't because of money," he argued. The government's neoliberal policies were causing miserly wage levels, he said, which deprived people of dignity and opportunity: "It pains me, I tell you, not to be able to dream of my child becoming a lawyer or a doctor. My son could make a living at soccer. Both sons. They play soccer well. But I don't have any possibility of sending them to the soccer clubs." In Juan Antonio's view, his children had neither the possibility of getting ahead with studies, nor even through sports. He made an identical point, in similar language, when reinterviewed three years later. In terms remarkably like Amartya Sen's, he said that poverty and unemployment created a "lack of liberty." He emphasized that his desired solution was not government welfare assistance, which he considered degrading. The solution, he said, required job opportunities and wage levels sufficient to support a family and to send children to high school.

Attitudes toward Inequality

The interviews revealed a broad consensus that some Argentines are restricted from fully participating in basic pursuits that are available to other Argentines. Many of those interviewed objected to this inequality of opportunity.[15] Many also focused on the unequal *outcomes* that resulted from this lack of opportunity, seeing luxury as an affront to misery and satisfied whim as an insult to unmet human rights.[16] The interviewees expressed a fundamental belief in equal rights as concern for the dignity of the individual regardless of social status. As Amanda put it, "We're all human beings. The rich aren't any better than the workers."[17] Or as Esperanza said, arguing against having different standards for poor and affluent, "I don't want a day care center for *villeros*, I want one where you too would bring your kids to be watched."

Those interviewed were not seeking absolute equal results. Interviews revealed widespread belief in the right of people to get ahead of others if they can, perhaps reflecting Argentina's immigrant tradition that helped establish a culture of ambition and mobility. This finding is consistent with previous studies (see Portes 1972, 283). For example, no one interviewed objected to some inequalities in salaries or questioned the norm that educational achievement justifies higher wages. Many people recognized inequality of educational opportunity as a problem that affected their families but no one suggested solving that problem by leveling the incomes of those who had the opportunity to get an education with those who had not. Several poor people of limited education mentioned that doctors, nurses, or teachers were low-paid in relation to their studies and their contributions to society.

Complaints about inequality of outcome are, like concerns about disparities in opportunities, expressions of frustration with constraints—specifically, with the social exclusion that comes from not having what others in society normally have. Comparing others' luxury to one's misery is not, essentially, a desire for equal luxury but for an end to misery. Rather than a call for egalitarian redistribution, those who complained about unequal distributions sought to eliminate extremes. In the statements from the interviewees that follow, there are no demands for mansions, BMWs, or Oxford educations. Rather, these people simply ask that some people not have luxuries when others do not have at all. They demand that their lives be rid of the fundamental structural constraints and anxieties of living without any legal home, any kind of car, or any higher education for their children. Thus it is not envy, but constraint, that is of greatest concern. The interviewees perceived the injustice to lie not in inequality per se but in such luxury *in the face of* misery.

For example, Diego, a political activist from a shantytown in the capital, decried global-level inequalities: "It's fine that you are all living well, but we should too. . . . We're not going to have a house with a car and a swimming pool, but at least [we should have] a house, and something to eat every day, and education for our children, and health care—things that we don't have here." Julio, a construction worker, argued that comparing one's lifestyle to that of others was inevitable. Describing the depression and alcohol abuse that he saw in poor neighborhoods, he described it as despair, bred by inequality: "Why do they have so much and the rest have nothing?! That's where [the problem] comes from. The decadence comes from this! . . . Because if I come from a province and live in a shack and then walk through Barrio Norte and I find grand apartments or two-story houses with gardens and pools and everything beautiful! . . . One doesn't have to be very intelligent to make the comparison. I compare my shack with those houses. And so, this image of the houses I see there and the image of the shack—it's crushing." Asked to elaborate, he said his objection was not a sign of envy but simply a feeling of being marginalized from opportunities in a society of haves and have-nots: "I don't consider it unjust that [a guy makes money as an] attorney. What I consider unjust is that I haven't also been given the chance to be an attorney." From Julio's perspective, individual initiative is not a feasible response to social conditions; opportunities are not taken or created by individuals but "given" by the economic and social structure that governments create. By this reasoning, governments should work to give better opportunities to poorer citizens.

However, not everyone agrees with Julio's viewpoint. Some, like Amanda, who was cited at the start of this chapter, argued that opportunities existed for hardworking individuals to claim. Occasionally others said that government was already creating as many opportunities as it could afford. Each of these perspectives was raised by people living with varying degrees of material constraints, but Julio was probably the most desperately poor of all the people interviewed. It may be that when all individual efforts to cope with material conditions have repeatedly failed, a person's only possible nonsuicidal response is to conclude that the state, the society, the next generation, or someone other than himself or herself must act to change the conditions.[18] To explore this point further, the next chapter presents evidence that the capacity to cope individually has an impact upon citizens' views of the state's responsibilities toward them.

Chapter

5

Coping Materially, Focusing Politically

One woman to another: "I started my
Christmas shopping fifteen days ago." "What
do you mean? I thought you said you were
buying nothing for Christmas," the other woman
said. "Exactly. I've bought nothing in fifteen
days."

SENDRA, Clarín (7 December 1991)

The last chapter examined how citizens respond to life with fewer material resources than perceived as normal in their society. The interviews revealed disparate reactions to objective material hardships. On the basis of interview
findings, the present chapter constructs a typology for understanding those
disparate reactions. This analysis underscores the complexity of perceptions
about political interests—perceptions resting on a mixture of concerns about
self, class, and nation. The chapter proceeds to examine the solutions that
people employ in order to live with their level of material resources and argues
that these solutions are relevant to whether or not they perceive their material
interests as political interests.

A Typology of Responses to Personal Material Interests

The interviews revealed attitudes about social justice; the social role and
actual capacity of the Argentine government; the material problems of daily
life and the means to solve them; conditions of inequality, poverty, and the
causes thereof; and hopes, dreams, and judgments about future prosperity.

These attitudes formed three patterns of thinking about political matters in relation to material concerns. Each of the three patterns is described briefly below and then six interviews are used to illustrate the patterns in some depth.

The first type of thinking about politics is microfocused, that is, focused on the person's own material problems with little thought to how government policies might have caused or might be able to alleviate those problems. Overall, people exhibiting a microfocus pursue their specific material interests at the lowest feasible level of resolution. They only perceive a political solution to their material grievances to the extent of using clientelistic relationships or local-level petitioning to address particular material needs. The experience as a client or petitioner does not bring these citizens further into the political system or enable them to perceive precise links between their material well-being and the activities of the national government, in which they remain largely uninterested. Their understanding of national politics and their preferences among national-level politicians and parties are rooted in simply understood party or class identities and general experiences as consumers. Their sole interest in the national economy is in what it is doing to them personally (thus they are not "sociotropic") yet they do not have the sort of precise understanding of the linkages between national political decisions and their own lives, which the social movements literature expects of a "conscientisized" voter who links pocketbook to policy. These may be the kinds of less-informed voters that some of the public opinion literature envisions when it disdains ignorant "pocketbook" voters who judge the government on the basis of their own circumstances; yet describing them as voting their pocketbook is unsatisfactory, for it raises questions of "what section of their pocketbook?" As the examples will illustrate, these people may have very serious and immediate pocketbook concerns that they ignore when thinking about national politics because their focus is so intensely on their own daily lives.

The second way of thinking about politics focuses on the meaning of politics for macrolevel affairs. Like those with a microfocus, macrofocused citizens also expect to resolve their own material interests through household-level efforts or perhaps local-level organizing and petitioning, and they do not demand that national government policies address their personal material interests. These people do, however, see a role for national government in solving material problems. While they do not expect their particular needs to be resolved politically, they express concern for government policy that addresses the needs of their social class generally and also of other societal groups that they consider particularly vulnerable or deserving of public concern (e.g., children, the elderly, the poor). People with this focal point believe politics is relevant to their material lives, but only at the very broad level of the macro-economy and the overall society. They recognize that macrolevel policies, such as monetary stabilization or economic restructuring, have an impact on the economy in which they have to function each day, but for their own particular needs they find household and local-level means to cope.

The third type of thinking focuses on the micro-macro link. People focused in this way perceived their own specific material problems, as well as those of people like them, as the product of larger forces, including the policies of the state. What people with this focus have in common is not their ignorance or their enlightenment, their education, social-class background, deprivation relative to others in society, objective level of need, or level of political activism per se, but rather their belief that their individual efforts are not sufficient to resolve the kinds of material problems they face.

While psychological factors may help explain why some have a microfocus and others a macrofocus, it should be emphasized that I am not suggesting that people are cognitively prone to focus or not focus on the micro-macro linkage. Someone who responded as a "micro-macro linker" did so under the conditions and contexts he or she faced at the time of the interviews. When facing different circumstances, the same person might not see any links between their conditions and the government. In short, this is not a typology of kinds of *people* but of kinds of *responses* to material conditions. I discuss which conditions and contexts engender the "linking" response later in this chapter. First, however, I present two cases to illustrate each type of response. These demonstrate the meanings of the three foci and also the considerations that I used to categorize the views of the other thirty-five people interviewed.

Microfocused Political Thinking

Citizens are microfocused when they simply do not perceive macrolevel behavior (such as national political activity) having much impact or significance to their current material interests. They may, like Jorge in chapter 1, be involved in local politics as a means to obtain specific things they want for their own families. They may discuss public affairs using anecdotal stories of a particular person's problems and the impact of government upon them. Yet mostly they do not understand national political actors and policies as having a substantial impact upon individual lives. Interviews with Oscar and Cecilia provide insight into this type of thinking.

Oscar.— Oscar, 43, was employed as a civilian janitor at an air force base. His wife was part of the growing "microenterprise" sector as a member of a sewing cooperative, and Oscar also shared in the sewing work. They lived with their school-age daughter in the outer suburbs of Buenos Aires in a relatively new settlement of self-built homes on developed lots. Not far away, rioting and looting had occurred during the 1989 crisis. Asked about the impact of the economic crises in Argentina upon his household, he insisted that the impact had been nothing other than that which was universally felt. "Everyone was affected" by the hyperinflation of 1989, he said, and "the economy affected us a lot" and "the fear made us suffer." He sought to explain to me that the universal experience was also not so severe as some had argued: "I saw the looting" and the people were stealing cognac, not flour. As he said, "They weren't dying of hunger." As for the specific impact of the national economic crisis in his own life, he said, "There wasn't much hunger in our own area. . . . we did not feel hit very much." Asked when his family had experienced the lowest income level, he dismissed the question, explaining that "Argentina has plenty of work. People who don't work, don't want to work." Asked further about the impact of the national economic crisis in his own life, he politely insisted that his family was doing fine: "I told you it didn't have much effect on us."

Oscar's claim that he had not been affected by national economic crises was belied by his work history. He had previously been employed in a textile factory, but the "industrial crisis," as he put it, caused the factory to shut down in 1982.[1] He was able to find new work within a few weeks, this time at a metallurgical factory. The job switch required some adjustment, he said, since the labor was much more physically demanding, but he chose to see the good side of change: "Later, it turned out to be good, because I wasn't stuck in one factory for forty years." He worked there for nine years before once again being laid off. Oscar admitted that the layoffs had consequences in his life. Every time you get a new job, he said, you lose money because you have to start over without any seniority built up and you also lose camaraderie and your way of working and have to learn new work skills. The shift from factory work to janitorial work was substantial, he said. Nevertheless, he was not embittered by the changes that had been forced on him. He looked at the bright side—new jobs keep life interesting, the air force treated its civilian employees well, and unlike other employers, they had given him credit for his previous years of work when they determined his vacations and pension. So, since he had been able to cope with the layoffs and find new—even if less desirable—work, he had not found the layoffs onerous.

Oscar was disillusioned by politics. His cynicism, however, did not stem from any negative impact that he perceived government policy having had in his life but rather from experiences that caused him to distrust parties and politicians. The *Movimiento al Socialismo* (MAS), a small party of the left, had been active in his neighborhood and he had once been favorably disposed toward them. During the early years of the debt crisis, people associated with MAS had promoted birth control as a solution to poverty. Now the father of only one, he regretted having listened to their advice, and he felt that they had misled people like him, taking advantage of their fear during difficult economic times. He stated, "The political system is necessary, but I stay out of it." He preferred what he called the "politics of the community," that is, the nonpartisan food cooperatives and catechism groups in which he had become active. Like the social movement experience of the people at Padelai (discussed in chapter 3), Oscar's exposure to community-based organizations had taught him that they were a means of civic participation and self-help, independent of and a preferred alternative to partisan forms of participation. "Politics is never going to do anything . . . but the churches are renewing everything," he declared. Rather than developing a consciousness of the linkages between government actions and his own conditions, exposure to social movements had taught Oscar to avoid macrolevel politics altogether and to focus on taking action within his own neighborhood community.

Cecilia.— Cecilia, a domestic worker and mother of school-aged children, provides a second illustration of a microfocus. Cecilia, her husband Jacobo, and their children had been evicted from a *casa tomada* where they had lived for almost eight years. They ended up with temporary shelter thanks to the assistance of a community activist organization associated with dissident Peronists (who later joined FREPASO). With help from that organization and an allied group, they eventually managed to obtain legal housing. As a legal resident from Uruguay, Cecilia could not vote in presidential elections. Asked about her political interests, she admitted to little knowledge about political affairs.[2] Yet when she was pressed about whether she had any particular political concerns, the first thing she mentioned, even though she was optimistic that her own housing problem had just been resolved, was housing. Her sense of what the government might do about housing, however, was not specific. Her mention of housing quickly turned into a general description of the Argentine economy. She implied that the president was responsible for economic performance but did not specify how: "They promise a lot to the people, but we'll see what happens. There are so many people walking about the streets. The president says 'yes [we'll do something about housing]'; but we'll see. The truth is that we didn't vote in the presidential election when Menem ran, but we wanted him to win. He seemed like a good person. I don't know. It seems that he has done a lot, that's what I say. I don't know. It seems that way to me. Other people say that he hasn't. . . . There's no lack of work. People who aren't working here don't want to work, because there are jobs."

So Cecilia said that she wanted the government to do something about homelessness, but there was no evidence that she evaluated the government on the basis of whether it had done so. Likewise, she implied that the government might have some role in promoting the economy and fomenting jobs, yet she dismissed those who criticized the government's performance in these areas as lazy individuals.

Precisely because of her limited knowledge of the political world and her focus on individual agency, we might expect her views to be based on simple reactions to personal circumstances. This is the expectation in the public opinion research that sees pocketbook voting as a function of ignorance. Likewise, the populism literature leads us to assume that she would support any political actors who had helped meet her most severe material need. Yet contrary to both of these expectations, Cecilia's miserable personal housing experience did not negatively affect her evaluation of the government, in spite of her professed belief that housing is an issue politicians should address. The fact that Menem had not yet addressed the housing deficit did not cause her to reject him. The fact that during Menem's term her family arrived home to find themselves evicted from their house and unable even to retrieve their furniture from the padlocked building did not cause her to blame the government for the desperation she suffered during its tenure. Of course she may simply have been feeling optimistic because they were about to have a home of their own, at last, but the fact that the people who helped her family find a means to permanent homeownership were vocal anti-Menemists did not seem to influence her or her husband's political loyalties: "To me, [politics] doesn't affect me much. I don't know how other people feel. In Argentina, we're living. If we were in Uruguay, there are many things that we wouldn't be able to buy, because it's more expensive. When my husband went [to visit Uruguay], the prices were horrible. The meat was very, very expensive. Here, we eat meat every day. When we were living there, we only ate meat at the end of the month when he got paid. . . . And we only bought sodapop for my daughter's birthday. Here, we buy sodapop every day."

As Cecilia's statements reveal, she talked about politics in material terms, and specifically, in terms of her own microlevel concerns rather than sociotropically. She claimed not to see the direct effects of government in her life (i.e., she denied a micro-macro link). Asked to talk about a macrolevel issue— her view of national politics—she based her answer on the quality of her consumption possibilities. Rather than speaking of the economy's health on the "sociotropic" basis of evidence in the news or the social conditions she witnessed around her (others' poverty, homelessness, etc.), she instead judged it favorably on the basis of her personal experiences as a consumer and worker.

Because she used personal experiences to make judgments, some scholars might see Cecilia simply as responding to her "pocketbook" and explain this response on the basis of her low level of political knowledge and socialization (cf. Mutz 1992; Goren 1997). Yet empirically, Argentine government policy has had a significant impact on consumer prices, so Cecilia's sense that when she enjoys low prices, the government is doing something well—however vaguely she may understand the linkage—should not be considered ignorant. Furthermore, although she uses her consumer experiences as a base of "information" by which to discuss the economy, the remarkable aspect of her political thinking is not her source of information about public matters but rather how little interest those matters hold for her, despite her objective needs. Like Oscar, she has an overriding conviction that national politics is not meaningful to her life. This is the opposite of the conviction of the micro-macro linkers, discussed below, who are mobilized to political action by the connection they see between their lives and government. Finally, knowing that she judges the economy by her concerns as a mother seeking affordable food and clothing for her family still begs the question of why she does not judge it as a mother seeking affordable housing.

Cecilia, Oscar, and other "microfocused" respondents were preoccupied with their own households' material interests. Their efforts to provide for those interests occurred through personal effort and community-level organizations. National-level politics appeared irrelevant to their material needs and therefore they paid little attention to it. As Betina, "microfocused" domestic worker and mother, put it (without intending irony) when asked if she voted, "Normally yes. At times yes—when it's very obligatory."[3]

Macrofocused Political Thinking

Political thinking is macrofocused when national-level political matters are discussed in broad impersonal terms without drawing connections to one's own worries, perceived needs, and current anxieties or to the anecdotal personal problems of individuals. Macrofocused thinking concentrates on the national or global economies; relationships between social classes; treatment of vulnerable social groups, such as the very poor, pensioners, or schoolchildren, to which the person does not belong; as well as nonmaterialist concerns such as nationalism or foreign policy; crime; and human rights. These concerns certainly might affect a person's own life but macrofocused thinking does not dwell on the personal impact. Rather, this type of thinking speaks of the good of a large community (be it a social class or a nation) to which the person belongs.

The reason for a microfocus versus a macrofocus appears to be largely idiosyncratic, rooted in particular family cultures and individual-level values, personalities, and motivations rather than in sociological causes. There was no consistent difference between the two groups in terms of formal education or of the level of economic anxiety or severity of need in their households. Asked about the basis of their macrolevel concerns, people said that one of their parents was active in a political party or that they were empathetic toward poor children because of their own childhood in poverty. Those who were microfocused did not necessarily face greater material problems nor were they more socially isolated than the others. They were simply people who were preoccupied by a quest to improve their families' circumstances to the point that all other matters were of little concern. It should be emphasized that people who are microfocused are not necessarily more self-centered than those who are macrofocused, nor are all of those with a macrofocus strongly interested in political affairs. The difference between them is that when they do engage in political behavior—talking about politics—those with a microfocus do not get beyond their personal-level concerns, while those with a macrofocus discuss politics as something affecting the larger community of which they are a part. To make the scope of the macrofocus clearer, I present the views of Andrés and Atilio as illustrative examples.

Andrés.— Andrés was born into poverty in a northern province but managed to get some postsecondary education and training in computers. He had used this skill in his jobs at several large corporations until economic crisis and corporate restructuring left him unemployed. After a divorce he lost his only capital asset, his apartment. Eventually he lost his job and the exorbitant rental fees of single-room occupancy hotels left him homeless. In an effort to resolve his housing situation he became involved in the MOI but eventually recognized that the housing movement's primary focus was not upon rental situations so much as on building occupations. To my knowledge he never found a substitute vehicle for political action on behalf of his own housing need. When told during our interview about an ideologically-oriented activist working on his sort of housing concern, Andrés rejected involvement with anyone who might be pushing a partisan or personal agenda.

When Andrés discussed politics, he never referred to his personal interests in housing or anything else. More knowledgeable and sophisticated about politics than Cecilia, and more interested in the news than Jorge, Andrés employed a coherent and thoughtful world view akin to social democracy. Although it was evident that pride prevented him from discussing his personal needs in more detail, one would expect that if his own needs were uppermost in his mind he would discuss them in general terms, such as talking about the problems of homelessness and unemployment in the country. Yet Andrés dis cussed politics in terms of the interests of those he considered much poorer and more vulnerable than he. Over several hours of conversation and several meetings, his political views were expressed in global terms, based especially on his concern for poor children and pensioners. He attributed his political empathies to having been poor and abandoned as a child. Eventually he turned his political activity away from housing and became involved in an NGO working for human rights for children.

Atilio.— Atilio also displayed a macrofocus. An older man born with a physical disability, he had lived a comfortable childhood but his disability and primary-level education had prevented him from obtaining economic comforts as an adult. He had depended upon relatives, street vending, and a tiny disability pension to support himself. He was not substantially more knowledgeable about politics than those classified as "microfocused," but he differed from the latter in that he was interested in talking about macrolevel affairs and he did not base his political judgments on his own experiences as a consumer. Atilio said he had always lived simply and had few material expectations. When he talked about politics, he focused on broad national concerns, such as civil "order," presidential leadership, corruption among President Menem's inner circle, and his complaint that the government did not serve "the people" and "the country." He had limited expectations of improving his microlevel conditions and did not perceive the government as responsible in any specific way for his standard of living. His focus was purely and fully macro.

Micro-Macro Linkers

People who focus on the micro-macro link are those who perceive a connection between their microlevel material interests and macrolevel politics and whose material interests then motivate the content of their political views. They do not perceive their material interests as ones to be resolved through clientelism or petitioning of local government officials but rather as rooted in decisions, or even systems, at the national level. When they express concern for the impact of public policies upon the class to which they belong, they do so in a way that personalizes the impact. Although they may also express concerns about macrolevel issues that do not directly affect them, their perspective differs from the macrofocus in that they do not solely express opinions about what the government ought to do for the country but rather see themselves as directly affected by the government's policies and frustrated by their inability to redirect those policies. Unlike the macrofocused discourse, which may express concern for class or for national community out of a generalized sense of identity with the interests of a larger collective, the micro-macro linkers see a *specific* cause-and-effect relationship between government action or inaction and their own lives. Nena and Tomás are two examples of this way of thinking about political affairs.

Nena.— Nena, 55, was an administrative employee in the Secretariat of Public Works. She was also an active member of the Association of State Workers (ATE), a public employees union that viewed Menem's policies as contrary to core Peronist values.[4] Menem's policies had their most visible effect in the public sector. His restructuring of the state cut employment in several ways: privatization of state corporations; downsizing of bureaucracies via early retirement buy-outs, forced retirements, and hiring freezes; contracting with private firms to do the work of civil servants; and transferring functions and employees to the provincial governments.[5] As a result almost 90,000 national administrative positions were eliminated from 1990 to 1991 and over 297,000 positions were cut between 1991 and 1992 (World Bank 1993b, table 3.10). State restructuring had also meant a change in the rules of the work place, as long-established promotion ladders were revised by a 1992 executive decree that went into effect a few months after my interviews. The ATE employees interviewed frequently mentioned this change in seniority practices. All in all, state restructuring meant that public employment—usually a bulwark against unemployment—had come to feel quite insecure. Nena felt these changes as direct hits on her personal security: "With the years I have left, I don't know how I'll get by. If I retire, they'll pay me a pittance. And I don't know if I can continue working. There's no job security. The state is being *greatly* reduced."

Nena said the years of economic crisis had affected her "terribly," that it was harder to make ends meet now than when she was raising her four now-grown children as a single parent years before. Moreover, she believed the painful adjustments were just beginning. With the constraints of the Brady Plan, she expected "we'll be much worse." Nena was not solely concerned about her own problems. She expressed dismay with the quality of education, health care, the judiciary, public safety, the labor market, and the welfare of the poor. She identified with the social justice message of traditional Peronism and felt it was betrayed by President Menem. Yet her position in the public sector and her union affiliation kept her focused not only on macrolevel policies, but on how those policies affected her own life.

In the public sector undergoing restructuring, the connection between the micro and the macro—between personal interests and public decisions—was obvious. Moreover, the ATE provided a discourse and an organization to encourage employees to see the link between their lives and the government's policies. When I interviewed the employees, they were anticipating a move to the Ministry of Economics as part of the reorganization of the state. The building in which they worked was largely vacant and on the floors where people still reported for work, many sections had little to do. Because the state budget for public works was low, there were no new projects for the computer analysts, engineers, project managers, and their clerical staffs to administer. During hours of empty time at work, employees' conversation in the onsite union office easily reinforced the link between Menem's broken promises and their own material insecurity.

Tomás.— Another example of thinking focused on micro-macro linkages is that of Tomás, 68, a retired professional accountant living with his wife in a dark, cold apartment, which he owned. Like those with a microfocus, described above, Tomás was single-minded in his interest in resolving his own particular material problem, which was that he received a government pension of $350 per month, only one-third of what he was legally due. Unlike the microfocused citizens, Tomás did not see his material hardship as something to be resolved through his own efforts. The size of his income was directly caused by decisions of the national government, which argued that fiscal constraints prevented the treasury from meeting its legal obligations to pensioners (see Powers 1995a, 107–9). He described his microlevel conditions as "the greatest possible indignity" and linked that indignity to macrolevel decisions that he termed "genocide" of the elderly. Not only was the attribution of responsibility clear (Feldman 1985), but it was also clear that the *solutions* to his problems were not ones he could create by himself.

Explaining Focus

To understand why some people would link their immediate material interests to their political views and others—more often—did not, we first need to understand how people deal with their material concerns. Most Argentines in the early 1990s managed to make ends meet despite low salaries, low pensions, or unstable employment. The majority interviewed discussed their material interests not as responsibilities of the government, but as problems to be handled by themselves. They were able to handle these problems by frugally watching how they spent their wages but more importantly, by supplementing and stretching those wages using personal, family, and community-level resources and assets.

Habits for Getting by

For many Argentines, their economic hardship did not appear suddenly and was not expected to end suddenly. Hardship became a way of life—a habit of self-denial and adjusting wants to possibilities in order to make ends meet. Paula, one of the poorest people interviewed, dreamed about purchasing an apartment one day. She said that she would choose a ground floor apartment because condominium associations typically do not charge the ground floor residents for the costs of running the building elevator. Clearly, her dreams were modulated by a frugality and methodicalness that had become second-nature.

Some people faced starker choices than others. The downwardly mobile working and middle classes who live above poverty-line levels made ends meet by eating cheaper foods, foregoing entertainment, skipping vacation, and rarely buying new clothes, books, or newspapers. The very poor were forced to make choices between more fundamental needs such as education, food, and utilities. All faced nonoptimal choices, but the more meager their economic resources, the more routinely they were forced to make choices that would never even occur to someone of moderate means: skipping dinner so there would be enough food for a guest; missing lunch in order to afford a newspaper; placating crying toddlers with plain bread and water; ordering only the smallest cup of coffee, without food, when joining a friend at a restaurant; buying clothes that will fit the children in two years and then altering them to fit now; not buying a television because there was money for some small kitchen appliances or for a TV but not for both. Each of these was a choice I observed in interviews among the poorest households studied.

No matter the income level, no two families made the same choices or sacrifices, and no matter how poor, people were not likely to be consistent pocketbook maximizers. This is not a sign of irrationality. After all, saving money today helps ease the stress tomorrow but spending money today on a rare pleasure can achieve the same goal. Hilda's husband, Ramón, worked twelve hours a day. One afternoon he spent seventy dollars taking the family on a trip to the zoo and taking photos of the children. "We could have paid more than five days' rent with that seventy dollars, but you get tired of always sacrificing. You need some pleasure once in a while, and so do the kids," he said.[6]

Strategies and Resources for Getting by

Making ends meet is not merely a question of how one spends one's wages. It also depends on nonwage income, resources, and assets that can be used to improve upon the level of living provided by earnings. Because household budget surveys cannot count these resources and assets accurately, they constitute small reserves that people use to live better than statistical surveys of household income indicate. The following sections describe some of the ways Argentines manage to cope without taking local or national-level political action.[7]

Human and Material Assets.— Some people are better able to cope with low income than others because of human assets. These include emotional as well as material support from family and friends. My interview sample included a number of families who managed to get by with the material and moral support of relatives. Gabriela, Amanda, and Carlos inherited or obtained housing through their parents; María José shared her apartment with her daughter and granddaughter; Atilio lived with his nephew; Pablo, at age 34, lived with his parents, sister, and brother-in-law, all sharing expenses. On the other hand, others interviewed, such as Andrés and Martín, wound up in their present living conditions after *losing* family support through divorce or estrangement. Immigrants or internal migrants, like Adriana, Cecilia, and Leonardo, were less likely to have family available to help when they found themselves in economic difficulty.

In comparing individuals living alone to those with family, one finds that the additional family members create additional expenses but they also increase opportunities for wage-earning and for finding solutions when one family member's income becomes insufficient. The people interviewed who had spouses who could work were better able to cope with their material circumstances than people whose spouse was ill or who were single.

Perhaps the most important asset people have is their own capacity for labor. In the early 1990s, low income Argentines frequently employed the strategy of working more hours, second jobs, or odd jobs known as *changas* in order to help make ends meet. For example, Francesca took care of a large family and worked four days a week cleaning houses, while her husband worked over ten hours at his day job and another four at his night job. Paula's husband took a position as a night-time bank security guard to supplement his full-time, formal-sector job at a detergents factory. The second income would possibly put their two-adult household over the poverty line and perhaps allow them to move to a better hotel but not to buy or rent a real apartment. However, their increased household income came at an exhausting price: Paula's husband had to get up at 4 A.M. to go to the first job and returned from the second at 11 P.M.

Marcela and her husband had built a small house in the outer suburbs of Buenos Aires on a lot purchased from a cooperative. To do so, she had depended on the availability of overtime pay. So she became frustrated that the restructuring of the public sector had included cutbacks on overtime: "I used to be accustomed to x, y, and z. I had a different salary, because until three or four years ago, we got a lot of extra hours. Everything that I have is thanks to that. For example with the house—it only came with the four walls—I had to do everything else. And now, I can't do anything. See? Now I can just barely buy things to eat and buy clothes, because that's necessary. But not much for the house."

Dependence on extra jobs and extra hours is common. A study of households whose incomes were below the poverty line in 1991 but above the line a year later found that 25 percent moved above the poverty line by increasing the number of hours worked and another 31 percent moved up by increasing the number of family members working (Minujin and López 1994, 101–3). The quality of life purchased with extra income may be undermined by its costs. For example, Amanda's family had to make considerable sacrifices for extra income: Amanda performed manual labor sixty hours per week, arriving home truly exhausted; her teen-aged children had to take shifts at home to watch their little brother; and her eighteen-year-old daughter worked full days as a janitor while trying to complete high school at night. As Andrés pointed out, the economy forced people to accept work days that the law had declared intolerable much earlier in the century: "The workers' movements succeeded in getting an 8-hour work day and half day on Saturday and such things. And in recent times, the process is beginning to reverse itself. And it turns out that the people today, in order to be able to survive and to be able, more or less, to eat, they have to, in addition to their 8-hour job, look for another 4-hour job. And so, once again, they are working 12 hours, as they did before. And they still haven't managed to get enough money to buy a family market basket.[8] It's a reversal!"

Many people coped with a weak job market and low wages by turning to the informal sector. In sixteen of the forty households studied, some or all of the household income came from informal sector work, including housekeeping and caregiving, craftmaking, skilled construction work, under-the-table arrangements to work in retail establishments, various skilled and unskilled odd jobs (*changas*), electrical work, and in one case, exceptional for its income potential, owning and driving a taxi. Recognizing the difficulty of defining "informality," and the debates over its significance (see Dietz 1998, 73–75), I categorize these varied activities together because they are all solutions that require going beyond the bounds of a regular job that has a "relation of dependence" (as the Argentines refer to legal employment with employee benefits). Each of the jobs categorized here as "informal," even the high-earning cabdriver, operates under conditions of precarious and fluctuating earnings. For example, even though Rafael, the cab driver, made a comfortable living for his family with his car, it was nevertheless an insecure occupation. He depended on extra work hours to cope—if he had a slow day, he was accustomed simply to driving for a few more hours. As more and more Argentines turned to the informal sector to make ends meet, the streets of Buenos Aires were becoming glutted with empty taxis and it was likely that Rafael would be spending more and more time on the road in order to make the same living. With a second-grade education, he did not have any skills to fall back upon as the supply of cab rides began to surpass demand. Another example of precariousness involves the opportunities for day laborers on construction sites, which vary both seasonally and with the national financial conditions that shape the building industry. When the informal market changes, informally employed workers do not have the protections of either job security, severance pay, or unemployment compensation that formal sector workers would have.

I recognize informal sector work as a coping solution, not simply a subtype of employment, because people turn to it in the absence of adequate possibilities for more secure formal-sector work. Eduardo, an unemployed fifty-year-old construction worker with four children, explains how odd jobs enabled him to support his family: "I work during the week by doing *changas*, as they say here, temporary things. I work two or three times a week, or four. So I can bring in, let's see, about 80 pesos a week. We try to stretch it out, as they say here, and get along as well as one can, no?" Another person who used the informal sector to cope is Ricardo, a retired factory worker whose pension at the time of our interview was only $180 per month. Unable to live on this, and unable to find any dignified or well-paid job because of his age, he finally took an under-the-table wage of $300, without benefits, for working through the night as a cashier in the video arcade at the bus station. Ricardo is an example of a citizen whose material resources imposed considerable constraints and difficulties in his life, although he would not be counted as poor by standard measures. During a lifetime of working two manufacturing jobs, Ricardo had managed to purchase his own apartment so he had a less precarious dwelling and a few more "comforts" (such as a private bathroom) than people living in hotels or *inquilinatos*. Because his married daughter lived with his wife and him, his total household income probably exceeded the poverty line. Given these conditions, the IPA or CEPA poverty studies carried out by the government would not have counted him as either "structurally" or "newly" poor. Yet finding that he could not make it "past the twentieth of the month," as he put it, he went out, at age 68, to work the night shift for a small wage. In short, material constraints had led him to accept fatigue as the price of greater material security.

For some people, the informal sector is the arena in which to supplement their income from low-paying, formal sector jobs. For others, the informal sector became their only workplace, for any number of reasons, including age, disability, low skills, poor education, plant closings, corporate downsizing, privatizations, or the weak formal labor market. In any case, they count on the informal sector as a flexible arena of opportunity to make ends meet.

The other human assets that help people cope are their own education, skills, and experience. The dignity and pay of *changas* are better when one has a specialty to offer other than mere manual labor, such as Betina's husband with his electronics training and Pablo, an experienced photographer. For Andrés, an older divorced man dependent on friends for shelter, finding employment was difficult, but for a time his training in computer programming was a marketable asset. He obtained occasional contracts for specific programming projects and borrowed a friend's computer to do the work.

In addition to human assets—family, friends, education, skills, good health, and hard work—material assets, or the lack of them, make a tremendous difference in the security a person feels on a low income. The most important asset, as I argued in chapter 3, is owning one's housing. Since most Argentines do not have monthly rent or mortgage payments, major government poverty studies have not even considered rent as a normal expense in calculating household budgets.[9] Those who are paying rent live considerably below the standard that their income level would otherwise seem to indicate. Those who do own their own apartments enjoy a level of relative material security that the people heard in chapter 3 were struggling to achieve. As Olivia put it, despite losing her job in the state restructuring, she owned her apartment, so if she did not find a job she might live with hunger and misery, she said, but she would not be without a roof over her head.

In-Kind Goods.— Argentines supplement the level of living enabled by their income in a number of ways. One is through *in-kind goods*, which sometimes provide for basic food, clothing, and personal needs when income cannot.[10] These goods may come from the government, political parties, private charity organizations, labor unions, or private businesses. None of this assistance is sufficiently regular or substantive for people to count on it to change their quality of life over the long term. No poor person attains a middle-income lifestyle on the basis of in-kind goods and fringe benefits. Yet these goods and benefits can ameliorate the sense of desperation by enabling people to make ends meet week to week.

Workers fortunate enough to be employed in the formal sector have various ways to get goods when they lack cash. Employees' fringe benefits often include lunches and company products, which can eliminate some basic costs from the household budget. For example, Paula never had to spend money on soaps or detergents at the grocery store because her husband worked for a multinational manufacturer of cleaning products. The corporation sold its products to employees at factory prices and once or twice a year gave a merit bonus consisting of a hefty carton of goods—sufficient to meet all of Paula's needs for cleaning products. Public sector employees also enjoy material fringe benefits. For example, employees of the Secretariat of Public Works received a free bus pass. This is not insignificant. For an administrative clerk commuting only within the capital, free transportation to work at 1992 prices was equivalent to a 3 percent increase in a clerk's $420 monthly salary. The public employees I interviewed took these benefits for granted, as the norm. Having the benefit did not make them feel any better off, but if it were eliminated as some of the meal allowances and overtime benefits they had once taken for granted were, they would notice and object to the new burden as they objected to those earlier changes in compensation.

Charitable and Partisan Patrons.— The human assets and in-kind employment benefits discussed above are used by both middle and lower income people to cope with and improve upon their material conditions. Additionally, for poor people simply trying to cope with food costs, assistance programs provide some relief. The food distribution outlets in Buenos Aires provided neither pride nor permanent relief to their beneficiaries but they did constitute "a help," as one interviewee put it. In some neighborhoods, the municipality sponsored a soup kitchen where children were given free meals. However, no one was *entitled* to a state-funded meal. The soup kitchens existed in ad hoc fashion, subject to political whim. Sometimes privately funded kitchens took up the slack where there were no municipally-funded kitchens. Eduardo, who lived in a *casa tomada*, said that some of his neighbors sent their kids twice a day to eat at a soup kitchen at a local evangelical church, but he was pleased that he had not had to resort to that coping strategy. Nevertheless, Eduardo pointed out that his kids benefitted from a small snack at school each afternoon. Every in-kind good helps a family conserve cash while improving its overall level of living.

Beyond prepared meals, food staples are distributed by both philanthropic and political institutions. The *Caritas* program of the Roman Catholic Church funds both soup kitchens and food pantries across the country. The parishes in Montserrat and San Telmo had monthly distribution programs for people living within their boundaries. A social worker visited the family's home in advance to qualify the person for assistance. About seventy-five families had qualified for aid at the Montserrat church where I volunteered, and more than one-third of those had shown up to seek food on a fall day in March 1992. In order to base the program on self-help and not mere charity, all but the most indigent paid $2.50 for their food. The food—typically a package each of rice, macaroni, sugar, flour, *mate* tea, powdered milk, and cooking oil—would cost about twice as much in the supermarkets.[11] The low attendance that day suggests that few people were in such desperate need as to be there each month at the appointed hour; on the other hand, the mere existence of the program and the fact that every month there was a crowd willing to wait in the registration line and then sit through a one-hour meeting/sermon while the food packages were prepared, all in order to receive two or three dollars worth of food, indicated that extreme need persisted.

Another source for food was a neighborhood political party office. The local political organizers told me that they would prefer to be out of the food distribution business and did not publicize their patronage. They provided food assistance, when asked, because they perceived that role as part of the political culture and difficult to change. Some neighborhood Peronist offices provided boxes of staples—similar to the church charity program, but more plentiful and without charge. Local Peronist leaders explained this assistance as charity given upon request or when surplus goods became available, not a systematic effort to reach out to neighborhood poor people. The leaders explained these goods merely as part of the party's role and obligation to help those in need, and particularly to show "solidarity" with nearby neighbors. They defended their goals as apolitical without acknowledging that to show solidarity with those of a particular socioeconomic status is a form of political expression.

Leaders of two local UCR offices were more forthcoming about the clientelist motives of giving direct aid, although they doubted whether the political payoff was worth the inconvenience. They preferred to help organize collective efforts to improve neighborhood services such as health and day care centers rather than engaging in ad hoc, individual-level patronage. They described food handouts as a distraction from their political work rather than part of it. During periods of extreme economic crisis in the late 1980s, some had engaged in systematic food distribution programs, but they said this role was more appropriately played by the social service sector. Despite their ambivalence, the local Radical organizers were willing to loan money, provide free legal advice, or more simply, deliver a rare treat from the pastry shop to some of those interviewed who were very poor and also active party members. All parties to the transaction understood that the organizers expected the recipient to help in the office at campaign time, but the relationship involved a long-term reciprocity between material support and campaign support, not just a simple quid pro quo.

Indemnifications.— Tens of thousands of Argentines were laid off in conjunction with the privatization of state industries, particularly between 1990 and 1993 (World Bank 1993b, 14–15). The impact of the layoffs on these workers' pocketbooks was ameliorated by laws dating from Perón's time, which required substantial severance pay. Workers were given one month's pay for each year with the employer, which enabled many people to maintain their household income level for several months after a layoff. In addition to legally mandated indemnifications, some companies downsized by offering early retirement buyouts.

Severance pay meant that despite the record unemployment levels, partly caused by privatization of state industries, unemployed workers did not all hit the streets, jobless and broke, at the same time. Many workers took their indemnification in a lump sum and used it as capital for a self-employment venture, as evidenced by the proliferation of taxis and kiosks in the capital city in the early 1990s. The saturated market made it increasingly difficult for such ventures to prosper, but it took some months for failure. Meanwhile, some workers would have found new employment. Thus, indemnifications served to soften the blow of the government's restructuring of the state and spread out the impact of large-scale layoffs.

This coping strategy was not available to those who lost their job in the informal market. Thus, for example, Olivia, who lost her bookkeeping job at a specialty savings bank following the November 1991 deregulation decree, waited through the summer to begin looking for a new job, knowing that she would be paid until midwinter. Eduardo, on the other hand, an unemployed laborer, had no indemnity and could not qualify for the government's newly implemented unemployment compensation program because his past earnings were all from the black-market.

Public Programs.— The Argentine state was also a source for food support, but not a reliable or adequate one. From 1984 to 1988, the Alfonsín government ran a national program (PAN) for distributing boxes of staples to poor people. At first the box contents met one-third of the monthly nutritional needs for a family of four, but by 1988, budget constraints forced a dramatic decrease in the food packages. President Menem restructured the program into a food stamp system and gave local authorities administrative responsibility, but eventually it was phased out (Midre 1992; Lo Vuolo 1997, 39).[12] A year after my fieldwork, new food assistance programs were incorporated into a poorly funded "Social Plan" that included vaccinations, job creation, sanitation systems, and other social development programs, as well as at least eight different nutrition programs targeted at particular groups, such as mothers and infants, the structurally poor, children, and the elderly without pensions (Lo Vuolo 1997, 40).

Only a few of those interviewed had benefitted from the food assistance programs. They said the food was somewhat helpful, but neither frequent, convenient, nor plentiful enough to constitute a reliable nutritional supplement. While they held inaccurate beliefs about the programs' funding and administration, they tended, like many opposition politicians as well as researchers, to be cynical about the programs' political intentions.[13]

Credit.— One of the tools that people the world over use to try to live beyond the level permitted by their income is credit. When the convertibility plan lowered inflation, credit on consumer goods became widely available. At the same time, trade barriers on imports were dropping. The result was that lower-income consumers were able to afford electronic and kitchen appliances for the first time in their lives. They also stretched limited budgets by purchasing school clothes, shoes, and other personal items with layaway-type plans that charge exorbitant total prices for the privilege of affordable monthly "quotas".

Credit is not a sustainable solution to inadequate resources. As students of poverty have long known, however, poor people often face worse choices than more affluent consumers. They cannot maximize their pocketbook even when they would prefer to do so, so they accept the future burdens and risks of credit as a means to get by in the present. For example, supermarkets have the lowest food prices in Argentina, but at the time of my fieldwork the large chains were mostly located in middle to upper-class neighborhoods. Montserrat and San Telmo together had only two modest supermarkets, although every block had an independent butcher, green grocer, or pantry. As one family explained, they recognized that the small shops had much higher prices than the larger chains, but they accepted the price as the trade-off for the convenient hours that the small shop owners kept and the chance to buy on credit that the neighborhood grocer allowed.

Reliance on Coping Mechanisms

Table 5.1 lists some of strategies, resources, and assets upon which the people interviewed depended in order to keep themselves and their families fed and sheltered. The list includes only physical resources (time, work, aid, assets).[14] My definition of "capacity to cope" excludes psychological capacities. The table includes any resources, assets, or strategies that provide the person with an advantage or tool by which to cope with the life afforded by wage and employment conditions in the economy. So, if a person works a *second* job in the *informal* sector, two coping tools are counted because that person's capacity to cope is a function not only of the effort put into working the second job but also of the access to such a job via informal means. These coping mechanisms are grouped according to the societal level at which they can be pursued, revealing that those interviewed relied primarily on household-level efforts and then assistance and activism within their local community.

The mechanisms listed are those that interviewees volunteered in the course of explaining their lives and their political views. In other words, I did not bias or limit the list toward household-level action; the weight of household-level activities in the list is a reflection of how people explained their lives. It is possible that the list undercounts community-level sources of support since people would hesitate to admit relying on charity and would forget to mention goods-in-kind or patronage. Since charity, patronage, and goods-

TABLE 5.1. COPING STRATEGIES USED

Solution	Interviewees using that Solution
Household-Level Strategies	
Working extra job or extra hours	14
Spouse works for pay	17
Children (living at home) work for pay	4
Relatives or friends providing shelter or material aid	10
Dependent on informal sector job	16
Wage-earner using educational or skill assets	11
Resource assets (home ownership or savings)	13
Local and Community-Level Strategies	
Goods-in-kind (e.g., from employer)	10
Charitable organizations	2
Local political party patrons	4
Grassroots action	16
housing or neighborhood organization [11];	
labor union [5]	
National-Level Strategies	
Social welfare programs	4
Indemnification following lay-off	1

in-kind are generally small items and *ad hoc* means of support, undercounting those would not substantially misrepresent the picture of how people cope. Since the interviews covered national-level politics, personal political activities, and national economic conditions extensively, I am confident that the proportion of national-level mechanisms and the incidence of grassroots activity are accurate reflections of the mechanisms being used by those interviewed.

Table 5.2 indicates the frequency with which the forty-one individuals interviewed relied upon or benefitted from these assets and resources and the range of reliance across the sample. It shows that they typically relied on three assets, resources, or strategies. At the upper extreme, Cecilia relied on eight of the thirteen mechanisms listed.

The tables show people first turning to remedies near at hand, those which they individually and members of their household could provide. Less commonly, they found solutions at the community or national levels. Direct political action in pursuit of material security was used by several of those interviewed, typically in addition to reliance on personal assets or resources and nonpolitical solutions. This political action was organized at the community level (by those involved in the housing movements described in chapter 3 and by four people involved in organizations to promote neighborhood activities) and at the national level (by the dissident public employee's union, ATE, with which five of those interviewed were involved to varying degrees and which constituted a form of political action to protect their salaries and benefits). Given that few of those interviewed were desperately poor, and given the weakness of the Argentine welfare state, it is not surprising that not many of those interviewed received substantial aid through the state's social policies.

These coping mechanisms are not, of course, all of equal value or kind. Owning a home adds much more financial security to a person's life than getting food packages from a local political party. Yet while buying a home would solve the major strain in the life of an employed homeless person, home ownership diminishes, but does not solve, the problem of the senior citizen with a

TABLE 5.2. RELIANCE ON COPING STRATEGIES

Type of Solution	Average per interviewee	Range
Household-level strategies	2	0–5
Local and community-level strategies	1	0–2
National-level strategies	0	0–1
Total strategies used	3	0–8

small pension check. Because coping tools are not equal and do not bring equal measures of relief to those who have them, a person with more coping tools does not *necessarily* perceive him or herself to have a greater capacity to cope; nevertheless, the interview data suggest a tendency for those who do not perceive themselves as coping successfully to be those with access to fewer household level assets and coping resources. As table 5.3 shows, the average number of household-level mechanisms used by people who felt they were *not* coping is below the mean for the thirty-three interviews that could be coded on the coping dimension, while the average number of mechanisms used by those who felt that they *were* coping is above the mean. Those who felt they were not coping were more likely to be those whose coping capacity depended upon national-level policies and programs, while those who felt they were coping were less likely to be coping with the aid of national-level mechanisms.[15]

Coping and Political Views

Scholars of social policy, poverty, and development are familiar with the multiple means that poor and downwardly mobile people use to make ends meet (cf. Dietz 1998, 26; Narayan et al. 2000; Nelson 1992). What is surprising is that the *political* importance of the capacity to cope has not been theorized. Analysis of interviews in which people explained their political views and priorities reveals that the difference between those who focused on the micro-macro linkage and those who did not is rooted in whether or not they perceived themselves to be coping with their material troubles adequately and at reasonable personal cost.

Cecilia, whose microfocus was examined earlier in this chapter, voiced the importance of being able to manage. Note her explicit statement that her coping capacity kept her from blaming the government for her poverty:

TABLE 5.3. PERCEIVED COPING CAPACITY BY AVERAGE NUMBER
OF COPING MECHANISMS USED

Self-Perception of Capacity to Cope	Household-Level Mechanisms	Local-Level Mechanisms	National-Level Mechanisms
Coping well (n=22)	2.68	0.77	0.18
Not coping well (n=11)	2.09	0.91	0.55
Mean (n=33)	2.48	0.82	0.3

I get help from all over. I can't complain about the government because they give me the PAMBA box with food. I go to another church this year where when I go they also give me food and clothes for the kids—new clothes, you see?—and also clothes for me. The truth is that I can't complain, neither about the government nor about Argentina, because to me, they've treated me well. I don't know. I don't know about other people. Lots of people complain. . . .The truth is I've been helped a lot. I've never ended up in the streets even though I've been evicted, [I've always been given a place]. The truth is we can't complain. The kids have everything. They eat every day. They don't lack for anything—sodapop, juices, whatever they want. So, one can't complain. . . .We don't lack for anything; quite the contrary, sometimes we go around giving away clothes because the closets are full. . . . We don't go out very much, you see?—because my husband works [such long hours]. Sometimes during vacation time, if there's something at the theater my husband takes them, if there's something for the kids to see. . . . Or if they're invited to a birthday party, I bring them. But I'm not one to go out much. So that's why the clothes get too small for the kids and we give them away. And on top of that, the church gives us so much besides what we buy ourselves. So really, I can't complain.

The majority of those interviewed *did* feel they could cope well with their material concerns at a household or local level. They might be struggling, but they perceived their material struggles as normal, surmountable, manageable, etc. They believed they could find ways to make do. This majority did not blame government for their material problems nor credit it for their successes, nor did they express a demand that the government do something to resolve the particular material problems they were facing. They were either microfocused or macrofocused.

Conversely, those who strongly focused on the links between their own material interests and politics were people who also were angered by what it took to try to cope. They saw their material conditions as too much to handle or unusually stressful, or they believed that coping required unacceptable choices or that their material conditions could not be improved upon meaningfully, despite their efforts. Table 5.4 summarizes these results, based on the thirty-three interviews that had sufficient comments to categorize the person's attitudes along the coping dimension. As reference points, the people discussed at length in this and earlier chapters are placed in the appropriate quadrants. Figure 5.1 depicts the association between perceived coping capacity and the three foci that people use to think about their interests.

TABLE 5.4. FOCUS AND PERCEPTION OF CAPACITY TO COPE (WITH EXAMPLES)

	Primarily Focused on Micro or Macro	Strongly Focused on Micro-Macro Link
Coping perceived as sufficient and normal	21 Jorge, Martín, Francesca, Amanda, Betina, Atilio, Andrés, Cecilia, Oscar	1 María José
Coping perceived as inadequate or onerous	3 Eduardo Marcela	8 Carlos, Graciela, Nena, Tomás, Ricardo

Impact of Material Interests on Perceived Coping Capacity

It might seem that an incapacity to cope, in material terms, would be related to the degree of poverty or to the frustration of facing new material constraints (as opposed to already being accustomed to them). Yet some poor people (such as Cecilia and Atilio) felt that they were managing to cope, while others who were no worse off (such as Carlos) did not. Some people with above-poverty level incomes (such as several public employees interviewed) felt frustrated and angry by their circumstances, while others—because of the assets of education or housing that their middle-class pasts had provided— were confident they could get through their moment of economic downturn.

Perceived capacity to cope was associated not with the severity or recency of material interests, but with the type.[16] Some types of material hardship can be addressed with coping mechanisms at the household or local level, while for others, coping will come about through national level action. An examination of the differences between three types of material problems—low pensions, poor housing, and hyperinflation—will demonstrate the point.

Pensions are set by national law and their disbursement depends upon the executive branch deciding that it has the resources to comply with the pensions law. Clearly, a low pension is solely a matter to be addressed by national leaders. Age discrimination, diminished mobility, and health problems leave senior citizens with considerably fewer options for self-help via supplemental employment. No one interviewed—whether a pensioner or a sympathetic fellow citizen—expected pensioners to cope with their low incomes through individual self-help. Ricardo, the pensioner interviewed who was trying to make ends meet with a late-night job as an arcade clerk, felt his coping effort was completely inadequate and he perceived a clear link between government policy and his own misfortunes.

In contrast, housing—although widely understood as a right of citizenship for which the constitution assigns responsibility to the state—was not, in fact, something that people expected the state to provide. The housing deficit in the country had been growing since the late 1960s and the state had not, during that period, had the wherewithal to make a dent in the problem (Lumi 1990). Housing was, unlike pensions, something that people could try to obtain for themselves without the aid of the national government. Therefore, even people for whom housing was their most severe material preoccupation did not react against the government's failure to implement an effective housing policy. Based on *context* (in this case, the recent history of housing policy in the country), they did not expect the national government to take care of their housing. Based on the *type* of material interest (housing), they did have self-help and local-level possibilities for resolution.

Hyperinflation is a problem with which people cannot cope adequately at a household or local level. It clearly demands national-level policy to resolve. Citizens' fears and anxieties under hyperinflation are greatly related to their incapacity to find individual-level means to save themselves from its cruel

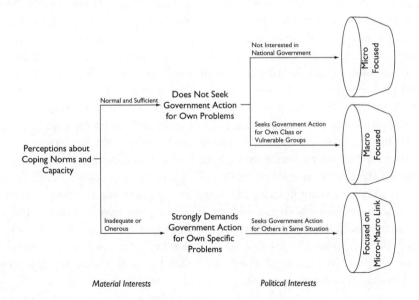

Figure 5.1. Impact of Own Material Interests on Political Interests

effects. When the Argentine voters punished Alfonsín's party at the polls in 1989 and rewarded Menem in 1995, they were linking their personal need for price stability to the government that oversaw monetary policy. People did not seek an end to inflation simply out of concern that inflation is bad for the national economy. They sought macrolevel policies to end inflation because of their microlevel need for income security. Every individual Argentine had learned, through their own microlevel, stress-filled experiences, that they could not cope with hyperinflation by themselves.

In sum, all material interests are not politically equal. To explain citizens' political foci we need to know the particular types of material interests they have. People are less likely to focus on what the national government ought to do to meet their own material interests if those interests can be handled through efforts at the household or local level. The *type* of material problem and *capacity to address it* are crucial to explaining whether they will expect remedies from the national government.

Learned Expectations, Timing, and Coping

The subjective feeling of being able to cope is also associated with expectations. Among those are expectations about one's standard of living and about whether one should make numerous efforts just to cope. These expectations can be caused by personal experience with material hardships and coping and/ or normative ideas about justice. Cecilia and Carlos, two people who always lived in poverty, provide contrasting examples. Cecilia, the Uruguayan mother and domestic worker described earlier in this chapter, struggled her entire life and does not question having to do so. This is not fatalism. She *has* hope, albeit modest, that her family can improve their standard of living and she feels pleased and relieved that she and her husband have found ways to keep their family afloat. Carlos has also struggled his entire life, but having been exposed to Marxist discourse through his political affiliations, he does not accept his struggles as normal or inevitable.[17] He wants to participate more fully in the life of his community and is angry that not only are his efforts insufficient to bring him out of the margins of society, but also that those efforts require so much time and energy that they further exclude him from the possibility of participating in politics. He feels that radical social change is necessary to make his life comfortable and that his own efforts to cope are utterly inadequate to the problem.

Expectations about what level of coping effort is "normal" and tolerable are not merely personal or idiosyncratic. They depend on context. One contextual influence may be political organizing, as the social movements litera-ture predicts. Among those interviewed who perceived their conditions as in-tolerable and focused on the link between their own problems and the political system, most were like Carlos, having been exposed to such criticism through leftist parties or through the dissident ATE. However, others who were so exposed, including Cecilia and the PADELAI leaders discussed in chapter 3, perceived their situations as manageable. Also, the set who saw cop-ing as onerous included Tomás and Julio, who did not draw upon ideas learned through political organizations so much as on frustration with their inability to resolve their material problems through their individual-level re-sources and assets. In the interviews, then, exposure to political organizers was not necessary nor sufficient to linking micro circumstances to macrolevel politics. A person's subjective sense of coping is shaped by a number of factors, which might include organized attempts to convince participants that their personal struggle to cope is unjust.

Furthermore, expectations about what degree of coping is normal and rea-sonable also result from a country's economic history and can be shaped by political discourse and dominant ideologies. In Argentina's case, history, dis-course, and ideology encompass both individualist and communitarian tradi-tions. As a land of opportunity for immigrants, Argentina has a political culture with a self-help tradition. At the same time, the Argentine constitution estab-lishes a role for the state in helping people succeed by guaranteeing social rights such as housing and education. Peronism too left a legacy that extolls "solidarity" and "social justice" as public virtues (Catterberg and Zayuelas 1992, 200–201; cf. Turner and Elordi 1995). Perón's legacy includes memories of government spending that improved people's daily lives. So while some ex-pectations of self-help exist, they are not present in Argentina in the same way as, say, in the United States.

While the political culture includes a role for government in ameliorating material concerns, that culture was modified by nearly two decades of eco-nomic turmoil, which substantially dampened expectations about the govern-ment's capacity to live up to promises of social justice or even to resolve national-level economic problems. Of the people interviewed for whom a per-spective was clear, twenty-one understood Argentina's economic decline to have been a long-term process, predating the Menem government. "It's been years since things have been good here," was a typical comment. People would say that things "used to be different" and when asked "When?" they would mention distant memories: "in the 1950s under Perón" or "in the early 1970s." Only six of those interviewed discussed their country's or their own economic difficulties as occurring solely under the Menem government and its policies. Because economic decline had been a long-term process, many Argentines learned not to depend on any government for quick solutions to the material problems they were experiencing.

They also learned that solving economic problems is not an easy task. President Alfonsín had two economic ministers, three major shifts in economic policy, and multiple minor ones in just six years (Smith 1991, 267–97). President Menem was on his third economic minister by the time of my interviews. This included eight major economic plans or plan amendments during his first two years in office (Lozano and Feletti 1991, 121–59). In each case, the economic ministers had to consider the policy pressures of international financial institutions and the economic realities of global market conditions and the country's substantial foreign debt. From observing these shifts in ministers and policies, as well as the effects of international economic forces, the Argentine public learned that national economic conditions *do* have a strong impact upon their personal material conditions—that is, that the micro-macro linkage exists—but they also learned that national governments are not in very firm control of what that impact will be. So, citizens turned to their own personal and local level devices to try to cope with whatever conditions the national and international economies threw their way.

Furthermore, Argentines learned in the 1980s and early 1990s that the economic hardships they experienced were widely felt. Everyone had struggled under hyperinflation. The decline in living standards through the 1980s had been so widespread that the people interviewed did not tend to have any friends or relatives who had not experienced material hardships. The near universality of the economic decline, ironically, softened its impact, because the sacrifices and efforts necessary to cope came to be perceived as normal, rather than onerous.

Relative deprivation research and historical studies of political instability have found that one factor causing mass dissent is sudden and rapid economic decline that follows a period of either economic development or stability (Davies 1962; Huntington 1968, 49–59; cf. Gurr 1970, 46–56). Rapid decline is more likely to cause violent reaction than incremental decline, even if the latter is severe (Tilly 1978, 207). Coping mechanisms provide an explanation for *why* sudden economic changes would be more politically charged than gradual changes. It takes time for an individual to develop the capacity to cope with economic challenges. Likewise, it takes time for a society to develop the capacity to help individuals cope because social policies, soup kitchens, and charity networks do not develop overnight. Sudden changes—such as hyperinflation or shock treatment policies—do not give consumers, or civil societies, time to figure out how to cope. This is why hyperinflation was such an electorally potent issue in Argentina and why hyperinflation and shock therapies were associated with violent protests there. Hyperinflation annihilates individual-level coping strategies because hard work, extra jobs, family assistance, or special skills cannot save people from the economy-level force that is destroying the value of their earnings. In contrast, *gradual* economic decline enables individuals, as well as societies, to develop coping strategies.[18] Those interviewed had a great deal of time to become accustomed to using household-level and local-level coping efforts as the means to survival and progress.

Figure 5.2 diagrams the factors, identified in this and the previous section, which shape perceptions about coping norms and capacity. Figure 5.2 precedes figure 5.1 (its right side matches the left side of figure 5.1) so that lined up together they portray the factors that affect 1) how material interests are perceived, and 2) whether those interests are perceived as political interests.

Subsidiarity and Neoliberalism

In a fiscally depleted state, individual-level solutions, which depend at least in part on a person's own initiative, appeared to most of those interviewed as the best way to take control of their lives. Neighborhood- and municipal-level politics appeared as the next plausible level at which to take action, if individual efforts were unsuccessful or insufficient. National-level politics appeared to citizens as the solution to material problems only if the specific type of problem could not be solved at a lower level. Citizens sought solutions with the most readily available means, thus implicitly following a principle of subsidiarity (that is, seeking local-level solutions where possible).

A subsidiarity principle is compatible with the neoliberal ideology of the Menem administration and the World Bank, with its emphasis on downsizing

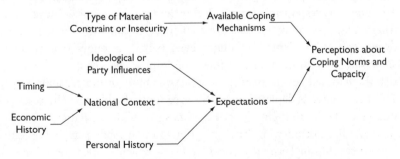

Figure 5.2. Development of Perceptions about Material Interests

the state, individual entrepreneurship, and decentralization (Prévôt Schapira 1996, 89; also see Neunreither 1993). Yet the Argentines interviewed for this research were not seeking household- and local-level mechanisms out of an ideological conviction that such was the appropriate level at which to solve their material problems. The majority spoke ardently of the national government's responsibilities for "social justice," and when asked what that entailed they mentioned housing, education, health care, pensions, and other areas of social policy that a neoliberal would believe can be handled by the private sector or at the level of the local community. In short, the people interviewed expressed their implicit sense of subsidiarity as a matter of practicality, not ideological conversion.

Conclusions

The people I interviewed took their serious material problems into their own hands rather than depend on government solutions. This does not mean they did not perceive a *general* responsibility for the state in social and economic matters, for nearly everyone did so.[19] In the *particular* case of their own material problems, however, only a minority of those interviewed thought the state could resolve them. The others were able to cope with their own material interests at "lower" levels, and so their personal-level material interests were not driving their evaluations of how the state handled its responsibilities.

The interviews included four exceptions to the generalizations just stated. One of these, María José, fell in the NE quadrant of table 5.4, which depicts a person who feels able to cope without government action and yet believes on principle that the government ought to be implementing economic and social policies that would make the person's own life more manageable. María José's assets and job, and the help of her adult daughter, enabled her to live without severe constraints, although much less well than earlier in her life. Despite being able to cope, she perceived that government mismanagement of the economy was responsible for the decline and stagnation of her level of living. Alternatively, some people believe that they are not fully coping with their own material problems and might even believe strongly that someone or something should help change their conditions, and yet they do not believe that the national government has the responsibility or the possibility to do so. This perspective is depicted by the SW quadrant of table 5.4. The three people interviewed who thought along these lines saw their capacities to cope as inadequate but not onerous. Their reactions to that inadequacy were tempered by partisanship or feasibility considerations, which shaped their conclusions about what the government ought to be doing. For example, Marcela expressed strong frustration with the financial constraints in her life that she perceived as due to national economic conditions and contrary to norms, yet she simultaneously recognized that relative to others in society, she was managing to get by. She was discouraged by what she perceived as the hardships that neoliberal policies imposed on the working class, and yet she was not convinced that Menem had any alternative but to follow those policies. In the cases of Eduardo and Paula, each occasionally saw links between the national government and their own hardships, but overall their strong partisan loyalties (one Peronist, the other Radical) served to focus their attention on macrolevel political issues and away from micro-macro linkages.

Whether or not the state is held accountable for one's material conditions is not merely a question of attributing blame for causing the conditions. It is also a question of assessing capacity and responsibility to improve the conditions. People who believed they had the capacity to solve problems by the efforts of their own households or through the local community did not tend to see those problems as ones the national government should be addressing. This chapter has argued that perceptions about whether the citizen or some other entity has the capacity to solve problems are shaped by the nature of the problems themselves and the timing and economic context in which solutions might be found. This is a crucial and often overlooked part of the explanation for how material interests become or do not become political interests, but it is not the entire explanation. Political factors also shape citizens' perceptions of the economic context—how they interpret the present situation and the possibility that an effective government could improve upon it. In cases such as those of Eduardo and Paula, seen in the SW quadrant of table 5.4, political factors may focus citizens' attention away from the link between material interests and the state's actions. Additionally, political factors influence which macrolevel issues are focused upon. These political factors are taken up in the next chapter.

Chapter

6

Political Interests in Context

To this point, this book has focused on individuals and their interests. In this chapter those individuals express themselves as citizens—members of a community and members with views about the political order and the public policies under which they live. The words and perceptions of those interviewed will reveal how their political interests are constrained and filtered by their social identities and by the historical, political, and economic contexts in which they live. Almost everyone featured in this chapter is someone who was categorized in the last chapter as employing either a macrofocus or "linking" their micro- and macrolevel interests. Those focused on the microlevel were not excluded from the chapter; rather, because of their microfocus they had little to say about the political and policy matters examined in this chapter.

Underlying Values, Identities, and Reputations

The first part of this chapter examines the underlying values, identities, and party reputations that Argentines employ in talking about political affairs.

The first two subsections examine hegemonic social values and class identities. The third subsection outlines the reputations of the two major parties in the eyes of their supporters and critics. Knowing these reputations is a necessary background to understanding the views heard later in the chapter.

Conserving Social Values

Many of those interviewed strongly believed that the state is responsible for providing for the general and specific welfare of the people. In other words, in a political climate offering few leadership or policy alternatives to satisfy their values, people were nevertheless certain of what they valued: well-paying jobs, state-supported health care and education, a decent standard of living for children and pensioners, and a decrease in homelessness and street children. Whether supportive of or opposed to Menem's policy changes, none questioned that the state had a legitimate role in these matters.

These values are rooted in the social teachings of the Catholic Church, codified by the labor and social guarantees in Article 14 of the constitution, and promulgated during nearly fifty years of Peronist discourse about social justice and solidarity.[1] These guarantees have always been *de jure*, not *de facto*. As one constitutional analyst wrote regarding the social guarantees in Article 14, "The effective realization of these propositions will depend, in part, on economic possibilities, and in part on future political decisions" (Pi de la Serra 1983, 110). While Menem aggressively moved away from a model of state-provided services, he did so with an argument based on budget necessity, efficiency, rationality, and the elimination of statist "privileges." He advocated individual liberty and initiative, but usually in the context of expressing concern for social justice and the common good. For example, he argued, "We must conceive a pluralist cultural project—respectful of private initiative, jealous of individual liberty, and eager for social justice. This is the project for the fatherland, one that is impossible to achieve without collective consensus" (Menem and Dromi 1990, 46). Working within the hegemonic value system, Menem made arguments that largely avoided the Calvinist discourse and divisive appeals to individual interest that have accompanied calls for state reform in the United States. When Menem spearheaded a revision of the constitution in 1994, the social guarantees of Article 14 were left untouched.

While appeals to budget necessity and "realism" may be used to persuade the public to undertake neoliberal reforms, the reforms will eventually create a new society legitimized not merely by pragmatism, but by a new set of dominant values. People interviewed were noticing this kind of change. Francesca, who was raised a Peronist and had voted for Menem, said that in Perón's day there was "humanity" and people were "united," but in contrast today "a guy who has money will just step on you." Her perspective was echoed by others:

> I think that right now, although they might wish [otherwise], things are sort of paralyzed, including this party, right? I think that at a global level, there's a turn toward the Right, toward conservatism, the very capitalist part, where the interest is in economic values. There's too much emphasis put on economic values. Other values are left aside, such as solidarity and trying to do things together. In Alfonsín's time, it was seen as propitious that people organize and join together to do things in common, but now I don't see it. Now it's propitious to save yourself if you can—if you have money, great, but if not, no one's taking care of the indigent, health care, or education. I see all of these being very neglected. (Olivia, laid off public employee and UCR activist)

Similarly, Soña, an artisan and lifelong Peronist, expressed, "Menemism is very harsh. It doesn't share or accompany [others]. It's liberalism, first and foremost. . . . Health, education, work, and food are really unprotected." In the sections that follow, Argentines discuss these core social values. These sections explore the reasons why Argentines differ in their interpretations about which leaders and policies would protect, augment, neglect, or abandon these values in their society.

Class Identities

The Argentines interviewed processed their life experiences and public options through class and party identities in order to come up with political conclusions. Their opinions about economic policies or the Menem government were often attributed to these identities rather than to personal material interests. There is no single source for such identities, although childhood upbringing established the party and class loyalties of many of those interviewed.

Some evidence for the extent of inherited political identity in Argentina comes from surveys in 1984 and 1991, which found 38 percent and 46 percent of Argentines respectively said they shared their parents' political attitudes (World Values Study Group 1994). Identities rooted in earlier periods help explain why political opinions do not necessarily reflect an individual's current socioeconomic status.[2]

The political importance of class is not surprising, but the relationship of class to interests merits additional comment. First, because class identity is a way that people identify their *differences* from others in society, class is inherently about inequality, not merely about quantity of material possessions. Those interviewed who expressed their political preferences in class terms preferred politicians who diminished their sense of inequality—who seemed accessible and familiar to people like them.

Secondly, class *identity* may not reflect current class *position*. With nearly half of Argentine workers employed in the informal sector, many are working in occupations below the levels of education, upbringing, and social status with which they identify themselves (cf., Sartori 1969, 83). Therefore, strong existing class identities may hinder the formulation of new ones based on shared problems in the current economy.

Third, because class position indicates inequality and no one wants to be treated unequally, people tend to disassociate themselves from powerlessness, by finding distinctions between themselves and others. People who identified themselves as "poor" would frequently talk about other poor people as having more difficult material problems with which to cope than they. It was also not uncommon to hear other people's material hardships being attributed to moral failings (laziness, ignorance, etc.), while their own were considered the result of fortune, society, or politics.[3]

Fourth, politicians, parties, and organizations promote class identity for strategic reasons (Przeworski 1985; Sartori 1969). Therefore, class identity is not merely a response to one's personal life circumstances but also to external forces. In Argentina, social class has been an important political identity, openly promoted by political discourse, for most of this century—a point explored further in the next section.[4]

Party Reputations and Identities

In Argentina, as anywhere, participation in party activities strongly reinforces the images of a person's own party and that of opponent parties. For true party believers, party is the first and last point of departure for evaluations of politicians, coloring their interpretations of their own and their country's interests and their evaluations of government performance. A couple of examples illustrate this idea. Mónica was a retired bureaucrat who participated in her neighborhood Radical *comité*.[5] She traced her UCR loyalties back to her grandparents, who were probably in the party's first generation of adherents. When asked to compare Alfonsín and Menem, Mónica seemed oblivious to the hyperinflation of 1989 under the former and the stabilization under the latter: "Under Alfonsín, things were much better, in the economic sense, than they are now. At least then we could live. Now under Menem, there's not enough money for anything—you almost can't live." When asked to describe something good that Menem had done, she was adamant: "I don't like Peronist politics, so I see nothing good." Similarly intense party loyalty and a similar use of party as the primary determinant of her political judgments can be heard in the interview with Gabriela, who helped run an *unidad básica* in her neighborhood. She was a "client" of a member of city council who had provided her with a "job" at city hall in return for her partisan activities. Her patron had supported Menem back in the 1989 PJ primaries and so she did too. Asked if she considered herself a Menemist, she insisted her loyalties were to the movement, not its current leader:

> No, no, no. We are Peronists of Perón. Understand? But if Alfonsín would have done things well, we would have supported Alfonsín. Not *voting* for him of course. But then, he didn't do things well. . . .
> Q: How would you have supported Alfonsín, if you wouldn't have voted for him? What *would* you have done to support him?
> Gabriela: Well, by supporting him, and by working for the country! eh?[6]

Later, when asked if she had ever or would ever not vote Peronist, Gabriela responded, "For example, Luder.[7] When Luder was running, I didn't agree with Luder. I never liked him. But I am a Peronist. You see? Therefore, if Peronism brings forward Luder, well then, if he was the captain—like General Perón said—he was the captain *[chuckle]* and I voted for him." And, asked if Menem and Perón were different or alike, she replied:

> They are different. For me, Perón was a visionary. What can I say? Peronism—how can I explain it to you? . . .He was a maestro. What can I say? The Old Man was everything for us, you see? He was a leader. . . .
> I open a book by Perón—*La comunidad organizada* or *La doctrina*, and it's as if the Old Man is alive and—because he's talking about things that are happening nowadays, and he already knew that they would happen.
> Q: For example?
> Gabriela: And, well, uh, the situation with the pensions.

While party loyalists were adamant and hyperbolic in their descriptions of their parties' strengths and opponents' weaknesses, people did not have to be politically active to have strong opinions and preferences about the parties. Importantly, these opinions and preferences were not built on policies or ideology. The parties have not differed significantly over the years in those terms. Each party favored developmentalist policies in their day and promoted neoliberal restructuring more recently. Divisions over particular policies were as strong among factions within any particular party as they were between the parties. Instead of using policy or ideology, the people interviewed described the PJ and UCR in terms of class affinity and historical performance. Despite both being "umbrella parties" with multiclass constituencies, the PJ and UCR have each relied on a particular class base and are each perceived as in sync with the interests of a particular class—the PJ with the working class and poor, the UCR with the middle class.[8] The parties' reputations are also deeply rooted in how each party acted during tumultuous moments in the twentieth century, in their differing styles of governance, their perceived "democraticness," and their achievements while in power. As Edgardo Catterberg and María Braun put it: "These two parties possess significant cultural political baggage, family tradition, and personal political histories. All of this contributes to the fact that the parties possess a diffuse yet considerable loyalty in the population, even beyond their registered members" (1989, 362).

This "baggage" constitutes two sets of conventional wisdom about the two major parties—the opponents' wisdom and the internal wisdom. Opponents of Peronism tend to see the Peronists as undemocratic, citing Perón's demagoguery and repressive tactics as well as the corrupt and heavy-handed leadership of Peronist-affiliated labor unions. They see Peronist voters as uneducated and easily deceived by simple promises. With a partisan desire to diminish the accomplishments of their opponents, at least four Radical supporters pointed out to me that the progressive social programs initiated by Juan Perón had in fact been conceived earlier by Socialist Party leader Alfredo Palacios. The conventional wisdom among Peronists, not surprisingly, is quite different. Although some acknowledge Palacios' ideas, all give great credit to Perón for the social policies he instituted. Although their own party does not emphasize democracy as a priority, Peronists argue that they are the only party that is democratic in the sense of representing the common person.[9]

The Peronists' "wisdom" about their opponents, the Radicals, is that the UCR has not shown a historical commitment to the constitution or to fair electoral competition. According to Peronists, the Radicals "always knock on the barracks door," as evidenced by their support for the 1955 coup that overthrew Perón and by their willingness to participate in presidential elections in 1958 and 1963, when the military had proscribed Peronist competition. On the other hand, the Radicals see their own history as evidence of democratic commitment: from their founder, Hipólito Yrigoyen, who won office after struggling successfully for electoral reforms, through Raúl Alfonsín, whose political discourse emphasized democratic values.

These broad party reputations filtered the thinking of many of those interviewed, as they talked about the policies and leadership offered by various Argentine politicians, starting with President Menem. The reputations have been inculcated over more than forty-five years of political discourse as well as passed along through family upbringing and experiences, as the following examples illustrate.

Vicente, a fifty-two-year-old skilled construction worker, traced his aversion to Peronism to his father's experience. His father's father had been an ardent Radical who taught his son to sympathize with the UCR. Vicente's father, however, "wasn't an affiliate [of the UCR] or anything. He [simply] wasn't a Peronist." Nevertheless, for failing to support the new Peronist party, he was harassed, beaten, and blacklisted from job opportunities in the interior province where they lived. From this family history, Vicente had taken not only a distaste for Peronism but also for dogma: "Starting from that experience, I don't respect nor have sympathy for anyone who wants me to think like he thinks or who wants to force me to think or do what he wishes. It's that simple."

Pablo, a thirty-four-year-old bank employee, was the son of a housekeeper and a waiter and had spent his childhood in a shantytown. He was not a loyal partisan. He said he had voted for Alfonsín in 1983 and Menem in 1989 and had a mixture of praise and criticism for Menem's performance in office. Nevertheless, he had affiliated with the Justicialist Party and said his parents also considered themselves Peronists. Why? "Because," Pablo said, "they come from a very humble background, and therefore, me too." Pablo chose his words very carefully; clearly he knew that people such as Vicente's father had been harassed by Peronist partisans. His sympathies for the party, however, seem to have led him to perceive the party as no longer suffering from the vices of which it is accused by the opponents' conventional wisdom:

> The Justicialist Party? I think it's a party that made its core with the poorest and neediest people. And that, in its early era, with Perón and Evita, well, excesses and abuses were committed, against the citizenry, because those people who never had anything suddenly found that they had a union, and they had housing, and they had some standard of living. Well, they themselves committed an outrage by their ignorance, no? For example, they became fanatics, believing that their own party was the very best and that everyone else was an enemy. I'm talking about the vast majority, of course. A minority manipulated all of this in its own favor, of course. Right? But the vast majority, I believe, acted this way because of the people's great ignorance and

naivete about someone who gave them something, someone who remembered them. They thought of him like a god. And therefore, they
became fanatical. Well. I believe that by today, the people have evolved
a great deal in this respect. In this respect, they've evolved. I believe
that the myths are dying, slowly. And I believe that the citizens are
moving [giant] steps forward toward a better democracy.

In sum, party identities were important filters through which citizens interpreted their political interests. The parties' "baggage"—their reputations from
past performance—served to reinforce existing identities and to shape citizens'
receptivity to, or antagonism toward, current behavior by the parties' leaders.
This reinforcing and shaping will be seen in the sections that follow.

Views about Argentine Government and Politics

This section presents views about the Menem presidency, examining how
partisan and class identities shaped interpretations of his performance. It
shows how social values, class and party identities, and party reputations influenced the views Argentines expressed about their government.

President Menem

Carlos Menem won election easily in 1989 because he represented an
alternative to the economic policy failures under the Radical Party's leadership
of Raúl Alfonsín. From 1987 to 1993, the Justicialist Party surpassed every
opposition party in congressional elections. During the early 1990s, Menem
portrayed the party's success as approval for himself and his economic policies. Despite Menem's success in this period, the interviews suggest that the
Peronists' electoral support from lower income voters was more likely attributable to their weak competition than to the popularity of their programs (a
point developed later in this chapter).

Neither class position nor level of living was sufficient to explain support
for Menem among those interviewed. Of the six people interviewed who had a
relatively positive view of President Menem and his economic policies, four
were structurally poor, living in dreadful housing.[10] Most were poorly educated and long-time Peronist supporters, and all identified strongly with the
working class. Yet the same could be said of many of those disillusioned by
Menem. To the extent political views were related to socioeconomic status,
those views were based on the voters' interpretation of, rather than empirical
experience of, their material and class concerns.

People do not all perceive the same reality in the same way, even independently of how that reality affects them personally. (Studies of juries, witnesses, teaching evaluations, and Rorschach test–takers, among others, make this clear.) How can we explain differences in perceptions of political phenomena? The differences among respondents' views of Menem were not usually rooted in their personal material conditions under the Menem presidency. That is, most of the interview set, as shown in the last chapter, did not link their micro-level conditions to their macrolevel evaluations. Their different views were also not rooted in differing information about Menem's policies nor in contradictory perceptions of the facts of what Menem had done—as in a Roshomon experience, where each remembers an event differently. Rather, Menem was praised or scorned on the basis of the *same* observed behavior. That behavior had been framed by elite-level discourse that could be heard in the news media (Gamson 1992). People interpreted that media content in light of their preexisting understanding of Peronism itself. The result was three patterns by which people interpreted Menem's behavior.

Disillusionment.— A number of people strongly identified with Peronism but were disillusioned by Menem's version of it. They perceived Menem's economic policies as a betrayal of his campaign promises and neglectful of the needs of the common person. They used words such as "defrauded" and "deceived" to describe how they felt after voting for Menem. This was a reaction to the president's campaign slogan, "Follow me, I won't defraud you."

These people perceived Menem as a betrayal of Peronism. Juan Perón had rejected the classical liberalism espoused by the oligarchy that ruled Argentina for most of its pre-Peronist history. Perón claimed to offer a "third way" between the liberal economics of capitalism and the collectivist economics of socialism. Menem, on the other hand, had appointed finance ministers and numerous senior-level officials from outside the Justicialist Party, who had strong ties to the business establishment (Gibson 1996, 180–209). He had also promoted policies to stop wage indexation and to eliminate Peronist-era labor legislation. For doing so, Menem was frequently described as "a liberal, not a real Peronist." Disillusioned Peronist voters said his actions contradicted either his prior promises or Peronist values. Typical of the sense that the political arena offered no good alternatives is Francesca, who said she had voted for Menem in 1989 but that if Menem were the candidate again in 1995 she would probably not vote for anyone (i.e., she would vote *en blanco*). Speaking of factory closings, Francesca, a domestic worker and housing activist, said: "Many of us blame the president. He's responsible for throwing people out in the streets. . . . Wages are hunger-level. . . . Menem just uses the Peronist banner.[11] . . . I'm very disillusioned."

Others held a similar perspective. Horacio, a maintenance worker in the public sector, stated, "I've always liked Peronism, but not Peronism mixed with other things. Because lots of things that they call Peronist aren't Peronism. . . . I voted for Menem. He promised a lot and we thought he'd follow the doctrine of Perón, but he didn't. . . . I won't ever vote for him again. I made a mistake and won't do it again." Soña, a self-employed artisan and lifelong Peronist, said, "We never dreamed that Menem was going to share power with the liberals. They weren't on the voting lists." Matilde, an artisan and seamstress, expressed, "[Menem and Perón] are completely different. Perón worried a lot about social assistance. . . . His was a labor government. Menem's is a rather conservative government."

Criticism.— Non-Peronist critics of Menem agreed with the view that his policies contradicted his campaign promises and Peronist tradition. They tended to view his neoliberal policies as not only contrary to Peronism but flawed as well. As the following interview excerpts illustrate, they believed Menem had sold out the concerns of the popular sectors, and either brought on, or failed to alleviate, economic hardships.

Diego: Menem isn't who he said he was.
Q: Prior to the election, did he have anything in common with the people you know? With people around here?
Diego: Look, I'm not a Peronist. My friend Esperanza here is a true Peronist militant and more Peronist than those good-for-nothings wandering all over.[12] The people, by nature, by feeling, are Peronists. The humble people. They're Evita, the General, Peronism. So those good-for-nothings played, they play, with the feelings of the people and use Peronism as a screen in order to win elections when they are completely the opposite and are dealing with the worst enemy. Perón kicked the U.S. ambassador, Braden, out of the country. . . .[13] The current president, no. I don't know who's governing today, the ambassador [of the United States] or Méndez.[14] (Diego, shantytown activist and leftist)

He's handing over the country in some ways. That's how I see it. Maybe I'm mistaken. And economically, it's a disaster. (Julio, construction worker with temporary employment, who votes for the left.)

He forgot all about his electoral platform from '89. Now he's leaning toward liberalism, toward the UCeDéists. He's more conservative. Many sectors are going down.

[Q: Which ones?]
The middle class and the lower middle. (Samuel, student and electrician, who had no party loyalties)

I didn't trust him at that time [i.e., at the 1989 election]. He seemed to be incompetent. . . . How do I see him now? I see him as a person at the service of big capital. He's following this path with complete coldness, without concern for the people, for what's happening to the poor. And this is something everyone says, no? . . . Well, the thing about Menem is that he's involved in the task of turning the country over—the riches of the country and with the riches, the people—to the people who have the power, here and in the rest of the world. No? He's into this and into intimidating the people, no? . . . Menem appeared and got the support of all the elements of the working people and part of the middle class, and then he also got the support—having spoken with them—of the church, the military, and the economic powers. . . . But it's a very immoral thing.
[Q: What was?]
This thing of deceiving everyone. That is, to have deceived the people by having made arrangements [i.e. with the centers of power]. (Andrés, informally employed vendor who had voted for Alfonsín in 1983 and could not remember whom [but remembers not backing Menem] he had supported in 1989)

Party Loyalty.— The statements from the opponents and the disillusioned Peronists reflect the depth with which certain of Perón's policy positions—nationalism, autonomy in foreign relations, autarchy in economic development, and opposition to liberalism—had come to be associated in the public's mind with Peronism and with the good of Argentina itself. Yet Perón's ideological position had never been fully coherent, much less consistently pursued.[15] Despite Peronism's image as an antiestablishment mass movement, it was persistently pragmatic. If Peronism stood for pragmatism, then Menem did not betray the movement. He argued that new times required new thinking, including integration into the global economy and a shift from diplomatic autonomy toward unprecedentedly friendly relations with the United States (Granovsky 1991). In a published effort to justify his promotion of foreign investment, privatization of state industries, and the dismantling of the powerful state Perón had created, Menem selectively borrowed statements from the canon of Perón's writings to show support for private capitalist interests. With pride, he claimed Peronist pragmatism as a progressive virtue in the face of ideological immobilism (see Menem and Dromi 1990, 22–23, 28, 31, 33). In one of many cases of convenient and clever citation, Menem defended the privatization of the industries that Perón had nationalized by citing Perón's argument *for nationalizing* them, in which Perón had vaguely promised that some day those nationalizations would be reversed. In other words, he used language that Perón had likely included to try to assuage critics of his policies as evidence that Perón would agree with the reversal of his own policy legacy. Menem insisted that Peronism was not about specific policies but rather that those policies were a product of particular circumstances, as were Menem's (opposite) policies (Menem and Dromi 1990, 37–38).

Some Peronist activists were very comfortable with the movement's pragmatism and the idea of an evolution in Peronism. Gabriela and her husband Raúl were lifelong Peronists who led an *unidad básica*. Consider the odd combination of partisan faith, philosophical flexibility, and historical selectivity evident in the following conversation with Raúl:

Q: Some people say that Menem is doing the opposite of what Perón did. What do you think of that?

Raúl: I believe that Menem is not doing things the way that, as you said, as Perón would do them. But let's not forget that these are different times. He inherited a country that was completely destroyed by the bad governments that were in before, by the military governments. . . . Not just economically destroyed, but also . . . during the period of the military *Proceso*, all of the student youth were disappeared—that is to say, the thinking youth. Right? These youth have disappeared completely. So therefore, Menem is doing a great deal with the little bit that he received. . . . Menem was criticized here because at the beginning he associated with Bunge y Born.[16] And who's he going to deal with if not with Bunge y Born, who has the money? . . . He's got to seek out capital, no? And since Perón was against capitalism, here's where there's a bit of a contradiction, no? *[laughs]*

Q: Sure, and the current government supports capitalism and liberalism.

Raúl: Clearly. Yes, they made an alliance with the liberals—something that never existed before. They never had anything to do with each other before! True Peronists feel shocked by this. Today we have this candidate, Porto, who isn't a Peronist and who doesn't have anything to do with Peronism.[17] And many Peronist people, you see, feel bad

about this. The thing is that they've never [read] Perón much either.
Because Perón [won] his elections with people [outside] the party. He
always had allies [who weren't] from the party.

The Peronist activists who were interviewed demonstrated an unquestion-
ing party loyalty, willingness to give the benefit of the doubt to their party's
leader, and a selective reading of events that found their party superior to all
opponents. As Eduardo, an unemployed laborer, claimed: "Alfonsín won because he lied. Politicians always lie. But Menem didn't lie. He didn't promise
anything." (The veracity of the statement is questionable, but the logic used is
even more interesting for what it suggests about the norms of democratic accountability. Eduardo sought to defend an elected leader on the grounds that
the leader offered voters no proposals for which to hold him accountable.)
   Eduardo accepted Menem's arguments that progress required persistence
with his economic plan, encouragement of foreign investment, and elimination of the high production costs caused by strong labor unions. He was
mildly hopeful that this progress might some day reach him. Like Raúl, quoted
above (and like Radical Party loyalists I quote later), Eduardo tended not to
blame his party's government for problems but instead perceived ongoing
problems as either irremediable or the fault of opponents or predecessors. This
tendency is illustrated in the following conversation about the problem of
"brain drain." Expressing frustration that Argentina once had a Nobel Prize
winner while today many of its best scientists emigrate, Eduardo said:

   They need to give more opportunity. There aren't opportunities.
   Q: Who has to give opportunities? The state?
   Eduardo: Yes.
   Q: Is Menem doing this?
   Eduardo: The answer is education—at all levels. But the Radicals con-
   trol most of the universities in the country, so we don't have much
   chance to change things. . . . Menem can't change things in three years
   if it's a problem that developed over thirty years.

Interestingly, Eduardo was less forgiving of the local Peronist Party than of
Menem. He had been a "ñoqui"—a party client collecting a paycheck as a ghost
employee of the city council. Losing that "contract" after a few months, Eduardo criticized the local party leaders for making false promises, exploiting
election volunteers like himself, and being unfaithful to the solidaristic
essence of Peronism. In the midst of what he already perceived as an unjust
world, he blamed the local party leaders for letting him and the Peronist ideals

down. In short, he exhibited the tendency towards subsidiarity, which was discussed in chapter 5. That is, he interpreted the local-level party organization as having a direct negative impact on his life but he did not look to national-level actors to resolve his problems.[18]

Menem's Leadership

Evaluations of Menem did not rest solely on opposition to, or justifications for, his policies. In many interviews, people commented upon Menem as a leader without reference to his leadership on particular policies, economic or otherwise. In their judgments they expressed preferences for a certain style and moral character of leadership.[19] As the discussion below shows, some of these judgments, although not all, corresponded to one of the two conventional wisdoms about Peronism. In other words, for some respondents, leadership evaluations were reinterpretations of their evaluations of the parties. They saw those leadership traits that they considered typical of Menem's party in Menem himself and then praised or criticized him on this basis. For other respondents, however, leadership style was judged independently of party images. In either case, judgments were offered in terms of leadership traits per se, not the material outcomes of the leader's work, which suggests that leadership character constituted an independent basis of political evaluation.

Most critics of Menem's leadership style were UCR voters and others who had long disliked the Peronist movement. They saw Menem as another example of the movement's populist and authoritarian heritage. In Ostiguy's (1997) terms, these citizens disapproved of Menem's "low" style. In this case, the critics' middle-class identities were evident in their rejection of what they perceived as Peronism's demagoguery. For example, Olivia said that she had never liked the personalistic and *caudillo* image that Menem had promoted during his 1989 campaign and she thought he handled the presidency with "frivolity—like a little kid with a new pair of shoes."[20] Mónica, the senior citizen and lifetime Radical partisan quoted at the start of the chapter, argued that "Menem spends more time on trips and soccer games than on other things." She repeatedly argued that Peronists "do whatever they want," while they ignore the economic conditions that had made her life difficult and harmed people much poorer than she.

Tomás, the retired bank accountant described in chapter 5, talked about his political interests only by focusing on the link between his own income and Menem's policies. Yet his political views had nonmaterialist roots much older than his own economic downturn. Tomás's father was a Basque socialist who had taken his family into permanent exile during Spain's Civil War.

According to Tomás, he learned from his father to reject authoritarian, populist, or dishonest leadership. These values were reiterated consistently over three hours of interview. Tomás was vehemently scornful of Menem and all Peronists, whom he saw as untrustworthy populists appealing to ignorant and short-sighted voters.

Some criticisms of Menem's leadership style were not filtered through partisan images and identities but were simply rooted in the person's standards for proper presidential demeanor. For example, Juan Antonio, who had been active in moderate left politics for many years, said that he voted *en blanco* in the 1989 presidential election rather than vote for Menem, whom he perceived as a "phoney from the provinces"—not presidential material. Atilio, a former Peronist voter, thought Menem was not serious about his responsibilities and did not govern for the good of the people. Menem, he said, was always "playing soccer, playing tennis, playing basketball—this isn't a presidential attitude."[21]

These criticisms repeated those in the media at the time. There had been widespread publicity about the president's jet set lifestyle, his preoccupation with his physical appearance, and his athletic activities. Catholic Church leaders had publicly questioned the "frivolity" of the government's attitudes toward social needs. The importance here is not the initial source of the criticism but the resonance that it found with some of those interviewed. Some people clearly responded to criticisms heard in the media, which were based not on retrospective evaluation of how particular policies affected either the person's own microlevel material interests or the national economy but rather on the president's leadership capacity and style. They perceived Menem's demeanor as inappropriate to his position, and they doubted, on grounds of his personality and moral character, his capacity to govern.

While critics of Menem disliked what they perceived as his authoritarian, populist style, this was precisely what appealed to some of his supporters, who perceived him as a take-charge, competent, and accessible leader. Blatantly populist acts, such as the *asados* (barbecues) that Peronists host to woo voters during their electoral campaigns, were widely criticized by non-Peronists. Amanda and her adult son, Pepe, however, thought the events were good. They fully recognized that the party was just trying to win votes but, in accordance with the literature on populism, the inclusion was the attraction. They appreciated that the party *wanted* their vote. Amanda's class identity led her to reject the other major party. She believed Radicals are "different from us" and "lean toward the upper class, while letting the lower class get even lower." Favorably predisposed to Menem because of their class identification with Peronism, Amanda and Pepe had clearly accepted the president's "spin" on many issues. For example, they told me that the president's pardon of the convicted *junta* leaders was necessary for national unity, that Alfonsín was so incompetent that he abandoned his responsibilities, leaving Menem to clean up the economic mess, and that Menem was "open and honest."[22]

Pepe explained Menem's leadership appeal: "Everyone says that Menem isn't a Peronist. Well, maybe he's not, but maybe he's simpler, and not so solemn. When he came to San Telmo, he gave me his hand to shake. So despite people saying that he's fake, he did that—and other presidents haven't done that and wouldn't have come to San Telmo." At the time of the president's election, Pepe's perception of Menem's accessibility was widely held. In a 1989 survey of metropolitan areas, 71 percent said Menem was "close to the people," compared to 30 percent for Radical candidate Angeloz. Also, 65 percent said Menem "is a simple person" (a compliment), as opposed to 43 percent for Angeloz (Catterberg and Braun 1989, 369). Perceiving a candidate as "close to the people" does not, of course, necessitate supporting that candidate. (Catterberg and Braun did not calculate the correlation between views of Menem's accessibility to the people and intention to vote for him.)

It is difficult to assess how important Menem's leadership style was in the overall evaluations of those interviewed. One should note, however, that several people made judgments about leadership style without mentioning how that leadership affected their own or the country's material interests. This suggests that leadership was an independent consideration in their thinking. Criticisms or praise of leadership style might be simple justifications offered in an interview to supplement a person's opinions rooted in other causes, including partisanship or material interests. On the other hand, it is unlikely that there is one root cause or dominant value for someone's political views. Rather, various compatible considerations may coalesce, mutually reinforcing the person's viewpoint. Thus, Tomás's opposition to Menem's populist style was consistent with his opposition to authoritarian behavior by the Argentine military. Likewise, Pepe's interpretation of Menem as accessible to people like him is consistent with Pepe's similar judgment about Menem's party.

Views about Alternatives

This section examines alternatives to Menem and his policies, analyzing views about the political opposition and noting once again the influence of partisan and class identities. I also examine how views are rooted in expectations that were created by the opposition's historic performance record. Finally, this section considers views about alternative economic policies.

Among those who had voted for Menem but become disillusioned with his policies, all said that they were unsure how to respond politically because of the weak alternatives. Skepticism was widespread:

> Well what happens is that they all make promises about what they are going to do, and then when they are elected, they don't do what they said. There are very few who fulfill their promises. (Betina, domestic worker)

> I would like to vote for Menem again—but I don't know. . . . So much corruption. I'm going to be among the "undecideds" *[laughter]*. (Marcela, public employee)

> I'm not in agreement with this [economic] model—not at all. And don't ask me for alternatives because I don't see any . . . not from any of the parties. . . . None of the parties is convincing to me right now. (Nena, public employee and ATE union member)

> Up until now, we've believed many of the lies that they tell us. Certainly after the experience of Menem, who told us about the productive revolution, the *salariazo*, and I don't know what other tales, the next guy who steps into a Menemobile and says the same thing isn't going to be believed. Because now we've *had* that experience! (Graciela, public employee)

While the disillusioned citizens were discombobulated and wondered where to turn to find policies promoting the working class, the Peronist loyalists thought that their party remained the only representative of their social class. Some Menem loyalists recognized Menem's broken promises but justified them as simply evidence of the corrupt and dirty nature of all politics. Some argued that common citizens inevitably pay for economic adjustments. They did not hold Menem accountable for the perceived burdens on the lower classes because they saw those burdens as the immutable result of social inequalities. As Eduardo, an unemployed laborer and Peronist activist, stated: "The one who pays the consequences [of the economic adjustment policies] is the last guy—the one on the bottom. That is to say, us. Here, and in every place in the world."

The UCR Alternative

Those who criticized Menem for his economic policies seldom favored Radicalism as an alternative. The most recent experience of Radical economic management had been the period of hyperinflation at the end of Alfonsín's term. As O'Donnell (1994) predicts of a "delegative democracy," those interviewed who were not Radical loyalists rejected Alfonsín and his party as alternatives. Although some recognized that Peronists had used obstructionist tactics that made it difficult for Alfonsín to implement his policies, nevertheless, the Radicals were perceived to have failed to take care of the national economic interests the last time they were delegated authority to do so.[23] An extreme version of this thinking was that of Betina's husband, superintendent of an apartment building, who said he assumed that if things did not go well under Menem there would probably be a military coup, because what alternative would there be? He said that when Alfonsín left office before his term was complete, the Radicals showed they did not have answers.

Not only was their record weak, but the Radicals at that time also offered little vision of an alternative future. They had obstructed some of Menem's proposals in Congress but overall they had not been active opponents of the philosophy or practice of Menem's economic adjustment and state restructuring policies.

UCR activists, of course, believed Radicalism was a viable alternative but they did not usually try to base that belief on the party's current proposals or past record. Just as with the Peronist loyalists described above, a selective reading of history and preexisting political biases shaped the Radical loyalists' discourse on material conditions. Paula's and Vicente's opinions exemplify two ways that longtime Radicals evaluated their party as an alternative to the incumbent government. Paula ignored and excused her party's record on economic policy. For example, rather than focus on the high inflation under Alfonsín, as most Peronist supporters did, she barely mentioned Alfonsín's difficulties with the economy. When she did, she said the problems were unavoidable because of the mistakes of Alfonsín's military predecessors. As a committed Radical, she gleefully waited for Menem's policies to fail. However, as an objective observer, she was not certain that would happen. Paula would have opposed Menem regardless of his economic policies because in her view he was demagogic and untrustworthy. She believed her party constituted the only viable alternative to Menem, but she worried that it had not come up with a strong, charismatic leader to oppose him.

Vicente, whose familial roots in Radicalism were discussed earlier in the chapter, demonstrated a less optimistic vision of the potential for the UCR to provide an alternative. His brief personal experience working in campaigns had made him aware of the seedier side of political competition and had diminished his interest and confidence in the political process. To be successful, he said, a politician had to be "a liar and a promisor." Asked to evaluate Menem, he immediately replied that the president's economic policies were "ferocious" for their impact on the popular sectors. As evidence he mentioned higher consumption taxes, stagnant wages, and penniless pensioners. Yet at the same time he recognized that the country's economy had been "in crisis because the government was administered so poorly for so many years" and he thought it remained to be seen whether Menem might be right that the sacrifices now would pay off for the next generation. He was much less certain than Paula that the Radicals could provide an alternative to Menem, saying that while he had always supported the Radicals, he was "not a Radical fanatic."

Overall, Vicente had few expectations that the political system had any alternatives with better solutions than Menem's. While he had voted for Radicals for president in the previous two elections, he believed it was just as well that Radical candidate Angeloz had lost in 1989 because the obstructionist tactics of Peronist opponents would have prevented Angeloz from effective governance just as they had not allowed Alfonsín to govern efficiently. He had heard reports of preelection deals between Menem and financial elites conspiring to assure that hyperinflation would seal the Radicals' fate in 1989. Three years after that election, Vicente saw the choices in the Argentine party system as neither well defined nor very appealing:

> I've watched the Radicals for a while now and have decided that over time they've been losing the essential base of Radicalism. Because Alfonsín's politics were a Radicalism of the left and ended up standing in the center and . . .the government we have now is completely of the right. Not even the Peronists are really Peronists and not even the Radicals are really Radicals. And all that I've read about Marx, about the Trotskyites, about the whole Communist line never ended up persuading me, because *[chuckle]* this understanding of the person is something that, no, no, *[searching for words to explain it]* this thing of man being subjected to man—I mean, the communist system. I have Cuban friends who've told me about Cuba and it's all national. [The attitude there is] either do what your Papa says or I'll give you a whipping.

Leftovers?

Vicente's views of leftist ideology were not uncommon. The overwhelming majority of the Argentine public had long been skeptical about socialist ideologies and wary of what they consider "extremes." The World Values Survey found only 18 percent of Argentines identified themselves as ideologically to the left—among the lowest percentages of the thirty-nine sites surveyed around the world (where the average was 27 percent). According to the survey, young Argentines identified with the left slightly more often than the oldest generation, not surprisingly, but there was no meaningful difference among income groups and only a slight variation by education (with greater affinity for the left among the most educated).[24] Likewise, in an in-depth study of ideology among Argentine workers in the mid-1980s, Ranis (1992, 144–45) found only 20 percent of his sample identified their personal ideology as left or center left, with differences by education and age being in the same direction as in the World Values Survey.

Wariness of the left was nurtured by decades of anticommunist political discourse, from Perón through the last military regime. The antipathy to the left was reinforced by experience with the guerrilla movement in the early 1970s. Although elements of the Montonero movement were not ideologically leftist (Ollier 1986), the general public painted all the movements with a similar ideological brush.

The left's reputation organizationally was no stronger than it was ideologically. For decades, the Argentine left had been divided into numerous and ever-transforming parties, fronts, and coalitions, ranging from the Stalinist hardliners of the Communist Party to center-left upshoots formed by those disillusioned with mainstream PJ or UCR politics. In the years between the democratic transition and the time my interviews were conducted, no one on the left had managed to attract even 10 percent of the vote. Reflecting and reinforcing that electoral weakness, the major newspapers and television newscasts paid little attention to the positions or proposals of these parties.[25] A voter had to attend a rally, buy a party-sponsored periodical, or be acquainted with party activists in order to learn about leftist alternatives to the dominant parties.

Given the left's image, low profile, and electoral weakness, it was not surprising that most of those interviewed did not even mention the left as an option.[26] When discussed at all, leftist parties were often portrayed as unrealistic and extremist in their aims, internally factious and exclusive, and electorally irrelevant. Pablo, a bank employee who identified with Peronism, illustrated these views about the left when he stated: "My opinion about the parties of the left here is that the majority are ultra left, ultraleftists, that is, they're practically fanatics. They cling to an idea, and they don't accept another one even though it might be better. And therefore, they end up being conservatives. There are parties—I think one is the Popular Socialists—that make a mixture, which is an improvement. But I don't know much about it. . . . [In the majority of the country] the leftist parties are very tied to their system, and I don't share that." Raúl, an unemployed taxi driver and PJ activist, expressed similar opinions of the left: "[The leftist parties] have disappeared here in Argentina, as in the rest of the world. There are four that are always saying the same thing as they always did before, but they don't [inspire?] anybody." As his statements in chapter 3 show, Martín perceived class identity clashes between members of the working class and those who joined leftist parties: "In Peronism the majority are workers—the base, I mean, the activists, are workers. And on the left, here in Argentina, the majority are university or tertiary or master's students—another level. And so there's always a bit of distrust too."

Some of those interviewed who had supported the left with their votes or their participation were also not confident about those parties either as representatives of their views or as effective alternatives for leadership. For example, Samuel, a university student and electrician, said that MAS's calls for Argentina to stop payments on the foreign debt were evidence of their "unthinking and impulsive statements." Samuel leaned toward the left, but not too far toward it. He saw his support of the left as a means to be "antiofficialist" —that is, against the government in charge. He did not want radical change but rather moderation and pluralism, which he expressed as some "sharing of power" and "balancing of things."

Another example is Juan Antonio, who had political experience with, and a record of voting for, the left. He had worked on the 1983 campaign for the *Partido Intransigente* (PI), a socialist offshoot from a much earlier split in the Radical party. He described what he learned from being a PI campaign volunteer:

> Within the party, they were the same as or worse than Radicalism or Justicialism, in terms of politics. "Hey, where's my posters?" "What about mine?!!" *[Here he imitates the bickering.]* That is, the things that usually go on within a political party. It wasn't any different from other parties, just smaller. . . .The growth that the PI had was what defeated it. . . . The leaders had never dreamed that the PI would grow as it did. And so, what did they start thinking? They didn't want to be council members anymore, they started thinking of becoming members of Congress and so on. Their political ambitions began growing and then they weren't careful and didn't realize that the people who were joining were from the left, especially lots of young people and lots of students who wanted to discuss and who wanted to participate in some way. They wanted some political space. And what happened? The leadership circle was very closed and as their ambitions grew and they put aside the city council issues, the people got tired of it and left the party. I think if they'd let the people discuss and let those who'd joined the party participate—not that the party's vote share would have gotten very much bigger, but at least the attitude of the party

could have been better. Then those voters felt disillusioned, but no other party managed to capitalize on the PI's success and win its voters.

While Juan Antonio was technically accurate when he described the PI as the "third force" in the 1983 election, its third place finish was not a "force" to be reckoned with. It won less than 3 percent of the valid votes in both the presidential and congressional races. That year, 91 percent of the votes for president and 85 percent of the votes for deputies went to the UCR and PJ (INDEC 1994, 248).

Andrés, an underemployed homeless man with some university education, had voted for socialist parties in the past. He saw small parties as an unknown quantity:

> I try to see the pros and cons of each [party]. At times, for example, a party has a good *[He searches for the noun, then rephrases.]*—offers good things, but at times it's with unknown people. So, at times, I am afraid that if these small parties got into government, where they'd have a lot of positions to fill, they are going to fill them with a not very selective group of people, who might bring on disaster. You have to be careful. So it's not just the intentions of the three or four great people at the top of the list that matter, but rather the people behind them. . . . Whereas with the big parties, you have some idea of the people who have been working with them for years who are going to be in these positions. . . . If it's for Congress, I could vote for a small party. But I wouldn't do it for president because of everything that enters with the president, such as the ministers and all that sort of thing.

In Argentina's electoral system, where the president is chosen by majoritarian rules and the Congress by proportional representation, Andrés's willingness to vote for small parties for Congress but not for president could be a strategy for not "wasting" his vote on lost causes—although Andrés's explanation did not rest on that calculation. Rather, his explanation implied having evaluated the parties "sincerely" on the basis of their leadership qualifications rather than according to their possibilities for winning election. Interviews with Samuel, Juan Antonio, and Andrés revealed people who were not unconcerned about the efficacy of their vote, but for whom ideology and competence determined the first "cuts" as they narrowed their options. Vote efficacy was a consideration, but only a secondary one.

Some citizens clearly did not think very much about wasted votes and strategic choices and thus made only one "cut"—on the basis of candidate/party qualities. One can consider the cases of Atilio, a senior citizen with an el ementary school education, and Julio, a construction worker with a second grade education. Neither man was particularly interested in politics, but both expressed great conviction and hope in their support for the left without calculating electoral possibilities. Atilio was adamant that he did not consider the candidate's potential to win but merely the candidate's potential to be a good national leader:

> "I have hope for the country, but we'll need to change a few heads and some of the people and topics out there. We also need to put things in order. . . . I vote to improve the whole country. Not my own life or to help me or him . . . I vote directly for the candidate. . . . Under Perón the country lived more or less better, according to my way of thinking about it. No? Later they defeated him and then he died and then Peronism no longer had ideas that I found likeable and so now I turned to the left."

Asked to explain his turn from Peronism to MAS, Julio, a construction worker, explained simply:

> MAS is the party with which I most sympathized. I liked it because there wasn't any other perspective, from my way of looking at it. It was the party I liked.
> Q: And what were the MAS ideas that you liked?
> Julio: Well . . . because MAS was for socialism. So that I can have things, just like any gentleman from Barrio Norte.

A person sufficiently informed about politics to be aware of the small leftist parties in Argentina would also be aware that they had never won a major election. Prior to 1995 most people voting for leftist parties would have known, at least subconsciously, that they were expending their vote on parties with no proven potential to win.[27] Certainly there was some "wishful thinking" involved in supporting parties of the left, but mostly support for the left constituted a means to *express* values, hopes, and dreams. Even if Atilio or Julio did not expect their votes to change the status quo, voting for the left was a means to avoid lending support to it.

Ignacio was a student with substantial exposure to socialist ideology through political organizations in his shantytown. He took a long-term view of his own efficacy. He wanted to help build the party organizations of the left in order to expand their capacity to express grassroots aspirations in the formal political system and also as a means to organize people to get involved in neighborhood-level self-help movements. From this long-term perspective, working for the left constituted not a waste of energy on a lost cause but an effort to turn the cause into a winner down the road.

In the last chapter, I explained a focus on the micro-macro link as the result of the individual's belief that personal and local efforts would not be sufficient to resolve the kinds of material problems faced. Leftist ideology promotes such an understanding of personal material problems. It encourages the development of "consciousness" about the structural connection between microlevel needs and the macrolevel state. Thus, it is not surprising that among those interviewed who had participated in leftist party organizations were people who recognized the links between their microexperiences and larger macro issues, such as Carlos, a garment worker, who expressed: "I have one thing clear, because as I see it, the capitalist system is never going to solve things for the working class. It's not going to resolve the problems of the vast majority."[28] Conversely, it is not surprising that none of those who were solely microfocused was a supporter of the left. Supporters of the left understood their microlevel circumstances not just as individual problems but as ones shared by others in their social class and caused by macrolevel structures and policies. Some were former Peronists seeking a better way to get to the Peronist ideal of social justice. Most of those interviewed who were attracted to leftist parties were poor from childhood. Their affinities for a more radical social discourse represented long-term class identities and experiences, not merely a response to immediate personal troubles. Therefore, although leftist citizens tended to perceive micro-macro linkages, voting for the left could not be well described by the concept of voting "one's pocketbook." That is, because the left was considered unlikely to win an election, voting for the left was not an effort to seek any immediate material gain for oneself. It was expressive rather than instrumental participation.

Military Populism?

A different way to express opposition to Menem's economic plans was to vote for the Movement for Dignity and Independence (MODIN). The campaign headquarters for MODIN's candidate in the 1992 Buenos Aires senatorial elections were located in Montserrat and a local party organizing office had been opened in San Telmo.[29] Three interviews came from this contact: María and her mother María José (interviewed separately), who were middle class but had suffered notable declines in their incomes during the democratic period, and Claudia, a housewife who enjoyed some of the comforts of the lower middle class but whose deteriorated family income and self-identity were consistent with the working class.

MODIN was a nationalist, populist party created by Aldo Rico, the former lieutenant colonel who had led a barracks uprising during Holy Week of 1987. The party leaders insisted that Rico had never intended to threaten the democratic regime with his Holy Week uprising but that he was merely trying to defend the military institution against further prosecution for its behavior during the previous regime.[30] While Alfonsín encouraged the public to see the uprising as a threat to democracy, Rico and his supporters perceived their uprising as an internal matter, intended to challenge the military high command for failing to protect them from prosecution (Norden 1996, 128). Yet, regardless of the institutional self-preservation or intrainstitutional conflicts that motivated their actions, the Holy Week uprising constituted a challenge to the authority of the judicial system as well as to the elected president who was spearheading the prosecutions. In so doing, the uprisings were not merely internal affairs, but a threat to the rule of law.

Five years later, discharged from the army and trying to become a politician, Rico fought his image as a coup-maker, insisting on his respect for democracy and his good faith participation in democratic elections. A party spokesman, anxious to project a positive image to a foreign author, claimed that MODIN saw itself as centrist, and he contrasted MODIN with the UCeDé, the major party on the right at that time, whose most prominent leaders had been associated with authoritarian governments.[31]

MODIN caused a stir when Aldo Rico received 10 percent of the vote in gubernatorial elections for the province of Buenos Aires in 1991, showing particular strength in areas of concentrated poverty. The fear among many democrats, and the hope of MODIN, was that the populist, nationalist message would appeal to low-skilled laborers abandoned by Menem's economic policies.[32] The people I met who supported MODIN were motivated in part by their economic decline and their concern about the low wages and high cost of living under Menem's economic policies. Claudia was strongly motivated by the economy, commenting that this was the most difficult period in which she had ever lived. María (who was well-educated and employed, living in diminished circumstances, but was not poor) had once been a Peronist; she expressed concerns about social issues and the living costs facing families in Argentina. María José had always voted for the Radicals but had lost her life savings after a devaluation under Alfonsín. Deeply dismayed by the decline in level of living for herself and the rest of the middle class, María José decided to vote for Menem in 1989, but three years later, she regretted the choice. By 1992, spurred on by her daughter María's involvement in the MODIN campaign, she decided to try a new choice, even though she increasingly saw the entire political process as illegitimate: "I hope and wish that MODIN is different, but I don't have too many expectations."

There is little doubt that MODIN offered an option for voters seeking material relief, but since parties on the left offered the same relief the support for MODIN cannot be fully explained as economic populism. Logically, other considerations had to be involved. My interviews confirmed this logic. MODIN's alternative on economic policy was never separated from other fundamental elements of the MODIN message: nationalism, indignation over corruption, and sympathy for the military.

To begin with the first of those elements, from MODIN's point of view the suffering of the Argentine poor and middle class was rooted in a failure to defend national interests. MODIN criticized the government's policies for allowing international economic integration, foreign imports, and foreign creditors to undermine national production and autonomy. The sense that nationalism is a positive value arose in most of the formal interviews and casual conversations with MODIN supporters. Nationalism was a priority for María and Claudia, although a lesser concern for María José. Claudia, the daughter of a Paraguayan mother and Argentine father, demonstrated a fervor in which her patriotic loyalty was superior even to her family ties: "My mom said that our war with Great Britain was a punishment for what we did to Paraguay. So I told her, you're my mom, but I'm going to defend my country under any point of view. Even though you're my mother, if you don't like what's going on here, you should leave the country. This is how you raised me to think and so I do! You married an Argentine, raised your kids as Argentines. I'm a nationalist in the sense that I defend the land of my birth."

Secondly, as most MODIN followers expressed it, corruption and strong-handed governance under Menem helped to delegitimize not only his government, but the regime. "This isn't a democracy, it's a dictatorship," exclaimed a very young man who frequented the San Telmo MODIN office. Later, he clarified his viewpoint by saying, "I didn't say I wanted a democracy." Thus, his primary complaint was not that the regime was undemocratic but that it was hypocritical because it espoused democracy but did not respect the rule of law. An organizer of the San Telmo office made a similar point about equivalence: "It's okay to claim that the military government was a tyranny, but this government is also [tyrannical]." Later, after saying that free expression is an important trait for a democracy, he said, "*First*, what we need to do is to clean things up," that is, get rid of corruption first and facilitate free speech later.[33] Party volunteers at the San Telmo office repeatedly stated that because corruption and not law determined government decisions, democracy did not exist in Argentina in 1992. Eliminating that corruption appeared to be more important than other democratic freedoms.

Furthermore, MODIN's military focus was rooted in the party's founding by a group of officers seeking to protect their institution from what they considered to be its dismantling by the Alfonsín government. The military con-

nection remained strong among MODIN activists. *All* of the MODIN supporters interviewed, and those I met at party offices, were not merely angered by
Menem's economic policies; they were also staunch nationalists, with
family members in the armed services or police forces. Despite its public
pronouncements of democratic allegiance, MODIN depended on the militaristic, personalistic image of its leader. For example, MODIN's posters for the
1992 senate campaign in the Federal Capital consisted of a large headshot of
Rico, a man best known for leading a military challenge to the Alfonsín government. Rico's name was in large letters. The actual senate candidate, Venturino, was not pictured, and his name was in smaller print. When those
interviewed were asked about MODIN, if they recognized the party at all, it
was usually by its association with Rico.

People who disapproved of military participation in government wanted
nothing to do with Rico's party, regardless of his economic message. Among
those interviewed who were not involved in some way with the MODIN organization and who disliked Menem's economic policies, almost none, including those who found some appeal in MODIN's economic message, gave any
credence to MODIN as a political alternative:

> Aldo Rico is crazy. He's got it wrong. . . . Although he's right when he
> says that as long as the savings of the country are leaving to pay the
> debt, the country will not go forward. (Tomás, retired bank adminis-
> trator)

> Aldo Rico. Well, this is a minority fraction of people who believe, for
> example, that the solution lies in eliminating, supposedly, the enemy,
> and that in that way they are going to move forward, no? I don't share
> this type of ideas. I believe that here, things are built on all of us, not
> on eliminating enemies, but trying to negotiate and trying to modify
> thinking with positive attitudes, not with violent attitudes or attitudes
> that don't lead to a logical reasoning. (Pablo, bank employee)

> I think that the man [i.e., Rico] is taking advantage of the times—that
> is, he has a point of view that at this moment makes for a good cam-
> paign. . . . But, at some point, a man like me, who is desperate, might
> feel attracted somewhat to this man, in spite of everything. . . . A per-
> son might feel like he's some kind of savior, but still he's a military
> man. But I don't know. At the same time, I don't trust him. (Julio,
> homeless, construction worker)

He's named Aldo Rico, but in politics, he's Aldo Pobre.[34] You have to show a viable alternative in politics, not just throw stones and criticize. He's trying to take advantage of the dissatisfaction. Besides, it's incoherent for someone who tried to break democracy to claim to be democratic. (Juan Antonio, maintenance worker)

Public opinion surveys show the same distrust of Rico that was expressed in these interviews (table 6.1). In a nationwide poll carried out in mid-1992, only 17 percent of respondents had a favorable impression of Aldo Rico. Even among people with promilitary or authoritarian attitudes, or among those seeking a change in the country's neoliberal economic model, the majority tended to have a negative opinion of Rico (see the "agree" columns in table 6.1); however those people were more likely to like Rico than were people who disagreed with militarist or anti-neoliberal positions (compare the "agree" and "disagree" columns in table 6.1). As the table also shows, attitudes

TABLE 6.1. ATTITUDES TOWARD MILITARY, DEMOCRACY, AND ECONOMIC MODEL
BY ATTITUDES TOWARD ALDO RICO (BY PERCENTAGES)[a]

	Military Govt. Is Efficient [b]		Democracy Is Threat to Order [c]		Should Change Neoliberal Model [d]		All
	Agree	Disagree	Agree	Disagree	Agree	Disagree	
Positive opinion of Rico [e]	37	11	26	12	23	16	17
Negative opinion of Rico	63	89	74	88	77	84	83
Total	100	100	100	100	100	100	100

Source: Estudio Graciela C. Romer y Asociados, Survey 11, May–June 1992.
[a] Percentages taken from positive responses (i.e., after eliminating "don't know" and "no answer" responses); number of positive responses varies among questions from 991 to 1071 out of a sample of 1250.
[b] Military governments have been more efficient than civilian governments. ("Strongly agree" and "agree" coded "agree"; "disagree" and "strongly disagree" coded as "disagree.")
[c] Democracy can cause dangerous disorder and disorganization. ("Strongly agree" and "agree" coded "agree"; "disagree" and "strongly disagree" coded as "disagree.")
[d] What do you think is the best thing for the country's development—continuing the economic direction chosen by the government or changing the economic direction? (Only 80 percent of respondents chose one of these answers.)
[e] What opinion do you have of the following people, considering that they occupy or could occupy important positions in Argentine politics? . . . Aldo Rico ("very good" and "good" coded "positive opinion"; "fair" and "bad" coded "negative opinion.")

toward military efficiency were stronger predictors of support for Rico than attitudes toward neoliberal economic policies. For example, of those who believed that military governments have been more efficient than democratic ones, 37 percent also thought well of Rico, while of those who shared Rico's belief that the country should change its economic policy direction, only 23 percent had a positive opinion of Rico.[35]

Field interviews revealed, and opinion polls corroborated, the nonmaterialist reasoning behind rejection of the Rico alternative. Rico's attempt to use populist arguments on economic matters failed not only because the arguments were not perceived as persuasive (a point discussed below), but also because the vast majority of those who shared his views on economic matters did not approve of his leadership on other grounds. Nonmaterialist considerations, that is, an interest in civilian, reliable, constitutional leadership, outweighed any attraction his economic populism held. The public's distrust of Rico and of military involvement in politics explain why MODIN was not perceived as an attractive alternative to Menem and his policies.[36]

National-level Data on Perceived Options

In interview after interview, many people expressed dissatisfaction with wage levels; social conditions such as poverty and the decline in health care, schools, and pensions; the labor market; corruption in government; and Menem's rejection of traditional Peronist positions. At the same time, only a few, who were activists in non-Peronist parties, expressed any confidence that the political arena offered a viable alternative. In short, most people interviewed expressed little support for President Menem but did not express strong support for anyone else.

The generalized nature of this lack of confidence in political actors' capacity to solve national problems and the public's dismay over the available alternatives is evident in a public opinion survey carried out in the same period as my interviews. I analyzed the survey data to see how respondents who did not approve of the government's economic policies—that is, those who would be most likely to be seeking alternative leadership—perceived their choices in the electoral arena.[37] From that set of respondents, figure 6.1 shows the median opinion on a four-point scale of the major political leaders of the early 1990s. In every case, the politicians were sufficiently well-known to elicit *some* opinion; that is, in no case was the median response "unknown or don't know" (represented by point 0 in the figure). President Menem and ex-president Alfonsín were both evaluated as "fair." Only two of eighteen leaders mentioned in the survey reached the level of "good."[38] None was considered "very good" and half were considered "poor"—the lowest rating.

I constructed figure 6.1 so that members of the same party are clustered together. The parties and the politicians within each party group are arranged from top to bottom in rough order of national prominence at that time. Therefore, leaders from the smaller parties and from opposition movements are situated on the bottom half of the figure. While none of the country's leaders elicited strongly positive evaluations, those on the bottom half of the figure are almost all rated "poor." Clearly, the public's perception that alternative leadership might be found from third parties was quite low in 1992.

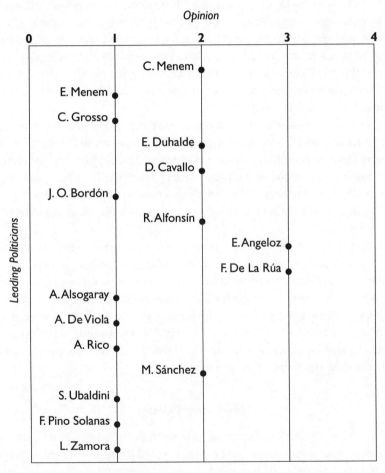

0 = Don't Know; 1 = Bad; 2 = Fair; 3 = Good; 4 = Very Good

Source: Estudio Graciela C. Romer y Asociados, Survey 11, May-June 1992.

Figure 6.1. Median Opinion of Political Leaders among People
Dissatisfied with Menem's Economic Model

As for the major opposition party of the period, the UCR, figure 6.1 shows that two of its leaders elicited positive evaluations from those who disliked the government's economic policies. One of these, future president Fernando De la Rúa, was a candidate for senator of the Federal Capital at the time. While his senate campaign issues included rhetorical calls for better education and pensions, less poverty, and a more "humanized" economy, De la Rúa never offered specific alternatives to the government's economic or social policies. Before the election, Menem tried to make the senatorial race into a referendum on himself and his policies in order to build support for his reelection proposal.[39] Thus, when De la Rúa defeated Porto some read it as a "vote against the government";[40] but Menem and his supporters quickly denied that the election had any such significance. Since De la Rúa had failed to define an alternative position, the government's new spin on the election was plausible.[41] De la Rúa himself claimed the election was about good government, not about a different government policy. Voters, he said, had not voted to punish Menem, but merely to control him.[42]

The other Radical who was rated positively in the opinion survey in figure 6.1, Eduardo Angeloz, had been defeated by Menem in the 1989 presidential race. By 1992 he sought to reassert his status within the party by presenting a more aggressive critique of the president's policies, but his efforts did not attract much attention outside the party.[43] As a provincial governor, not involved in any election at the time, Angeloz's name seldom came up in my interviews in Buenos Aires.[44]

Using the same set of respondents as above, figure 6.2 gives further evidence that those who were dissatisfied with the government's policies did not have much confidence in political institutions generally. On a scale of zero to ten, where zero means "no corruption," the median respondent considered political parties—along with all of the other major institutions of government plus the labor unions—exceptionally corrupt. By comparison, nongovernmental actors fared better, although only the Catholic Church was widely considered below the midpoint of the corruption scale.

Alternative Policies

The previous section illustrated how parties of the left, center, and right carry historical baggage—a public image based on their record—that obstructed their efforts to be perceived as credible alternatives to Menem on the merits of their policy proposals and current leadership capacity. Apart from their views of the actors who offered an alternative to Menem, did citizens who were discouraged by Menem's policies believe that any alternative policies were viable?

Argentines have lived through about twenty years of repeated economic turmoil. Few people doubted that the country was in difficult financial straits and needed to implement some kind of new policies when Menem took office. Stokes (1996, 506–7) labels this as a view that government is the "antidote"— that is, that while new policies are tough to endure, they are necessary given the poor health of the economy. Regardless of ideological or partisan position, the people interviewed often accepted that facing Argentina's foreign debt necessitated an economic readjustment program. Despite the illegitimate way in which much of the debt was accumulated by the previous military government, the majority of those who discussed the debt justified its payment as the moral or practical choice. Some people believed that the country's budget could not afford the costs of better pensions or schools. A few offered the resigned justification that austerity policies were a necessary burden that always fell on workers.

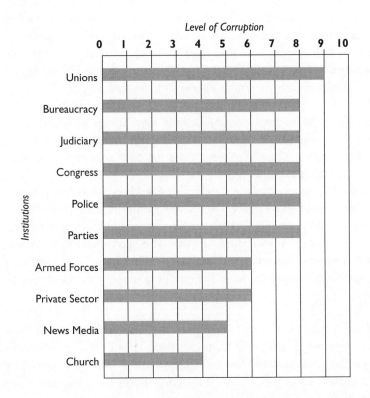

Source: Estudio Graciela C. Romer y Asociados, Survey 11, May-June 1992.

Figure 6.2. Median Opinion of Corruption Level in Institutions among People Dissatisfied with Menem's Economic Model

Even critics of Menem's policies were not certain that the policies were in error:

I don't know if privatization is the answer. There are countries with state industries that work and countries with private industries that work, so it doesn't seem that privatization makes the difference. Menem has it in his head that privatization is the answer, so we'll see. (Samuel, student and electrician)

Today, economic power rules over political power, a lot, which means some very good leaders can't do anything. (Juan Antonio, maintenance worker)

We're in crisis. We're in crisis because the government was administered poorly for so many years that at some point it had to be noticed. Some time or other, one has to pay, no? That's why, if all of this works—and it's not working for me, but if I knew that my kids were going to have a better standard of living than me, and I could prove that, then I'll give my vote to the person who's capable, not simply on a whim to some Radical [i.e., his own party] who's not doing things well. (Vicente, construction worker)

Marcela, a public employee: Apparently, now things are status quo, things are calm, prices are constant, and things are getting much better. But the one who suffers—a lot—is the poor person, the worker, the pensioner, the public employee. . . .
Q: Could it have been done differently? Could there have been a better way to make these changes, without harming so many people?
Marcela: I don't know much about how to explain politics/policy to you. But from what I see now, [the one who had to pay] to move the country forward was thanks to [sic] the working class. . . .Perhaps carrying out the economic plan is the only way to move the country forward.

Reiterating these views later, Marcela revealed that the reason she thought there was no remedy other than for the working class to bear the costs of economic progress was that the "business class" would not make any sacrifices "because that's the way it is." Asked if the government could not demand more from that class, she simply replied, "There are a lot of interests."[45]
Some of those interviewed argued that alternatives might be found if the

government had the political will to do so. They sought to balance realism with their sense of the injustice of social conditions that they perceived to be worsening. They suggested that a different strategy of debt negotiation would have left more money for social policies and pensions. Nevertheless, they tended to be vague on the details of how that could have been accomplished:

> I think that there's money, but the issue is whether it's used to pay off the foreign debt or to help the poor a little bit. To split it, no? Let's pay a little less on the foreign debt and help the people a little more. (Andrés, former computer programmer)

> Yes, I think the debt has to be paid—even though the government during the dictatorship had nationalized it, since there were lots of private debts and they nationalized them, which I think was dreadful. . . . But it could be that the costs of the foreign debt don't have to be paid in such a way that the people pay them, because the adjustments are taken from the wages of people who have the least. No? I think that there could have been other [solutions]. . . . There have always been economic groups here that have a lot of money. So it should come from them! Nevertheless, when taxes are imposed on the big capitalists or big landholders, they're the first ones with the power to say, "Hey, it's not going to be that way." And those on the bottom are the ones without the power to do anything. (Olivia, laid off bookkeeper)

A third example is María who, after lamenting the problems of cholera, senior citizens without medicine, poor quality health care, inadequate AIDS prevention, and malnutrition, was asked what any government could do about these things. She replied:

> The government could try to divide things a bit more and get to a more, let's say, diplomatic and elastic rapprochement with the great, traitorous [laugh] powers. . . .The foreign debt is a very great block. Because we pay and pay and pay and still there's always more foreign debt, so I don't know how they're reducing the foreign debt. And so I think a government that calms the population . . . At one time, for example, I was able to buy six or seven pairs of shoes per season, so I was giving a hand to the shoe industry because it wasn't just the shoe but the people who made all the parts, so lots of people ate from the

shoes I was able to buy. Now that can't be done. So all the industries have been cut back. So if we had a government that recomposed the wages of the middle class, and the skilled workers, and even the unskilled ones—without ignoring the debt we owe—and for this, we need order, honesty, and dignity—not a corrupt government.

María's answer employed some of the campaign rhetoric and goals of the MODIN party to which she belonged, but like Andrés and Olivia, she did not offer any specific alternative policies to those of the Menem government.

Some of those interviewed were aware that constraints on the national budget were not just due to the foreign debt but were exacerbated by low revenues. Juan Antonio, Pablo, and Eduardo said that enhanced tax collection would enable the government to ease the debt burden paid by consumers. Their descriptions of this tax collection problem revealed their biases for or against Menem and his policies. Juan Antonio (a critic of Menem and neoliberalism) emphasized the government's responsibility to manage a budget and enforce the tax laws, while Pablo and Eduardo (both supporters of Menem who tolerated neoliberal policies as necessary evils) placed the blame for budget deficits on the irresponsibility of corporations and wealthy citizens, who failed to pay their taxes.

A common way of explaining Argentina's economic problems was to blame problems on the Argentine national character rather than on particular policies, parties, or institutions. Frustrated by the development problems in the country, people put the blame upon cultural proclivities, real or imagined. For example, Martín said that Argentines lacked the thrift of their Italian and Spanish immigrant ancestors. María José repeated a common joke that God gave Argentina an unfair natural advantage over every other nation and then compensated for the abundant resources by giving the country the supposed burden of the Argentine people. To her the country's problems were caused by a deeply rooted corruption among the people, particularly those in leadership positions. Similarly, when asked whether economic problems in Argentina are principally the fault of the government, the democratic system, or something else, Pablo responded by critiquing the irresponsible ethos that he felt permeated both Argentine citizens and the leaders who emerge from the citizenry: "The problem is us—the mentality that we have. That is, if people here would become conscious of what a true economy is, and if they would take care down to the last penny . . . . well then, that would be something else. And the people who govern, the governors, they are people who were common citizens before, and now, they're governors, and so, not much can be expected of them either." Pablo believed this "mentality" was promoted through popular culture, such as movies, television shows, and tango lyrics: "Not working, for example, was encouraged here. . . . This education encouraged a point of view that, for example, seeks to make easy money without working; for example, playing the horses or playing cards or games. The smart guy is the one who doesn't work and the fool is the one who does. And, well, this idea was encouraged so much that I believe that this is, like, inside of the people and, well, it's going to be very difficult to root this out."

This culturalist way of thinking about the causes of Argentina's problems suggests that alternative policies would not make much of a difference. It has implications not only for what people expect of the government but also for their views of democracy because it implies that the country's problems cannot be solved through political processes. It uses cultural and individual values to explain problems rather than examining the institutions that embody national values and the electoral processes through which individuals of high character might be chosen for leadership. Appeals to this type of thinking could be used by authoritarians offering solutions that put aside political institutions and seek to inculcate "better" cultural values.

Conclusions

The people interviewed cared a great deal about the economic performance of the incumbent government. They presumed that one of the president's primary responsibilities was economic policy and they knew that such policy could affect them personally. Yet if we tried to predict their political views on the basis of either broad macrolevel indicators or their own pocketbooks, we would fail. In this chapter, the interviews revealed that two kinds of factors colored citizens' evaluations of economic conditions and guided and constrained their political views. These factors were personal identities and national contexts.

Argentines repeatedly filtered their views through the lenses of class and party identity. Microfocusers, who paid little attention to national politics or its influence in their lives, often relied heavily on class identification as an easy means to make decisions when required to vote or express an opinion. Likewise, macrofocusers and micro-macro linkers also frequently used identities to guide their more complicated analyses of political processes.

In studies of social movements, scholars see identity as an important part of political mobilization. It is a means by which microlevel concerns can be linked to macrolevel politics, as people come to identify themselves on the basis of shared microlevel conditions in opposition to some "other" perceived as responsible for causing those conditions (Gamson 1992; Oxhorn 1995).

Properly mobilized and updated, identities serve to facilitate recognition of micro-macro connections. This chapter reveals, however, that when identities were created long ago, they may still mobilize people—for example, Paula will always work for the Radicals and Gabriela for the Peronists. However, the identities may no longer serve them as a means to connect their microlevel interests to the political arena. To put it differently, static identities may constitute obstacles to micro-macro connections. For example, class identities, rooted in differing childhoods, prevented people who were similarly left out of Menem's policies from seeing they had common political interests. Strong identification with Peronism prevented people who were disillusioned with Menem's policies from believing any macrolevel political alternative might solve their microlevel concerns.

One should note that while it is common for an Argentine to root party identity in class identity—which Peronism encouraged over the years—nevertheless, the association cannot be taken for granted. It is not uncommon to find people like Vicente or Juan Antonio who strongly identify with their class as workers and who seek leaders who will serve their class but who judge Peronism negatively because of its leaders and leadership style. Through exposure to non-PJ political movements, these people have put aside static identities and identified alternative vehicles for representing their class interests.

In addition, contexts are critical. Political, economic, and historical contexts shaped the way citizens evaluated macrolevel conditions and their solutions. (This statement does not apply to microfocusers, who largely ignore macrolevel conditions and the contexts in which they occur.) Studies of collective action have found that social protests are facilitated by the right "opportunity structure," such as accessible political institutions or divisions among elites (Tarrow 1991, 32–35). Similarly, individual citizens evaluate their opportunity to "protest" policies (in their thoughts, conversation, voting, or by other means) by considering the structure of possibilities. In the early 1990s, the political arena offered little hope that things could be different. Political institutions were not very accessible to nonelites in an age of discredited labor unions, extensive use of executive decrees, and executive manipulation of the courts. At that time, the principal public voices criticizing the impact of economic policy upon the poor, workers, and the declining middle class were voices from weak corners of the political system: the militaristic MODIN, the dissident Peronists who had not yet organized into FREPASO, and the Catholic Church. Prior to the constitutional assembly elections of 1994 (when FREPASO emerged as a viable party), the Catholic Church was the most effective of these three in getting media attention to its critique of government policy, but the Church did not constitute a political vehicle for citizens who agreed with its critique.

In chapter 5 I argued that people formed expectations about what the government might be able to do to improve their material conditions within the context of their historical experiences of economic decline and policy failures. Interviews in this chapter reveal that historical experiences likewise affect political expectations—about what leaders from different political parties or from the military might be able to accomplish while in power. In chapter 7, I turn to people's expectations about democracy. Again, the interviews will show that historical experiences help structure people's expectations about what the regime should accomplish.

Chapter

7

Perspectives on Democracy

> As I heard a political sociologist say,
> what happened in Peru is representative of the
> fact that the democracy isn't sufficiently
> consolidated in Latin America.
>
> PAULA, answering question about state of
> democracy in Argentina

The genesis of the research for this book was my concern about the effects of unaddressed poverty and impoverishment upon the stability and quality of democracy.[1] Would a government based on popular elections maintain public support if its policies increased inequality and neglected poverty? When a democratic government turns away from the social commitments of previous elected governments, do the former beneficiaries of such commitments see the democracy as formal and biased toward affluent citizens? Do poorer citizens see democracy as chaotic and unable to address their interests? The answers to these questions—and the explanations for the answers—depend upon what citizens understand by the word "democracy"; what it is, if anything, that they value in the concept, as they understand it; and whether or not they find those values in the regime under which they live.

The argument of this chapter is that democracy in Argentina has managed to maintain widespread legitimacy as a valued system of government despite its inability to produce governments that could create a decent standard of living for all. The historical context in which Argentina finds itself has created a keen awareness in most Argentines, although not all, of the difference be-

180

tween the government and the regime and a recognition of the value of a liberal democratic regime. This chapter is divided in three sections; the first describes and analyzes how those interviewed understood the meaning of democracy. The second section examines whether they valued this thing they understood as "democracy" in light of how it is practiced in Argentina. Each of these sections draws its own conclusion by synthesizing the main findings. The third section examines the quality of democracy in Argentina. Drawing on insights from chapters 4 and 5, this section analyzes democratic citizenship as it is undermined by low levels of material resources. In this section I take a close look at the interview with Carlos to understand the interplay of material resources and the exercise of citizenship.

I used both direct and indirect methods to uncover these views. A number of explicit questions about democracy were on the interview schedule, and I used as many as time and interview conditions permitted in order to "get at" the democracy issue from various angles and to elicit as many insights as possible. For example, in addition to asking people directly to define democracy, I asked their opinions of alternatives to it (e.g., Given the many different opinions one hears about the last military government, how would you describe it?). Likewise, I asked their opinions of specific current events that had democratic implications (such as Peruvian President Alberto Fujimori's 1992 "self-coup," in which he closed down the Congress). The interviews also included a number of questions designed simply to engage people in talk about elections, the leadership of Alfonsín and Menem, and politics generally. As they spoke about these topics, they revealed their attitudes about freedom, elections, law, order, authority, and participation. I listened for what behaviors were described as "democratic" or "not democratic."

Each interview was studied closely for the definitions of democracy the interviewees employed, the importance they placed on a democratic regime as opposed to alternatives, the reasons they were ambivalent or indifferent toward democracy, and the attitudes they expressed toward the actual regime. I examined each interview numerous times both in its parts and as a whole. The dozens of interview parts—phrases, answers to particular questions, examples used, etc.—identified the three major categories of traits by which democracy was *defined*. When examined holistically, the interviews fell into four categories of thinking about democratic *legitimation*.

The Meanings of "Democracy"

In the interviews Argentines employed three ideas of "democracy." These ideas are not mutually exclusive or mutually incompatible, but in about half the interviews only one of the three meanings was employed, and only rarely did all three arise. This suggests that the salience of the characteristics that distinguish life under a democratic regime varies among ordinary Argentines.

Democracy as Freedom

Some interviewees understood democracy as *freedom*, primarily as individual rights and freedom of political expression and also as freedom from repression, curfews, and other sorts of control, harassment, or intimidation imposed by officers of the state. Following this first pattern, democracy was defined by Walter, a supermarket employee, as the ability "to live, basically, [where one can] speak one's thoughts, with lots of tranquility; give criticisms, whether good or bad, to the government." Marcela, a public employee, saw democracy as "freedom. Lack of freedom is something that I don't remember too much, but I remember that you couldn't go out at night to go to a dance, you couldn't do this and that, in that era." Soña, an artisan, said that "democracy is one of the best ways of living in community in a country. It means individual liberty. To develop yourself without anyone telling you what you have to do." Free expression benefits not just the individual but also the society at large. Amanda's son Pepe volunteered that democracy had enabled public revelations of social problems, such as drug use, that had previously been hidden: "Thanks to the democracy, things are more out in the open. Before, with the military dictatorship, you couldn't talk, nobody could do anything. Now, with the democracy, journalists can speak more and discuss more, and . . . a person can say what he wants in the street, one can think what he wants, can express himself more." Moving beyond the freedom to publicize ideas and information, occasionally a respondent focused on the progress derived from the freedom to *exchange* ideas. That is, democracy was expected to include debate, discussion, political activism, and pluralism. An eloquent expression of this view came from Pablo:

> I understand democracy as thinking that is being constructed, no? That it's okay that in a democracy there are, for example, completely different thoughts because things can be drawn from those thoughts in order to elaborate something better. For example, the liberal says that we need to free up the market, and that . . . the production per person needs to improve because that means the individual improves. No? And on the other side, there's the leftist discourse that says, for example, that the liberals give lots of importance to capital and forget about the human being. And the liberals say to the leftists that the latter worry more about the humanistic part and forget about the economy, which is very important, no? It's a discourse ping-ping-ping that's like ping-pong.

Democracy as Institutions and the Rule of Law

Additionally, democracy was defined in terms of institutions and the rule of law. Some people focused on representative institutions, the holding of elections, or the equal right to vote or have input into decisions as evidence of democracy. Some saw democracy as restraint on the concentration and arbitrary use of power. Others associated democracy with constitutional government. Since the Argentine constitution requires a government established by a vote of the people, elections were presumed to be part of "constitutional" rule. Illustrations of defining democracy in this way include these statements:

> Rule of the people: "demo" "cracia." This would be the election of governors by popular vote. I think this is the base. . . . Every segment of society—or every group—having its representation; that is, that the representation in parliament should be proportional to the voters, no?[2] (Andrés, former computer programmer)

> Democracy is the free play of all the institutions; the institutions working the way they are supposed to work and if they aren't working, fixing themselves. (Olivia, bookkeeper)

> Vicente: Democracy means respecting the constitution. If it's only being half respected, then it isn't real democracy. The dictionary definition would be: respecting the freedom of the people who live in society and they in turn respecting moral principles and living within the law. . . .
> Q: Are elections part of any democracy—a fundamental part of a democracy?
> Vicente: Elections are within the constitution.
> Q: Could there be a democracy where elections weren't in the constitution?
> Vicente: I don't know any other constitutions.

If the constitution is the touchstone for defining democratic behavior, it is, according to some, not a sufficient basis for establishing democracy. Eduardo argued that democracy implies constitutionalism but that the elected governments of Radical Presidents Frondizi and Illia had been "constitutional" but "not democratic," because the Radicals had won their elections at a time when the Justicialist Party was proscribed from electoral participation.

Beyond the simple idea of "government by the people," which came up periodically, only a handful of respondents remarked upon elections per se as a key element of a democratic regime. Many more, however, clearly assumed that electoral competition was intrinsic to democracy. If asked directly whether elections were essential to democracy the usual reply was either an automatic yes or puzzlement; both answers revealed that the person took elections as part of what "democracy" typically involves for granted. Yet the fact that elections were seldom mentioned without prompting suggests that the actual choosing of leaders through the vote is not the part of democracy that was most salient in respondents' minds.

Oftentimes, the interviewees automatically labeled the regime since 1983 a "democracy" without implying a set of substantive characteristics. This was consistent with the lexicon established in public discourse during the presidency of Raúl Alfonsín, who emphasized that the country was undertaking a dramatic shift from the repression and illegality of a military regime toward a new legal order. So, in one sense, *democracy* was a shorthand term many used to mean "not military," given all of the infringements on freedom and on the constitution that "military" implied.

Democracy as Popular and Participatory

The third way of conceptualizing democracy, which arose somewhat less frequently (in thirteen interviews), was democracy as *popular* government in the Spanish sense of that term, meaning "of the people." People with this perspective saw democracy as government that is based on citizens' participation and is dedicated to citizens' welfare. One example of this viewpoint is the argument that democratic governments are those that are inclusive, giving stature and enacting policies that serve all citizens, particularly the poor. For example, Francesca said that she would like to see the kind of "democracy" that existed under Perón, when she said there was more "humanity" and "respect for both rich and poor alike. . . . Democracy is, for me, good policy. Government like that of Raúl Alfonsín, which supposedly was a dignified democracy, is not. . . . Democracy is respect. It's the unity of the people— something that we don't have. We aren't united. The guy who has money will step on your head." Another take on the *popular democracy* perspective sees democracy in public input. This explains, for example, what Leonardo meant by saying that when President Fujimori closed the Peruvian Congress in 1992 he acted democratically, because Fujimori had widespread public support.

All three views of democracy—as freedom, as institutions, and as popular participation—are heard in the interview with Julio. He began defining democracy in electoral terms but then added that elected governments had not resolved people's needs. Talking out his dissatisfaction, he decided that in the posttransition period the military's legacy continued, so the people were afraid to speak freely or participate; this fear created an undemocratic situation.[3] As he talked through his thoughts, he moved from his initial focus on elections and political freedom to state that the illiberal legacy of authoritarianism was a situation in which average citizens are excluded from public life: "There were many years of domination. There was always a dictatorship. And so, people are afraid . . . to ask a question. They're afraid that if they're seen somewhere in the morning they'll be put on the Black List and things like that. So things are a bit prohibited. And so it isn't . . . *[He changes his thought mid-way through the sentence and begins again.]* What would democracy be?! Democracy is also participation—making everyone actors instead of always being spectators!"

Conclusions

Out of forty-one interviews, democracy was described in terms of freedom in nineteen interviews and in terms of institutions and the rule of law in nineteen interviews also. A number of people used both meanings; thus twenty-nine of the forty-one interviews either employed the ideas of *democracy as freedom* or *democracy as institutions and law*, or both (cf., Ranis 1992, 153). These conceptualizations are consistent with the process-oriented understanding of liberal democracy most political scientists use today. The dominant literature tends not to consider popular input, participation, or benefits as essential to democratic process although they might be seen as desirable (cf. Alvarez et al. 1996, 18–19; Huber, Rueschemeyer and Stephens 1997; Schmitter and Karl 1991). Interestingly, however, while respondents clearly associated elections and freedom with democracy, only a few spoke of the competition for power that elections provide. Elections were taken for granted as part of democracy but they were not the characteristic that stood out in Argentines' minds. For political science, a defining characteristic of democracy is the competitive process to determine leadership (cf. Dahl 1971, 4; Schumpeter 1947). For those interviewed, the defining characteristics of liberal democracy were ones with which they, as nonelites, could identify through personal experience: freedom from repression, the rule of law, and popular sovereignty.[4]

The Legitimacy of Democracy

Knowing how people define democracy is only the prelude to discovering how people evaluate the legitimacy of the actual regime in Argentina. Here I follow Juan Linz's use of the term *legitimacy* that, drawing upon the Weberian understanding of sources of authority, sees legitimacy as the free belief that a regime deserves obedience because it is preferable to any alternative arrangement of political institutions (Linz 1988; Weber 1978, 212–16). Legitimacy impels obedience to the political regime, independent of one's views of specific governments or their policies. Linz argued that "obviously no government is accorded legitimacy in this sense by all its citizens, but no government can survive without that belief on the part of a substantial number of citizens" (1978, 16).

Regime legitimation depends, first of all, on whether or not democracy itself is valued—that is, whether people consider democracy an ideal form of government and the sole legitimate regime type. If most citizens prefer democracy but believe the actual regime does not meet their definition of democratic, or alternatively, if they believe the actual regime meets their definition of democratic but they do not value democracy as a regime type, then the legitimacy of the actual regime is weak.

How do material interests shape the evaluation of the regime under which one lives? When democracy is defined in the procedural terms of freedom, individual rights, elections, and the rule of law, and when those processes are considered indispensable, then the regime's performance would logically be judged in those procedural terms rather than by the material conditions brought about under the regime. When democracy is defined in procedural terms but those processes are *not* considered indispensable, then one might expect a regime's performance to be judged on substantive grounds, including material conditions. Finally, when democracy is conceptualized as popular government, in which nonelites are not merely voters and clients but active participants and primary beneficiaries of government decisions, then the citizen has raised the bar for the regime, expecting that a democratic regime offers not only process but outcomes. As the last section explained, this more demanding conception of democracy was not the dominant one found in my fieldwork; nevertheless, citizens who hold this viewpoint are those whose material hardships could be expected to cause them to disdain the current Argentine regime.

Absolute Liberal Democracy (AL)

The most frequent legitimation pattern heard in interviews was an absolute commitment to liberal democracy (AL). People with this perspective believed that the best regime is a democratic one and they understood "democratic" to include freedom, institutions, or both. For several of them, freedom or institutions were necessary but not sufficient. That is, several also conceived of democracy as popular government and were highly concerned that the regime produce governments that would respond to the material needs of the lower classes; however, their interest in substantive outcomes did not supersede their baseline commitment to the minimal protections of elections, constitutional rule, or individual freedom. They put legal process ahead of desired outcomes. They wanted the regime to be improved, not replaced, and considered the actual Argentine regime to be democratic as compared to past regimes; however, most believed it not as democratic in its processes—nor as fair, in terms of social justice—as it could be. These were people who put a priority on following the constitutional rules of the game, abhorred the human rights record of the previous authoritarian regime, and unequivocally rejected the military as an alternative source of leadership to solve the country's problems.

Nearly all those who expressed an absolute commitment to liberal democracy were either macrofocused or macro-micro linkers when they discussed their political interests, meaning that they focused their evaluation of politics on national-level government actions. Many were angry about the harshness of economic conditions under Presidents Alfonsín and Menem. Yet in keeping with their conception that the bottom-line of democracy is freedom or the rule of law, they judged the *regime* by the process, not the outcomes. They saw liberal democracy as legitimate and they judged the performance of the regime in those procedural terms. Only the particular *government* of President Menem was judged (and only in part) on the results of its economic policies.

Their strong support of democracy was indicated by their rejection of claims that the people's needs could be met outside democratic institutions. Events of April 1992 enabled me to ask many interviewees about a news statement by Peruvian President Fujimori in which explained his "self-coup" by saying, "I had two choices left: to defend the interests of a political minority or to defend the majority of the Peruvian public. Obviously I chose to do the latter." The people for whom legitimacy rested only in absolute liberal democracy rejected Fujimori's statement that he had served the majority. They tended to be distrustful of self-designated saviors. Nena expressed, "To pretend to defend the majority is a lie." Andrés stated, "It's a lie, a lie, a lie. This thing about his not having any other choice is of course something that's always said, and that he did it for the majority. . . . Here, every time there was a military coup, the discourse also came out saying that 'we did it for the *Patria*, for the citizens,' and I don't know what else, and 'the poor folks in the governments are thieves and can't be tolerated.' It's all lies." Eduardo declared, "I don't agree with Fujimori. The majority of the Peruvian people voted for there to be a Congress. Fujimori got bad advice. He even lost the consensus of Latin America and lost the support of the USA. Fujimori had never even worked in politics. In any country where the leader doesn't have experience and comes in as a Messiah, this always happens. And the people, humble, workers—they're the ones who always pay." People who thought about regime legitimacy in absolute liberal democratic terms believed that the current regime needs improvement, not elimination. As Nena put it, "Democracy is the best system. . . . but we need to perfect it. Argentine democracy is still in its infancy."

Effective Liberal Democracy (EL)

Like the first thought pattern, the second one also defined democracy in terms of its processes—rights, freedoms, elections, or constitutions.[5] Again, as in the first pattern, these processes were described as valuable. Yet in the second pattern interviewees revealed *some* ambivalence about the value of democratic processes compared to other values. Those processes were not as sacrosanct as they were to the absolute liberal democratic mind. Those seeking effective liberal democracy (EL) perceived the maintenance of public order, macroeconomic conditions, or social justice as high priorities that might sometimes justify a heavy hand, some abridgments of citizens' rights, or a temporary departure from the constitutional order.

Some ambivalence about the priority of democratic practice was revealed by those who did not rule out some limitations on liberal rights for the sake of other desired ends. Walter expressed an ambiguous, even contradictory view of liberty. He stated his opposition to "murderers" in the last military regime, but then when asked about military regimes generally said that "all evil is necessary sometimes" to "purge" society of antisocial ideas. In one interview, Leonardo used the pejorative *milicos* to describe the military, claiming he never liked the former regime, that it was a "disaster" featuring corruption, disappearances, repression, and ever-changing heads of state; he also stated that the military lacked the professional training to be in the business of government. A month later, his focus had shifted from valuing liberty to valuing order. He told me he had some fondness for MODIN because ex-military leaders would know how to stop immorality in society and he thought it would be good to have a government that included *some* active duty military officers so that liberty would not become license. In interviews with others I also encountered this liberty versus license distinction twice. This is a minority concern in Argentina but one that is regularly heard. Ranis (1992, 162–63) found 20 percent of Argentine workers surveyed in 1985–86 expressed some fear about excesses of liberty turning into license.

The people with an EL perspective include those who were ambivalent about rigorous maintenance of the constitution. To observe the difference between the first two patterns, one can compare the replies in the previous section to my question about Peruvian President Fujimori's *autogolpe* with the following:

> Well Perón also closed the Congress. He had a majority in Congress and still closed it. Yes, this was right. They weren't doing things that he needed to do. Peru's been in bad shape because of the guerrillas, who are powerful and kill anybody. It depends on the results. If things are better, then it's ok that he closed the Congress. (Martín, laborer and lifelong Peronist)

> Well, at least if Mr. Menem would close the Congress and dedicate himself to attending to the people, well good, that would be welcome. But this guy doesn't do one thing nor the other. Why does he have them there inside, those council members or deputies—to drink coffee and smoke? To chat? . . . The people are paying—are they paying for that?! . . . Like with this issue of the, what's it called, the Previsions Law. Have a plebiscite and you're going to find out if the people are for it or not. But this guy says no, do it by decree. So, what's the Congress for, if he's going to decide? Get rid of all the lazy bums inside and then close the Congress. I don't know!
> Q: Would that be better?
> If he does this for the people. But he doesn't do everything he does for the people. He does it, let's say, for his party and for his boss. (Atilio, retired street vendor)

Martín was a lifelong Peronist, long active in partisan activities and now active in grassroots neighborhood work. Democratic process was part of his life and he talked about politics with the expectation that elections were the norm. Atilio previously had expressed clear dislike for the military or for nonconstitutional regimes. He had defined democracy for me as freedom to express political views and to vote (although he suggested that voting might take place in plebiscites). He was also concerned about institutions; in the statement above he expressed anger that Menem made so many policy changes by decree, bypassing Congress. Yet rather than demanding that Congress fulfill its institutional role in the democracy, he was willing to see an alternative process that enabled popular participation and that might serve the popular will, even if the constitutionally-established, popularly-elected Congress were undermined in the process. Similarly, Martín saw no contradiction between his desire to have widespread freedom of expression for alternative political positions and his acceptance of a president closing the Congress in which such free expression might take place.

Evidently, among those seeking EL democracy, the analytical distinctions that political scientists might make between democratic and nondemocratic methods of decision making tended to be blurred, and the civil libertarian's rigorously consistent commitment to the rule of law was absent. Is inconsistency evidence of a poor education and an inability to perceive inherent contradictions in one's attitudes? Or is consistency the hobgoblin of small minds and inconsistency a recognition of complexity? Contradictory (and thus ironic) as it may seem, I think the answers are yes, and yes.

A firmly articulated conviction that liberal democratic processes should be held inviolable, regardless of other concerns, appears to be associated with either educational or experiential backgrounds that emphasize consistency in thought and democratic practices in action. As table 7.1 shows, those who thought along AL democratic lines tended to have more formal education than those seeking EL democracy. Those in the first group who lacked substantial formal education were, with one exception, people who had been active in local party politics and thereby socialized to use democratic practices and accustomed to thinking about politics in terms of interparty competition. In contrast, those whose thinking was less absolutely committed to liberal processes tended to have relatively little formal education and, with only two exceptions, were not active in party politics.

Yet while consistency and logical ordering of preferences may be learned through education, and an absolutist commitment to process may be learned through involvement in the process, there is more to the ambivalence and apparently contradictory preferences of those following the second legitimation pattern than simple ignorance or inexperience. Inconsistent views are a re-

TABLE 7.1. LEGITIMATION PATTERN USED BY EDUCATION LEVEL ATTAINED

	Primary or Incomplete Secondary	Secondary School Complete or Higher
Absolute liberal democracy	5	9
Effective liberal democracy	10	1
Popular, justice-based democracy	2	1
Results-based regime	4	2
Totals*	21	13

*All interviews not counted because of insufficient information either on education level (n=5) or legitimation perspective (n=2).

sponse to a complex reality, where all goals cannot be maximally fulfilled simultaneously. Solving one problem (such as crime) may exacerbate other problems (like police brutality). The citizen sincerely cares about less crime *and* less police brutality, but the odds are good that the individual citizen will not personally have to live with the negative consequences when society trades either one for the other. So when average citizens talk about their political interests, rather than hold fast in absolutist fashion to one valued thing, democracy, they wishfully aspire to several things—order, economic stability, social justice, and popular input, as well as democratic process. It is not that they are indifferent or have no preferences among these valued things. Rather, they do not weigh their preferences and choose democracy or nondemocracy because they are not in a position to have to choose. Multiple priorities can coincide during political periods where the choices are not starkly presented. So, as citizens discussing politics with an interviewer in the early 1990s—or debating with a relative, or watching a news program, or even deciding to march in a rally—people need not weigh their preferences or organize them into a coherently ordered whole. Even as they vote, they may not need to make hard choices between conflicting value priorities: they can vote a split ticket or they can vote for a politician who espouses incompatible promises.

In some comparative politics literature, some of those I have identified as using "effective liberal democracy" as their basis for legitimation would have been categorized as lacking in democratic orientation or "civic culture" (Almond and Verba 1963; Putnam 1993). In other studies they might be described as "populists" owing to their willingness to see strong leaders do things for the people even when doing so involved tampering with institutions (Coniff 1982; Roberts 1995). Yet there is an important difference between the thinking of those seeking effectiveness within a generally liberal democratic regime and the thinking of those willing to support the authoritarian populism of someone who would rewrite the constitutional rules, such as, Venezuela's Hugo Chávez. Both ways of thinking seek take-charge governments that can get things done for the people, but the EL pattern acknowledges the legitimacy of some institutional constraints upon the actions of those governments. EL thinking condones some weakening of those constraints for the sake of action but does not condone elimination of the constraints—and the difference between weakening institutions and eliminating them is substantial.

To summarize this thinking then, the pursuit of "effective liberal democracy" involves recognizing and valuing the liberties enjoyed under a democratic regime. Those who think in this manner understand the difference between the actions of the government and the freedoms and institutions of the regime and they do not judge the regime on the policy successes or failures of the government. They tend to see liberal democracy as the *best* type of regime but they are willing to have less of that democratic regime to have more of some additional values. Those other values are both material and nonmaterial: social order and a sound national economy were equally common interests among these respondents. Social justice was also valued. Those seeking EL democracy were neither fond of nor indifferent about the previous military regime. At the same time, the previous regime was not highly salient for them so they were not preoccupied by fear of unconstitutional or repressive government. They tended to find politics more distant and less interesting or meaningful to their lives than the people with an absolutist approach to liberal democracy did. Nearly all of the people seeking effective liberal democracy discussed politics in macrofocused terms. In short, from the effective liberal democracy perspective, liberal democracy was a valued thing, all other things being equal; but since all other things are seldom equal, this perspective was not averse to placing *some* limitations on democracy for the sake of other goals.

Popular, Justice-based Democracy (PD)

People who employed the third pattern of thinking about the Argentine regime, PD, sought popular democracy based on social justice. Although only a few respondents thought in this way, their ideas constituted a different pattern than those of the other respondents. Each had been exposed to socialist ideology through grassroots organizations and political parties and, consistent with that ideology, perceived the world in terms of social class struggle and had disdain for the formalities of democratic process. Two interviewees focused primarily on macrolevel conditions without discussing how those conditions affected their personal material conditions. (Indeed, Francesca proudly claimed not to be affected.) The other two drew some connections between the macrolevel policies they opposed and the material conditions in which their own families lived.

In this pattern, democracy was defined solely in popular terms rather than in terms of freedom or institutions. Furthermore, they valued democracy as the best type of regime. These respondents disdained the elitism and inequalities of power found in contemporary liberal democracies and therefore felt the liberal democratic regime in Argentina fell far short of their conception of "democracy." As Diego, a shantytown activist, expressed, "The supposed democracy today doesn't give you selection—it gives you either 7-Up or it gives you Coca Cola. There's only one boss. They are different colors—no they're not different colors, they are different shades of blue. There's no red, there's no green. . . . The democracy that exists is false. It's a lie. The people don't have choices."

Those people for whom regime legitimation rests on justice-based popular democracy were outcome oriented. They strongly opposed Menem's turn toward neoliberal economic policies and tended to be impatient with liberal political processes that they saw readily used to the advantage of economic elites. They showed substantial ambivalence about the value of the current regime and its institutions, and with one exception, hoped some day that a revolution would bring about social and political equity. Although they did not believe the extant regime was the best alternative in an ideal world, these respondents accepted it for the time being, seeing it as absolutely superior to the alternative of military authoritarianism. They were willing to work within the existing regime to participate in electoral politics and nonviolent social movements as means to making small gains in social justice.

Ignacio, who was ambiguous in his commitment to liberal processes and instead prioritized processes allowing grassroots participation, illustrates the PD pattern. A part-time college student from a shantytown, he had been exposed to Marxist social critique through various political activists in his neighborhood and family. Ignacio thought poor people would benefit from liberal democracy because they would be free from military repression. He rejected what he considered the unrealistic strategy of the guerrillas who had called for revolution over elections in the 1970s. He worked within the electoral process as a campaign volunteer for the Frente del Sur (a coalition of parties from the left that several reorganizations later became FREPASO); however, using concepts common among the Latin American left through the years (see Barros 1986), he explained elections as a tool to promote a better life for poor people, not an end in themselves. He was not confident that the left would be allowed to implement dramatic social change if it won office. So he concluded that while he would prefer peaceful routes to change, over the long-term he expected violent struggles would occur once poor people made more expansive political demands. In short, Ignacio valued the freedom and the process of liberal democracy, but he found it insufficient because, he said, it is "a democracy in which many people are left out." His commitment to democratic practice over the long-term seemed tempered by his belief that liberal democracy is structured and supported by elites so that certain people are left out permanently. Because Ignacio and the others seeking justice-based popular democracy did not consider a military regime an acceptable alternative to imperfect liberal institutions, their dissatisfaction with the limits of the current regime undermined regime legitimation in Argentina less than that of those using the fourth category of regime legitimation.

Absolute Results Regime (AR)

In the fourth pattern of thinking about democracy and the Argentine regime, people sought Absolute Results (AR). This pattern occurred among eight respondents. With two exceptions, which are discussed below, people fitting this pattern defined democracy in terms of institutions or liberty. None spoke of democracy in popular terms. Yet while they understood democracy in procedural terms, they did not have strong faith in the legitimacy of those processes because they judged their political world on the basis of results, not processes. For these Argentines, regime legitimation depended on achieving desired ends, including economic, physical, and national security. In some cases, this results-oriented perspective meant the person did not clearly distinguish the government from the regime because they did not appreciate the regime as a set of processes rather than a means to obtaining desired ends. Even those who did recognize the difference between the government and the regime were not convinced that the regime mattered. The use of force, through military means, was considered a reasonable option for meeting desired ends.

Two people who fit this pattern were the only people interviewed who did not define democracy using any of the three definitions discussed at the start of this chapter. They simply equated democracy with physical comfort and security. Apparently, the hegemonic normative preference for democracy had become distorted into the notion that "good things" are called "democratic." Thus, they said that the military governments, although admittedly not democracies according to usual usage, were indeed democratic. Claudia, a homemaker, declared, "The majority of Argentines will tell you that they lived better under military governments than under democratic governments. And the military was democratic, because we were happy then. We could safely go out to the park at five in the morning!"[6] When he was interviewed, Rafael, a cab driver/owner stated:

> I accept the democracy.
> Q: Yet you also accepted the military period.
> Rafael: The military period, for me, was democracy too.
> Q: Why was it a democracy too?
> Rafael: Because I lived well. I didn't have any problems. My children didn't have problems. Because I trained my children. You don't have to have your kids on the TV or in the newspapers [shouting] in order to say that you're in a democracy. I always live by showing respect, and so do my children. I do like it that under a democracy there are lots of people saying whatever they want.[7]

The apparent contradictions in Rafael's words indicate that he knew that a democratic regime offers more freedom of expression than an authoritarian one, but he did not consider this extra freedom essential to his or his children's quality of life. Rafael's and Claudia's imprecision in defining a concept such as democracy and in distinguishing the traits of different regimes is likely a reflection of the facts that both had minimal education and, until recently at least, little exposure to public affairs.

Within the group of those using a results-based regime legitimation, there were degrees of tolerance for coercive regime alternatives. On the least tolerant side were those generally supportive of elected governments and opposed to authoritarian ones but not unequivocally so. Horacio, for example, said that most military governments had not done much good for Argentina, but that "as far as I can remember, the only military government that was okay was Lanusse's because prices stayed stable." So while generally critical of authoritarian regimes, like an EL, Horacio was willing to consider them "okay" if they met the country's economic needs. Other people fitting the AR pattern supported authoritarianism without ambivalence. They claimed to support democratic rule but were also staunch defenders of the previous military regime, adapting the military's rationale that it had eliminated subversion, preserved the social order, and kept citizens secure. These respondents recognized that under the regime in power from 1976 to 1983, abuses of authority, as they considered the repression, had occurred but they did not condemn unequivocally the use of military repression to restore order. In my set of interviews, the unabashed apologists for the repressive tactics of the previous regime were people with family members currently or formerly in the armed or police forces (where they would have been indoctrinated with the rationale for repression), plus one person who had lived out of the country for many years and had missed the period when the grim details of the military's repression were revealed through public trials.

One of these apologists was María, a college-educated MODIN activist described in chapter 6. She believed that Argentines were frustrated because once-powerful institutions such as the military and the labor unions had become weak. María said she would like to have a democracy "like in the United States" and that if democracy means government of those elected by the people, then she felt it was a good thing: "But at the same time, you need a *mano dura* (a firm hand) to get rid of vices. . . . Thinking from the nation's point of view, I hope we never have a coup d'etat again. Personally, I'd like to see a coup to recompose things, but from the country's perspective, it would be good to keep growing with elections." María had little confidence that electoral processes would actually be able to meet the serious social needs of the country. Asked about Fujimori's actions in Peru, she said that one would need to understand the situation from a Peruvian's perspective, but she also stated, "It seems that Fujimori did not have a choice. If he hadn't done what he did, there would have been chaos."

The greatest degree of tolerance for authoritarianism occurred among people who were simply indifferent about all political regimes. For these interviewees, the state's primary role is to provide a high standard of living and a stable economy. So while the regime under which the state operates may have the advantage of more political freedom and constitutionality, they did not judge the regime by its rules but by the outcomes produced by the governments operating under that regime. They recognized political freedom as positive, all other things being equal, but felt it could be eliminated for the sake of the economy. The conversation with Rafael, cited above, provides one illustration of this perspective. Matilde, a middle-aged artisan, provides another. In her interview she declared, "Right now we have freedom of expression and ideas—democracy, but we always end up saying we're in a democracy and perhaps doing things that aren't good. For example, leaving people without jobs. Such as the people laid off from SOMISA . . . If this is democracy, I don't know what benefits there are in it."[8] A domestic worker named Betina demonstrated most clearly the inability to distinguish between the regime and the government, which may occur under this pattern. She said, "When the military were in, my mom said, one lived very well in that military period. Because nothing happened, nothing was done, people didn't stay out. Everyone was in his house. The way of life was more strict. But now it's not." Betina could not say whether she would support a military government in the future because she said there is no way to know if the next military government would also provide a good standard of living. She then summed up her goals for political life by stating, "For me what's most important is what [the government] is going to do. If it's military, Peronist, UCeDé, or communist, or whatever, for me what matters is what does this person *think about* doing for us, that is, the most humble people." Betina judged regimes based on their governments' expressions of concern for the poor and working class and was unconcerned about democratic process.

The majority of those who fit the AR pattern of regime evaluation were macrofocused as they discussed politics just like the majority of those seeking liberal democracy in the first two patterns. A couple were microfocused and only one was a micro-macro linker. In other words, for most people illustrating the fourth perspective, *personal* material interests did not motivate the content of their political views. This means that their tolerance for authoritarianism cannot be understood simply as a reaction to their own material interests. Indeed, they tended to be better off than those who fell into the other three patterns, and while some were worse off compared to their own pasts, this was not a dominant pattern.

Those citizens who thought about politics from the AR perspective did not picture politics as a means to self-governance but as a means to an end: it provided order, economic progress, coping, etc. The low value they placed on democracy seems to have resulted in some cases from their lack of awareness, due to weak political socialization, of the liberal purposes of democratic politics. Half of those who sought a results-based regime had not finished high school. Most had little or no interest in political affairs, and those who did were motivated by strong nationalist interests, rooted in family upbringing. The exceptions, María and her mother María José, who were reasonably knowledgeable about politics, had been strongly socialized in an authoritarian direction, learning in their military household to place a higher value on order than politics and to see the military as honorable leaders, not repressors.

The indifference of Betina, Matilde, and Rafael differs from the disillusionment of those who employed PD conceptions of democratic legitimacy. While both groups wanted better outcomes from a regime, those with a PD perspective would not accept military rule regardless of the short-term economic stability or growth that a military regime might deliver. Advocates of popular democracy recognized that in recent Argentine history, military governments had been even less likely to encourage participation and benefits for the poor than liberal democratic ones. Similarly, the AR thinkers' priority for results differs from the concern for effectiveness found in the EL thinkers because again people who think along AR lines care only about results and are willing to eliminate process completely for the sake of those results; in contrast, the EL patternists seek some optimal combination of both results and process but oppose the elimination of process.

Conclusions

In nearly three quarters of the interviews, democratic regimes were considered valuable for their promotion of civil rights and nonarbitrary rule, regardless of their social and material benefits. This strong majority was socialized to that position by paying attention to political affairs during the Alfonsín administration. By prosecuting the former military junta in public trials, Alfonsín promulgated a widespread recognition that democracy meant an alternative to the human rights violations of the military era. Because of those violations, the majority of Argentines no longer saw the military as an acceptable alternative regime, even under difficult economic circumstances. Political scientists have recognized that the experience with state repression under military regimes followed by the efforts of governments such as Alfonsín's to publicize the actions of those regimes turned elites on both the left and right into faithful supporters of liberal democratic institutions (Barros 1986; Linz and Stepan 1989, 46–48). The interviews discussed in this chapter show nonelites— democracy's citizens—also had learned that lesson. They came to define and value democracy as the rule of law and legal institutions and freedom from repression.

Significantly, the differences between those who saw democracy as uniquely legitimate and those who believed a regime must justify itself on the basis of its economic success cannot be distinguished from each other by their personal economic conditions or their self-perceptions of being materially insecure. Indeed the people who tolerated authoritarian regimes in the pursuit of results tended to have a higher standard of living than the people who thought along one of the other three patterns.

In-depth interviews are designed to uncover patterns and illuminate the reasoning and influences behind those patterns. While not designed to detect the same nuances in thinking, survey research allows observations about the generality of attitudes. Here I compare my findings from in-depth interviews to the general findings from two surveys. The late Argentine political scientist Edgardo Catterberg carried out pioneering survey research to measure civic culture in his country. In surveys from the 1980s, Catterberg found, as I did later, a "lack of consensus for any alternative legitimacy" other than democracy. He feared, however, that memories would fail over time, and the military regime would begin to look effective compared to the democracy (1989, 146–47). In my research about four years later, memories had not faded; the only people who suggested the military would be effective governors were those like Rafael and Betina who were unable to distinguish regime types or those like María José who supported military regimes out of respect for the armed forces and the keeping of order without regard to their economic effectiveness.

Catterberg said that democracy itself was not strongly valued in Argentina. On average only half of his sample answered closed-end questions about tolerance, censorship, party competition, and state authority in ways that suggested they valued democratic liberties and competitive processes. Liberal values, as indicated by the survey questions, had peaked at the end of the military regime and then declined again (1989, 63–65). The in-depth interviews used here showed EL pattern thinkers were not always "democratically correct" in their attitudes toward liberal processes, yet as I argued above, it is possible for people to express views not consistent with a rigorous political libertarianism and yet nevertheless show no interest in replacing the existing regime.

Catterberg feared that results-based thinking dominated Argentine political culture. After five years of the new democratic regime, he saw "considerable permanence" in certain "populist" attitudes rooted in "demands and expectations that perceive democracy more for its association with material success than as a set of rules." This "populist political culture," in Catterberg's terms, undermined the legitimacy of democracy, because "there's a very close relationship between acceptance of the democratic system and perception of the efficacy of that regime" (1989, 144–45). The bases of Catterberg's conclusions included first, a relationship between those who expressed dissatisfaction with conditions in the country and those who said military governments were more efficient than civilian ones, and secondly, a question in which people were asked to choose one of several traits as "most important in the democracy." A plurality of respondents (38 percent) chose "it should satisfy economic needs" (1989, 55–60 and 144 n. 1).

On the second question I suspect that Catterberg interpreted his own data too negatively. The closed-end survey question about the most important democratic trait included four choices that might express a respondent's priority for liberal democratic process: "the vote," "the right to criticize and protest," "the existence of various parties," and "respect for minorities." While no single one of those traits was chosen more often than the "satisfy economic needs" choice, nevertheless, a majority of respondents (54 percent) did not choose "satisfy economic needs" as the most important aspect of democracy but picked one of the four liberal traits instead. Similarly, in regard to the military efficiency question, while Catterberg's cross-tabulations showed that the percentage of those who perceived military governments as most efficient increased as dissatisfaction with personal or national economic conditions increased, they also showed that the majority of people did not respond to their dissatisfactions in that way. Those who were dissatisfied with both the country's situation *and* their personal pocketbooks were the people most likely to agree that military governments were most efficient, and yet most did not do so. Over half of them (57 percent) disagreed with the statement "military governments are more efficient than civilian ones" (1989, 57).

By 1992, results from another national-level survey showed an even stronger consensus against the claim that military governments are more efficient than democratic ones (77 percent). Consistent with Catterberg's data, the later survey also showed that those who felt their pocketbooks or the country were in bad condition had a slightly stronger tendency to perceive the military positively, but the more important conclusion that came from the data is that they, like Argentines overall, overwhelmingly rejected the military as governors (see tables 7.2 and 7.3). In sum, surveys from 1988 and 1992 suggest that material dissatisfactions were a deciding factor in delegitimizing democracy for a small minority of Argentines, but not for the majority. This corroborates the conclusion drawn using qualitative techniques in my interviews.

On other questions too the survey taken in the same period as my interviews confirms a generally strong support for democratic processes and very weak support for authoritarianism, even for the sake of solving difficult problems. Asked to imagine that the country was once again experiencing the political situation it faced in the last days of Isabel Perón's administration and to select among four possible solutions, only 12.5 percent of those surveyed said that in that situation "the military should take over the government to restore order and return to democracy," another 13.5 percent thought "some constitutional guarantees should be suspended so as to establish order," while 35 percent chose the more institutionally respectful statement "the Congress should govern until new elections are held." The plurality of respondents, 39 percent, chose the response that most respects legal process: "it would be best simply to do nothing, waiting until the term elected by the people is finished."[9]

Looking at surveys taken during the Alfonsín government, Catterberg argued that the new democracy raised Argentines' material expectations, thus setting up the possibility that the regime would fail to meet those expectations. He posited that such failure could encourage a selective memory about the military's record and a discontent that would engender illiberal beliefs, but it might also lead to more modest expectations, as too-high expectations were not met (1989, 146–47). I have argued in chapter 5 that the latter situation, not the former one, has occurred. By the early 1990s, expectations of how material conditions might improve under democracy had been considerably diminished. Political and economic contexts had changed from the first years of the democratic regime, and with them, citizens' bases for evaluating the regime. Immediately after the transition to democracy, Argentines may have

TABLE 7.2. VIEW OF MILITARY EFFICIENCY BY RETROSPECTIVE VIEW OF
POCKETBOOK, MID-1992 (BY PERCENTAGES)

Own Economic Situation Compared to One or Two Years Ago Is:					
Better	Slightly Better	The Same	Slightly Worse	Worse	Total
Military govts. are more efficient than civilian:					
Agree	23	19	21	24	29	23
Disagree	77	81	79	76	71	77
Totals (%)	100	100	100	100	100	100
n	261	264	339	87	214	1165

Source: Romer & Associates, Survey 11, May–June 1992. National adult sample from Federal Capital, Greater Buenos Aires, and six other metropolitan areas. Archive no. ARROMER92-TOP011 at Roper Center for Public Opinion Research. "Don't know" or "no response" eliminated.

seen democracy as a solution to the economic crisis attributed to the military regime. By 1992, having gone through the experience of the debt crisis, hyper-inflation, and multiple changes of economics minister and economic program under two elected presidents, Argentines knew that democracy was not, by itself, the cure to their country's economic problems. This knowledge did not lead them to widespread rejection of the regime but instead to rejection of any expectations that a regime change could be an economic cure.

Moreover, as the regime aged, the structure of the political situation changed in ways that made it more likely that the public would perceive responsibility for economic policy as resting with particular governments, not entire regimes. As the second president of the democratic regime, leading a different party from his predecessor, and with the military increasingly controlled by civilian authorities, Menem saw his competition for power as coming from the political opposition, not the armed forces.[10] Alfonsín, the first leader after the transition to democracy, worked to convince the public that the new *regime* could meet their material interests better than authoritarianism.[11] In contrast, Menem sought to convince the public that his party's *government* could meet their material interests better than the democratic opposition. Thus, as the democratic process worked—as political parties competed for votes and the military threat receded—the public's comparative reference point shifted from regimes to governments. The public had learned to distinguish the accomplishments of the regime from those of a government. They had learned, from Alfonsín's rhetoric and from their comparative experiences with the military, to value democracy on its own procedural terms. Catterberg ended his book on the hopeful note that the passage of time would favor democracy; it appears that his hope has been fulfilled (1989, 147).

TABLE 7.3. VIEW OF MILITARY EFFICIENCY BY RETROSPECTIVE SOCIOTROPISM, MID-1992 (BY PERCENTAGES)

Country's Economic Situation Compared to Two Years Ago Is:			
	Better	The Same	Worse	Totals
Military govts. are more efficient than civilian:				
Agree	22	23	25	23
Disagree	78	77	75	77
Totals (%)	100	100	100	100
n	744	259	161	1164

Source: Romer & Associates, Survey 11, May–June 1992. National adult sample from Federal Capital, Greater Buenos Aires, and six other metropolitan areas. Archive no. ARROMER92-TOP011 at Roper Center for Public Opinion Research. "Don't know" and "no response" eliminated.

The Quality of Argentina's Democracy

Democratic Processes

The previous section showed that the procedural benefits of liberal democracy—freedom, elections, and the rule of law—were considered valuable by many of those interviewed, independently of the material results they might bring. These interviews indicate a pattern of political thinking in which material hardships do not cause citizens to question the legitimacy of the liberal democratic regime. They valued a democratic regime for its personal and political freedoms, not for its material payoffs to themselves or to the country. This suggests that the current regime should be able to maintain legitimacy, in the Linzian sense of there being no acceptable alternatives, despite ups and downs in the country's economic conditions.

Maintaining legitimacy is important to maintaining the regime, but legitimacy is not the same thing as support. People may believe that the democratic regime in Argentina is preferable to any alternative and yet be very dissatisfied with the quality of the regime. Among those interviewed who valued democracy were people who were highly concerned that under the existing regime, neither the rule of law nor political freedoms were well protected. In practice, Argentine democracy seemed riddled by corruption and partisan obstructionism, and as discussed in chapter 6, elections seemed to offer poor options. As Diego expressed, "The people say 'I don't want anything to do with politics.' Because politics is corrupt, it's screwed up, it's dirty." These views were reactions to the practice of democratic politics in Argentina. President Menem's switch to neoliberal policies, following the populist tone of his campaign, encouraged the belief that politicians are dishonest. Other experiences with the supposedly deliberative and representative processes of liberal democracy also left many Argentines skeptical. These occurrences included partisan wrangling and parliamentary gamesmanship in Congress (during both the Alfonsín and Menem presidencies) as well as the policy deadlock between the Congress and a president who was uncompromising on certain presidential initiatives such as labor "flexibility" (during the Menem administration).

Menem's use of decree powers to implement many of his economic reforms was an example of the failure of democratic processes frequently cited by interviewees. Non-Peronists saw his ready use of executive power as a lack of respect for democratic norms. At the same time, some people assumed that since Menem was doing so much by decree, the members of Congress must be incompetent or unoccupied—and thus not worthy of their generous salaries. Similarly, the municipal and neighborhood council members were criticized frequently for making big salaries while playing politics. Elected officials were not perceived as representatives of the public will. Although those interviewed did not express the problem in the social science terms of institutionalization, they were, in effect, complaining about the weakness of democratic institutions in Argentina (see O'Donnell 1994). They cited Menem's well-publicized manipulation of the judiciary, numerous scandals in which high-ranking officials were accused of misappropriating public funds, and the executive branch's threats to cut back on advertising purchases from the newspapers that investigated the scandals. These and similar events suggested to people that the constitution was not being respected and the rules of the political game were not followed.

Democratic Citizenship

One need not define democracy in terms of what it produces for "the people," nor in terms of bottom-up participation, in order to see the quality of citizenship as fundamental to the quality of the regime. The political processes of liberal democracy—universal suffrage, freedom of expression, freedom to participate in political life as a candidate or party member—are founded on a principle of equality of citizenship. If people are not considered equal in their citizenship it makes no sense to give them an equally weighted vote.[12]

While the majority of those interviewed did not value the democratic regime on the basis of its material outputs, many observed that their material inequality left them without the capacity to exercise fully the political rights of citizenship. To begin to understand these views about citizenship, my arguments in chapter 4—that the impact of low income in a person's life is best understood in terms of how material conditions constrain the person's participation in society—should be recalled. One of the areas in which lower-income people are most restricted is in their ability to participate in political society. First of all, they encounter time constraints—and the poorer they are, the stronger these constraints. Washing clothes by hand; having to go to places in person because one lacks a phone; walking dozens of blocks home to save bus fare—these and myriad other examples illustrate how the time of Argentines who do not have the money to purchase conveniences that the middle class takes for granted (i.e., washing machines, telephones, cab rides, etc.) is wasted. The time that poor people spend surviving is time that more affluent people in society spend on recreation, leisure, and rest; on getting an education or skills training which could improve their income potential; and also on social and political activities (UNDP 1997, 62).

In chapter 5 I argued that people find numerous ways to cope with their constraints and, to the extent that they can cope, they are less likely to see those constraints as problems requiring government amelioration. Yet while citizens' coping mechanisms may mean they demand less that the government meet their material interests, these mechanisms may simultaneously reduce the quality of their citizenship. Political organizations often hold their meetings during the evening hours, when many poorer citizens work second jobs. Moreover, because overtime hours, second and third jobs, and other forms of coping create fatigue, lower-income Argentines have little energy left for participating in partisan politics, or even for self-help social movements. Those interviewed who did participate in political activities to better their living conditions, such as the Padelai organizers, mentioned repeatedly that their political work was burdensome because it caused them to spend less time with their families. Time away from family is, of course, the price paid by any political activist, rich or poor; but unlike more affluent activists, those like Jorge or Francesca who live with meager resources cannot pay for nannies, housekeepers, hired home repairs, or after-school recreational activities to keep their families and homes cared for while they go to political meetings.

Carlos.— A particularly clear explication of these constraints comes from Carlos. In his interview, one can hear two types of limitations experienced by those with relatively low levels of material resources and assets: first, constraints from above, that is, from those who disdain people of a lower social class, and secondly, constraints from below, that is, from weariness (caused by poor material conditions) or from the educational and social background of the poorer person.

Carlos lived with his pregnant wife and two sons in a one-room stucco dwelling of irregular title, which he spent his weekends working to rehabilitate.[13] He had been raised in a poor northern province by his single mother, who had only a fourth grade education. Having moved to Buenos Aires and obtained some high school education and a formal sector job in the garment industry, and having an employed wife, Carlos appeared better off than he had been as a child. Materially, his family lived much better than the poorest Argentines. They had a safe dwelling and his sons had clean, contemporary clothes and calculators for their schoolwork. Although the family shared a bathroom with other families, they enjoyed their own television, stereo set, a new electric space heater, and a refrigerator.

Carlos expended considerable effort to rise above the educational and social disadvantages that he saw as typically leading to diminished political awareness. He was current on political affairs and used concepts and arguments drawn from Marxist ideology. He had become familiar with Marxism through work in leftist parties including the Communist Party (PC), an orthodox, perennially tiny force in the Argentine party system. He had run for a seat on the *Consejo Vecinal* (Buenos Aires Neighborhood Assembly), and though he was unsuccessful, was pleased with the level of support he had received as a political newcomer. Later, however, he became less active, having become disillusioned with the party's closed leadership.

Not surprisingly, given his leftist exposure, Carlos linked micro and macro issues when he discussed politics—and the linkage was complex. Contrary to what some public opinion literature predicts, when Carlos blamed the macrolevel "system" for his problems it was not on the basis of political ignorance or because of his failure to understand how individual-level effort could improve his pocketbook. Carlos knew where his individual efforts had brought him since his childhood, and he planned to continue those efforts to improve his sons' chances; however, he also saw severe limits to microlevel effort. Carlos perceived the micro-macro linkage from both directions: he saw microlevel material conditions as a product of the larger political and economic systems, but he also felt they were a hindrance to his capacity to affect those systems.

Despite his efforts to improve his ability to participate in society, Carlos still felt strongly excluded by barriers that he could not overcome. For example, for a person of his material means, being well-informed on public affairs had tangible material costs. He bought the *Clarín* newspaper daily but could only afford to do so by sacrificing something else, like lunch or cigarettes. He credited his militancy in leftist parties for teaching him the importance of reading, but he was bitterly aware that he could not afford all the books, newspapers, and other accouterments that he considered necessary, not for physical survival, but for civic survival. He resented the social elitism from above, that excluded people like himself from positions of authority and from expressing their political convictions: "People here have the idea that the cultured guy is the one with the most education. This is a totally erroneous concept. That's not so. . . . I've been working since 1976 and do you know that I never, ever had job stability [well, not until the last three years, since I've been at a small shop] and do you know why? Because I don't sell out or compromise. Because there are things that I don't accept, see? . . . Do you know what they told me once at the factory? 'I want *negros*[14] who work, not who think.'" Carlos lamented that most working class people were not raised to be independent thinkers. From his perspective, they do not take much interest in political affairs or protest their conditions. One cause for this situation, as he saw it, was their socialization. Drawing upon his own experience, he argued that many poor people were raised in poor or troubled families or families headed by young single mothers. He felt the second reason that poor people were not more politically involved was the workers' lifestyles, which leave little time to ponder politics:

> Even in the parties of the left, there's a social class that runs things—the bourgeoisie. That's why I said that it's very difficult for a worker to end up in the leadership of something. Why is it difficult? Because of all the problems they have. We've got housing problems, children problems, problems with . . . *[garbled]*, family problems, we have to work sixteen hours. What time do you have left to think? If when you get home from work you go to sleep. . . . The working class here doesn't think. Why doesn't it think? Because they aren't allowed to think. The system doesn't let them think. . . . The guy who is at the factory for twelve hours—what time does he have to think? He's sleeping on the bus on the way home and when he turns on the television, what does he see?—nonsense.
>
> The leaders of the PC, as of other parties, have their problems resolved. They have their homes and autos and they want the workers in the party to do what they are told—to paint slogans on walls—but they won't let a worker move up to leadership. Besides, a worker doesn't have time or energy because of problems at home and responsibilities.

Even the two hours he spent that night talking with me were a "sacrifice," although he said it was one he was willing and able to make because he had clearly thought through his political ideas (and he apparently took some pleasure in talking about them since we talked at length on three separate occasions).

Related Views on Citizenship.— Carlos's conviction that full citizenship is only available to Argentines with comfortable financial positions was echoed by many other respondents who lamented the disparity in citizenship and political power between elites and masses. I did not prepare any of the interview questions with the design of detecting interviewees' criticisms of the elite power structure or the de facto disparities in citizenship, so generally this concern was raised by them. While in material life (as discussed in chapter 4) Argentines wanted less inequality but not full equality, in politics, they expected that democracy should offer absolute equality of citizenship. Contrary to these expectations, they felt weak in the face of self-interested and distant political representatives. María lamented, "Just like in any other country in the world, I'd like to have a government where public officials walk freely down the street [and talk to people]. That happens everywhere in the world. Here that doesn't happen, because the public official—who is stealing away everything and robbing everything—is a great celebrity, almost a god." Asked later to elaborate, she explained: "City council members sit over there in the city council but they don't attend to the population, they don't attend to the neighbors, they don't attend to their fellow citizen. You can't reach a council member. He's a celebrity, as if he were, almost, the pope. You can't reach him. You'll speak to the secretary of the secretary of the secretary of the secretary of the [aide]. You'll get to the council member if someone has sent you, if you have a calling card—this is the country of calling cards—it's still a place of recommendations and influences." Mónica, retired civil servant and staunch critic of Menem, concurred; she declared, "[The Peronist government] should be giving more help to the poor . . . rather than filling the pockets of the legislators the way they're doing, without thinking about others."

Twelve people expressed the conviction that self-interested capitalists have disproportionate influence over the political process and the economic system. These interviewees came from the range of class identifications and material resources included in this study. For example, Juan Antonio, a janitor in the public sector, lamented the problems of leadership in Argentine history. He explained that when good leaders arise they cannot accomplish their goals because "what happens here is that the economic powers manage things; they determine a lot of politics." Speaking of the burden of the foreign debt, Olivia, a laid-off bookkeeper and active Radical, said that it would seem that there should have been some way to pay the debt other than by tightening the salaries of people with the least money. She pointed out that the government *has* imposed taxes on wealthy people and on "big money and landowners" but those powerful interests protest the taxes, whereas people at the grassroots have "neither strength nor power" to protest policies imposed upon them to pay the debt.[15]

Until this point in this section, I have focused upon the ways in which people felt their political rights were undermined by disparities in material resources and assets. Additionally, people expressed concern that they did not have equal civil rights to those of more affluent members of society.[16] They identified a right to equal treatment under the law not merely with "democracy" but with an older ideal in the country's public discourse, social justice.

[Social justice means] that things are governed for the people, specifically. For all of the social classes, not just for one, for all: blue collar workers, the powerful, and, and white collar workers—and on the basis of equality. Because it's not equality if a guy who did some horrible thing—murder or something—and the judge lets him out on $3,000 bail and he gets out. This guy should be inside. He can't be out just because he has a lot of money with which to get out. Bail doesn't work. It shouldn't even exist. Judgments should be carried out. Because it's very easy if you have money to commit crimes. . . . This is not social justice. (Paula)

Francesca said that under Perón, there had been "respect for both the rich and the poor alike." To illustrate how that was no longer the case, she told how the local police had refused to take a statement from a group of Padelai leaders who went to report a crime problem in their building. The officer claimed that the appropriate person was not available to take the complaint, but Francesca was sure that they were being ignored because they were poor.

Conclusions

Most of those interviewed did not discuss or evaluate democracy as a means to substantive ends for themselves or for the society at large. The authoritarian-tolerant pattern (AR) was not adopted primarily by the poorest people interviewed, but rather by people who identified themselves as comfortable in relation to others. Also, most interviewees did not link their personal material interests to their evaluation of the democracy's worth. Although the popular, justice-based democracy pattern was only found among people who were born into poverty, who continued to live in substandard housing, and who strongly identified with the lower class, the other three legitimation patterns were not limited to any particular class identity or standard of living. Furthermore, the thinking pattern of those seeking PD democracy was not simply a reaction to their own poverty. It was an interpretation of that poverty drawing upon socialist concepts to which they had been socialized, including the conceptualization of democracy as popular and participatory, and the materialist evaluation of regime worth. Among the majority of those interviewed, material interests did not drive their evaluations of regime legitimacy. They had been socialized by the elite discourse in contemporary Argentina and by their experiences with military regimes to define and value democracy for its freedoms and institutions, not its substantive outcomes.

The widespread defining of democracy in liberal terms is context driven. The historical experiences, elite-level political discourse, and current political opportunity structure in Argentina have combined to create an environment in which democracy is defined liberally and democratic practices are valued. This constitutes a substantial shift at the grassroots level from the more substantively and popularly focused understandings of democracy that inspired debates and political movements a generation ago.[17]

The legitimacy of democracy in Argentina has also been driven by context rather than by any ideological recognition of democracy's inherent values. Linz's conception of regime legitimacy rests not on citizens' approval of the regime but on their refusal to consider alternatives to it. Liberal democracy has legitimacy for most Argentines because the alternative that they know best— military authoritarianism—is perceived as intolerable owing to its well-publicized record of abusing human rights. As long as the memory of the previous military regime remains negative—and human rights groups through the 1990s used international fora, the press, the streets, and the courts to assure that it would—it is unlikely that Argentines will support military solutions to their own or their country's material suffering.

The Argentine public's recent experience of democracy as "not military" has been good; but they have been disappointed by their experiences with a democracy that does not measure up to "the rule of law," "freedom of the press," "equal treatment of citizens," or "government that responds to the expressed will of the people." Most of those interviewed would not support a military regime that offered them material comforts, but many were angered by a democratic regime that seemed to allow political insiders to live well from corruption or high salaries while the general population was asked to make sacrifices during economic adjustments. While the occasional interviewee thought a military hand could impose some honest behavior, more often respondents hoped that improvements in Argentina's democracy would come about through individual morality, specifically, through more honesty on the part of public officials.[18] Overall, these results suggest that while citizens were dismayed by the poor quality of democracy in Argentina, their contextual reference points and their understanding of democracy in largely procedural terms led most to wish to improve the current regime rather than to replace it.

Chapter

8

Conclusions

The daily lives, life experiences, and words of the Argentines in this book reveal the complexity of material interests and the complicated path from objective material problem to perceived material interest to perceived political interest. The people interviewed were not well off and the vast majority did not like the incumbent government, yet when they explained their criticism of the government, it was only occasionally a criticism of how the government's policies affected them materially. As human beings, they were motivated by material as well as idealistic interests. As citizens, their personal material concerns only became the foundation of their political interests under certain conditions.

To understand interests, rather than take them for granted—and particularly to understand the apparent priorities that citizens place on some objective material conditions as opposed to others—we need a fine-grained approach. General economic conditions, such as poverty or economic growth, cover up a diverse set of material conditions and diverse resource and asset capacities for coping with those conditions. Expectations that government should solve a material problem depend upon what the problem is, what kinds of constraints it creates, and what it takes to attempt to resolve those constraints. Also, material conditions are not experienced in a vacuum. Citizens evaluate their material conditions using additional objective information—the historical, political, and economic contexts in which those conditions are experienced—and using subjective identities that affect their perceptions of both personal material conditions and the contexts in which they occur.

Economists and policy scholars studying other parts of Latin America have often commented on the heterogeneity of material interests, which this book has emphasized. At first, scholars observed that economic restructuring policies caused differential impacts upon various social groups (Nelson 1989). As targeting became the buzzword for social policy in the 1990s, policy makers started finetuning their social categories beyond broad class or income labels. Those labels, such as "poor," obscure significant differences in the resources and assets, both human and material, to which people have access. Glewwe and de Tray (1991, 50–52) found that even identifying narrow socioeconomic groups, such as landless peasants or public employees, was an inadequate means to identify groups with common levels of resources and assets. The interviews in chapter 4 illustrated this diversity. Similar socioeconomic status did not explain the different views of Rodrigo and Graciela, or Amanda's as compared to those of her son Pepe. They perceived their similar situations differently because their ages and life circumstances created different degrees of constraint on their freedom to pursue the lives that they considered should be within normal expectations.

While scholars of social policy and economics have noted the heterogeneity of material interests, as well as the individual, community, and state means for coping with periods of economic crisis, few analysts of politics have paid attention to these mechanisms.[1] There are two reasons for this omission, both discussed in detail in chapter 1. First, political science focuses much more on elites than nonelites. Even research literatures that study the politics of the grassroots in one way or another, via the study of public opinion, populism, or social movements, typically do so in order to understand the relationship between elites and nonelites or the effect of one upon the other. This means that the daily experiences of life at the grassroots get little attention. Secondly, political scientists tend to take material interests as givens. Some political scientists have paid attention to the contexts against which the public sets its expectations and then measures its gains or losses (see Weyland 1996, 190), but overall, concepts of "gains" or "losses" are not clearly defined and types of gains or losses are often not disaggregated. The literature does not explain why, when faced with trade-offs among interests, people prioritize one type over another. This book argues that we can make such distinctions, which

vastly affect whether gains or losses take on political meaning, if we pay attention to how objective conditions will affect security, freedom, and a sense of
fitting in with the normal levels of living in society. In particular, we need to
pay attention to the conditions, policies, and timing that affect coping capacity. By examining material conditions in the light of expectations and coping
mechanisms, we can better explain how objective conditions become subjective political interests.

The critical point is that political scientists should start their analyses at
an earlier point on the path to the formation of political interests. If we understand the bases of material interests, rather than taking them for granted, we
gain insights into why some objectively difficult material conditions cause
much greater political reaction than other conditions that seem equivalently
difficult. Building on the work of Amartya Sen, Peter Townsend, and others,
we can see that the basis of material interests is best understood not in terms
of accumulation or acquisition but in terms of freedom from material conditions that constrain opportunity, security, and social participation. Adding
those insights into a larger analytical framework, which includes but is not
limited to the elite-mobilized identities and elite-created contexts through
which grassroots-level evaluations are filtered, we end up with a more comprehensive, less elite-centric explanation for the relationship between a country's
material conditions and the political views citizens express. We also have an
explanation for the legitimation of democracy, which looks up from the perspective of the demos rather than down from the actions of elites.

The Path from Material to Political: A Summation

Understanding citizens' political response to their material problems begins
with understanding how they experience those problems and how they might
resolve them. The Argentines studied here did not discuss their material conditions in simple quantitative terms, where more is better. They were certainly
materially motivated but did not desire material goods for their own sakes.
Rather, they spoke of alleviating the constraining effects of their material
condition—insecurity, inability to plan for the future, stress, fatigue, and restricted opportunities. They wanted material goods not for the sake of accumulation but to be included in the normal lifestyle of the society. The case
study of housing revealed that equally deteriorated but qualitatively different
housing conditions caused different types of constraints, insecurities, discomforts, and stresses, and different possibilities for resolution.

People who perceive their material conditions as limiting may or may not
perceive those hardships as ones that the government can or should help them

resolve. The reasons for this perception are rooted in the material problems themselves and the perceived options for coping with those problems. First of all, the person's goal is to solve the problem, regardless of who solves it. Often the most readily available means to cope with a problem are not political ones. Different types of problems will pose different possibilities for finding solutions at the individual or local level, rather than through the state. People also possess differing resources and assets with which to cope with their material constraints. Many of those coping mechanisms are available at the individual, family, or local level. In addition, the contexts in which people in a particular society experience their material hardships affect their possibilities for coping with the problems as well as their expectations about such possibilities. These contexts include the suddenness and speed with which the material hardships appeared, the organizations and programs in place to enable people to cope, political discourse about the ease or difficulty of improving economic conditions, and historical experiences that shape expectations about what kind of conditions and coping are "normal."

Of course, one might argue that anyone not dying from exposure, malnutrition, or medical neglect evidently has found some capacity to cope with their material conditions. The point here is that people want to be able to cope with the specific condition considered a problem—their low pension, joblessness, or lack of housing. They also want to be able to cope with that problem without substantially increasing fatigue, insecurity, exclusion, and other constraints that their material circumstances have created. When they have a variety of coping mechanisms, they are more likely to perceive coping as feasible. When the best options for coping with their problem are out of their hands (i.e., when government policy change is the only means to improve coping), then they are more likely to perceive their material problems as political ones.

Because most material interests were ones with which people could seek to cope at levels "below" that of the state, their personal-level material interests did not usually shape their evaluations of the state, its leaders, or the political process. That is, most of the people I interviewed did not make the micro-macro connection linking their specific material interests to past or future actions by the state. Some people took little notice of national politics, perceiving it as not interesting to them or as not having much impact on their lives. In this book, their perspective was called a "microfocus." Others, called "macrofocusers," perceived political activity as important to the nation overall but did not focus on its impact on themselves personally. They perceived the impact of the state upon the economy and upon certain classes or groups in society, such as the poor or the elderly, but they perceived their own material problems as separate from these macrolevel policies and processes. Only those who faced problems for which the best coping mechanism was a change in national policy (such as pensioners and public employees) and who perceived other efforts to cope as onerous or inadequate were focused on the micro-macro linkage. While many Argentines did not focus their political views on the personal material problems they wanted resolved, most felt that the state had a responsibility to create a general climate of economic prosperity and social justice.

The path to these three types of foci was summarized in figures 5.2 and 5.1. If we know where someone focuses a camera, then we know what the person is looking for but not what the person sees in the picture. Similarly, knowing the focus of citizens' political interest does not tell us the content of their political views. As chapters 6 and 7 argued, the content of their views comes from their examinations of alternative leaders, parties, policies, and regimes through the filters of class and partisan identities and economic, political, and historical contexts. Figure 8.1 (which connects with figure 5.1) depicts this process. Like camera filters and background lighting, these identities and contexts change how reality is perceived—whether solutions are expected to be found through government, who or what is blamed for a country's problems, who is perceived as most capable of fixing the problems, and what kinds of policy or regime solutions are perceived as feasible and acceptable.

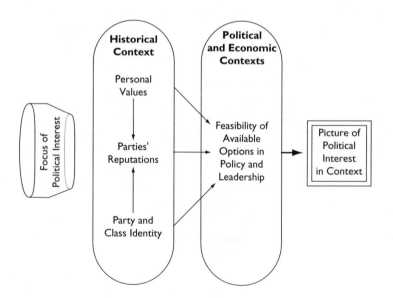

Figure 8.1. Forming a Picture of One's Political Interest

Reexamining Literature on Material-Political Links

Chapter 1 outlined the divergent perspectives of three political science literatures with markedly different insights about how citizens link their material concerns to their political ones. Despite addressing the same fundamental relationship between the material and the political, these literatures—on economic voting in Western democracies, on populism in Latin America, and on social movements—often diverge yet rarely confront each other. The grassroots-level interviews in this book reveal some strengths, shortcomings, and conjunctures in the ways these literatures explain micro-macro linkages.

Explaining Sociotropic Thinking

The economic voting literature reviewed in chapter 1 draws heavily upon public opinion surveys in long-established democracies to find that sociotropic thinking is common. A finding of sociotropic thinking in a particular case and time simply begs the question of why people evaluate their political interests in terms of national-level conditions, where those conditions do not match their own. It also begs the question of why people would pay attention to the government's effect on some of their interests more than on others. As reviewed in chapter 1, the voting studies literature seeks to address those questions by focusing on attributions of blame and on access to information about national conditions. The attention is on the sources external to the voter, which influence the making of a micro-macro connection.

This book has sought to explain when, where, and why the link is made or not made by examining the micro *and* macro levels separately in order then to uncover the conditions and reasoning under which they are brought together. Certainly my findings concur with the argument that attributing blame is important. Often, whether blame might be attributed is inherent in the kind of material interest (such as pension levels or public employee salaries). Likewise, this work has paid attention to the information people have about national conditions—not to the accuracy of their knowledge but rather to the historical, political, and economic contexts in which they judge whether national conditions are normal, whether alternative solutions are feasible, and whether their own personal problems are normal and solvable at a household or local level.

The media's coverage of national-level interests certainly might, as Mutz (1998) proposed, cause people to believe that their problems are atypical and thus purely personal. Its effect, however, could also be the opposite. Recalling Julio's despair at the end of chapter 4 and making use of the concepts from

Townsend's (1970) work on poverty, one can better understand that, particularly in highly unequal societies, the media may simply serve to convince people that they are not sharing in what is normal in their society or in what they had formerly expected would be their normal standard of living. The poorer people interviewed sometimes mentioned wanting to live *como la gente* (like comfortable folks). If their media, politicians, or own observations suggest to them that comfort is the norm, then they expect to share it. If those sources suggest that "we're all poor these days," then their expectations of what they should be able to achieve will be moderated.

Furthermore, while interviews clearly revealed the influence of media coverage and political exposure in people's discourse, they also revealed that whether linking takes place is not just a question of whether people are informed or sophisticated. Contrary to the normative assumptions of some works on sociotropic voting, linking one's microlevel interests to macrolevel politics is not typically ill-informed or illogical—quite the opposite. This is particularly the case in developing countries, where the debt crisis, high inflation, devaluations, and shock treatments have made it obvious that state policies affect individuals' lives in ways beyond their control. Logic and good information scream out for making a connection between the micro- and macrolevels. Social movements (and to a more controlled extent, populists) work hard to show people these connections. Yet often the people interviewed focused their political attention on macrolevel conditions, particularly economic ones, while ignoring direct ways, evident to an observer, in which government policy had affected their personal lives. They did not hold government accountable for their personal problems because they expected to resolve those problems individually or locally or they did not believe the problems were resolvable. While macrolevel solutions might be more comprehensive and permanent, microlevel coping is more tangible and individually efficacious. This means it is not a "leap of logic" to hold government accountable for one's personal conditions—but given the felt distance between many citizens and their governments, it may be a leap of faith. Consequently, if people can find personal or local-level means to cope at what they consider to be normal and tolerable degrees of effort then they tend not to look for macrolevel solutions. Whether or not such coping solutions are perceived depends, in turn, on the types of material interests, people's capacities for resolving them without government intervention, and their confidence, within particular contexts, that government intervention is feasible and could be helpful.

Two additional points arise from my analysis. First, since types of interest and the state's capacity to address those interests vary across cases and time, I would like to emphasize that we cannot assume *a priori*, nor should we expect to find empirically, that sociotropism (or any other linking or nonlinking pattern of thought) is typical, sophisticated, or informed. Secondly, the voting literature generally assumes citizens are narrowly self-interested and that sociotropism is simply a sophisticated means of being instrumentally rational. The interviews in this book certainly show plenty of instrumental and materialist reasoning but also call our attention to the need to expand our understanding of the vote beyond that reasoning. The "sincere" voters of the left, discussed in chapter 6, remind us that many acts of citizenship, particularly by the less powerful, begin as expressive acts without yet having any likelihood of being instrumental ones.

Linking and Consciousness

The social movements literature as discussed in chapter 1 finds that grassroots organizing and participation can raise consciousness of the micro-macro linkage. Stokes (1995) has argued that such consciousness only develops in those grassroots organizations that confront authority rather than ingratiate themselves to it through clientelism. My interviews suggest, however, the need for additional investigation of which movements develop awareness of micro-macro links. Chapter 3 showed that the activists at Padelai were staunch proponents of confrontational rather than clientelist tactics. Their organizers aspired to the social movement ideal of consciousness-raising. Indeed, the Padelai residents did change their thinking in certain ways as the result of their participation in the housing movement, learning to be tolerant of diverse opinion, to value democratic decision-making, and to believe in their own capacity to bring about favorable political decisions on specific demands. They did not, however, become conscious of the ways that their overall material conditions existed in a larger social, economic, and political arena. They were narrowly focused on gaining their own housing, and precisely because of the quintessential social movement strategy of avoiding partisan alignments, they perceived their political activity at the local level as unrelated to their views about national level political issues. Among Argentines interviewed who were micro-macro linkers were some people influenced by their participation in organizations; these were not participants in new social movements but rather in traditional parties and labor unions, which urged their members to perceive their hardships as owing to national government policy.

This book did not focus on movements themselves, but its findings about how the material-to-political link occurs suggest certain hypotheses about why "consciousness" is so difficult to raise—even among movement activists. First of all, the type of problem around which a movement forms seems to affect whether or not participation in a movement is likely to engender micro-macro linking. People join a movement as a means to cope with a problem. If the movement is organized around problems that are best addressed in the local community, then like the Padelai residents, participants are unlikely to see the bridge from their own local-level activism to national-level politics. Secondly, where national party identities are strong, as they have been in Argentina, national politics are organized by and around partisan debates. Thus, the nonpartisan strategy of a social movement does not give the movement's members a clear path to perceiving how their interests might be connected to national-level politics. Furthermore, consciousness could be expected to be raised best by those collective organizers who are explicitly concerned with both national politics *and* material interests—such as leftist parties and labor unions. In addition, the micro- to macro linkage involves both retrospective and prospective thinking—that is, it involves assigning blame as well as seeking solutions. Social movements seeking to engender this linkage may be hindered by the preexisting identities of movement participants and by the contexts in which participants evaluate their conditions. Preexisting identities color perceptions of who is to blame for material conditions, and contexts shape perceptions about what kinds of solutions are feasible. Therefore, static identities—such as those of the Peronists who remained loyal to the PJ even while they disagreed with Menem's policies—can become obstacles to the acknowledgment of micro-macro connections. In these ways, identity and context factors may interfere with the perception of a micro-macro linkage, despite the efforts of movement mobilizers.

The People's View of Populism

As pointed out in chapter 1, often the literature on populism concentrates on the populist and not the populace that follows him. Understanding why populists are successful requires knowing not just what they do and the context in which they do it (which is the literature's emphasis), but how people evaluate the populist's appeals to their many and varied interests as well as the contexts in which they make those evaluations. The implication of the evidence from Argentina is that people evaluate politicians not on the basis of the quantity or distribution of material goods, but on the opportunity, security, leisure time, and coping capacity created by the particular type of good or policy provided.

The examinations of material interests in chapter 4 and of class and party identities in chapter 6 show people interpreting politicians' appeals in terms other than their material promises. As some populist literature implies, pop-

ulists offer their followers not just progress but also inclusion. The antiestablishment discourse typical of populism offers people a sense of identity and a
feeling of membership in the economic and political life of their society. That
Perón succeeded in this endeavor became evident in the statements from
Peronists in chapter 6.

The assumption in some of the literature that the popular sectors value
material payoffs more than democracy did not surface in many of my interviews. Most of those interviewed evaluated the benefits of a democratic regime
in nonmaterial terms. The way people respond to their political leaders, then,
is more complicated than a simple reaction to what they receive materially
from the government, yet it is not (in either of the contrary ways proposed in
the public opinion and social movements literatures)[2] merely a matter of political sophistication. While this book was not focused on responses to populists
per se, it has argued that citizen-level views about politicians are formed in response to the alternatives available in the political context. This means that
people may determine that it is in their *political* interest to support a particular
leader not because the leader offers a positive solution to their material interests or other interests but simply because they perceive the leader as less negative than the alternatives. This distinction is often overlooked by observers
who misinterpret this conditional support of the "least worst" alternative as a
positive endorsement of the leader's "populist" policies or persona.

Finally, by examining the strategies and discourse of leaders, rather than
the thinking of potential followers, the populism literature may overestimate
the appeal of populist style. Statements in chapter 6 from those interviewed reveal people inspired by the inclusiveness and common touch associated with
Peronism, as well as people—including people of equivalent socioeconomic
level—repelled by it.

Argentine Politics through the Nineties

Knowing how people think about their material conditions and the factors
that shape their expectations of political leaders, we are in a better position to
examine grassroots political opinion in Argentine politics as it evolved
through the 1990s. Starting in about 1993, signs appeared that significant portions of the public disapproved of Menem's economic policies and saw those
policies as having a negative impact on their own lives. These citizens were
mobilized at first by public employee unions and senior citizen groups, whose
members could see the direct impact of government policy upon their personal economic security. By mid-decade, a large segment of society was involved. The Radical Party, a center-left coalition called the Frente del País

Solidario (FREPASO), and on occasion, the otherwise pro-Menem General Workers Confederation (CGT) helped sponsor mass street protests as a means to build support or pressure the president.

The first of these signs of emerging opposition had appeared in the interior provinces, when, after months of unpaid wages, public employees were told they would suffer new austerity measures (see Powers 1995a, 122–24). Public employees rioted in Santiago del Estero and Tucumán at the end of 1993, a massive public march from the north to Buenos Aires was organized in July 1994, and police clashed with public employees in Viedma, La Plata, and Jujuy in December 1995.

By the presidential election of May 1995, the Argentine public faced three major alternatives—an unknown rural governor from the well-established UCR, a well-known governor from the newly-established FREPASO, and the well-known president from the well-established PJ. Facing these alternatives, about half the public voted for Menem and the other half divided their votes among his opponents.[3] Menem's defeat of hyperinflation was crucial to his popularity in his first term, for it restored citizens' capacity to cope with their daily lives. Moreover, his steadfast commitment to the Convertibility Plan meant that many voters saw him as an ongoing guarantor of that coping capacity. Menem's success with inflation led many voters to feel confident that he could be similarly successful in tackling the new constraint, unemployment, that had arisen by 1995. At a moment of international financial crisis and an unprecedentedly difficult domestic labor market, there was insecurity about trusting the economy to unproven newcomers (cf. De Riz 1998, 143 and Szusterman 1996, 111). One opposition party had a strong organization but a weak candidate and a poor performance record. The other had a strong candidate but a weak organization with no record. Both opponents focused their campaigns more on issues of character and leadership than on policy. Neither was able to convince a sufficient number of voters that he could tackle the new problems better than the incumbent.

After the 1995 election, the opposition flourished and Menem's support shrank. In the Federal Capital, just five months after Menem won 42 percent of the city's vote, his party got only one of every four votes for the capital's senator and deputies. The senate seat was taken by FREPASO, thereby establishing a new level of credibility for the upstart coalition. In the austral spring of 1996, labor unions called a successful nationwide work stoppage, 36-hour general strike, and massive rallies. In May 1997, unemployed laborers blockaded highways in the northern province of Jujuy. As the national guard responded violently, sympathizers emerged nationwide with marches by public employees, pensioners, and the unemployed, and a "teach-in" by students at the University of Buenos Aires.[4] In August, another nationwide one-day strike took place, led by two labor federations that had broken with Menem. By the October 1997 congressional races electoral support for the president's party had fallen considerably. The PJ won only 36 percent of the overall vote, losing its majority and thirteen seats in the lower chamber. By March 1998, a poll showed 49 percent of Argentines viewed Menem negatively, while only 15 percent viewed him favorably, with the rest unsure.[5] As the 1999 election year progressed, unemployment and fiscal crises at the provincial level were prominent concerns. Protests against unemployment and unpaid public sector wages took place in Tucumán, Corrientes, Neuquen, and Tierra del Fuego.[6] By the time Menem turned over the presidency to Fernando De la Rúa in December 1999, a poll taken in major urban areas showed nearly 80 percent of respondents held negative opinions of him.[7]

The collective action involved in organizing public demonstrations or opposition campaigns depends on organizers' resources and mobilization opportunities, but it also depends upon the perceived interests and alternatives of the individuals who decide to express themselves through collective actions. Based on the understanding of interests developed through this book, we can analyze why perceptions of interests evolved through the 1990s.

One must first consider which types of material problems Menem addressed and which he did not. Menem failed to provide solutions to several types of material hardship. He reneged on the *salariazo* promised during the 1989 campaign, and his early policies ignored poverty and social policy shortfalls (Minujín 1992, Minujín 1993). Faced with widespread criticism that his economic plan neglected the poor, his initial response was denial rather than amelioration (Powers 1995a). As seen in chapter 6, some people took Menem to task on these matters, sometimes because they themselves had hoped to enjoy the promised pay raise but more often because they perceived his attitude toward salaries and poverty as evidence of a retreat from Argentine or Peronist values of social justice. Nevertheless, while failing to provide some types of material goods, he did provide others. Although people disliked the stagnant salaries, they universally approved of the unchanging prices of consumer goods. So even while not providing all of the economic payoffs he had promised, Menem did resolve the inflation problem—a problem that citizens felt the state should resolve and one that had plagued his predecessors. In doing so, he enabled people to cope with their poverty or their low salaries on their own and reduced the insecurity of life on a lower income budget. He also opened the way for an explosion of consumer credit, which further lessened the constraints of life on a small monthly paycheck. In short, while Menem failed to meet all the interests he had promised to meet in his 1989 campaign, he enhanced individual-level coping capacity when he lowered inflation and kept it low. A substantial portion of the public, who supported his economic policies, apparently decided they could take care of their other problems on their own.

If this reasoning, derived from individual-level analysis, is correct, it explains why opposition to Menem was muted in the early years and only surfaced from pensioners, public employees, and the like, who needed additional state action to be able to cope. This also explains why ending inflation generated such good will toward Menem, whereas ignoring poverty, inequality, and social policy problems did not engender equivalent bad will.

By the mid-1990s, many Argentines faced a new type of material problem, unemployment. The impressive economic growth from 1991 to 1994 favored workers with high technical skills and did not produce sufficient jobs to meet the demands of less-educated workers.[8] The problem was exacerbated by the collapse of the Mexican peso in 1994, which triggered disinvestment throughout Latin America. The Argentine government was forced to institute austerity measures and the country went into a short recession. Unemployment climbed to the historically unprecedented level of 18.4 percent in May 1995, at which point most people, jobless or not, recognized it as one of the country's major problems.[9] With the high level of unemployment, poverty levels began to increase again.[10] Within a year of the Mexican peso crisis, the Argentine economy had recovered from recession but the impact of unemployment remained through the decade and the economic growth was short-lived (see table 8.1).

The way a person or household copes with joblessness or poverty depends on the national unemployment context. As unemployment levels soar, competition for extra and part-time *changas* increases. Thus, as unemployment in Ar-

TABLE 8.1. ECONOMIC AND SOCIAL CONDITIONS IN ARGENTINA, 1991–1999

	1991	1992	1993	1994	1995	1996	1997	1998	1999
Growth[a]	9.2	8.2	4.5	4.4	-4.1	4.1	6.6	2.6	−4.5
Wages[b]	100.4	101.7	100.4	101.1	100.0	99.8	99.3	98.2	99.2
Inflation	84.0	17.6	7.4	3.9	1.6	0.1	0.3	0.7	−1.7
Poverty[c]	28.8	19.3	17.8	16.1	22.2	26.7	26.3	24.3	27.2
Unemployment[d]	6.5	7.0	9.6	11.5	17.5	17.2	14.9	12.9	14.5

Source: ECLAC (1999) and SIEMPRO (1999). 1999 data are preliminary.
[a]Change in GDP/capita in 1995 prices.
[b]Index of average real manufacturing wages, 1995=100
[c]Population below the poverty line, Greater Buenos Aires, per May (or April) survey.
[d]Average annual rate of urban unemployment.

gentina grew, it undermined the effectiveness of coping measures, such as taking a second job, working an informal sector job, or making one's spouse or child work, routinely used by the poor and near-poor in earlier time periods.[11] As Juan Antonio told me in a reinterview in 1995, it was no wonder that violence erupted among the unemployed because of the feelings of "impotence" (in his terms—or incapacity to cope, in mine)—that people experienced. The fact that political protests occurred most frequently in the smaller cities in the north and south is explained by the particularly scarce alternatives for individual-level coping in those regions, where small consumer markets, widespread poverty, and a small private sector left few avenues for making a living beyond public employment, which was being reduced.

People fortunate enough to have full-time employment were also constrained as the national labor market worsened. They were often asked to work more overtime hours in order to keep their jobs. By 1997, a 10-hour work day was the norm in the formal private sector.[12] These extra hours help account for how economic growth occurred in 1996 and 1997 without substantial improvements in employment rates.[13] Furthermore, people employed in the private sector no longer had the job security or job benefits that they once enjoyed. Reforms in the labor laws in 1991 had enabled some employers to hire workers on six to twenty-four month contracts with no provisions for benefits or severance pay.[14] By late 1997, 17 percent of wage earners did not have permanent contracts, an increase of 7 percentage points in just one year (ECLAC 1998a, 95). So even when new jobs were created in the 1990s, often they were not ones that enhanced people's feelings of security or diminished their feelings of constraint.[15] In sum, once unemployment and underemployment became national problems on a large scale, they became problems that were less amenable to individual-level coping solutions and more likely to be linked to national government performance.

Menem responded to the unemployment crisis in two ways. He instituted policies that enabled the poorest people to cope somewhat in the short term. This was done through a World Bank-funded program that created temporary jobs for the poor. The jobs were in infrastructure development so the program had the added benefit of providing funds and labor for projects to improve water, sewage, roads, schools, health clinics, and housing.[16] While a temporary jobs program would enhance the recipients' capacities to cope with their poverty, the program was not designed to provide permanent jobs and so could not create long-term security or social inclusion. The jobs paid a very minimal wage, sufficient to allow workers to avoid malnutrition but not to live at even minimal standards in Argentine society.[17] The second of Menem's solutions was intended to create jobs over the long-term. The president argued

that unemployment would only be reduced by eliminating the last vestiges of
Peronist-era labor laws in order to lower the cost of doing business in Argentina, attract investors, and eliminate the costs of firing which served as disincentives to hiring.[18] In 1995, changes were made for small- and
medium-sized firms. With the encouragement of international financial institutions and the business community, he then proposed changing the law applicable to large firms, including ending the system of indemnifications for
severance. This change would have eliminated an important coping mechanism—the lump sum payment based on seniority that so many laidoff workers
in the 1980s and early 1990s had used to start new businesses. A promise that
easy firing encourages job creation at the national level does not resolve the
short-term coping problem of the individual employee who loses his or her
job and faces the insecurity of a "buyer's" labor market. The Confederación
General de Trabajo (CGT) and its Peronist allies in Congress fought long and
hard against the reform proposals. After more than three years of negotiations,
Congress enacted new labor legislation in September 1998, which was a bare
skeleton of the proposal sought by business and the International Monetary
Fund.[19] Severance pay was not eliminated in the end although the method of
calculation changed, diminishing the size of payments to employees laid off
after less than two years with a firm. By facilitating the firing of new employees, the law created a new level of insecurity in an already weak labor market.
In 2000 President De la Rúa continued Menem's focus on labor law reform. By
May, he had persuaded Congress to enact changes to the collective bargaining
law and longer probation periods so that large employers could hire workers
for up to three months without incurring obligations to pay severance. Although indemnification protections for long-term employees remained in
place, and although the labor law reforms are supposed to foment job-creation,
the changes offered little that would increase workers' job or income security.

Not only did the types of material problems and the possibilities for coping with them change through the course of the 1990s, but so did the political
context in which citizens judged Menem, Peronism, and alternatives to them.
The emerging context offered citizens more feasible and credible means to attempt to redress their material interests through politics. Labor organizations
(including on several occasions the long-Menemist CGT) were energized by
the rise of unemployment. Their mobilization offered citizens new opportunities for treating their personal material problems as political interests.

Although the major parties did not propose dramatic shifts in economic
policy (and given Argentina's agreements with the IMF, it is unlikely that any
would), nevertheless, opposition leaders gradually became more combative by
the mid-1990s. They also gained credibility as leaders capable of opposing the

government. In the early 1990s, the UCR had been so badly discredited by its performance in the government and Menem was riding so high on the success of the Convertibility Plan that the Radicals meekly took up a strategy of retaining any influence they could. In 1994, Alfonsín, acting as UCR party leader, made a pact with Menem, in advance of the constitutional assembly, in which they agreed on the amendments to come out of that assembly, including the one that would allow Menem to run for reelection. The end-run around the constitutional assembly was widely criticized, both within and outside the UCR. The effect inside the UCR was to create factions that eventually resulted in new leadership and strategies, but outside the pact further discredited the UCR. The party realized the extent of its decline in reputation when it came in third place in the presidential elections of 1995 with a mere 17 percent of the valid votes.

In the early 1990s, the center-left parties were young. As chapter 6 showed, most people I interviewed, accustomed to many powerless parties on the left of the Argentine party system, did not perceive them as capable of bringing about policy change. The 1994 constitutional assembly elections gave one of these parties, the Frente Grande (precursor to FREPASO), a unique opportunity by which voters could vote their consciences without the risk of electing a third party too weak to govern.[20] The Frente Grande won nearly 13 percent of the vote nationally and 37.5 percent in the Federal Capital. By doing surprisingly well in the unusual electoral circumstance of a constitutional assembly election, the Frente Grande gained credibility, and in the next general elections, when it had evolved into the FREPASO, 28 percent of all voters were willing to risk their vote on the center-left newcomer. Following FREPASO's 1995 success and the UCR's debacle, the two opposition forces formed the Alliance for Work, Justice and Education, running on a single ticket in the 1999 presidential election. The Alianza offered a stronger opposition to the incumbent party than the UCR or Frepaso alone—an option citizens did not have in the first half of the decade. Thus, the new political context offered Argentines more opportunities than earlier in the decade for seeing their personal material interests as resolvable in political ways. The Alianza's presidential candidate, Fernando De la Rúa, was a well known commodity, having been a senator as well as mayor of the city of Buenos Aires. He won the election with over 48 percent of the vote to the Peronist candidate's 38 percent.[21]

In conclusion, Menem's declining popularity in the late 1990s may be explained by conditions that undermined capacities to cope on an individual basis, leading people to begin to link their economic dissatisfactions with their views of the macropolity. It also reflects changes in the economic and political contexts, which changed the ways people evaluated their opportunities in the economy and their alternatives in the political arena.

The Analysis in Comparative Perspective

Through inductive methods, this book constructs a typology of political thinking—of focus—and seeks to explain the conditions under which a linking focus might develop. It is, quite consciously, not a typology of citizens. While some readers may wish to know what portion of Argentines fit each type of thinking, that would be, in certain ways, contrary to the point. We should not expect to find a fixed or predictable proportion of citizens who are macro- , micro- , or linking-focused across time and space precisely because time and space strongly affect interests and coping capacities and thus affect foci. In principle, for a particular moment and set of conditions one could use survey methods to uncover the material hardships, expectations, coping mechanisms, constraints, and foci of a particular population, but existing survey instruments are not designed for this purpose. The goal of this research has been to build the theoretical framework and related concepts necessary to think comprehensively about the relationship between individual-level and societal-level factors that influence the formation of political interests among ordinary people living with material difficulties and yet having diverse interests. With those tools in hand, future researchers could measure the concepts and test their relationships.

In the discussion that follows, I use secondary sources that are largely derived from the public opinion survey approach to doing research on economic voting. Those studies suggest that the analytical framework developed in this book is on track, but again the tools are not designed for a fine-grained examination of how people understand their interests. With further in-depth work of the kind I have done, scholars could explore further both what and how citizens of newer democracies think about their interests.

Before putting the Argentine case in comparative perspective, it should also be emphasized that we cannot generalize on the basis of the *content* of the Argentines' responses to their regime and government. My argument here rests on the fact that the content was determined by the people's particular material problems, their resources and assets for coping with those problems, and the contexts under which the problems were confronted. Therefore it would be contrary to my argument if I were to generalize about the effects of unemployment or inflation or any particular factor. Whether those become political interests depends upon how they are experienced and the opportunities for coping with them in a particular place and time. Since the analytical framework presented here provides a means to account for case-specific conditions, there is no reason to expect that the analysis itself cannot "travel" to explain material-political relationships beyond Argentina. This section begins by putting that analysis to work in Latin America. Then it turns to the very different transition context of Eastern Europe, showing that the book's analysis identifies the appropriate concepts and relationships for understanding findings reported in the literature on grassroots-level political and economic viewpoints in that region.[22]

Comparisons within Latin America

Although there is much diversity on specific policies or particular macro-economic problems, many Latin American countries have faced political and economic conditions relatively similar to those of Argentina in the late twentieth century. While Argentina's debt levels and its experiences with hyperinflation were more extreme than those of the majority of its regional neighbors, it shared many overall challenges in common with them. The 1980s are called a "lost decade" for the region, in which every country but Chile, Colombia, Cuba, and the tiniest countries of the Caribbean experienced a net decline in GDP/capita over the course of the decade (CEPAL 1989, 3). Often provoked by their debt burdens, many countries of the region began with substantial oversight from international financial institutions to restructure their economies. Like Argentina, the goals were to pay foreign debts, promote economic growth, and tame inflation by enacting policies to stabilize the monetary system, limit deficit spending, increase trade, diversify, foster domestic investment, and privatize parastatals. The pace and progress of democratization varied across the region, as did the timing of economic restructuring relative to the democratic transition, but many of the countries experienced the challenge of doing two difficult things at once during the past twenty years.

As Latin American citizens faced these material burdens, they coped using the kinds of mechanisms described in this book: informal sector jobs, more family members working, longer hours, and recourse to no-rent housing, assets, friends, charities, and where they exist, social services. Barrera described the soup kitchens, cooperatives, and community day care centers that the Chilean popular sectors have come to depend on as "a veritable social safety net" where the public one is inadequate (1998, 144). Lustig showed that after Mexico implemented austerity policies in 1982, causing severe declines in real wages, consumption remained above income levels. This was possible because 23 percent of the average household's income came from non-wage sources, both monetary and in-kind (1995, 74–75). In Latin America, informal sector

work has become the normal means to cope, with more than half of all working people informally employed. In the early1990s, 84 percent of new jobs
came from that sector, according to the International Labor Organization
(ECLAC 1998b, 178; also Narayan 2000).

The Peruvian case provides a particularly interesting example of the relationship between coping and politics. When President Alberto Fujimori became
president of Peru in 1990, the country was in severe economic crisis, having
experienced 4-digit annual inflation rates for three years straight, which
peaked at an annual rate of 7649.6 percent in the election year. A study in
Lima showed an astounding 55 percent decline in adjusted per capita consumption levels during the prior five years affecting every income bracket of
society, with a nearly 63 percent decline for the poorest population decile
(Glewwe and Hall 1994, 696–97).

With the major party leaders discredited by corruption scandals at the
highest levels, and the leading party's candidate proposing to solve the problems with painful austerity measures and orthodox restructuring policies,
Fujimori capitalized on the situation. He employed the classic populist tactic
of identifying with the grassroots and against the established power structure.
When he gained power, he lacked a support in the party system so, again
consistent with the literature on populism, he ruled via direct appeals to the
public and sought to legitimate his actions in plebiscitary style with referenda
and opinion polling. He used decrees extensively and appealed to the people's
cultural identities by being photographed wearing traditional ponchos and
hats or dancing at local festivals. He was widely accused of using public
money not to meet human needs efficiently but to gain votes efficiently.[23]

In April 1992, after months of fomenting conflict with members of Congress, Fujimori closed the judicial and legislative branches of government.
Polls showed the public overwhelmingly supported this authoritarian act. He
later manipulated the writing of a new constitution that allowed him to run
for reelection in 1995. His high approval ratings carried him to an easy victory
with 64 percent of the valid vote. (During his second term Fujimori became
increasingly authoritarian, relying on the support of the military as he thwarted
independent action by the judiciary, Congress, and media. He won a third
term in a 2000 election, but most observers thought the victory owed more to
manipulation of the electoral process than citizen support for a regime viewed,
by then, as corrupt and under military control.)

In economic matters, Fujimori took on, in 1990, one of the most troubled
economies of the world and managed to bring it back to stability although not
widespread well-being. Within days of his inauguration, Fujimori implemented a shock treatment program similar to the one his election opponent

had proposed. One of the policies he instituted was the elimination of subsidies on many basic goods, which resulted in soaring food and gasoline prices. However, Fujimori's policies stabilized the monetary system quickly and inflation fell to 139.2 percent in the first year and 10.2 percent in the 1995 election year. The decline continued through the end of the 1990s. With the end of hyperinflation, the real value of wages improved although they remained far below their levels at the start of the 1980s. Unemployment levels rose early in his first term but then remained fairly constant in the mid- and late 1990s, averaging 8.5 percent over the period, although underemployment was also high.[24] By the late 1990s, the economy was in recession, and while inflation remained at record lows, the currency was devalued 15 percent, further diminishing the value of wages (Chauvin 1999).

Menem and Fujimori are frequently compared as examples of neoliberal populists (Roberts 1995; Weyland 1996). The important similarities, as well as crucial differences, between Argentine and Peruvian politics in the 1990s can be identified with the help of the analysis presented here. The critical similarity between the two leaders is not, as frequently claimed, that each used populist tactics. Fujimori fits the populist mold much more than Menem, since the latter relied heavily for his support not on his own appeal but on workers' preexisting identifications with the CGT–loyal labor unions and the Peronist party. Fujimori operated much more in the institutional vacuum that scholars associate with the rise of populism. Also, while Menem was identifed as engaging in a populist leadership style (see chapter 6), the content of his policies, discourse, and political alliances often exhibited an elitism that does not fit well with scholars' conceptualizations of populists (see chapter 1).

More than populism, the key similarities between Menem and Fujimori were the type of problems they solved and the alternatives available in the political system. In their first terms they each won the public's confidence that they could enhance material security better than their opponents. First of all, both alleviated insecurities arising from a particular problem, hyperinflation, which people could not stop simply with individual-level coping strategies. Second, they operated in similar political contexts, in the sense that their predecessors' failures left citizens with little confidence in alternative leaders or policies.[25]

Based on the Argentine case, I have argued in this book that if people vote for a president who brings hyperinflation under control, they do not necessarily vote this way out of a sociotropic sense that what is good for Argentina is good for themselves. These citizens do not vote for an economic manager but instead for individual-level security; they vote for the freedom that comes from not wondering how they will make a paycheck stretch through the month when prices rise daily. In the case of Peru, statistical analyses of public opinion likewise suggest that inflation is not simply one more kind of macroeconomic condition that people think the government should manage but that it is interpreted differently by people in different social classes and separately from other macroeconomic conditions. In a regression analysis of the relationship between presidential approval in Peru and various macroeconomic variables over a thirteen-year period, Carrion (1998, 65–68) found that of the different variables only inflation explained changing approval levels. Stokes's (1996) analysis of support for Fujimori and his policies also examined the particular impact of different types of material conditions (an approach, obviously, endorsed by the argument of this book). She found falling inflation correlated with rising support for both Fujimori and his economic program, yet rising real wages were not associated with rising approval levels. The poorest Limeños seemed to interpret wage increases as a signal of impending inflation since that had been their country's prior experience. In other words, they judged their future interests by present realities, a thought pattern Stokes terms "inter-temporal."

Stokes' research also noted that the popularity of Fujimori's economic policies during his first term was nearly always substantially less among the poor than among the rich. So while on the whole Fujimori gained approval by enhancing material and personal security, and he managed to win reelection easily, observers must interpret that approval and electoral support in context. In neither Peru nor in Argentina were people of low resources particularly enthusiastic about many of Fujimori's or Menem's economic programs, which they perceived to be beneficial to the affluent. They simply were not more enthusiastic about any of the alternative programs and feared a return to hyperinflation.

It should also be noted that the Peruvian public's interest in personal security was not merely economic. A couple months after the self-coup, the Shining Path guerrillas renewed violent attacks on public spaces and private homes. These events played into Fujimori's hand, as his authoritarian style was touted as the necessary means to fight terrorism (McClintock 1993). The broad support for Fujimori from the self-coup until the next election, even as support for his economic plan was falling, suggests that the public's security interests were not merely in monetary stability (Stokes 1997). They also sought protection from another terrifying threat with which they also could not cope at an individual or neighborhood level: guerrilla violence.

Turning now to the regime level, the analysis of democratic legitimation in chapter 7 sheds light on a crucial difference between the Argentine and Peruvian cases. In Argentina, the legitimacy of the democratic regime was a separate issue in people's minds from the effectiveness of the government's policies. The repression under the previous regime had discredited nondemocratic processes as means to other ends. Although Menem's discourse and practice frequently showed a rather reckless disregard for democratic process, he did not disrupt the process as Fujimori did.[26] When Fujimori executed his self-coup, he declared that the people were more interested in "breaking the chain of corruption" by partisans in Congress than in his "breaking with the constitutional order." He said he had no choice but to "defend the majority of the Peruvian people" against the political minority.[27] His gambit was undoubtedly based on his having reason to think the public would agree. A 1991 poll in the capital found that 75 percent preferred democratic regimes but 81 percent said they would be supportive of a "'government that is not elected by the people but that is just and improves the situation'" (Pásara 1993, 28). This suggests a strong majority of Peruvians thought about regime legitimation in terms of its popular and justice base rather than its institutions and rights. The large support found in the poll for a nonelected regime that "improves the situation" shows a blurring of the distinction between the rules and rights of a regime and the effectiveness of a government.

Why was it easier to blur the distinction between regime and government in the Peruvian case rather than in Argentina? Peru's recent experience with authoritarian regimes was exceptionally benign compared to Argentina's. The government of General Velasco took power in 1968 with an agenda of social reform, not of antipopular reaction. They initiated grassroots level projects to address poverty and reform land tenure. While their top-down methods were incompatible with their bottom-up rhetoric, and therefore they did not succeed in creating the legacy of social change they had tried to implement, the generals nevertheless did not leave the legacy of fear that the Argentine military had left (see McClintock 1989, 348–51). Thus, when Fujimori openly argued that the constitutional regime was less important than the security and economic success he could provide if given free rein, Peruvians did not have a historical context for fearing for their personal security. Given the historical, economic, and political contexts in which they lived, hyperinflation and two active guerrilla groups created more palpable fear than authoritarian rule.

Comparisons with Eastern and Central Europe

In Eastern Europe, the historical context—the communist experience—made the link between state and individual abundantly clear. Obviously, people just recently removed from state socialism would not doubt that the state could directly affect how they live. The dramatic posttransition changes in people's daily lives further revealed the micro-macro link. Indeed public opinion and voting studies in Eastern Europe have found evidence of micro-macro linkages in citizens' thinking (cf., Przeworski 1996, 527 n.11; Powers and Cox 1997), although not all citizens took from the communist experience the same lessons about what role the state *ought* to play in their posttransition lives (Miller et. al 1994).

In Eastern Europe, the introduction of market economics, rooted in the idea that prosperity derives from risky dynamic economic relationships, created tremendous insecurity for people accustomed to a context of planning, control, and social security nets. As in Argentina, one of the areas in which insecurity has been most clear is pensions. In Bulgaria, Hungary, and Poland, pensioners were hard-hit by a combination of inflation and fiscal constraints. They are more limited than younger people in their possibilities for supplementing their income or developing new income-generating skills, although some pensioners try to cope by selling crafts or their garden vegetables (Engelbrekt 1992). Because the elderly have more limited coping options, and because a restructured economy only indirectly and over time offers to address their inadequate pensions, senior citizens are more likely to oppose than tolerate current economic hardships. In Bulgaria, the Movement for Protection of Pensioners, Unemployed, and Socially Handicapped Citizens, a group affiliated with traditional communist parties, might well have called itself the Movement of Sectors Least Able to Cope under Capitalism.[28]

Like poor people throughout the world, Eastern Europeans use local-level coping mechanisms to get by, as new work by a team of World Bank researchers makes clear (Narayan 2000). That is, East Europeans depend upon the kinds of coping mechanisms identified in Argentina in chapter 5. As in Argentina, as economic restructuring proceeded the informal sector in Eastern Europe became an important means to deal with joblessness or to supplement insufficient incomes. The New Democracy Barometer survey of people in ten East European countries, taken in late 1992, found only one-third could live on their formal sector wages, but when informal sector work was included, 60 percent could get by without taking on debt or using up savings (Rose 1993, 28).

In addition, East Europeans looked to state welfare programs as a means to cope with the changing economy—and in this case the state as a coping mechanism was much more readily available than in Argentina. The communist experience had created a norm that the state should assure individuals the means to cope. Rather than coping first on their own and then turning to the state when self-help was insufficient, people living under communism had learned to expect the state to assure the basic resources and assets they needed to cope with life, such as health care and education, affordable shelter and food, and a job guaranteeing an income. So East Europeans were accustomed to seeing the state as a starting point for coping, relying on self-help as a fallback measure when the state could not support them adequately. Although this way of thinking reverses the order of subsidiarity I described in chapter 5, the underlying relationship is consistent in all of the cases: historic, economic, and political contexts created coping mechanisms and also created expectations about what degree, kind, and source of coping are normal.[29]

As in Argentina, in Eastern Europe scholars find that citizens base their political views not simply on their reactions to national economic conditions, but also on their considerations of the insecurities they face and the available solutions to ease that insecurity. Repeatedly, the literature shows that historical, political, and economic contexts shape people's perceptions of solutions to their present material insecurities. Denise Powers and James Cox (1997), for example, found that Polish voters' support for communist parties in 1993 was due less to discontent with personal material conditions than with whether voters believed the communist past or the postcommunist reformers were responsible for causing those conditions. Studying the former Soviet Union, Finifter (1996) emphasized that context, not education level, explains different views about who should solve welfare problems. She argued that public opinion about whether the individual or the state is responsible for material welfare is not due to ideology or education level but to the respondent's need for "personal security and survival" (1996, 149). Weyland (1998a, 1998b) used prospect theory to argue that citizens accept the risks of drastic reforms by unknown leaders because of their inability to cope with present hyperinflation.

The Polish case demonstrates how any relationship between material conditions and political views depends on the particular types of material interests and means of coping with them as interpreted in a particular economic, historical, and political context. In Poland, the first democratically elected government after the transition quickly implemented a shock treatment intended to bring down soaring inflation. Johnson and Kowalska (1994) and Przeworski (1996) argue that this shock was initially tolerated because the public understood it as the necessary cure for inflation. Additionally, public hope for success from the shock therapy was high because the new team of technocrats, strongly supported by international actors, was perceived as well prepared to tackle macroeconomic problems. This was particularly so because the less radical reforms implemented at the end of the communist regime had proven ineffective (Johnson and Kowalska 1994, esp. 194 and 199–200). Thus, the difficulties of coping with high inflation led to a demand for a solution, and the domestic and international contexts shaped Poles' expectations that the solution would require austerity. Even when the shock treatment did not quickly bring down inflation, Przeworski uses survey data to argue, Poles were tolerant of the policies. Their expectations of what alternatives existed had been shaped by the political and historical contexts. Policy makers had warned citizens that past errors had created the inflation and that the shock treatment could not remedy the problem overnight. Consequently, when inflation did not indeed fall rapidly, Przeworski argues, the public "exonerated" the new government. They interpreted the high inflation as an indication that the tough remedies were still needed (1996, 540).

In contrast, Przeworski found that the Polish public used different standards when assessing other material conditions, such as unemployment. As elsewhere in Eastern Europe, where the communist state had assured every person a job in Poland, the prospect of unemployment was terrifying even when the incidence was not high by European standards (1996, 534–35; also Kohl 1995, 110). Przeworski found that negative opinions of the government's economic policies were most strongly associated with unemployment growth. Furthermore, reaction to unemployment was not limited to the unemployed— in other words, people were not merely responding to their own, *current* circumstances. Rather, he argued, the public's fear of unemployment occurred in the context of market reforms that created new possibilities that one might lose one's job and in a historical context in which people, under communism, expected that access to the social safety net came through their place of employment. After the transition, the government's unemployment compensation program was neither broad nor deep enough to assure the jobless any means to cope with the new economy. This created insecurity even for those who were not jobless at the time (1996, 534–41). In other words, given the full employment policies under communism, even low levels of unemployment constituted a situation of great insecurity, one that was exacerbated by undeveloped public or private coping capacities. Przeworski's findings in Poland, then, are wholly consistent with the argument in this book that the expectations and coping capacity associated with particular kinds of material conditions determine actual and perceived insecurities, which in turn affect whether people link microlevel conditions with their evaluation of macrolevel policy.

On the question of whether harsh economic conditions undermine support for the democratic regime, the Eastern European situation was complicated by the fact that the transitions to democracy and capitalism occurred at the same time and therefore became conflated in most citizens' minds. Thus, researchers anticipated that citizens would not distinguish the new governments and their austerity policies from the democratic regime. They found, however, results compatible with those I found in Argentina. Using surveys conducted in eight countries of Eastern Europe, Evans and Whitefield (1995, 501–2) found that commitments to democracy were based significantly more on democracy's political benefits than its economic achievements. Just as most Argentines examined democracy on the basis of their memory of its antithesis rather than on the basis of their pocketbooks, so too did most East Europeans. Using a five-country survey, Rose and Mishler (1994, 170–72) found that 80 percent of those surveyed evaluated the democratic and communist regimes in opposite ways, favoring one and opposing the other (rather than being skeptical about or accepting of both). The strongest support for the democratic regimes was found in Bulgaria and Romania, where authoritarianism had been "most intense and extreme."

Studies of Eastern Europe, whose economic and political situations were substantially different from Argentina's, identify the same factors of coping and context that I have identified in this book. East Europeans, like Argentines interviewed for this book, see material interests first in terms of security and opportunity, not quantity. Their feelings of security and opportunity are augmented or undermined by the specific objective resources and assets available for coping with a specific material problem. Objective capacities to cope are shaped in part from context (e.g., whether there has been time to develop the coping measures). Perceptions about capacity to cope and about the capacity of the state or particular political actors to improve capacity to cope derive in part from expectations rooted in national-level contexts of history and politics.

Democracy and Citizenship

Material Expectations of the Regime

The introduction to this book raised the question of whether material satisfaction is a prerequisite to regime stability. One side in this scholarly debate argues that most people do not judge the worth of a democracy by its material output. The evidence in chapter 7 supports this position. Most Argentines did not reject the democracy for its failure to live up to Alfonsín's promise to feed and school them. Why not? In Argentina, the experience with nondemocratic regimes taught a society-wide lesson in the value of accountability and civil and political rights. Yet while most Argentines I interviewed did not confuse the democratic process with the policy record of elected governments, they were nevertheless not absolute idealists. They balanced their respect for the freedoms and processes of democracy with their expectation that governments are responsible for assuring a prosperous economy. In this balancing act, most of those interviewed rejected regime change, but many accepted some limitations on liberal democratic process for the sake of material outcomes. That is, the existence of democracy does not appear threatened by material conditions because political and historical contexts have created a situation in Argentina in which democracy is understood as a regime based on liberal processes. The quality of that democracy, however, is undermined by material conditions to the extent that citizens are willing to tolerate some divergence from ideal democratic process for the sake of effective economic management.

Coping and Citizenship

The conclusions of this research raise questions about the quality of democracy in a second way. On the one hand, the conclusions suggest that most people do not react to political situations (whether governments or regimes) in a knee-jerk way based on their own material interests. Rather, they more often showed a macrofocus. Under certain conditions, this focus benefits democracy. A macrofocus is a sign that a person sees him- or herself as part of a larger community (class or nation) and recognizes that a democratic government exists to serve the many interests in that larger community beyond the individual. The fact that many people interviewed expressed their political interests in terms of concerns about social justice, honesty in government, national pride, and the needs of those worse off than themselves indicates that they did not have the narrowly self-serving viewpoint that economistic approaches presume.

On the other hand, where objective links exist between the quality of an individual's life and the policies of the government and government is not held accountable for that impact on its citizens, then the quality of the democracy is weak.[30] That is why social movements seek to teach participants to recognize and focus upon micro-macro links. The micro-macro focus is a means to claim their citizenship and exercise their citizenship rights.

Those objective links exist everywhere. Although in some societies the state has a larger and a more overt impact on individuals' lives than others, in both advanced economies and developing ones the state's actions and inactions shape the conditions under which workers, consumers, employers, renters, pensioners, savers, parents, and students live and work. People are particularly unlikely to notice the micro-macro link when they are beneficiaries of the state's policies and those policies are not in jeopardy. Middle-class Americans, for example, tend to see their comfortable homes as solely the products of their own efforts, ignoring the substantial housing assistance the state provides in the form of tax deductions for mortgages. They see their degrees and the corresponding incomes as rewards for hard work, forgetting the state's contributions in subsidizing their university, giving them student loans, etc. Whether in Argentina, the United States, or the poorest country of the world, people who are living comfortably and whose interests are routinely protected by governments can afford to be sociotropic, ignoring the state's influence over their lives until the rare occasions when it threatens to turn negative. Conversely, people who are living with substantial material constraints shortchange themselves as citizens if they do not recognize the impact of public policies on their own lives.

My point is not that poorer people should engage in single-issue voting or ignore broad macrolevel issues in favor of solving their personal problems. It is beneficial to democracy that citizens weigh their concerns about how the state affects them with their concerns about effects upon others in society as well as concerns about justice, nationhood, a clean environment, or other general values. Nor should the state be held accountable for addressing every material interest. Government, and particularly the national government, is often not the most effective level at which to solve problems or the easiest level at which citizens can exercise real input. Life experiences teach people that lesson, which is one reason they have low expectations of what government might be able to accomplish. Moreover, the political process takes time and patience; it is reasonable that people would look to solve their problems not through political measures but through private and local solutions found more readily at hand. So linking is not absolutely the best or most democratic strategy.

The quality of democracy, therefore, depends not on the extent to which people perceive linkages between their own concerns and those of the state, but rather on the *reasons* why people in a particular society do not link their material and political interests. If they do not recognize a linkage because objectively there is none (e.g., their low income is due to a job loss after a fight with the boss), or because the link has proved beneficial (i.e., the state has anticipated citizens' needs and responded to them with long-term solutions, such as with mortgage deductions), then the quality of citizenship is not at risk. Also, if citizens *choose* to look locally for solutions or choose to prioritize general values over personal ones, this is different than if they do so because they are unable to envision the state doing anything to improve the constraints and stresses of their individual lives. On the other hand, if the presence of adequate coping mechanisms leaves people less inclined to expect action by the state, then the disheartening conclusion one can draw from this research is that, given propitious contexts, elected governments *can* get away with ignoring deep structural problems and great inequities as long as they pacify citizens with palliatives that enable them to cope without too much distress.

The dominant economic and social policies in Latin America through the 1990s focused the state's attention on assuring that, first and foremost, investors perceived a positive link between *their* conditions and the state's policies. The capacity of the state was undermined by fiscal constraints and delegitimized in many cases by charges of corruption. Hamstrung by tight fiscal conditions and focused on maintaining a positive investment climate, governments "targeted" social spending to those with the fewest coping resources. Everyone else was left to seek local-level and private solutions to their material interests. The economic rationale for targeting is its efficiency in matching limited resources with direst needs. The political rationale is preventing public opposition to economic reforms. By helping indigent citizens to cope, the state tries to undermine the potential that those citizens would turn their material interests into political causes.[31]

In light of the arguments of this book, the trend toward a narrower role for government in addressing material needs poses two final issues concerning the emerging quality of democracy. First, it remains an open question whether (and if so, how) local and private institutions, plus the engine of the market, will provide all citizens not merely with the capacities to cope, but with the means to participate fully in the normal life of their society. Heated controversy in the streets (from southern Mexico to southern Argentina and from Seattle to Washington) and much academic research have broached these questions. Much more debate will occur before any consensus develops.

Second, as governments urge all but the very poorest citizens to look elsewhere to meet their private material interests, the state, in effect, tells citizens not to be micro-macro linkers. It sends the message that it cannot or will not help most people to cope with most types of material interests. The risk in such a message is that as states reduce their functions, ordinary citizens may gradually lower their expectations about the state's capacity to meet *any* of their interests, private or macrolevel. Of course, a lean state that promotes self-reliance, decentralized power, and fiscal prudence is salutary, but caution is warranted about unintended side effects. If ordinary citizens do not see the state as a means to address either their own needs or their broader concerns for their society, they have little reason to be engaged in civic life.[32] If they disengage (becoming microfocused), then they cannot hold their elected officials accountable effectively—a point not lost on politicians. If nonelites expect little from the state, political elites inside and outside the government have more room to maneuver for their private benefits. Politicians become free to compete for office with little effort to serve the broad interests of citizens.

These final thoughts on the quality of democracy are preliminary. The fears for the quality of citizenship in an age of globalization are many—but so too are the hopes. One of the striking findings in my interviews was just how hopeful most people were about their own capacities to find ways to meet challenges. Certainly there is hope that societies have similar capacities. My own hope for this book is that by "listening" to people at the grassroots, as they thought aloud about the constraints and insecurities in their lives, their expectations for improving those conditions, and their views about the political community in which they live, readers have perhaps thought in a new way about how ordinary citizens picture politics.

Appendix 1

Methodology

Whether by coincidence or harmony with the rest of this book, the appendix includes both a micro- and a macrofocus. It begins with the mechanics of how I carried out my fieldwork and then turns to a discussion of the broader issue of qualitative interviewing as a methodology. I hope it proves useful not only to understanding this project but also to those contemplating carrying out qualitative research of their own.

The Research Design

This book is based on in-depth conversations I had with forty-one people in Buenos Aires. Those interviews are interpreted against a background of fieldwork that included over seventy interviews with neighborhood, intellectual, and political elites (typically an hour or more in duration), eighteen preliminary short interviews in a public housing complex and a nearby neighborhood, which helped me better understand socioeconomic conditions, and months of participant observation at meetings of political, civic, and charity organizations. The reasons that Argentina suited the questions of this study were outlined in chapter 2. Here, I take up the question of whether the Argentine case is a reasonable basis upon which to draw general conclusions about political interest formation. I then examine how the interviews were set up and conducted.

There are no "typical" countries; however, one would not wish to choose a case for study that is an outlier on the particular issues under study. Since materialist and nonmaterialist responses to politics are at the core of this book, the World Values Surveys on those two dimensions can give us some idea of whether Argentina was an outlier. On the dimension of survival values versus well-being values (essentially materialism versus postmaterialism), Argentina was just about at ground zero in Inglehart's factor analysis of these values for all countries studied. That is, Argentines surveyed in 1990 displayed materialist and nonmaterialist values about equally. This suggests that Argentina is not culturally predisposed toward either materialism or postmaterialism. Therefore, since the population did not—relative to other populations in the world—lean one way or the other, it was a good setting in which to investigate to what extent people reacted to their government and regime on the basis of their material conditions and on the basis of other nonmaterial considerations such as human rights and democratic practice (Inglehart, Basañez, and Moreno 1998, 15, citing Inglehart 1997).

Having chosen the country for study, I then set about identifying appropriate people to interview. Overall my approach was strongly influenced by the research of Lane (1962) and Hochschild (1981). Their specific techniques for identifying interviews, however, which had worked for them in the United States, were not applicable in my research setting. In Argentina, voter registration lists were not available and the postal and telephone systems were not reliable or were not accessible to many of the people targeted for interviews. Furthermore, Argentines do not typically welcome a stranger into their homes on the basis of a letter addressed to them after randomly choosing their name from a voting list. Contacts were crucial—and I spent substantial field time building up these contacts, arranging interviews, and hoping the person showed up for the appointment.

The primary means used to identify suitable subjects was geographic. I focused on the old established central city area of southern Buenos Aires, where I could come to know Argentine life and meet people in the places they lived, worked, and did politics. I lived in the neighborhood of San Telmo during fieldwork in the austral winter of 1990 and in the adjacent neighborhood of Montserrat from October 1991 through June 1992. My goal was not to study neighborhoods; rather, because of the area's characteristics, it was a logical place for locating people who were poor or who had recently experienced economic decline. This is a socioeconomically diverse area; San Telmo has pockets of greater poverty and areas of greater wealth than Montserrat. This area of Buenos Aires has only a handful of shanties hidden beneath bridges or on abandoned lots, but it also has many tenement houses, single-room occupancy "hotels," and abandoned buildings occupied by squatters (MOI 1992). The poorest people interviewed lived in those circumstances. Surrounding these residences are multistory apartment buildings, which are home to people from the downwardly mobile middle class and stagnant working class, who typically lived in small apartments that they purchased years before. The main streets are lined with stationery or home supplies shops, fruit vendors and bakeries, pizzerias and kiosks, and other small merchants.

From this geographic base, I observed daily life and got to know neighbors, local political party organizers, neighborhood civic and social activists, and charity workers. Using these sources as contacts, I identified people to interview. Existing Argentine sociological literature described the living conditions, education levels, and employment situations of the poor and "new poor," who had suffered under Argentina's economic changes (INDEC 1990). Armed with this empirical profile, I asked contacts if they knew of someone who fit it—unemployed, in an unskilled job, on a pension, laid off due to privatizations, etc. (A few interview subjects were identified without regard for geographic base on the basis of this socioeconomic profile.) I told my contacts that I was interested in talking with people who were having a difficult time economically and that my goal was to understand how ordinary Argentines dealt with economic difficulties and what they thought about politics regardless of their level of political involvement. In Montserrat, the offices of the then-secretariat of public works provided a ready means to meet people strongly affected by policies to restructure the state.

To construct a diverse sample and avoid the danger of any neighborhood patrons diverting the study to the sorts of views or people they considered interesting, I made the most varied contacts possible. No more than five interviews derived from any single source. This research design assured I received a set of interviews with people from diverse party sympathies, political activism levels, occupations, residential and family statuses, and ages. (See appendices 2 and 3.) The set is evenly divided by gender.

All of those interviewed were permanent residents of Argentina but four retained citizenship in the neighboring country where they were born. Two of these had been active in partisan or political affairs in Buenos Aires. The views of these disenfranchised members of Argentine society about their material interests and about the impact of government decisions upon their lives did not disappear or become meaningless simply because they did not have the right to vote in national elections. In a free society, they were able to express themselves politically through conversation and activism regardless of their passport. Therefore, I kept these interviews in the sample and I have used the word "citizen" rather loosely in this book to refer to any resident living in the community under democratic rule in Argentina.

All of the interviews were in-depth conversations I conducted in Spanish with the participants. Interviews were guided by a lengthy schedule of open-ended questions about political actors and events, economic conditions, and democracy. The questions were designed to gather data on the effects of national economic conditions at the individual level, to identify factors that might shape the person's political ideas (lifestyle, background, and demographic characteristics), to learn what those political ideas were, and to learn what reasoning, knowledge, and history people used to think about their politcal and economic experiences. I consulted several studies, including Hochschild

(1981), Lane (1962), Nun (1989), and Catterberg (1989), for question ideas. The question schedule was a starting point. A strong reason for choosing in-depth conversational interviewing is that the relaxed environment encourages the informant to speak candidly and fully, unencumbered by the interviewer's presuppositions about what topics are important or interrelated. Therefore, creating the rapport through which such conversation can take place was a priority over covering every item of interest, particularly given that people var-ied in talkativeness, political knowledge, and free time. Perceptions of the boundaries of privacy also varied among interviewees, as did sensitivities about monetary or educational accomplishments. This explains why some results re-ported in the book have fewer than forty-one respondents (cf., Oxhorn 1995, 337–41). My goal was always to preserve a comfortable interview atmosphere in order to solicit the most open and profound discourse.

The text describes the life circumstances of particular individuals inter-viewed and quotes them at length. The goal is two-fold: first, to give a full fla-vor of popular political discourse and allow the voices of those interviewed to speak directly to the reader; secondly, to help document for the reader the bases upon which I drew conclusions about the respondents' political ideas. Sometimes a response may seem to skip from one idea to another. Some lack of clarity is to be expected when people are asked to speak in more detail about their political views than they might usually do. Interviews are not grad-uate-level oral exams or forensics exercises, in which people are held account-able for non sequiturs or for failure to completely address the question asked. My goal was to understand views as the person interviewed wanted to explain them, not as I would do so.

The average interview involved nearly two and a half hours of project-re-lated conversation (almost always preceded and followed by social conversa-tion). The longest one totaled nine hours over several visits. In about one quarter of the cases, our conversations took place over two or three visits. In-terviews usually took place in the person's home, but they occasionally oc-curred at work or in a café. At every step of the process—in arranging the interview, explaining its purpose and ground rules, introducing and wording the questions, and listening to answers—I was careful to avoid biasing, steer-ing, intimidating, or abbreviating the individual's answers.

All first names which appear in the text without surnames are pseudo-nyms, whether used to denote the person interviewed or a family member or acquaintance. All of the forty-one nonelites interviewed were assured of confi-dentiality and were advised that our mutual acquaintance would not be in-formed of their views. Many of the forty-one interviewees volunteered that they would be happy to be quoted by name in my book, but in accordance with professional norms I have treated all interviews with nonelites as equally confidential. In about one quarter of the cases, and only when the changes were inconsequential, I have also changed minor personal details, such as their real occupations, number of children, or place of birth, substituting a sociologically equivalent value in order to assure that certain individuals could not be positively identified by knowledgeable neighborhood folks.

I have used actual names for organizations, neighborhoods, and places. My fieldwork included a great deal of elite-level interviewing. Where anyone is quoted or cited by first and last name, of course, those are actual names.

In about three of four initial interviews, I was able to use a small, inconspicuous recorder—always with permission. Otherwise, I took copious notes, both during and immediately after the interview. Even while taping, I typically took notes too. I discovered notetaking provided an important safeguard if background noise made the tape difficult to decipher. Notetaking also enables the researcher to record a smile, smirk, hand motion, or other information not conveyed by words on a tape.

Qualitative Methods

The goal of qualitative research is to deepen understanding so as to build hypotheses and construct frameworks for further analysis. By giving people time to flush out their thoughts and to link ideas, qualitative interviews offer a means to uncover how people reason about their material situations and their government. The literature using qualitative interviews to explore political thinking at the nonelite level includes works by Lane (1962), Hochschild (1981), Porter (1983), Passerini (1987), Patai (1988), and Oxhorn (1995).

Qualitative interviews in the context of fieldwork always serve a dual role as means to collect information about the "field" or the context being studied and as means to collect data for analysis. Some research designs emphasize one role or the other. For example, my interviews with neighborhood organizers and party elites were primarily for the purpose of collecting background information. That is, I was not studying the organizer and his or her views per se but simply trying to understand more about the organization or party itself and its activities. Other qualitative research uses interviews primarily as the means to collect data about how people think, as I did with the interviews with nonelites that are the foundation of this study. Regardless of the main purpose served by the interview, qualitative interviewing provides access to the other purpose. The duality is not avoidable and is part of the richness of the technique. While interviewing people about housing, I learned not only how they thought about their housing problems but also how they lived with those problems. That is, I gained *data* about their views as well as *information* about the empirical conditions that underlay their views. In addition, the physical presence in the field—in a person's kitchen, shopping in their neighborhood, attending meetings of a neighborhood association—allows the qualitative researcher to observe directly the physical and social conditions in which people live and work.

Even when specifically told (as my interviewees were) that the purpose of my study was to collect data about their views, the conversations nevertheless at times involved the interviewee explaining empirical realities as the person understood them. Particularly when the interviewer is from outside the interviewee's milieu, people may see themselves as presenting factual information about how things work. This information may be useful to the researcher in its own right since it makes a researcher aware of political events and processes for further investigation, but it also constitutes data about the way people understand their world. The interviewees' descriptions of reality reveal their understanding of causality. Furthermore, "empirical" statements also constitute data, for the information a person believes is worthwhile for the researcher to know is an indication of the person's values and priorities. Foreign researchers can be advantaged here because they have the luxury of being able to ask deliberately naive questions that a local could not credibly ask in order to hear how the person explains some political or economic reality.

Drawing conclusions from qualitative interviewing entails judgment calls by the researcher—interpretation, as Geertz (1973) put it. Accurate analysis requires a constant awareness of the context and manner in which the interviewee made a particular point. In this case, I reviewed the contents of the interviews countless times, first identifying themes and points of variation, and then coding and categorizing interviews along several dozen dimensions so they could be examined systematically. Particular statements were examined in the context of the whole interview, before I drew any conclusions about how to categorize a particular person's focus or beliefs. The benefit of a method that necessitates some discretion is that it also offers opportunities for insight that only exist because an active listener, rather than a passive form-filler, is recording a person's views. For example, the researcher can hear the influence of elite-level discourse and behavior in the mass-level political conversations. The interview method is particularly suited for uncovering fundamental values and logics in popular discourse because as people talk and explain themselves, *they* identify their primary concerns. They reveal what makes them angry, what they respect, and what is of minor concern to them. They demonstrate the causal connections they perceive between politics and economics and between politics and themselves.

As with survey research, in-depth interviews put people on the spot. They may feel that they should sound intelligent and to do so may rely on information they have heard recently in the news—the "top-of-their-head answer," as Zaller (1992) put it. Qualitative interviewing, however, can minimize these problems because it gives a person a chance to talk through their top-of-the-head responses. Sometimes the interviewee will offer an immediate response to a question yet reveal a contrasting perspective as she or he talks about the issue. Upon hearing contradictory positions expressed, the qualitative interviewer can ask the person to explain, clarify, or justify the apparent contradiction. In the process, the researcher gathers more data about how the person puts ideas together, what he or she values, and how he or she understands and evaluates the empirical world.

A qualitative interview carried out with a sense of leisure and informality offers the great benefit of time—time through which people can ponder, explain, clarify, and emphasize what is really on their minds. With qualitative interviewing, the researcher is also able to tell from the response whether the question was understood as intended, whether the conviction is strong or tentative, and whether the person thinks the issue is important and interesting. In short, qualitative interviewing can get past *what* people thought at a particular moment in time to find out *how* they thought—that is, the linkages they made between interests, and the role of personal values, identities, and contexts in the development of ideas.

Of course, views about the world are not constant. If a mind is open at all, it is subject to change when confronted with new information, ideas, situations, or arguments. However, the qualitative interview technique, because of its priority for depth, makes it more likely that the views the interviewee expresses constitute expressions of conviction rather than convenience. In almost every case where I interviewed the person on more than one occasion, I found the person expressed very similar interests from one meeting to the next. Moreover, returning to the field three years after the initial interviews, I again found the same consistency. While there were some shifts in interpretation in response to changing realities (as support for or opposition to Menem grew weaker over the three years), I did not find that people shifted dramatically in their worldviews or ways of discussing politics. In the case of Juan Antonio, a comparison of interview notes shows he described his material interests using the very same example from his sons' poor opportunities, and in some of the same words, in interviews held more than three years apart. Clearly the example had not been used at the first interview simply because it was top-of-the-head.

Qualitative method uncovers the logic and concerns that underlie thinking. If the people interviewed are outliers, then that logic and those concerns should not prove useful in understanding the larger picture and the rest of the interviews. Conversely, if the insights that emerge from one or more interviews help to interpret many interviews and help provide a logical explanation of how political interests are formulated in Argentina and in other parts of the world, then indeed there is much to learn from investigating deeply why a few people talk about their interests as they do.

Demographic Profile of Persons Interviewed

ALIAS	AGE					HOUSING	OCCUPATION/VOCATION
	<30	30-39	40-49	50-60	>60		
Adriana			•			Irregular, room	Domestic/Janitorial
Amanda			•			Inquilinato	Janitor
Andrés				•		Homeless, residing with friend	Mostly unemployed/trained computer technician
Atilio					•	Inquilinato	Pensioner (due to disability)
Betina	•					Apartment	Domestic worker
Carlos		•				Irregular, room	Garment worker
Cecilia		•				Casa tomada	Domestic worker
Claudia			•			Own apartment	Housewife
Diego		•				Shantytown	Community organizer
Esperanza				•		Shantytown	Community organizer
Eduardo				•		Casa tomada	Odd jobs (ex-laborer)
Francesca		•				Casa tomada	Domestic worker
Gabriela			•			Rental apartment	Political aide/patronage
Graciela	•					Rental apartment	Data processor
Gregorio		•				Inquilinato	Unemployed electrical technician
Hilda	•					Hotel	Housewife (ex-domestic worker)
Horacio		•				Own house	Maintenance worker
Ignacio	•					Shantytown	Student
Jorge		•				Casa tomada	Pipefitter
Juan Antonio		•				Shantytown	Maintenance worker
Julio			•			Hotel—temporary	Construction worker
Leonardo		•				Hotel	Factory worker
Marcela	•					Own house	Secretary
María			•			Own apartment with relative	Sales manager
María José					•	Own apartment with relative	Clerical worker
Martín				•		Casa tomada	Landscaper
Matilde				•		Own house	Microenterprise/crafts
Mónica					•	Rents room at retirement home	Retired (public administrator)
Nena				•		Own apartment	Clerk, public sector
Olivia				•		Own apartment	Bookkeeper (laid off)
Oscar			•			Own house	Maintenance worker
Pablo		•				Rental apartment	Bank clerk
Paula					•	Hotel	Shows apartments for realtor
Rafael			•			Own apartment	Cab driver (owner)
Ricardo					•	Own apartment	Pensioner and cashier
Samuel	•					Irregular title	Student/Electrician
Sara		•				Hotel	Clerk for large corporation
Soña			•			Own house	Artisan
Tomás					•	Own apartment	Pensioner (ex-accountant)
Vicente				•		Casa tomada	Skilled construction worker
Walter		•				Inquilinato	Grocery employee
Totals	6	12	9	8	6		

Political Profile of Persons Interviewed

ALIAS	PARTISANSHIP/IDEOLOGY		POLITICAL EXPERIENCE?		
	Strong	Leans toward	Yes, in party	Yes, other	Not significant
Adriana		UCR	Y		
Amanda	Peronism				N
Andrés		Socialism			N
Atilio		Left			N
Betina		Peronism			N
Carlos	Socialism		Y		
Cecilia					N
Claudia	MODIN		Y		
Diego	Left			Y	
Esperanza	Peronism		Y		
Eduardo	Peronism		Y		
Francesca		Peronism/Left	Y		
Gabriela	Peronism		Y		
Graciela		Peronism		Y	
Gregorio	Left			Y	
Hilda		UCR			N
Horacio	Peronism			Y	
Ignacio	Left		Y		
Jorge				Y	
Juan Antonio		Left			N
Julio	MAS (Left)				N
Leonardo		UCR			N
Marcela		Peronism			N
María	MODIN		Y		
María José		MODIN			N
Martín	Peronism		Y		
Matilde		Peronism			N
Mónica	UCR		Y		
Nena		none		Y	
Olivia	UCR		Y		
Oscar		none		Y	
Pablo		Peronism			N
Paula	UCR		Y		
Rafael	UCR				N
Ricardo	UCR		Y		
Samuel		Left			N
Sara		none			N
Soña			Y		
Tomás		Socialism			N
Vicente	UCR		Y		
Walter		Peronism			N
Totals			16	7	18
Peronism	6	7			
Radicals (UCR)	6	3			
Left	5	6			
MODIN	2	1			
None		3			

Notes

Introduction

1. Gallup Argentina, "Estudios de opinión pública," October 1994, cited in Díaz (1995, 91).

2. Since many interviews were carried out in the person's home, privacy was not always possible. The forty-one count does not include a few spouses or other individuals whose views are occasionally discussed in this book and who participated in the conversations.

3. A significant recent exception is Dietz (1998).

4. On consumers, see Perlman (1976, 153–60); on politicians considering the public's reaction to policies, see Goldrich, Pratt, and Schuller (1967, 16).

5. Some key sources in this literature include Cornelius (1974); Goldrich, Pratt, and Schuller (1967–1968); Perlman (1976); Piven and Cloward (1977); Portes (1972); Scott (1976, 1985) and Sharpe (1977).

6. The relationships between either inequality and democratic survival or economic performance and democratic survival have been examined in numerous cross-national quantitative studies but with differing results (cf. Bollen and Jackman 1985, 1995; Gasiorowski 1995; Muller and Seligson 1987; Muller 1995a, 1995b; Przeworski et al. 1996 and Wang et al. 1993). Because of their level of analysis (as well as the problems of measuring and comparing situations of growing inequality), these studies tend to augment but cannot test speculations in the literature about how citizens at the grassroots might react to particular performance or inequality conditions. Unlike the present book, studies comparing macroeconomic conditions and regime stability are not designed to reveal the political processes or political thinking through which either growth or declining inequality would or would not affect democracy.

7. The Latinobarómetro survey of seventeen countries is discussed in Lagos (1997). In all countries but Honduras, 50 percent or more of respondents agreed with the statement "Democracy is preferable to any other kind of government."

Chapter I. Political Views at the Grassroots

1. A more detailed account of Jorge's work and views is found in Chapter 3.

2. The distinction between resolvable "problems" and "malaises" comes from Sharpe (1977, 118–29).

3. My thinking about the dichotomy between micro- and macrolevel politics was clearly influenced by O'Donnell (1983), although I employ the dichotomy for a different purpose here than O'Donnell did.

4. In other words, this definition is, for all practical purposes, limited by instrumental evaluations of feasibility and priorities, and therefore is close to Easton's (1965, 45–47) conception of "subjective interests."

5. For a review of the objective and subjective approaches to defining interests, see Cohen (1989, 51–54). Cohen's research purpose and mine differ. He chooses to use a subjective definition of interest yet one that allows for the objective judgment that people have mistaken the appropriate means to their subjective ends. Here my purpose is not to judge the efficacy of citizens' political judgments but rather to analyze the formation of them.

6. Of course, correlations might be analyzed to find associations between what is on people's minds and their education, media exposure, employment status, or other objective factors that might be causal, but the causality is determined by the researcher, not revealed by the respondent.

7. Those causes are multiple, however; therefore, saying that there are observable causes that tend to engender certain perceptions of interests is quite different from saying that interests themselves are objective and inherent in, say, a particular class position.

8. A word of caution: like all analogies, this one is imperfect and is not intended as an analytical tool to be stretched out in all its implications; it is meant as a handy metaphor to summarize simply the major arguments.

9. The public opinion literature derives from study of the United States and Western Europe, but is a literature increasingly cited in study of the developing world as elections become widespread there. The other two literatures have strong roots in scholarship on Latin America.

10. It should be emphasized that the purpose here is to examine how these literatures conceptualize and explain material and political interests—*not* what they say about the political behaviors that follow. The scope of this project does not include a comprehensive review of these literatures. I focus only on those points that shed light on grassroots-level political thinking.

11. I thank Jeff Mondak for several personal conversations that have helped shape my understanding of this literature. Of course, he is not responsible for my assessment of it.

12. Even if personal and national material conditions are judged to be overlapping, the literature tends to assume that the basis of the voter's political evaluation remains sociotropic. That is, it assumes the voter relies on information gleaned from observing how the government manages the economy overall, rather than information from personal experiences. The assumption, following Weatherford (1983, 161), is that the "rational voter [is] attempting to arrive at a summary judgment of the quality of incumbent economic management. . . ." Thus the very research design sets aside the broader question of whether and how citizens hold governments accountable for governing *on their behalf.*

13. Recently public opinion scholarship has moved toward studying subnational sociotropic judgments—that is, the group, neighborhood, or class-level observations that give people information about government performance (Conover 1985; Mondak, Mutz, and Huckfeldt 1996; Mutz and Mondak 1997). The focus is still on information sources, which I find problematic for the reasons noted below, but the effect may be to uncover some of citizens' subnational and noneconomic interests, that is, the variety of things that citizens might wish to have taken care of on their behalf.

14. For review of this point in the literature, see Mutz (1998, 108).

15. Consider this example talking about group-level sociotropic judgments: "Presumably *information* about the interests of salient groups will have more personal relevance for an individual than assessments of national well-being" (Conover 1985, 140, emphasis added).

16. *Interests* might be reduced to *information* if *information* were conceived so broadly as to render it meaningless for explanatory purposes (e.g., if "information" included everything

one has heard, experienced, or learned that might engender wants, stress, insecurity, joy, opinions, values, pleasure, or complaints, whether obtained from media, school, daily living, historical experience, others' accounts, etc.). Thankfully, the concept in the literature is not conceived so broadly.

17. For reports of two (controversial) studies showing growth in income inequality, see L. Kim Tan, "U.S. Income Gap Widens; Advocates: Tax Rules Hurt Wage-Earners." *The Boston Herald* (January 19, 2000), 7.

18. A point made to me by Jeffrey Mondak in a personal conversation.

19. This is true of all societies, regardless of development level, although certainly the state may have a larger impact in some societies than others.

20. Thus, the potential role for the media and other political actors is not merely to disseminate accurate *information* about "others' experiences," which individuals might connect to their own experience (the "Tocquevillian" thesis, Mutz [1998, 147ff] takes up), but also to explain the complex policies and decisions that cause those experiences.

21. For a contrasting view that eschews the role of organization and focuses instead on the structural conditions that facilitate or obstruct popular mobilization, see Piven and Cloward (1977, 18–37).

22. While Mutz (1992) and Mutz (1994) reach different conclusions about whether the media encourages sociotropism or politicizes pocketbooks, respectively, both articles suggest media exposure as a causal variable to explain sociotropic or pocketbook thinking.

23. Interestingly, public opinion scholar Stanley Feldman (1985, 155) also recognized that sociotropism is a political position not a logical one when he observed that sociotropic thinking reflects norms about self-sufficiency and individualism.

24. Occasionally the populism literature deals, in certain ways, with expectations, which are shown in figure 1.1 on the lower left side (Madsen and Snow 1991; Weyland 1998b), but it ignores the middle of the process altogether.

25. For helpful overviews of the populism literature as well as efforts to refine the conceptualization of the term *populism* in light of the vast and sometimes contradictory approaches in the literature, see Roberts (1995) and Weyland (1999). Important earlier collected works include Conniff (1982); Ionescu and Gellner (1969) (see especially the chapter by Wiles); and Weffort and Quijano (1976).

26. There are some exceptions. Oxhorn (1994) stresses that populism occurs where popular collective identity is weak. Madsen and Snow (1991) use the political psychology literature (rather than the populist literature) to examine citizen responses to a populist's charisma. De la Torre (1999) focuses on symbolic means for "seducing" the popular sectors in order to construct an identification as one of them in opposition to elites. Di Tella (1965) wrote of unfulfilled expectations at the base, which arose owing to the "demonstration effects" brought on by media coverage of more affluent countries. Ianni (1975, 48) is a partial exception. He deplores the earlier literature's depiction of a docile, manipulated mass and sees instead an internally conflicted, heterogenous base of support; overall, however, he treats interests as objective, class-based phenomena and thus does not explore the subjective interests of the popular sector.

27. Cf. Ianni (1975, 48ff), who contested the view that populism occurred in a political vacuum.

28. For example, in the case of Argentine President Menem, Roberts (1995, 111) argues that he divided the labor movement in order to foster direct, dependent relationships between himself and his supporters.

29. A Gallup poll showed 61 percent of Americans favored greater spending on military,

health care for the elderly, and education over a tax cut. A *Wall Street Journal* poll found only 9 percent mentioned the tax burden as a national problem. William Claiborne and Eric Pianin, "GOP Kicks Off Tax Cut Campaign; Illinois Autoworkers Are Skeptical of Hastert's Pitch," *Washington Post* (August 12, 1999): A-3.

30. It should be noted that Weyland admits that Argentina is a "partial exception" to his thesis about the new type of "neopopulism" arising along with neoliberalism, but overall he tries to fit Menem into his thesis in a way that I find is not supported by evidence from the field.

31. Weyland (1996, 12, 14) acknowledges this point but downplays it, as his article is generally concerned to show that Menem's neoliberalism, not merely his Peronism, was popular.

32. For an argument that public opinion is largely measuring the reception of elite-level messages, see Zaller (1992).

33. There are important exceptions. Levine (1992 and 1993) pays considerable attention to what he calls the "voices" of the popular sectors in Latin America. In the same vein, Guidry (1996) focuses on the experiences and values that shape ordinary Brazilians' discourse.

34. For an example of the latter, see (Eckstein 1989, 14).

Chapter 2. The Political and Economic Context

1. For a seminal English-language history of Argentine politics and economic development, see Rock (1987). Electoral conditions before 1930 and the rise of the UCR are discussed on pp. 129, 189–90, respectively.

2. For analysis of the developmental and political consequences of Peronist ISI policies, see Waisman (1987). For a structural interpretation focused on the changing alliances between state and classes, in the context of Argentina's ISI development model, see O'Donnell (1978); O'Donnell (1979, chapter 4); O'Donnell (1988), and Smith (1991). For analysis of the development of the party system, see Mainwaring and Scully (1995) and Gibson (1996).

3. On Perón's development of ties to the labor movement, see Ranis (1992, 17–27) and McGuire (1997, 56–59).

4. The repressive conditions of 1951 are discussed by Rock (1987, 303–6).

5. These policies, and opponents' evaluations of them, are described further in Rock (1987, 262–66) and Ranis (1992, 17–27).

6. For fuller explanation of the political and economic tensions described in this paragraph, see Rock (1987, 289–319) and Smith (1991, 26–32).

7. For a brief account of Perón's overthrow and of Aramburu's government, respectively, see Rock (1987, 314–18 and 334–37).

8. For analysis of the "impossible game" that politics became, when the largest political party was prevented from holding office, see O'Donnell (1979, chapter 4). A detailed historical account of this period of political "deadlock" is also found in Rock (1987, 320–66).

9. See O'Donnell (1979; 1988) and Smith (1991).

10. The ideological, tactical, and political divisions during the 1955–76 period both within Peronism and within the left were complex and dynamic. For close analyses, see Hodges (1988) and Ollier (1986). Re: the nationalist factions of the guerilla movement, see Rock (1993, 205–22).

11. The 30,000 figure is commonly cited by human rights groups in Argentina, but Pion-Berlin (1994) suggests 15,000 is a more reliable upper limit. Other figures are from

John P. King ("Comparative Analysis of Human Rights Violations under Military Rule in Argentina, Brazil, Chile and Uruguay," *Statistical Abstract on Latin America* 27 (1989): 1049–50) as cited in Pion-Berlin (1994, 108).

12. On the economic policies of the authoritarian regime, see Smith (1991).

13. For an analysis of the bases of electoral support for Alfonsín in 1983 and comparisons with the previous presidential election in 1973, see Mora y Araujo (1985).

14. For a provocative retrospective on the trials by one of the key players, see Malamud-Goti (1996, esp. 59–70), who also provides an overview of the main events, trials, barracks uprisings, and legislation related to Alfonsín's handling of the military's human rights record.

15. In the World Values Survey carried out in Argentina in 1991, Argentina ranked among the bottom third of countries around the world in terms of the percentage of its population expressing strong confidence in the congress, the armed forces, the police, the civil service, the education system, the legal system, the Church, the press, and labor unions. Only 7 percent of Argentines surveyed had substantial confidence in the civil service, 17 percent in the congress, and 8 percent in labor unions—the lowest confidence levels of any of the forty-two countries/cities surveyed (Inglehart, Basáñez, and Moreno 1998, V272–80).

16. I have relied on the close analysis of the regime's economic policies in Smith (1991, 231–66). See also Barsky and Bocco (1991).

17. Smith (1991, 254), citing figures from José Miguel Candia, "Cambios en el mercado de trabajo en el período 1976–1981 y perspectivas," in *Argentina: políticas económicas alternativas* (Mexico City, Mexico: CIDE, Estudios de Caso Num. 1, Serie Instituto de Estudios Económicos de América Latina, September 1982, table 3, 68).

18. Ten years after coauthoring Menem's campaign book, the PJ's 1999 presidential candidate, Eduardo Duhalde, admitted, "I'm proud of having written *La revolución productiva*, and still believe in it. That stage was finished, but the *salariazo* is still missing." (Paola Juárez, "Duhalde: falta el salariazo," *La Nación Line* [5 May 1999], 13).

19. He repeated this phrase in his May Day speech to congress in 1992 (*La Prensa* 2 May 1992, 1).

20. Examples are plentiful. Two illustrative ones are Bocco and Repetto (1990) and Moscona (1990).

21. *Clarín*, (editorial, 9 April 1992, 18) and *Clarín* ("Pros y contras del Brady," 8 March 1992, Suplemento Económico, 7).

22. An example of both unexpectedly low price and numerous improprieties is the sale of the state steel company, SOMISA. See McGuire's description (1997, 220, 230).

23. John J. Duffey first pointed this out to me based on his meetings in 1992 with government and labor union officials interested in creating the needed regulatory systems. The government waited until October 1994 to begin creating an umbrella organization to oversee the existing utility regulatory bodies and provide an avenue for consumer complaints. World Bank staffers, summarizing Argentina's privatization program, acknowledged that regulatory frameworks were not as well developed as had been hoped but apparently did not make real monopoly regulation a condition for lending (World Bank 1993b, 22). Much harsher criticism of the regulatory gap came from Menem's critics in the press and the opposition.

24. The complete text of this massive set of changes can be found in a special supplement printed with *Clarín*, (1 November 1991). For a brief description, see Newfarmer (1995, 186).

25. For a description of the Convertibility policy, see Starr (1997) and Erro (1993, 215–19). See also Palermo's (1998) analysis, which sees Menem's first term policies as "moderately" populist, on the basis that they stimulated demand rather than recession.

26. From *La Nación*, (17 June 1992, Sec. 3, 3), citing National Statistics Institute (INDEC) figures.

27. Cf. *La Nación*, (7 May 1992, 16) and *Clarín*, (7 March 1992, 27). From the start of the Convertibility Plan through December 1993, during which time wages and exchange rates essentially held steady, rents increased 157 percent and medical services 93 percent (FIEL 1993, 7).

28. See World Bank (1995, 7), which shows that since 1976 poverty has risen and fallen roughly in sync with inflation although the decrease in poverty levels between 1990 and 1993 was not nearly as sharp as the decrease in inflation.

29. The poverty levels reported by national and international agencies, as well as by private researchers, vary markedly in magnitude, although not usually in direction of change over time. The Study of Argentine Poverty (known as IPA [INDEC 1990]) and the CEPA studies (1993a, 1993b, 1993c), which were carried out by the Alfonsín and Menem governments respectively, are not strictly comparable, not only because of different measurement decisions but also because of a different data base. IPA used specially trained interviewers working on a specially drawn sample from selected sites around the country while CEPA used the existing Permanent Household Surveys (EPH) that are done biannually. Most poverty data reported from Argentina are based on the biannual EPH data, which are collected by INDEC, the national statistics agency. Even when researchers use the same database, poverty measurements will vary substantially (for a comparison of poverty levels found in eleven major studies in Argentina during the 1974–1993 period, see World Bank 1995, 6). The variation in magnitude results from decisions made in establishing a household's poverty line and in measuring the household's income. These decisions include: how to account for the different nutritional needs of household members of various ages and genders (i.e., computation of adult equivalencies), whether and how to account for variation in housing costs (e.g., imputing rental costs), whether and how to correct for underreporting of income, and assumptions about the proportion of the household budget spent on food (i.e., the size of the Engels coefficient). For an analysis of the effects of various measurement decisions upon poverty levels, see Minujin and Scharf (1989), Beccaria and Minujin (1985 and 1991), and CEPA (1993a). For a review of these issues, including the methods and findings in various Argentine poverty studies, see Powers (1995a, 92–98 and 1995b, chapter 3). I thank IPA researcher Elsa Pallavicini for valuable insights on the measurement process.

30. Based on data from Greater Buenos Aires. The Gini coefficient is a widely used measure in which 0.0 indicates perfect equality and 1.0 indicates perfect inequality.

31. Gallup poll, reported in Díaz (1995, 71).

32. Minujín and Kessler (1995, 65) report that over two decades the average income fell 40 percent.

Chapter 3. Housing Interests

1. This point is recognized in Minujin and Vinocur (1989, 36) and Golbert and Tenti Fanfani (1994, 33).

2. A similar point is made in Castells (1983, 185–86) drawing on Ricardo Infante and Magaly Sánchez, *Reproducción de la fuerza de trabajo es la estructura urbana la condición de la clase trabajadora en zonas segregadas de Caracas* [sic] (Caracas: Universidad Central de Venezuela, Instituto de Urbanismo, 1980, 4 volumes).

3. Paraphrased statement, per author's interview with Andrés, 6 June 1992.

4. My attention to the heterogeneity of material conditions, here and throughout the book, has its intellectual roots in the works of Katzman (1989) and Murmis and Feldman (1992).

5. Golbert and Tenti Fanfani (1994, 39) make a related argument.

6. Author's interviews with Martín and Hilda.

7. Data from Secretariat of Housing and Environmental Quality. See Rubén Correa, "El 40% de los argentinos sufre el déficit habitacional," La Nación (7 June 1992, 21).

8. The 3 percent is my calculation of those whose housing was considered inadequate based on data from the 1991 census published in CEPA (1993c, 6, 8, 16, 19). Available data are not consistent. A frequently quoted figure, attributed to the 1980 census, states that 3 percent of housing in the capital was residence hotels and an additional 3 percent was rooming houses (inquilinatos); see Cuenya (1991, 52) or Peñalva and Arroyo (1991, 37). Cuenya puts the population in these hotels and rooming houses in 1980 at 150,000 (5 percent of the total population), while Peñalva and Arroyo estimate that as of 1990 there were 300,000 people in the hotels, rooming houses, and occupied buildings of Buenos Aires. A 1986 survey estimated only 111,645 people in hotels and rooming houses (Gazzoli, Agostinis, and Jeifetz 1987, 16). The difficulty of getting accurate results from the study of people living in often irregular, clandestine, or humiliating circumstances means that all estimates, including the 1991 Census data, must be considered only rough approximations.

9. For a description of the varieties of self-constructed squatter settlements in the Buenos Aires area with some analysis of differences in their potential for political organization, see Silva and Schuurman (1989, 54–58).

10. Estimates vary but all agree that at the start of the 1990s about four times as many people in the Federal Capital lived in residence hotels and inquilinatos as in shantytowns. Cf. Peñalva and Arroyo (1991, 37); Reynals, Giglio, and Kömkle (1991), and Labado, Ladillinsky, and Garmendia (1991, 43–44). In some sections of the country, such as the southern cities of Neuquen and General Roca, inquilinatos (but not hotels) have been a common lodging for the poor; but in most parts, shanties are a more typical kind of precarious housing (see INDEC 1990, 343).

11. Figures are from the Encuesta de Situación Habitacional, as reported in Rubén Correa, op. cit.

12. For a fascinating ethnographic study of a toma (taking over) of one neighborhood in Greater Buenos Aires, see DuBois (1998).

13. In addition to interviews and observation of meetings of occupants working to legalize their housing, my observations here benefitted from a brief history of neighborhood housing arrangements prepared and shared with me by Nélida de Naveiro, social worker at the parish of Nuestra Señora de Montserrat (unpublished mimeo, no date, no title). As well, this section rests on conversations with Néstor Jeifetz, MOI member and cofounder, and a grant proposal he and his colleagues prepared (MOI 1992). I am grateful to both of them for their insights and willingness to share their work.

14. Author's interview with Julio. Also, Silvina Schuchner, "Casa tomada," Clarín (30 June 1991, 10–11).

15. Author's interviews with Jorge and Martín. Written accounts of this man's bullying are found in MOI (1992, 6–7) and Centro de Estudiantes de Ingeniería (1991, 87).

16. In the face of complaints, the U-24 zone was cut nearly in half in 1982, but the oldest parts of San Telmo and Montserrat remained part of it. Eventually, in December 1991, the municipality enacted a new ordinance intended to help rejuvenate the neighborhoods by fo-

cusing only on the preservation of historically significant buildings. Sources: "Distrito U.24," *Buenos Aires, nos cuenta: San Telmo* (October 1987); "Se aprobó la ordenanza que reemplaza a la U-24: ¿Periodismo—ficción?" *Alsur* (December 1991, 8); and PROSUR (Program for the Revitalization of Southern Buenos Aires City), public service advertisement, in *Buenos Aires en blanco y negro* (May 1992, 30).

17. Property taxes increased dramatically at the start of the military regime. See Oszlak (1991, 88–89). For the story of one such rental property, abandoned by its owners, and gradually occupied by previously paying tenants as well as newcomers, see Eduardo Pogoriles, "Los vecinos del inquilinato allanado acusaron a un grupo de peruanos," *Clarín* (4 July 1991, 39).

18. Sources on organizational difficulties include interviews with Jorge and Julio and observation of several meetings of the Squatters and Tenants Movement (MOI) or of residences affiliated with MOI.

19. MOI (1992, 2) argues that occupied houses are more insecure than shantytowns, which have "relative stability." Of course, this stability is a feature of posttransition Argentina. During the military regime, vast shantytowns in the Federal Capital were razed and their residents forced to move to the outskirts (Oszlak 1991, 147–98).

20. Grillo (1995, 10) also observes these political ties.

21. Per author's interview, 4 June 1992.

22. Altogether, three of the families included in this study had children who suffered serious falls at home. Buildings in disrepair are not merely dangerous for children. For example, a residence hotel in the neighborhood of La Boca collapsed in the middle of the night after renovations had been made without reinforcing a load-bearing wall. "Se siguen derrumbando 'Hoteles'," *Alsur* (June 1991, 9).

23. A thorough study of hotels and *inquilinatos*, including a comparison of demography and conditions in each type of shelter, is Gazzoli, Agostinis, and Jeifetz (1987, esp. chapter 2). I have used it extensively to prepare this section of the chapter to supplement and corroborate my own field observations. A brief summary of the study is found in Gazzoli (1991). Labado, Ladillinsky, and Garmendia (1991, 41–50) focus on the "juridical chaos" that exists in place of hotel regulation. For a discussion of the history of hotels in the urban housing market, including the profitability for owners, see Cuenya (1991).

24. Per author's conversation with sociologist Silvia Agostinis, 11 March 1992, and interview with Gregorio, one of the forty-one interview subjects, who is also an organizer of *inquilinato* residents, 29 February 1992. Of those interviewed Cecilia, Martín, Paula, Sara, and Andrés are known to have been living in circumstances that represented downward mobility in their quality of shelter.

25. See 1980 census definition in Labado, Ladillinsky, Garmendia (1991, 42).

26. Per shantytown organizer, Guillermo Villar, quoted in Zaffaroni and Armada (1991, 64).

27. Observation at meeting at the Casa del Sur, 30 April 1992.

28. Reinterview, August 1995.

29. These people would fit the categorization of the "old poor"—i.e., those no longer expecting upward mobility—in Golbert and Tenti Fanfani's proposed typology of urban poverty (1994, 33).

30. Per author's interviews with Paula and Andrés.

31. Reynals, Giglio, and Kömkle (1991); "Menem entregó las tierras a los ocupantes de tres villas," *Clarín* (23 June 1992, 38); and Zaffaroni and Armada (1991).

32. A similar observation is found in Zaffaroni and Armada (1991, 59).

33. Indeed, in a study done in the late 1980s, two researchers had concluded that the capital's shantytowns were very poor prospects for successful housing movements (see Silva and Schuurman 1989, 58).

34. Oxhorn (1995) noted comparable things in his study of shantytowns in Chile.

35. My understanding of these events has been shaped by interviews with active members of the residents' cooperative (Francesca, Jorge, and Martín), as well as with local journalists, Américo García and Livio Fort (21 February 1992), NGO-affiliated organizers Nestor Jeifetz (22 August 1995) and Silvia Agostinis (11 March 1992), Alejandra Oberti (involved as a university student, interviewed 31 March 1992), as well as two written accounts by Jeifetz (MOI 1992) and by the students (Centro de Estudiantes de Ingeniería 1991). Not surprisingly, "success has a thousand fathers" as the saying goes—that is, while the various accounts are substantially the same, albeit with slight differences in chronology, there are some differences in the credit given to various actors. In comparing accounts and synthesizing them here, I have leaned toward the residents' version over that of their technical associates.

36. The city council approved the proposal in the early hours of 20 December 1991, just a few months before I interviewed Jorge, Francesca, and Martín. The municipality later authorized the first one million dollars of design and construction funds but never issued the check. Nearly four years later, I returned to find the former organizers discouraged and uninvolved. The leadership of the cooperative had changed, as residents became disillusioned by the slow pace of the promised improvements. Residents took their frustration out on their cooperative's elected leaders rather than on City Hall, where the Padelai's affluent political opponents had gained new strength. By 1999 the funding had not been released and city officials showed signs of reconsidering the residents' rehabilitation project, perhaps because the building is in the tourist heart of colonial-era San Telmo. See "Discriminan a mis hijos por ser pobres," *Clarín digital* (8 June 1999) and Gabriel Reches, "Nadie sabe qué hacer con el edificio donde estaba el Padelai," *Clarín digital* (3 January 1999).

37. For a review of the literature on how organizations and movements frame issues for individuals, who would otherwise tend to attribute their problems to personal rather than social causes, see McAdam, McCarthy, and Zald 1988, 713–14.

38. For a close examination of the tensions between parties and urban social movements, see Oxhorn (1995, 27–33).

39. Compare the views just expressed with those described in Centro de Estudiantes (1991, 89).

40. Interviews with Diego, Esperanza, Gregorio, Carlos, and Ignacio.

41. Oxhorn (1995, 164–65) found the same thinking in Santiago, Chile.

42. These include shantytown activists Esperanza and Diego, as well as MOI participants Julio, Cecilia, her husband Jacobo, Vicente, and Andrés.

Chapter 4. Material Interests

1. Attention here is to the article's argument, not its figures, which are erroneous. Prior to this excerpt, the article asserted that INDEC's poverty line was at about $1000 per month, which is at least double the correct figure. 230 pesos would constitute severe poverty approaching indigence, certainly not enough to fund even the dreary existence the journalist describes. Unfortunately, I do not know the precise level of the poverty line at the time of this research because it was not an "official statistic" at the time and therefore INDEC refused to release it. A year later, Minujin and Kessler (1995, 63) placed the 1993 poverty line at $420 per month for a family of four, which seems reasonable, given "off the record" information provided me by an INDEC researcher and my own estimates.

2. For example, see the basic needs identified in two government studies of poverty (INDEC 1990, CEPA 1993c).

3. Thus, this finding is consistent with the point made earlier that perceived "needs" increase as objective conditions improve.

4. My stress on exclusion should not be mistaken for a reprise of the "marginality" and "culture of poverty" literatures of the 1960s, which saw poverty as a self-perpetuating set of social problems and cultural values by which the poor exclude themselves from mainstream society. Rather, by focusing on the way conditions beyond the individual exclude people from fuller participation in society and attainment of their goals, the argument here is consistent with the literature that so effectively *criticized* marginalization theories (cf. Portes 1972; Perlman 1976). As Perlman described the poor, "rather than being passively marginal in terms of their own attitudes and behavior, they are being actively marginalized" (1976, 195).

5. The tables list only the changes that the person revealed in the course of interview questions about their jobs, living conditions, and pasts. Because I was not aware of the extensiveness of this flux until I had interviewed many people, I did not systematically ask each one to name all the major changes or insecurities in their lives. Thus, the full level of flux in their lives is *at least* as shown in the tables and probably greater.

6. The Spanish word "*ajuste*" means adjustment, as in structural adjustment, but has the double meaning of belt-tightening.

7. Note that this conversation took place at the second interview, which occurred after she took on the extra four-hour work shift.

8. Similarly, in interviews with Oscar, Francesca, and Cecilia—all working in janitorial or domestic cleaning—each stated that there were plenty of jobs available for people who were willing to work. Francesca's comment illustrates their convictions that there was pride in labor well done, regardless of its status: "In my opinion there are jobs. If I look for it, I'll find it, but people have a lot of pretensions. You have to be willing to work. If I'm out of work and someone offers me a job pushing a broom, I'll do it."

9. The partial exceptions to this generalization were Jacobo (Cecilia's husband) and Claudia, who both insisted that while they thought their children would study and develop a skill, they would not care if their kids were street sweepers as long as they were honest and upstanding.

10. These families, the so-called "new poor," are identified as people with incomes below the poverty line but who possess other qualities of life (safe housing and sanitation and a sufficiently educated head-of-household) that suggest their impoverishment is relatively recent. In contrast, the "structurally" poor were identified as those lacking safe housing, sanitation, and adequate wage-earning capacities.

11. Unpublished data from SIEMPRO, Secretaría de Desarrollo Social, based on INDEC figures.

12. Even though the terms of the question about a newborn's opportunities tended to focus respondents' attention on structural causes (class status and class-based resources) rather than policy ones (how government policies affect the life chances of people of lower means), some people nevertheless mentioned that policy decisions or government incompetence could increase or hinder existing inequalities. These views are discussed below.

13. The view that the poor are fatalistic was promulgated in the so-called "culture of poverty" literature that arose in the 1960s (e.g., Lewis 1961) on the basis of interviews with people expressing views like Eduardo's.

14. I thank José Nun for recommending to me this approach to evaluating hopes for upward mobility. I asked an open-ended question derived from one he had used. See Nun (1989, 163).

15. In addition to interviews previously cited, this aspect of inequality was a concern expressed by Carlos, Eduardo, Graciela, Martín, Pablo, Ricardo, Tomás, Walter, and Amanda's son Pepe. For discussion of inequality as exclusion from participation, see Townsend (1970) and Miller and Roby (1970).

16. In addition to those cited, this second conception of inequality was used by Andrés, Betina, Gabriela, Graciela, Jorge, Juan Antonio, Leonardo, María José, Martín, Soña, Tomás, and Vicente.

17. Per reinterview in August 1995. Field notes from 1992 reveal Amanda's teenaged daughter saying the same thing in identical language, which probably indicates this was a frequently expressed viewpoint in their household.

18. Julio said, "I don't know what one can do. Because one isn't superman." Shortly afterward, I asked what view he took from his difficult life experiences, and he volunteered, "I haven't lost my hope, let's say, because that's always the last thing left to a man is hope. . . . If one loses hope, one doesn't have anything left, and you kill yourself. I have hope for a change, but I don't know how. But something is happening. . . . In the new generations, there's hope."

Chapter 5. Coping Materially, Focusing Politically

1. The factory closing Oscar experienced would have occurred in the context of the severe economic crisis at the end of the authoritarian regime, which included sharp declines in industrial production (a 15.2 percent decline) from 1980 to 1981 and continued decline (another 4.7 percent) in 1982 (Smith 1991, 245–48).

2. My set of interviews included four people without full Argentine citizenship—one Paraguayan, one Bolivian, and two Uruguayans. While Cecilia's lack of full citizenship rights might seem to be the reason for her failure to pay more attention to the impact of political affairs on her life, that would not be a very satisfying explanation. There is no reason to anticipate a microfocus as typical or logical for a long-time resident without full citizenship. Two of the other foreigners interviewed were macrofocused and had been politically active. Macrolevel politics affects the lives of those who cannot vote for the president at least as much as the lives of those who can. (I say "at least as much" because in 1999 the Menem government tried to use workers from neighboring countries as scapegoats for the country's stubbornly high unemployment.)

3. Voting in Argentina is mandatory so I asked her if some elections were really more obligatory than others. Betina assured me, "Certainly, yes, yes."

4. For a brief overview of the ATE and its stance early in Menem's presidency, see Jeppesen (1994, 81–83).

5. The first three items are per author's interview with E. Sainz, an ATE administrator, 29 May 1992. The last item is per World Bank (1993a, xvii).

6. No doubt some reader might judge that these people have simply made bad choices. Ramón could have chosen a less expensive respite than the day at the zoo. Yet my purpose here is not to argue the moral injustice of the material hardships suffered, and thus there is no need for moralistic counterarguments. The question is, given the choices people do make and their empirical circumstances as they perceive them, how do their material circumstances affect their political views?

7. Nelson (1992) identifies some of the same coping strategies as here, although she focuses on differences in coping capacities between classes in order to judge differential costs of economic adjustment. Here I emphasize coping difficulties that are not necessarily defined by class, and I use coping capacity as part of an explanation of crosscutting political attitudes.

8. The family market basket (*canasta familiar*) is a reference to the cost of a household's basic nutritional needs. Most Argentines are familiar with the concept because newspapers routinely write cost-of-living stories by comparing the cost of a market basket of goods (not necessarily the same "basket" measure used by government poverty studies) to average wages.

9. Particularly in the Federal Capital, people may have condominium fees, but these are a relatively small portion of the average household budget. The reason that the poverty line calculation has not taken account of housing costs is that the Permanent Household Surveys (EPH) are carried out in Greater Buenos Aires, an area where housing costs are a minor percentage of the average family budget. According to EPH food is the major item in the budget of lower income households (Teubal 1989, 96) The EPH determines the percentage of the average family budget spent on food; the reciprocal of that percentage is multiplied by the costs of a food basket to calculate the poverty line. The result is that the poverty line is set too low to identify many renters living in poverty. Neither the INDEC 1990 nor CEPA 1993 studies corrected their methods to accurately measure poverty among renters although, because the number of renters in the populous suburbs of Buenos Aires is low, the failure to correct did not significantly miscount the incidence of poverty overall (Beccaria and Minujin 1991, 30–31).

10. María del Carmen Feijoó reminded me of this point in a personal conversation. Also, see Townsend (1970), who incorporates in-kind employment benefits into his conceptualization of the types of resources the lack of which identified poverty.

11. I volunteered for five months and the staples were always approximately the same, occasionally a bit more generous. My estimate of value is only approximate, using INDEC (1992, 11).

12. The municipality of Buenos Aires created a program called *Programa Alimentario de la Municipalidad de Buenos Aires* [Buenos Aires Municipal Nutrition Program], known by the acronym PAMBA, which involved the distribution of food boxes to qualified recipients. It appears that PAMBA was related to Menem's restructuring of PAN. One interviewee told me that the frequency of PAMBA boxes had fallen considerably, which would be consistent with information from the World Bank (1993a, 213) stating that the 1992 budget for the food subsidy program was only about 11 percent of its original level.

13. On the PAN program, see Del Franco (1989) and Midré (1992). The latter also describes Menem's short-lived National Emergency Solidarity Bond program. Auyero (1995) provides a fascinating analysis of how politicians and policy makers in different periods of recent history have shaped the image of poverty and the discourse on the rights of the poor, including under the PAN program.

14. Credit does not show up in table 5.1 because I did not collect sufficient data about which people I interviewed were relying substantially on credit.

15. Reiterating a point from chapter 4, I do not intend "coping" as a synonym for "surviving." Citizens' perceptions about what constitutes successful coping are expressed as expectations about *normal* standards of living in the society, not mere physical survival.

16. My attention to different types of needs is influenced by the literature on the sociology of poverty, which emphasizes the heterogeneity of material hardships as well as the so-

cial heterogeneity of people living at similar income levels. See Golbert and Tenti Fanfani (1994); Katzman (1989); Murmis and Feldman (1992).

17. Carlos is described in more detail in chapter 7.

18. This timing factor also affects firms. See Acuña and Smith (1994, 31).

19. This point is discussed further in the beginning of chapter 6.

Chapter 6. Political Interests in Context

1. A useful anthology of Peronist discourse is Iturrieta (1990). For a review of the emergence of social and labor rights in statute and later in "new Article 14" of the 1957 constitution, see Pi de la Serra (1983, 106–10).

2. This finding concurs with voting studies of the industrialized world, concerning how ideology and partisanship shape political views (cf., Lewis-Beck 1988, 57–67).

3. Similar observations are made by Golbert and Tenti Fanfani (1994).

4. For an in-depth discussion of Argentine class identity, see Ranis (1992, chapters 7 and 8).

5. Argentine parties have neighborhood level organizing units, called *comités* (committees) in the UCR and *unidades básicas* (basic units) in the PJ. The neighborhood activists who set up these storefront organizations are typically loyal to, and subsidized by, a particular faction or politician in the party.

6. I believe that by "supporting" him, she meant "not actively resisting his policies," that is, not doing what the Peronists had done.

7. In the 1983 presidential election, after a bitter primary campaign between Herminio Iglesias and Antonio Cafiero, Italo Luder emerged as compromise PJ candidate (see Rock [1987, 388]).

8. On the Peronist movement, the Justicialist Party, and changes in the movement over time, see Chumbita (1989), Levitsky (1998), and McGuire (1997). On Peronist identity, see de Ipola (1987), Miguens and Turner (1988), Ostiguy (1997, 1998), and Ranis (1992). Ostiguy's work also discusses anti-Peronist identities.

9. On Perón's position on democracy, see de Ipola (1987, especially 338ff).

10. The interview set deliberately included diverse partisan attachments, so it was not surprising to hear a variety of evaluations of Menem. The overwhelming majority of those interviewed had a negative opinion of him, but my conclusions rest not on the numbers from this nonrandom sample, but rather on the reasoning employed to evaluate the president, as revealed by in-depth interviews.

11. Francesca's exact words in Spanish were, "El Perón lo usan de bandera,"

12. Diego's words, in Spanish, were, "Más peronista que todos esos atorrantes que andan por ahí."

13. U.S. Ambassador Spruille Braden tried to influence the 1946 election in a number of ways, including spreading charges that Perón had collaborated with the Axis during World War II. Perón turned the interference to his advantage with a campaign slogan suggesting the voters' choice was "Braden or Perón." Braden was subsequently recalled by the U.S. State Department. Diego's claim that Perón "kicked Braden out" stems from Perón's version of events—a version not backed up by historical accounts but now part of Peronist mythology (Page 1983, 92–105, especially 101; Rock 1987, 261 and 275).

14. Méndez—one of the most ordinary surnames in Argentina—was a derogatory reference to Menem.

15. Non-Peronist authors frequently comment upon the inconsistencies and vagaries of Justicialist thought (cf., Page [1983, 221]; Rock [1987, 264]). A more sympathetic view is

that there have been "diverse Peronisms, both across historical time and across socio-cultural space" and that the "ideological and policy contradictions that are historically manifested in the heart of Peronism reflect those in an exclusionary society. . . ." (Jordi Borda, in prologue to Iturrieta [1990, 14–15]). Readers can judge for themselves, in the chronological anthology of major statements from Perón through Menem, found in Iturrieta (1990).

16. One of the country's oldest and largest holding companies, with interests including food processing, grain exporting, and finance, Bunge y Born epitomizes the business establishment. William Smith has described the firm as "long a reviled symbol of *vendepatria* capitalism" for Peronists (1991, 300).

17. In the June 1992 election for senator of the Federal Capital, the PJ formed a coalition with the UCeDé and chose Avelino Porto, a businessman with no ties to Peronism, as their candidate. Porto was soundly beaten by the UCR's Fernando De la Rúa.

18. Eduardo's tendency *not* to link his material and political interests was explored more extensively in chapter 1, as well as late in chapter 5, where the effects of his partisanship on his thinking were introduced in the discussion of table 5.4.

19. For a detailed and nuanced discussion of Argentines' preferences for certain leadership styles, see Ostiguy (1997), which identifies a pattern of "high" and "low" style in Argentine politics, with Peronism associated with "low" style and the UCR with a "high" style. Ostiguy's typology is based on findings in the field consistent with my own, and I have found it very helpful in thinking through the relationship between leadership traits and party identity in this section.

20. The *caudillo* image she mentions refers to the long sideburns Menem used to wear to imitate Facundo Quiroga, a nineteenth-century *caudillo* who came from Menem's home province of La Rioja.

21. In contrast, Eduardo, a Peronist loyalist, mentioned Menem's tennis and soccer playing as a positive thing because it demonstrated that his position and power did not change his daily routine.

22. Pepe's precise words were, "Transparente y recto." Note that this was not a description often attributed to the president by anyone but himself because of the numerous corruption scandals associated with his administration.

23. Dietz (1998, 17) found similar behavior in Peru.

24. See Inglehart, Basañez and Moreno (1998, n.p.), regarding their variable 248. Identification with the left was operationalized as those who chose points 1–4 on a 10-point left-to-right scale.

25. A slight exception was the leader of the Movement toward Socialism (MAS), who garnered some press by advocating that Argentina refuse to pay the foreign debt acquired under the military regime and received further publicity by breaking away from his own party in 1992.

26. Both because of the nature of in-depth interviews and owing to some respondents' lack of political knowledge, not everyone was asked, or had an opinion, about the parties of the left.

27. Special circumstances surrounding the constitutional assembly in 1994 enabled the "third" party, FREPASO, to emerge as an electorally viable option, thus changing strategic calculations of some voters by 1995. See chapter 8.

28. Carlos talked mostly about macrolevel problems, not his own, but underlying the conversation was a constant reference to himself in class terms ("lower income," "working class," "poor") together with a discourse on politics that was based on the same class terms.

He clearly saw his personal fortunes as largely controlled by inequities at a system-level, and thus I classified his thinking as focused on the micro-macro link.

29. I interviewed Major Ojeda, the director of the capital campaign at the headquarters, and visited both offices several times, conversing at length with party organizers, volunteers, and supporters from the neighborhood who stopped by the San Telmo office.

30. For a detailed account of the Holy Week uprising, its motivations and outcomes, see Norden (1996, 128–30). Norden's account of participants' perceptions of their actions is consistent with that of the MODIN members I interviewed.

31. This is not a personal interpretation. In our second meeting, 21 May 1992, the spokesman said that he spent two hours with me because he sought to get the party's message out correctly.

32. MODIN's hopes, per author's interview with Major Ojeda, 21 May 1992.

33. Based on visit to the San Telmo office, 23 June 1992.

34. This is a play on the Spanish words *rico,* which means rich, and *pobre,* which means poor.

35. To the extent the belief about economic policy affected approval of Rico, the effect was interactive: approving of Menem's economic policies did not cause those polled to disapprove of Rico (who wanted to change those policies) as much as disapproving of Menem's policies caused respondents to approve of Rico. This interactive effect, however, was not strong.

36. Ultimately, Venturino won only 6 percent of the vote in the 1992 senatorial race. MODIN's popularity peaked at 9 percent in the constituent assembly elections of 1994. Afterward the party disintegrated owing to leadership conflicts and disillusionment among party activists over Rico's political bedfellows and perceived ethical lapses. By 1995 the party had broken apart. Some leaders retired from public life and grassroots activists sought other outlets in their search for leadership clean of corruption and opposed to the neoliberal economic model (per 15 August 1995, reinterview with María and a party colleague). By the time I reinterviewed María and Claudia in 1995 both had moved on politically. Although still distrustful of the left, each had voted for the FREPASO candidate in 1995 as a protest vote against Menem's policies and perceived corruption.

37. I selected all survey respondents who had expressed the opinion that "it would be best for the development of the country if the economic path chosen by the government were changed."

38. Eighteen politicians were mentioned in the poll, but in the interests of space, I've excluded from the figure two of the less prominent ones, both Menem allies, whose median ratings were "poor."

39. Manuel Mora y Araujo, "Rechazo a la concentración de poder," *El Cronista* (29 June 1992), 10; and José M. Pasquini Durán, "Al cuarto oscuro," *Página 12* (27 June 1992), 4.

40. Edgardo Siblerkasten presented De la Rúa as a "moderate" critic of the government's policies, in "Menem sufrió su primera derrota," *El Cronista* (29 June 1992), 8. The more radical *Página 12* claimed the election constituted a "punishment vote." Its postelection banner headline declared, "El Castigo Capital: Casi 70 por ciento de la Capital Votó contra el Oficialismo" (Capital Punishment: Nearly 70 Percent of the Capital Voted against the Government).

41. The day after the election, Menem was quoted as saying, "This wasn't about Carlos Menem," in Daniel Santoro, "Menem quiere ser el gran elector del '95," *Clarín* (29 June 1992), 6. The conservative *La Nación* editorialized, "The Radical candidate centered his pre-

election campaign on essentially political issues and publicly expressed his adherence to the monetary stability and the general orientation that has been impressed upon the economy during the last 15 months," in "La elección de senador en la Capital," *La Nación International Weekly Edition* (30 June 1992), 2. Polling expert Manuel Mora y Araujo offered the interpretation that despite the government's attempt to make the election a plebiscite on its administration De la Rúa's election did not constitute a vote "for or against the government's administration or programs" (but contradictorily, Mora y Araujo went on to claim that the vote did represent a vote for "continuity in economic policy"); see Araujo, op. cit., 10. Edgar Mainhard said that "De la Rúa isn't very different in many of his ideas," from those of the PJ/UCeDé alliance candidate he defeated. See "Ahora la izquierda y no la UceDé ocupa el 3er lugar," *Ambito Financiero* (29 June 1992, 25).

42. Fernando De la Rúa, "Un voto 'control'," *Página 12* (29 June 1992, 4–5).

43. "La economía divide al angelocismo," *Clarín* (10 April 1992, 15).

44. Any expectations that Angeloz might offer an alternative in the short-term were greatly diminished in 1995 when he stepped down from his long tenure as governor of Córdoba amidst rioting by unpaid provincial employees, and further in 1996, when he was charged with illicit enrichment in office. See Reuters (19 April 1996). He was never convicted.

45. The translation of "interests" should be read as "interested parties," or "pressures brought to bear," not interests in the way that term is used elsewhere in this book.

Chapter 7. Perspectives on Democracy

1. The chapter epigraph, taken from the interview with Paula reveals that a concern about consolidation had moved beyond academic circles to inform everyday understandings about democratization as a slow process.

2. Here Andrés assumed that the proportional representation system that he has experienced as a congressional voter in Argentina is the only democratic way to choose representatives.

3. Note that Julio's view that people still fear to speak out was not typical among the interviews. This excerpt is presented not to illustrate the fear but to illustrate the view that a "democracy" would be inclusive.

4. On this point, see also the study of Argentine workers carried out by Peter Ranis in 1985–86. Ranis (1992, 152–55) used a slightly different categorization of thinking patterns, which blends together those who focus on freedom with those who focus on elections or the rule of law, and which subdivides the group I've identified as favoring "popular government." Categorizations aside, our findings concur.

5. Of twelve people whose thinking seemed to best fit the "seeks EL democracy" profile, only three had used the popular conception of democracy discussed earlier and only one of those had used it exclusively.

6. Of course, opponents of military rule would disagree with Claudia's perceptions because they did not feel safe going out after dark during the military regime, due to the chance of being harassed, or worse, by the police.

7. Rafael grew up in poverty and had only a partial primary school education. He migrated from a northern province as a teenager and, when interviewed, lived a modest but solidly middle-class lifestyle. He reported that the economic crisis had not affected him much because as a self-employed driver he could simply put in more hours when his family needed extra income. His views were included in this study because of the precariousness that his combination of education and employment gave him (see chapter 5).

8. SOMISA was the state-owned steel manufacturer that was privatized shortly before this research project was done.

9. Data from national survey in eight major metropolitan areas by Romer and Associates, Survey 11, May–June 1992, available as Archive ARROMER92TOP011 from Roper Center for Public Opinion Research.

10. Examples are ubiquitous. For one, in a 1994 newspaper interview, while denying that his government was engaged in fiscally irresponsible preelection spending, Menem compared himself to his *elected* predecessors: "Public deficit was what we used to have under the UCR administration because of all the state-owned companies." (7 Dec. 1994, per *FBIS-LAT-94-240*, translation from the Spanish by FBIS). This is a cynical political claim given that the poor condition of the state-owned companies preceded the UCR's government, and moreover, that the president's party had been the major opponent of Alfonsín's attempts to privatize state companies.

11. For example, in a speech that closely echoed his campaign theme, Alfonsín declared upon election that "heading toward democracy means restoring law and—to subordinate military power to political power. However, our democracy will not only meet the demands of citizens as such but also of men of flesh and blood. Therefore, our democracy will allow the people to vote, as I have always said, to eat, to cure their ills, and to have access to education." Press conference, 31 October 1983, *Foreign Broadcast Information Service* (1 Nov., 1983), B4.

12. For a detailed discussion of this point and the literature that supports it, see O'Donnell (1998).

13. Carlos emphasized that he was not squatting illegally and his home had regular electric service (which is not available to squatters). He explained it as a residence "hotel" whose owners had died thirty some years ago and whose residents had simply remained there, apparently passing on the space to other families over the years. Because taxes could exceed the value of an old building, this sort of abandonment is not unusual in central Buenos Aires.

14. Carlos at one point told me that "*negros*" is simply his term for "workers," but the connotation of the term is pejorative. As used by the boss, "*negros*" refers to workers such as Carlos, who are from (or descended from parents who are from) the poorer northern provinces where mestizo populations predominate.

15. Olivia spoke of *los grandes capitales* and simply *los grandes*.

16. On the distinction between political rights and civil rights, see O'Donnell (1998).

17. For insights into debates about democracy a generation ago in Latin America, see Lehmann (1990) and Ollier (1986). Also, to observe how thinking about democracy has evolved, contrast my typology of the three conceptualizations I heard in interviews in 1992 with MacPherson's typology of the three competing conceptions of democracy in the 1960s (1972, 35–37).

18. This is a false hope since corruption is often systemic, not merely due to moral lapses by individuals. Nevertheless, I heard nothing in interviews to suggest that the citizens hoping for more morality would not also be supportive of systemic changes that could inspire moral behavior via institutional mechanisms to ensure greater accountability.

Chapter 8. Conclusions

1. An important exception is Nelson (1989 and 1992).

2. See chapter 1 of this book.

3. When blank and null ballots are included (4 percent), Menem won 47.7 percent, Massaccesi (UCR) won 16.4 percent and Bordón (FREPASO) won 28.2 percent (Ministry of Interior data reported by De Riz (1998, 143). Because the government chose not to count blank (i.e., protest) ballots as valid for purposes of determining if the threshold for election on the first round had been met, the results are usually reported as percentages of valid ballots, as Menem 49.8 percent, Massaccesi 17 percent, and Bordón 29.3 percent (cf. Szusterman 1996, 110 and 112).

4. "La Gendarmería volvió a reprimir en Jujuy y se extienden los conflictos," *Clarín* (Buenos Aires, 23 May 1997).

5. Poll taken by Center for Study of the New Majority, reported in "Argentina: Shades of Perón," *Luxner News South America Report* (1 March 1998). Available through http://web.lexis-nexis.com, Newsletter Database.

6. "Bid to Contain Wave of Provincial Unrest: Concessions Could Have Impact on Fiscal Targets," *Latin American Weekly Report* (17 August 1999): 99, no. 32, 378.

7. Poll carried out for the *Clarín* newspaper by the *Centro de Estudios para la Opinión Pública*. See Ricardo Rios, "La gente cree que ahora habrá menos corrupción y desempleo." *Clarín digital* (11 December 1999).

8. From 1991 to 1997 employment levels among those with high school and university diplomas increased 20 and 30 percent respectively, while falling almost 30 percent and 6 percent respectively among those who had not completed primary school and those who completed primary school but not secondary school (ECLAC 1998b, 25). A helpful analysis of the Argentine labor market in the 1990s is Pessino (1997).

9. In a national level survey carried out in May and June 1995, by the Mora y Araujo, Noguera & Asociados firm, 85 percent of those polled named unemployment as one of three major problems facing the country. I thank Manuel Mora y Araujo for access to the data.

10. Miguel Angel Rouco, "Hay 3.200.000 pobres en la Capital y el conurbano," *Clarín digital* (9 May 1997); and Marcela Valente, "Government Labor Policies Exacerbate Poverty," *Inter-Press Service* (24 June 1998).

11. For example, in the biannual national-level Permanent Household Survey (EPH) of May 1999, 8.9 percent of the economically active population were working part-time but actively seeking additional work. They were competing against another 14.5 percent who were unemployed but actively seeking work. Figures from *Instituto Nacional de Estadística y Censos* at http://www.indec.mecon.arsinopsis/trabajo.htm. (25 October 2000).

12. Ministry of Labor data from October 1997, reported by Ismael Bermúdez, "Los argentinos trabajan más horas y ganan menos," *Clarín digital* (9 March 1998).

13. Marcela Valente, "Economy: Argentine Government Lowers Unemployment with Subsidies." *Inter-Press Service* wire report (19 December 1997).

14. For an overview of labor law changes, see Pessino (1997, 188–92).

15. Marcela Valente, "Argentina—Labor: Job Instability, High Unemployment Seen." *Inter-Press Service* (4 December 1997).

16. "World Bank Approves Loan for Third Social Protection Project in Argentina," World Bank Group, (30 June 1998, News release no. 98/1863/LAC). Also, see Epstein (1998).

17. Marcela Valente, "Government Labor Policies Exacerbate Poverty," *Inter-Press Service* (24 June 1998) and "Argentina—Labor: Job Instability, High Unemployment Seen." *Inter-Press Service* (4 December 1997).

18. For an economist's rendition of the case for "flexibility" in hiring and against sever-

ance payment laws, see Edwards (1997, 137–41). For a critique of the case for labor "flexibility," see LoVuolo (1997).

19. A brief account of the law can be found in *Latin America Weekly Report* WR-98-35 (8 September 1998), 410.

20. On the Olivos Pact between Menem and Alfonsín and the elections to the constitutional assembly, see De Riz (1998, 138–41).

21. Election figures per Ministry of Interior data per the Political Data Base of the Americas (1999). Argentina: Elecciones Presidenciales de 1999. [Internet]. Georgetown University y Organization of American States. In http://www.georgetown.edu/pdba/Elecdata/Arg/Pres99.html. (20 July 2000).

22. Throughout this chapter, I use "Eastern Europe" to indicate the former Soviet bloc countries although they might more precisely but awkwardly be called Eastern and Central European countries.

23. Useful sources, both general and more theoretical, on Fujimori's economic and social policies, political tactics, and populism, include Arce (1998), Epstein (1998), Graham and Kane (1998), McClintock (1993), Pásara (1993), Roberts (1995), Stokes (1997), Weyland (1996), and Wise (1994).

24. All data from official sources, reported by CEPAL (1989) and ECLAC (1999).

25. For a detailed analysis of these two processes in the Peruvian case, see Panfichi (1997, 221–32, especially 226).

26. Examples of Menem's actions include his manipulation of the judiciary, his extraordinary utilization of executive decrees, accusations of intimidation of journalists, his rewriting of the constitution to assure his own reelection, etc.

27. Per EFE and Reuter's report carried in *Clarín* (9 April 1992): 30–31.

28. This movement is identified in "Leftist Organizations Form 2 New Fronts," *FBIS Daily Report* (24 January 1997), FBIS-EEU-97-017.

29. After the collapse of communism, East European states continued to provide a variety of social guarantees far beyond the social coverage typically found in developing countries. In the unusual case of the former East Germany, the already developed and fiscally sound West German state stepped in to raise pensions, negotiate pay raises, and subsidize temporary work, job training, and other means of maintaining employment (Headey, Andorka and Krause 1995, 257–59). More commonly, fiscal constraints kept the level of social coverage modest such that the state's provision of coping capacity varied both within and among the former communist states (Centeno and Rands [1996, 381]; Kohl [1997]).

30. Important works in the growing literature on the quality of democracy in posttransition regimes and the relationship between citizens and the state include Agüero and Stark (1998), Chalmers et al. (1997), Mainwaring, O'Donnell and Valenzuela (1992), O'Donnell (1996 and 1998), Oxhorn and Ducatenzeiler (1998), Sassen (1996), Smith and Korzeniewicz (1997), van Steenbergen (1993), and von Mettenheim and Malloy (1998).

31. Lustig (1995b) includes numerous case studies of how countries "cope" with economic austerity at a macroeconomic level and with compensating social policies. For a brief but insightful analysis of this issue, see Bresser Pereira and Nakano (1998, 32–36).

32. Advocates expect a lean state to enable greater individual freedom and to be better able to carry out basic functions, but as O'Donnell (1993) pointed out, some Latin American states have simply become too weak to carry out their most basic roles effectively.

References Cited

Acuña, Carlos H. and William C. Smith. 1994. "The Political Economy of Structural Adjustment: The Logic of Support and Opposition to Neoliberal Reform." In William C. Smith, Carlos H. Acuña, and Eduardo A. Gamarra, eds., *Latin American Political Economy in the Age of Neoliberal Reform: Theoretical and Comparative Perspectives for the 1990s*. New Brunswick, N.J.: Transaction Publishers.

Agüero, Felipe, and Jeffrey Stark, eds. 1998. *Fault Lines of Democracy in Post-Transition Latin America*. Miami, Fla.: North-South Center Press at the University of Miami.

Almond, Gabriel A., and Sidney Verba. 1963. *The Civic Culture: Political Attitudes and Democracy in Five Nations*. Princeton, N.J.: Princeton University Press.

Alsur (San Telmo neighborhood newspaper). Buenos Aires. Various editions.

Altimir, Oscar. 1982. *The Extent of Poverty in Latin America*. Trans. D. R. J. Black. World Bank Staff Working Papers, no. 522. Originally published as *La dimensión de la pobreza en América Latina. Cuadernos de la CEPAL* No. 27. Santiago, 1979.

————. 1996. "Economic Development and Social Equity: A Latin American Perspective." *Journal of Interamerican Studies and World Affairs* 38, nos. 2/3 (Summer/Fall): 47–71.

Alvarez, Sonia E. 1990. *Engendering Democracy in Brazil: Women's Movements in Transition Politics*. Princeton, N.J.: Princeton University Press.

Alvarez, Mike, José Antonio Cheibub, Fernando Limongi and Adam Przeworski. 1996. "Classifying Political Regimes" *Studies in Comparative International Development* 31, no. 2: 3–36.

Ambito Financiero. 1992. Buenos Aires. Various editions.

Angell, Alan. 1993. "The Transition to Democracy in Chile: A Model or an Exceptional Case?" *Parliamentary Affairs* 46: 563–78.

Arce, Moises. 1998. "The Political Consequences of Targeted Poverty Alleviation in Contemporary Peru." Paper presented at the 1998 meeting of the Latin American Studies Association. Chicago, September 24–26.

Auyero, Javier. 1995. "Language of Rights, Language of War: Encoding Poverty in Contemporary Argentina." Paper for the 1995 meeting of the Latin American Studies Association, Washington, D.C., September 28–30.

Baloyra, Enrique, ed. 1987. *Comparing New Democracies: Transition and Consolidation in Mediterranean Europe and the Southern Cone*. Boulder, Colo.: Westview.

Barrera, Manuel. 1998. "Macroeconomic Adjustment in Chile and the Politics of the Popular Sectors." In Philip D. Oxhorn and Graciela Ducatenzeiler, eds., *What Kind of Democracy? What Kind of Market? Latin America in the Age of Neoliberalism*. University Park: Pennsylvania State University Press.

Barros, Robert. 1986. "The Left and Democracy: Recent Debates in Latin America." *Telos* 68: 49–70.

Barsky, Osvaldo, and Arnaldo Bocco, eds. 1991. *Respuesta a Martínez de Hoz.* Buenos Aires: Imago Mundi.

Beccaria, Luis A. 1993. "Estancamiento y distribución del ingreso." In Alberto Minujin, ed., *Desigualdad y exclusión.* Buenos Aires: UNICEF/Editorial Losada.

Beccaria, Luis, and Alberto Minujin. 1985. *Métodos alternativos para medir la evolución del tamaño de la pobreza.* INDEC Documento de trabajo no. 6. Buenos Aires: INDEC.

———. 1991. *Sobre la medición de la pobreza: Enseñanzas a partir de la experiencia Argentina.* Documento de trabajo no. 8. Buenos Aires: UNICEF Argentina.

Beccaria, Luis, and Pablo Vinocur. 1991. *La pobreza del ajuste o el ajuste de la pobreza.* Documento de trabajo no. 4 Buenos Aires: UNICEF Argentina (March).

Bocco, .Arnaldo, and Gastón Repetto. 1990. "La política económica de Menem." *Realidad económica* 97 (November): 5–27.

Bollen, Kenneth A., and Robert W. Jackman. 1985. "Political Democracy and the Size Distribution of Income." *American Sociological Review* 50: 438–57.

———. 1995. "Income Inequality and Democratization Revisited: Comment on Muller." *American Sociological Review* 60 (December):983–89.

Boltvinik, Julio. 1992a. "Conocer la pobreza para superarla." *Comercio Exterior* 42, no. 4 (April), 302–9.

———.1992b. "El conocimiento y la lucha contra la pobreza en América Latina: Una guía para el lector." *Comercio Exterior* 42, no. 5 (May), 483–89.

———. 1992c. "El método de medición integrada de la pobreza. Una propuesta para su desarrollo." *Comercio Exterior* 42, no. 4 (April), 354–65.

Bresser Pereira, Luiz Carlos, and Yoshiaki Nakano. 1998. "The Missing Social Contract: Governability and Reform in Latin America." In Philip Oxhorn and Graciela Ducatenzeiler, eds., *What Kind of Democracy? What Kind of Market? Latin America in the Age of Neoliberalism.* University Park: Pennsylvania State University Press.

Cardoso, Ruth Correa Leite. 1989. *Popular Movements in the Context of the Consolidation of Democracy.* Working Paper no. 120. Notre Dame, Ind.: Helen Kellogg Institute for International Studies.

Carrion, Julio F. 1998. "Partisan Decline and Presidential Popularity: The Politics and Economics of Representation in Peru." In Kurt von Mettenheim and James Malloy, eds., *Deepening Democracy in Latin America.* Pittsburgh: University of Pittsburgh Press.

Castells, Manuel. 1983. *The City and the Grassroots: A Cross-Cultural Theory of Urban Social Movements.* Berkeley: University of California Press.

Castro Rea, Julian, Graciela Ducatenzeiler, and Philippe Faucher. 1992. "Back to Populism: Latin America's Alternative to Democracy." In Archibald R. M. Ritter, Maxwell A. Cameron, and David H. Pollock, eds., *Latin America to the Year 2000: Reactivating Growth, Improving Equity, Sustaining Democracy.* New York: Praeger.

Catterberg, Edgardo. 1989. *Los argentinos frente a la política: Cultura política y opinión pública en la transición Argentina a la democracia.* Buenos Aires: Planeta.

Catterberg, Edgardo, and María Braun. 1989. "Las elecciones presidenciales Argentinas del 14 de mayo de 1989: La ruta a la normalidad." *Desarrollo Económico* 29, no. 115 (Oct.–Dec.): 361–74.

Catterberg, Edgardo, and Carmen Zayuelas. 1992. "Social Mobility and Politics in Argentina." In Frederick C. Turner, ed., *Social Mobility and Political Attitudes: Comparative Perspectives.* New Brunswick, N.J.: Transaction Publishers.

Centeno, Miguel Angel, and Tania Rands. 1996. "The World They Have Lost: An Assessment of Change in Eastern Europe." *Social Research* 63, no. 2 (summer): 369–402.

Centro de Estudiantes de Ingeniería. 1991. "Una experiencia de trabajo con la comunidad. El ex-Patronato de la Infancia." In Rubén Gazzoli, ed., *Inquilinatos y hoteles*. Buenos Aires: Centro Editor.

Chalmers, Douglas A., Carlos M. Vilas, Katherine Hite, Scott B. Martin, Kerianne Piester, and Monique Segarra, eds. 1997. *The New Politics of Inequality in Latin America: Rethinking Participation and Representation*. Oxford, England: Oxford University Press.

Chauvin, Lucien O. 1999. "Peru: President Alberto Fujimori Looks to Recapture Magic." *NotiSur* (15 January). University of New Mexico.

Chumbita, Hugo. 1989. *El enigma peronista*. Buenos Aires: Puntosur.

Clarín, various dates, 1990–92.

Cohen, Youssef. 1989. *The Manipulation of Consent: The State and Working-Class Consciousness in Brazil*. Pittsburgh: University of Pittsburgh Press.

Comisión Económica para América Latina y el Caribe (CEPAL). 1989. *Balance preliminar de la economía de América Latina y el Caribe 1989*, nos. 485/486 (December). Santiago, Chile: United Nations.

———.1991a. *Indicadores macroeconómicos de la Argentina*. Buenos Aires: CEPAL.

———. 1991b. *La equidad en el panorama social de América Latina durante los años ochenta*. n.p.: CEPAL.

———.1997. *La brecha de la equidad: América Latina, el Caribe, y la Cumbre Social*. Santiago, Chile: United Nations.

Comisión Nacional Sobre la Desaparición de Personas (CONADEP). 1986. *Nunca Mas: Informe de la Comisión Nacional Sobre de la Desaparición de Personas*. 14th edition. Buenos Aires: EUDEBA.

Comité Ejecutivo para el Estudio de la Pobreza en la Argentina (CEPA). 1993a. *Necesidades Básicas Insatisfechas: Evolución intercensal 1980–1991*. Documento de trabajo no. 1. Buenos Aires: INDEC (June).

———. 1993b. *Evolución reciente de la pobreza en el Gran Buenos Aires 1988–1992*. Documento de trabajo no. 2. Buenos Aires: INDEC (August).

———. 1993c. *Hogares con necesidades básicas insatisfechas. (NBI) 1980–1991*. Documento de trabajo no. 3. Buenos Aires: INDEC (October).

Conniff, Michael L., ed. 1982. *Latin American Populism in Comparative Perspective*. Albuquerque: University of New Mexico Press.

Conover, Pamela Johnston. 1985. "The Impact of Group Economic Interests on Political Evaluations." *American Politics Quarterly* 13, no. 2: 139–66.

Cornelius, Wayne A. 1974. "Urbanization and Political Demand Making: Political Participation among the Migrant Poor in Latin American Cities." *American Political Science Review* 68 (September): 1125–46.

Cuenya, Beatriz. 1991. "El submercado de alquiler de piezas en Buenos Aires." In Rubén Gazzoli, ed., *Inquilinatos y hoteles*. Buenos Aires: Centro Editor.

Dahl, Robert A. 1971. *Polyarchy*. New Haven, Conn.: Yale University Press.

———. 1989. *Democracy and Its Critics*. New Haven, Conn.: Yale University Press.

Davies, James C. 1962. "Toward a Theory of Revolution." *American Sociological Review* 6 (1971): 5–19; reprinted in James C. Davies, ed., *When Men Revolt and Why*. New York: Free Press.

de la Torre, Carlos. 1999. Neopopulism in Contemporary Ecuador: The Case of Bucaram's

Use of the Mass Media. *International Journal of Politics, Culture and Society* 12, no. 4: 555–71.

de Ipola, Emilio. 1987. "La difícil apuesta del Peronismo democrático." In José Nun and Juan Carlos Portantiero, eds., *Ensayos sobre la transición democrática en la Argentina.* Buenos Aires: Puntosur.

del Franco, Analía. 1989. "Consideraciones organizacionales acerca del Programa Alimentario Nacional (PAN)." In Bernardo Kliksberg, ed., *Cómo enfrentar la pobreza?* Buenos Aires: Grupo Editor Latinoamericano.

de Riz, Liliana. 1998. "From Menem to Menem: Elections and Political Parties in Argentina." In Joseph S. Tulchin with Allison M. Garland, eds., *Argentina: The Challenges of Modernization.* Wilmington,Del.: Scholarly Resources.

Diamond, Larry. 1992. "Economic Development and Democracy Reconsidered." *American Behavioral Scientist* 35: 450–99.

Diamond, Larry, Juan J. Linz, and Seymour Martin Lipset, eds. 1989. *Democracy in Developing Countries: Latin America.* Boulder, Colo.: Lynne Rienner.

Díaz, Rodolfo Alejandro. 1995. "El empleo: cuestión de Estado." *Libro blanco sobre el empleo en la Argentina.* Buenos Aires: Ministerio de Trabajo y Seguridad Social.

Dietz, Henry. 1998. *Urban Poverty, Political Participation, and the State: Lima 1970–1990.* Pittsburgh: University of Pittsburgh Press.

di Tella, Torcuato. 1965. "Populism and Reform in Latin America." In Claudio Veliz, ed., *Obstacles to Change in Latin America.* London: Oxford University Press.

Drake, Paul W. 1982. "Conclusion: Requiem for Populism?" In Michael L Coniff, ed., *Latin American Populism in Comparative Perspective.* Albuquerque: University of New Mexico Press.

DuBois, Lindsay. 1998. "The Politics of the Past in an Argentine Working Class Neighborhood (1972–92)." Ph.D. diss. The New School for Social Research.

Easton, David. 1965. *A Systems Analysis of Political Life.* N.p.:John Wiley & Sons.

Economic Commission for Latin American and the Caribbean (ECLAC). 1992. *Economic Survey of Latin America and the Caribbean 1990.* Vol. 2. Santiago, Chile: United Nations.

———. 1993. *Economic Survey of Latin America and the Carribean 1991.* Vol. 2. Santiago, Chile: United Nations.

———. 1998a. *Economic Survey of Latin America and the Carribean, Summary 1997–1998.* Santiago, Chile: United Nations.

———. 1998b. *Social Panorama of Latin America 1997.* Santiago, Chile: United Nations.

———. 1999. *Balance preliminar de las economías de América Latina y el Caribe.* Santiago, Chile: United Nations.

Eckstein, Susan. 1989. "Power and Popular Protest in Latin America." In Susan Eckstein, ed., *Power and Popular Protest: Latin American Social Movements.* Berkeley: University of California Press.

Edwards, Alejandra Cox. 1997. "Labor Market Regulation in Latin America: An Overview." In Sebastian Edwards and Nora Claudia Lustig, eds., *Labor Markets in Latin America: Combining Social Protection with Market Flexibility.* Washington, D.C.: Brookings Institution Press.

Engelbrekt, Kjell. 1992. "Growing Poverty among Bulgaria's Pensioners." *FRE/FL Research Report* (28 February): 64–66.

Epstein, Edward C. 1998. "Participation by the Poor in Government Anti-Poverty Programs: The Cases of Chile, Peru, and Argentina Compared." Paper presented at the 1998 meeting of the Latin American Studies Association. Chicago, September 24–26.

Erro, Davide G. 1993. *Resolving the Argentine Paradox: Politics and Development 1966–1992.* Boulder, Colo.: Lynne Rienner.

Eulau, Heinz, and Michael S. Lewis-Beck, eds. 1985. *Economic Conditions and Electoral Outcomes: The United States and Western Europe.* New York: Agathon Press.

Evans, Geoffrey, and Stephen Whitefield. 1995. "The Politics and Economics of Democratic Commitment: Support for Democracy in Transition Societies." *British Journal of Political Science* 25: 485–514.

Feijoó, María del Carmen. 1984. *Buscando un techo: Familia y vivienda popular.* Buenos Aires: CEDES.

Feldman, Stanley. 1982. "Economic Self-Interest and Political Behavior." *American Journal of Political Science* 26, no. 3 (August): 446–65.

———. 1985. "Economic Self-interest and the Vote: Evidence and Meaning." In Heinz Eulau and Michael S. Lewis-Beck, eds., *Economic Conditions and Electoral Outcomes: The United States and Western Europe.* New York: Agathon Press.

Finifter, Ada W. 1996. "Attitudes toward Individual Responsibility and Political Reform in the Former Soviet Union." *American Political Science Review* 90, no. 1 (March): 138–52.

Foreign Broadcast Information Service (FBIS). Various editions.

Freire, Paulo. 1974. *Concientización: Teoria y práctica de la liberación.* Buenos Aires: Busqueda.

Fundación de Investigaciones Económicas Latinoamericanas (FIEL). 1993. *Indicadores de coyuntura,* no. 330 (December).

———.1994. *Indicadores de coyuntura,* no. 340 (October).

Galin, Pedro, and Marta Novick, eds. 1990. *La precarización del empleo en la Argentina.* Buenos Aires: Centro Editor.

Gallart, María Antonia, Martín Moreno, and Marcela Cerrutti. 1991. *Los trabajadores por cuenta propia del Gran Buenos Aires: Sus estrategias educativas y ocupacionales.* Buenos Aires: Centro de Estudios de Población.

Gamson, William A. 1992. *Talking Politics.* Cambridge, England: Cambridge University Press.

Gasiorowski, Mark J. 1995. "Economic Crisis and Political Regime Change: An Event History Analysis." *American Political Science Review* 89: 882–97.

Gay, Robert. 1993. *Popular Organization and Democracy in Rio de Janeiro: A Tale of Two Favelas.* Philadelphia: Temple University Press.

Gazzoli, Rubén, ed. 1991. "Inquilinatos y hoteles en la ciudad de Buenos Aires." In PROHA, *Alojamiento para sectores populares urbanos: Buenos Aires, Montevideo, San Pablo y México.* Buenos Aires: Ed. Plus Ultra.

Gazzoli, Rubén, Silvia Agostinis, and Néstor Jeifetz. [1987]. "Inquilinatos y hotels de Capital Federal y Dock Sur: Características de los establecimientos, población y condiciones de vida." TMs.

Geddes, Barbara. 1995. "The Politics of Economic Liberalization: A Review Essay." *Latin American Research Review* 30, no. 2: 195–214.

Geertz, Clifford. 1973. *The Interpretation of Cultures.* New York: Basic Books.

Gibson, Edward L. 1996. *Class and Conservative Parties: Argentina in Comparative Perspective.* Baltimore, Md.: Johns Hopkins University Press.

Gibson, John, and Anna Cielecka. 1995. "Economic Influences on the Political Support for Market Reform in Post-Communist Transitions: Some Evidence from the 1993 Polish Parliamentary Elections." *Europe-Asia Studies* 47, no. 5: 765–85.

Glewwe, Paul, and Dennis de Tray. 1991. "The Poor in Latin America during Adjustment: A Case Study of Peru." *Economic Development and Cultural Change* 40: 27–54.

Glewwe, Paul, and Gillette Hall. 1994. "Poverty Inequality and Living Standards during Unorthodox Adjustment: The Case of Peru, 1985–1990." *Economic Development and Cultural Change* 42: 689–718.

Golbert, Laura, and Emilio Tenti Fanfani. 1994. *Poverty and Social Structure in Argentina: Outlook for the 1990s*. Translated by Judy Lawton. Democracy and Social Policy Series Working Paper No. 6. Notre Dame, Ind.: Kellogg Institute.

Goldrich, Daniel, Raymond B. Pratt, and C. R. Schuller. 1967–68. "The Political Integration of Lower-Class Urban Settlements in Chile and Peru." *Studies in Comparative International Development* 3, no. 1. St. Louis, Mo.: Social Science Institute, Washington University.

Goren, Paul. 1997. "Political Expertise and Issue Voting in Presidential Elections." *Political Research Quarterly* 50, no.2 (June): 387–412.

Graham, Carol, and Cheikh Kane.1998. "Opportunistic Government or Sustaining Reform? Electoral Trends and Public-Expenditure Patterns in Peru, 1990–1995." *Latin American Research Review* 33, no. 1: 67–104.

Granovsky, Martín. 1991. "Política exterior: Las relaciones carnales con EE.UU." In *El Menemato: Radiografía de dos años de gobierno de Carlos Menem*. Buenos Aires: Letra Buena.

Green, Duncan. 1995. *Silent Revolution: The Rise of Market Economics in Latin America*. London: Cassell.

Grillo, Oscar. 1995. "Notas sobre las formas de asentamiento de los sectores populares en relación con los impactos de las políticas de ajuste." In Oscar Grillo, Mónica B. Lacarrieu, and Liliana Raggio, eds., *Políticas sociales y estrategias habitacionales*. Buenos Aires: Espacio Editorial.

Guidry, John Alexis. 1996. "The Everyday Life of Politics: Class, Democracy and Popular Discourse in Urban Brazil." Ph.D. diss. University of Michigan.

Gurr, Ted Robert. 1970. *Why Men Rebel*. Princeton, N.J.: Princeton University Press.

Haggard, Stephan, and Robert R. Kaufman. 1995. *The Political Economy of Democratic Transitions*. Princeton, N.J.: Princeton University Press.

Haveman, Robert H. 1987. *Poverty Policy and Poverty Research: The Great Society and the Social Sciences*. Madison: University of Wisconsin Press.

Headey, Bruce, Rudolph Andorka, and Peter Krause. 1995. "Political Legitimacy versus Economic Imperatives in System Transformation: Hungary and East Germany 1990–1993." *Social Indicators Research* 36, no. 3: 247–72.

Hennessy, Alistair. 1969. "Latin America." In Ghita Ionescu and Ernest Gellner, eds., *Populism: Its Meaning and National Characteristics*. N.p.: The Macmillan Company.

Hochschild, Jennifer L. 1981. *What's Fair?: American Beliefs about Distributive Justice*. Cambridge, Mass.: Harvard University Press.

Hodges, Donald C. 1988. *Argentina 1943–1987: The National Revolution and Resistance*. Revised edition. Albuquerque: University of New Mexico Press.

Huber, Evelyne, Dietrich Rueschemeyer, and John D. Stephens. 1997. "The Paradoxes of Contemporary Democracy: Formal, Participatory, and Social Democracy." *Comparative Politics* 29, no. 3 (April): 323–42.

Huntington, Samuel P. 1968. *Political Order in Changing Societies*. New Haven, Conn.: Yale.

Ianni, Octavio. 1975 [first reprinting, 1980]. *La formación del estado populista en América Latina*. Mexico City, Mexico: Ediciones Era.

Inglehart, Ronald.1997. *Modernization and Postmodernization: Cultural, Economic, and Political Change in 43 Societies.* Princeton, N.J.: Princeton University Press.

Inglehart, Ronald, Miguel Basañez, and Alejandro Moreno. 1998. *Human Values and Beliefs: A Cross-Cultural Sourcebook.* Ann Arbor: University of Michigan Press.

Instituto Nacional de Estadística y Censos (INDEC). 1988. *Encuesta de gastos e ingresos de los hogares: Estudios INDEC No. 11.* Buenos Aires: INDEC.

———. 1990. *La pobreza urbana en la Argentina.* Buenos Aires: INDEC.

———. 1992. *Estadística mensual IPC 2,* no. 3. Buenos Aires: INDEC.

———. 1994. *Anuario Estadístico de la República Argentina.* Buenos Aires: INDEC.

InterAmerican Development Bank (IADB). 1993. *Economic and Social Progress in Latin America: 1992 Report.* Washington, D.C.: IADB.

Ionescu, Ghita, and Ernest Gellner, eds. 1969. *Populism: Its Meaning and National Characteristics.* N.p.: The Macmillan Company.

IPSA Audits and Surveys. 1985–86 and 1988–90. Estudio RISC. Unpublished survey research. Buenos Aires: IPSA.

Iturrieta, Aníbal, ed. 1990. *El pensamiento peronista.* Madrid, Spain: Ediciones de Cultura Hispánica/ Instituto de Cooperación Iberoamericano.

Jelin, Elizabeth, ed. 1987. *Movimientos sociales y democracia emergente/2.* Buenos Aires: Centro Editor.

Johnson, Simon, and Marzena Kowalska. 1994. "Poland: The Political Economy of Shock Therapy." In Stephan Haggard and Steven B. Webb, eds., *Voting for Reform: Democracy, Political Liberalization, and Economic Adjustment.* Washington, D.C.: World Bank/Oxford University Press.

Karl, Terry Lynn. 1996. "Dilemmas of Democratization in Latin America." *Comparative Politics* 23 (October 1990): 1–21; reprinted in *Democracy in Latin America: Patterns and Cycles,* ed. Roderic Ai Camp. Wilmington, Del.: Scholarly Resources. 21–46.

Katzman, Rubén. 1989. "La heterogeneidad de la pobreza. El caso de Montevideo." *Revista de CEPAL,* no. 37 (April): 141–52.

Kiewiet, D. Roderick. 1983. *Macro-Economics and Micro-Politics: The Electoral Effects of Economic Issues.* Chicago: University of Chicago Press.

Kilpatrick, R. W. 1973. "The Income Elasticity of the Poverty Line." *Review of Economics and Statistics* 55, no. 3: 327–32.

Kinder, Donald R., and D. Roderick Kiewiet. 1979. "Economic Discontent and Political Behavior: The Role of Personal Grievances and Collective Economic Judgments in Congressional Voting." *American Journal of Political Science* 23: 495–527.

Kohl, Richard. 1995. "Sustaining the Transition: Are Social Contracts the Answer?" *World Policy Journal* 12, no. 3 (Fall): 109–17.

Labado, Alejandro, Alfredo Ladillinsky, and Susana Garmendia. 1991. "Inquilinatos y hoteles en la ciudad de Buenos Aires." *Cambios* 1 (June): 41–50.

Lagos, Marta. 1997. "Latin America's Smiling Mask." *Journal of Democracy* 8, no. 3 (July): 125–38.

Lane, Robert E. 1962. *Political Ideology.* New York: Free Press.

La Nación, various dates, 1990–92.

Larkins, Christopher. 1998. "Judiciary and Delegative Democracy in Argentina." *Comparative Politics* 30, no. 4: 423–42.

Lawton, Jorge A. 1995. "Conceptualizing Development: Moving Beyond Linear Northern Perspectives." In Jorge A. Lawton, ed., *Privatization amidst Poverty: Contemporary Chal-*

lenges in Latin American Political Economy. Miami, Fla.: North-South Center Press at the University of Miami.

Lehmann, David. 1990. *Democracy and Development in Latin America.* Philadelphia: Temple University Press.

Levine, Daniel H. 1992. *Popular Voices in Latin American Catholicism.* Princeton, N.J.: Princeton University Press.

———. 1993. "Popular Groups, Popular Culture, and Popular Religion." In Daniel H. Levine, ed., *Constructing Culture and Power in Latin America.* Ann Arbor: University of Michigan Press.

Levitsky, Steven. 1998. "Crisis, Party Adaptation and Regime Stability in Argentina: The Case of Peronism, 1989–1995." *Party Politics* 4, no. 4: 445–70.

Lewis, Oscar. 1961. *The Children of Sánchez.* New York: Modern Library.

Lewis-Beck, Michael S. 1988. *Economics and Elections: The Major Western Democracies.* Ann Arbor: University of Michigan Press.

Linz, Juan J. 1978. *The Breakdown of Democratic Regimes: Crisis, Breakdown, and Reequilibration.* Baltimore, Md.: Johns Hopkins University Press.

———. 1988. "Legitimacy of Democracy and the Socioeconomic System." In *Comparing Pluralist Democracies: Strains on Legitimacy*, ed., Mattei Dogan. Boulder, Colo.: Westview.

Linz, Juan, and Alfred Stepan. 1989. "Political Crafting of Democratic Consolidation or Destruction: European and South American Comparisons." In Robert A. Pastor, ed., *Democracy in the Americas: Stopping the Pendulum.* New York: Holmes & Meier.

Linz, Juan J., and Alfred Stepan. 1996. *Problems of Democratic Transition and Consolidation: Southern Europe, South America, and Post-Communist Europe.* Baltimore Md.: Johns Hopkins University Press.

López, Artemio. 1997. *La derrota del padre: Pobres estructurales y nuevos pobres en las elecciones de Capital Federal y Provincia de Buenos Aires.* Buenos Aires: Instituto de Estudios sobre Estado y Participación.

Lo Vuolo, Rubén M. 1997. "The Retrenchment of the Welfare State in Latin America: The Case of Argentina." *Social Policy Administration* 31, no.4: 390–409.

Lozano, Claudio, and Roberto Feletti. 1991. "La economía de Menem: Cambio estructural, crisis recurrente y destino incierto." In *El Menemato: Radiografía de dos años de gobierno de Carlos Menem.* Buenos Aires: Letra Buena.

Lumi, Susana. 1990. "Restricciones y posibilidades de la política habitacional argentina." In Eduardo S. Bustelo and Ernesto A. Isuani, eds., *Mucho, poquito o nada: Crisis y alternativas de política social en los '90.* Buenos Aires: UNICEF.

Lustig, Nora. 1995a. "Mexico: The Social Costs of Adjustment." In Jorge A. Lawton, ed., *Privatization amidst Poverty: Contemporary Challenges in Latin American Political Economy.* Miami, Fla.: North-South Center Press at the University of Miami.

Lustig, Nora, ed. 1995b. *Coping with Austerity: Poverty and Inequality in Latin America.* Washington: Brookings Institution Press.

Macpherson, C. B. 1972. *The Real World of Democracy.* Clarendon Press, 1966; reprint, New York: Oxford University.

Madsen, Douglas, and Peter G. Snow. 1991. *The Charismatic Bond: Political Behavior in Time of Crisis.* Cambridge, Mass.: Harvard University Press.

Mainwaring, Scott. 1987. "Urban Popular Movements, Identity and Democratization in Brazil." *Comparative Political Studies* 20, no. 2 (July): 131–59.

Mainwaring, Scott, Guillermo O'Donnell, and J. Samuel Valenzuela. 1992. Issues in Democratic Consolidation: the New South American Democracies in Comparative Perspective. Notre Dame, Ind.: University of Notre Dame Press for the Helen Kellogg Institute for International Studies.

Mainwaring, Scott, and Timothy R. Scully, eds. 1995. *Building Democratic Institutions: Party Systems in Latin America.* Stanford, Calif.: Stanford University Press.

Malamud-Goti, Jaime. 1996. *Game Without End: State Terror and the Politics of Justice.* Norman, Ok.: University of Oklahoma Press.

Maslow, A. H. 1954. *Motivation and Personality.* New York: Harper Brothers.

McAdam, Doug, John D. McCarthy, and Mayer N. Zald. 1988. "Social Movements." In Neil J. Smelser, ed., *Handbook of Sociology.* Newbury Park, Calif.: Sage.

McClintock, Cynthia. 1989. "Peru: Precarious Regimes, Authoritarian and Democratic." In Larry Diamond, Juan J. Linz, and Seymour Martin Lipset, eds. *Democracy in Developing Countries: Volume 4 Latin America.* Boulder, Colo.: Lynne Rienner.

————. 1993. "Peru's Fujimori: A Caudillo Derails Democracy." *Current History* 92, no.572: 112–19.

McGuire, James W. 1996. "Strikes in Argentina: Data Sources and Data Trends." *Latin American Research Review* 31, no. 3: 127–50.

————. 1997. *Peronism without Perón: Unions, Parties, and Democracy in Argentina.* Stanford, Calif.: Stanford University Press.

McSherry, J. Patrice. 1997. *Incomplete Transition: Military Power and Democracy in Argentina.* New York: St. Martin's Press.

Menem, Carlos, and Eduardo Duhalde. 1989. *La revolución productiva: De la Argentina especuladora a la Argentina del trabajo.* 2nd ed. n.p.: Fundación Lealtad.

Menem, Carlos, and Roberto Dromi. 1990. *Reforma del estado y transformación nacional.* Buenos Aires: Editorial Ciencias de la Administración S.R.L.

Midré, Georges. 1992. "Bread or Solidarity?: Argentine Social Policies, 1983–1990." *Journal of Latin American Studies* 24 (May): 343–73.

Miguens, José Enrique, and Frederick C. Turner, eds. 1988. *Racionalidad del peronismo.* Buenos Aires: Planeta.

Miller, S. M., and Pamela Roby. 1970. "Poverty: Changing Social Stratification." In Peter Townsend, ed., *The Concept of Poverty: Working Papers on Methods of Investigation and Life-styles of the Poor in Different Countries.* New York: American Elsevier.

Miller, Arthur H., Vicki L. Hesli, and William M. Reisinger. 1994. "Reassessing Mass Support for Political and Economic Change in the Former USSR." *American Political Science Review* 88: 399–411.

Minujin, Alberto. 1991. "New and Old Poverty in Argentina: The Consequences of the Crisis." Paper delivered to the International Statistics Institute, Cairo.

————., ed. 1992. *Cuesta Abajo—Los nuevos pobres: efectos de la crisis en la sociedad Argentina.* Buenos Aires: UNICEF/Losada.

————., ed. 1993. *Desigualdad y exclusión: Desafíos para la política social en la Argentina de fin de siglo.* Buenos Aires: UNICEF/Losada.

Minujin, Alberto, and Gabriel Kessler. 1995. *La nueva pobreza en la Argentina.* Buenos Aires: Editorial Planeta.

Minujin, Alberto, and Néstor López. 1994. "Nueva pobreza y exclusión: El caso Argentino." *Nueva Sociedad* (Caracas), no. 131 (May–June): 88–105.

Minujin, Alberto, and Alejandra Scharf. 1989. "Adulto equivalente e ingreso per capita:

Efectos sobre la estimación de la pobreza." *Desarrollo Económico* 29, no. 113. (April–June): 113–23.

Minujin, Alberto, and Pablo Vinocur. 1989. *¿Quiénes son los pobres?* Documento de trabajo no. 10. IPA: Buenos Aires. (July)

MOI. 1992. "The Federal Capital Squatters and Tenants Movement (Buenos Aires, Argentina): A Proposal for Organizational Development." Prepared by Néstor Jeifetz, Carla Rodríguez, and Daniel Rossi. (Mimeo, April).

Mondak, Jeffery J., Diana C. Mutz, and Robert Huckfeldt. 1996. "Persuasion in Context: The Multilevel Structure of Economic Evaluations." In Diana C. Mutz, Paul M. Sniderman, and Richard A. Brody, eds., *Political Persuasion and Attitude Change*. Ann Arbor: University of Michigan.

Montoya, Silvia, and Oscar Mitnik. 1994. *Acumulación de capital humano: ¿Determinante de la pobreza?* Córdoba, Argentina: Fundación Mediterranea.

Mora y Araujo, Manuel. 1985. "La naturaleza de la coalición Alfonsinista." In *La Argentina Electoral*. Buenos Aires: Editorial Sudamericana.

Moscona, Rafael. 1990. "Al gran pueblo Argentino, ¿salud?" *Argumento político* 1, no.1.

Muller, Edward N. 1995a. "Economic Determinants of Democracy." *American Sociological Review* 60 (December): 966–82.

———. 1995b. "Income Inequality and Democratization: Reply to Bollen and Jackman." *American Sociological Review* 60 (December): 990–96.

Muller, Edward N. and Mitchell A. Seligson. 1987. "Democratic Stability and Economic Crisis: Costa Rica, 1978–83." *International Studies Quarterly* 31: 301–26.

Munck, Gerardo L. 1998. *Authoritarianism and Democratization: Soldiers and Workers in Argentina, 1976–1983*. University Park: Pennsylvania State University Press.

Murmis, Miguel, and Silvio Feldman. 1992. "La heterogeneidad social de las pobrezas." In Minujin, ed., *Cuesta Abajo—Los nuevos pobres: efectos de la crisis en la sociedad Argentina*. Buenos Aires: UNICEF/Losada.

Mutz, Diane C. 1992. "Mass Media and the Depoliticization of Personal Experience." *American Journal of Political Science* 36, no. 2 (May): 483–508.

———. 1994. "Contextualizing Personal Experience: The Role of Mass Media." *Journal of Politics* 56, no. 3 (August): 689–714.

Mutz, Diana C. 1998. *Impersonal Influence: How Perceptions of Mass Collectives Affect Political Attitudes*. New York: Cambridge University Press.

Mutz, Diana C., and Jeffery J. Mondak. 1997. "Dimensions of Sociotropic Behavior: Group-Based Judgments of Fairness and Well-Being." *American Journal of Political Science* 41, no.1: 284–308.

Narayan, Deepa, with Raj Patel, Kai Schafft, Anne Rademacher, and Sarah Koch-Schulte. 2000. *Voices of the Poor: Can Anyone Hear Us?* New York: Oxford University Press for the World Bank.

Neal, Arthur. G., and Melvin Seeman. 1964. "Organizatoins and Powerlessness: A Test of the Mediation Hypothesis." *American Sociological Review* 29: 216–26.

Nelson, Joan M. 1989. "The Politics of Pro-Poor Adjustment." In Joan Nelson, ed., *Fragile Coalitions: The Politics of Economic Adjustment*. Washington, D.C.: Overseas Development Council.

———. 1992. "Poverty, Equity, and the Politics of Adjustment." In Stephan Haggard and Robert R. Kaufman, eds., *The Politics of Economic Adjustment*. Princeton, N.J.: Princeton University Press.

Neunreither, Karlheinz. 1993. "Subsidiarity as a Guiding Principle for European Community Activities." *Government and Opposition* 28, no.2 (spring): 206–20.

Newfarmer, Richard S. 1995. "Argentina's Progress from Insolvency to Recovery." In Jorge A. Lawton, ed., *Privatization amidst Poverty: Contemporary Challenges in Latin American Political Economy.* Miami, Fla.: North-South Center Press at the University of Miami.

Norden, Deborah L. 1996. *Military Rebellion in Argentina: Between Coups and Consolidation.* Lincoln: University of Nebraska.

Nun, José. 1989. *Crisis económica y despidos en masa.* Buenos Aires: Legasa.

Nun, José, and Juan Carlos Portantiero, eds. 1987. *Ensayos sobre la transición democrática en la Argentina.* Buenos Aires: Puntosur.

O'Donnell, Guillermo. 1978. "State and Alliance in Argentina, 1956–1976." *Journal of Development Studies,* no. 15: 3–33.

———. 1979. *Modernization and Bureaucratic-Authoritarianism.* Berkeley: University of California Institute of International Studies.

———. 1983. *Democracia en la Argentina: Micro y macro.* Working Paper no. 2. Notre Dame, Ind.: Kellogg Institute for International Studies.

———. 1988. *Bureaucratic Authoritarianism: Argentina, 1966–1973, in Comparative Perspective.* Berkeley: University of California Press.

———. 1993. "The Browning of Latin America." *New Perspectives Quarterly* 10 (Fall): 50–53.

———. 1994. "Delegative Democracy." *Journal of Democracy* 5, no. 1.

———. 1996. "Illusions about Consolidation." *Journal of Democracy* 7, no. 2 (April): 34–51.

———. 1998. "Polyarchies and the (Un)Rule of Law in Latin America." In Juan Méndez, Guillermo O'Donnell and Paulo Sérgio Pinheiro, eds., *The (Un)Rule of Law and the Underprivileged in Latin America.* Notre Dame, Ind.: Notre Dame Press.

O'Donnell, Guillermo, Philippe C. Schmitter, and Laurence Whitehead, eds. 1986. *Transitions from Authoritarian Rule.* Baltimore, Md.: Johns Hopkins University Press.

Ollier, Maria Matilde. 1986. *El fenómeno insurreccional y la cultura política (1969–1973).* Buenos Aires: Centro Editor.

Ostiguy, Pierre. 1997. "Peronismo y anti-peronismo: Bases socioculturales de la identidad política en la Argentina." *Revista de ciencias sociales* 6 (September): 133–215.

———.1998. "Political Identity and Social-Cultural Differentiation: Peronism and Anti-Peronism in Argentina." Ph.D. diss., University of California at Berkeley.

Oszlak, Oscar. 1991. *Merecer la ciudad.* Buenos Aires: HUMANITAS-CEDES.

Oxhorn, Philip. 1994. "Where Did All the Protesters Go? Popular Mobilization and the Transition to Democracy in Chile." *Latin American Perspectives* 21, no. 3 (summer): 49–68.

———. 1995. *Organizing Civil Society: The Popular Sectors and the Struggle for Democracy in Chile.* University Park: Pennsylvania State University Press.

Oxhorn, Philip, and Graciela Ducatenzeiler, eds.1998. *What Kind of Democracy? What Kind of Market? Latin America in the Age of Neoliberalism.* University Park: Pennsylvania State University Press.

Page, Joseph A. 1983. *Perón: A Bibliography.* New York: Random House.

Página 12, various dates.

Palermo, Vicente. 1998. "Moderate Populism: A Political Approach to Argentina's 1991 Convertibility Plan." Translated by John Collins. *Latin American Perspectives* 25, no 4: 36–62.

Panfichi, Aldo. 1997. "The Authoritarian Alternative: 'Anti-Politics' in the Popular Sectors in

Lima.'" In Douglas A. Chalmers, Carlos M. Vilas, Katherine Hite, Scott B. Martin, Keri-anne Piester, and Monique Segarra, eds. *The New Politics of Inequality in Latin America: Rethinking Participation and Representation.* Oxford, England: Oxford University Press.

Pásara, Luis. 1993. "Peru: Into a Black Hole." *Hemisphere* (winter/spring): 26–30.

Passerini, Luisa. 1987. Fascism in Popular Memory: The Cultural Experience of the Turin Working Class. Trans. Robert Lumley and Jude Bloomfield. New York: Cambridge University Press.

Patai, Daphne. 1988. *Brazilian Women Speak.* New Brunswick, N.J.: Rutgers University Press.

Peñalva, Susan, and Daniel Arroyo. 1991. "Cambios en la regulación estatal y crisis de la política social: Los actuales dilemas de la gestión municipal." *Cambios* 1 (June): 31–40.

Perlman, Janice E. 1976. *The Myth of Marginality: Urban Poverty and Politics in Rio De Janeiro.* Berkeley: University of California Press.

Pessino, Carola. 1997. "Argentina: The Labor Market during the Economic Transition." In Sebastian Edwards and Nora Claudia Lustig, eds., *Labor Markets in Latin America: Combining Social Protection with Market Flexibility.* Washington, D.C.: Brookings Institution Press.

Pi de la Serra, Miguel. 1983. *Constitución y República.* Buenos Aires. Ediciones El Cronista Comercial.

Pion-Berlin, David. 1994. "To Prosecute or to Pardon? Human Rights Decisions in the Latin American Southern Cone." *Human Rights Quarterly* 16, no. 1:105–30.

Pion-Berlin, David, and George Lopez. 1991. "Of Victims and Executioners: Argentine State Terror, 1975–79." *International Studies Quarterly* 35 (March): 63–86.

Piven, Frances Fox, and Richard Cloward. 1977. *Poor People's Movements.* New York: Pantheon Books.

Porter, Marilyn. 1983. *Home, Work and Class Consciousness.* Manchester, England.: Manchester University Press.

Portes, Alejandro. 1972. "Rationality in the Slum: An Essay on Interpretive Sociology." *Comparative Studies in Society and History* 14, no. 3: 268–85.

Powell, G. Bingham Jr., and Guy D. Whitten. 1993. "A Cross-National Analysis of Economic Voting: Taking Account of the Political Context." *American Journal of Political Science* 37 (May): 391–414.

Powers, Denise V., and James H. Cox. 1997. "Echoes from the Past: The Relationship between Satisfaction with Economic Reforms and Voting Behavior in Poland." *American Political Science Review* 91, no. 3 (September): 617–33.

Powers, Nancy R. 1995a. "The Politics of Poverty in the 1990s." *Journal of Interamerican Studies and World Affairs.* 37, no. 4 (winter): 89–137.

———. 1995b. "Poverty Looks at Democracy: Material Interests and Political Thinking in Contemporary Argentina." Ph. D. diss., University of Notre Dame.

———. 1999."Coping with Economic Hardship in Argentina: How Material Interests Affect Individuals' Political Interests." *Canadian Journal of Political Science* 32: 521–49.

Prévôt Schapira, Marie-France. 1996. "Las políticas de lucha contra la pobreza en la periferia de Buenos Aires, 1984–1994." *Revista Mexicana de Sociología* 59, no. 2 (April–June): 73–94.

Przeworski, Adam.1985. *Capitalism and Social Democracy.* Cambridge, England: Cambridge University Press.

———.1991. *Democracy and the Market.* Cambridge, England: Cambridge University Press.

————. 1996. "Public Support for Economic Reforms in Poland." *Comparative Political Studies* 29, no. 5 (October): 520–43.

Przeworski, Adam, Michael Alvarez, José Antonio Cheibub, Fernando Limongi. 1996. "What Makes Democracies Endure?" *Journal of Democracy* 7: 39–55.

Putnam, Robert D. 1993. *Making Democracy Work: Civic Traditions in Modern Italy.* Princeton, N.J.: Princeton University Press.

Raggio, Liliana. 1995. "Un lugar en la ciudad: Alternativas habitacionales en los tiempos de la crisis." In Oscar Grillo, Mónica B. Lacarrieu, and Liliana Raggio, eds., *Políticas sociales y estrategias habitacionales.* Buenos Aires: Espacio Editorial.

Ranis, Peter. 1992. *Argentine Workers: Peronism and Contemporary Class Consciousness.* Pittsburgh: University of Pittsburgh Press.

Remmer, Karen L. 1991. "The Political Impact of Economic Crisis in Latin America in the 1980's." *American Political Science Review* 85: 777–800.

————.1996. "The Sustainability of Political Democracy: Lessons from South America." *Comparative Political Studies* 29, no. 6 (December): 611–34.

Reuters wire service reports, via Nexis-Lexis.

Reynals, Cristina, Mónica Giglio, and Nelda Kömkle. 1991. "Programa de radicación de villas y barrios carenciados de Capital Federal: De la marginalidad a la integración." [photocopy] Paper issued by the Secretaria de Planeamiento, Municipalidad de la Ciudad de Buenos Aires.

Roberts, Kenneth M. 1995. "Neoliberalism and the Transformation of Populism in Latin America: The Peruvian Case." *World Politics* 48 (October): 82–116.

Rock, David. 1987. *Argentina 1516–1987: From Spanish Colonization to Alfonsín.* Berkeley: University of California Press.

————. 1993. *Authoritarian Argentina: The Nationalist Movement, Its History and Its Impact.* Berkeley: University of California Press.

Rodrik, Dani. 1994. "The Rush to Free Trade in the Developing Wold: Why So Late? Why Now? Will It Last?" In Stephan Haggard and Steven B. Webb, eds., *Voting for Reform: Democracy, Political Liberalization, and Economic Adjustment.* Oxford, England: Oxford University Press for the World Bank.

Rose, Richard. 1993. "The Bad News is also the Good News in Eastern Europe." *The American Enterprise* 4, no. 4 (July–August): 26–29.

Rose, Richard, and William T. E. Mishler. 1994. "Mass Reaction to Regime Change in Eastern Europe: Polarization or Leaders and Laggards." *British Journal of Political Science* 4, no. 2 (April): 159–82.

Rosenthal, Gert. 1989. "Latin American and Caribbean Development in the 1980s and the Outlook for the Future." *CEPAL Review* 39 (December): 7–17.

Sabato, Hilda, and Marcelo Cavarozzi, eds. 1984. *Democracia, orden político y parlamento fuerte.* Buenos Aires: Centro Editor.

Sartori, Giovanni. 1969. "From the Sociology of Politics to Political Sociology." In Seymour Martin Lipset, ed., *Politics and the Social Sciences.* New York: Oxford University Press.

Sassen, Saskia. 1996. *Losing Control: Sovereignty in an Age of Globalization.* New York: Columbia University Press.

Schmitter, Philippe C., and Terry Lynn Karl. 1991. "What Democracy Is . . . and Is Not." *Journal of Democracy* 2, no. 3 (summer): 75–88.

Schumpeter, Joseph A. 1947. *Capitalism, Socialism and Democracy.* 2nd ed. New York: Harper.

Schvarzer, Jorge. 1992. "The Argentine Riddle in Historical Perspective." *Latin American Research Review* 27, no. 1: 169–81.

Scott, James C. 1976. *The Moral Economy of the Peasant.* New Haven, Conn.: Yale University Press.

———. 1985. *Weapons of the Weak: Everyday Forms of Peasant Resistance.* New Haven, Conn.: Yale.

Sen, Amartya. 1987. *The Standard of Living.* Ed. Geoffrey Hawthorn. Cambridge, England: Cambridge University Press.

Sharpe, Kenneth Evan. 1977. *Peasant Politics: Struggle in a Dominican Village.* Baltimore, Md.: Johns Hopkins.

Sherraden, Michael. 1991. *Assets and the Poor: A New American Welfare Policy.* New York: M.E. Sharpe.

Shue, Henry. 1980. *Basic Rights: Subsistence, Affluence, and U.S. Foreign Policy.* Princeton, N.J.: Princeton University Press.

Sistema de Información, Monitoreo, y Evaluación de Programas Sociales (SIEMPRO). 1999. "Informes de Situación Social 1999." Buenos Aires: Ministerio de Desarrollo Social y Medio Ambiente. Online at http://www.siempro.org.ar/

Silva, Juan, and Frans J. Schuurman. 1989. "Neighborhood Associations in Buenos Aires: Contradictions within Contradictions." In Frans Schuurman and Ton Van Naerssen, eds., *Urban Social Movements in the Third World.* London: Routledge.

Smith, William C. 1990. "Democracy, Distributional Conflicts and Macroeconomic Policy-making in Argentina, 1983–89." *Journal of Interamerican Studies and World Affairs* 33, no. 2: 1–41.

———. 1991. *Authoritarianism and the Crisis of the Argentine Political Economy.* Stanford, Calif.: Stanford University Press.

Smith, William C., and Roberto Patricio Korzeniewicz, eds. 1997. *Politics, Social Change and Economic Restructuring in Latin America.* Miami, Fla.: North-South Center Press at the University of Miami.

Starr, Pamela K. 1997. "Government Coalitions and the Viability of Currency Boards: Argentina under the Cavallo Plan." *Journal of Interamerican Studies and World Affairs* 39, no. 2: 83–133.

Stokes, Susan C. 1995. *Cultures in Conflict: Social Movements and the State in Peru.* Berkeley: University of California Press.

———. 1996. "Public Opinion and Market Reforms: The Limits of Economic Voting." *Comparative Political Studies* 29, no.5 (October): 499–519.

———. 1997. "Democratic Accountability and Policy Change: Economic Policy in Fujimori's Peru." *Comparative Politics* 29: 209–26.

Szusterman, Celia. 1996. "The Argentine Elections." *Electoral Studies* 15: 109–16.

Tarrow, Sidney. 1991. "Struggle, Politics, and Reform: Collective Action, Social Movements, and Cycles of Protest." *Western Societies Program Occasional Paper No. 21*, 2nd ed. Ithaca, N.Y.: Cornell Studies in International Affairs.

Teubal, Miguel. 1989. "Hambre y alimentación en la Argentina." *Realidad Economica*, no. 89 (4th bimonthly): 85–103.

Tilly, Charles. 1978. *From Mobilization to Revolution.* Reading, Mass.: Addison-Wesley.

Tironi, Eugenio. 1989. *¿Pobreza = frustración = violencia? Crítica empírica a un mito recurrente.* Working Paper no. 123. Notre Dame, Ind.: Helen Kellogg Institute for International Studies.

Torrado, Susana. 1992. *Estructura social de la Argentina: 1945–1983*. Buenos Aires: Ediciones de la Flor.

Townsend, Peter. ed. 1970. *The Concept of Poverty: Working Papers on Methods of Investigation and Life-Styles of the Poor in Different Countries*. New York: American Elsevier.

Turner, Frederick C., and Carlos A. Elordi. 1995. "Economic Values and the Role of Government in Latin America." *International Social Science Journal* 47, no. 3: 473–88.

United Nations Development Program. 1997. *Human Development Report 1997*. New York: Oxford.

van Steenbergen, Bart, ed. 1993. *The Condition of Citizenship*. London: Sage.

von Mettenheim, Kurt, and James Malloy, eds. 1998. *Deepening Democracy in Latin America*. Pittsburgh: University of Pittsburgh Press.

Waisman, Carlos H. 1987. *Reversal of Development in Argentina*. Princeton, N.J.: Princeton University Press.

Walton, John. 1993. *Urban Poverty in Latin America*. Latin American Program Working Paper No. 202. Washington, D.C.: Woodrow Wilson Center.

Wang, T. Y., with response by William J. Dixon, Edward N. Muller, and Mitchell A. Seligson. 1993. "Controversy: Inequality and Political Violence Revisited." *American Political Science Review* 87: 979–93.

Weatherford, M. Stephen. 1983. "Economic Voting and the 'Symbolic Politics' Argument: A Reinterpretation and Synthesis." *American Political Science Review* 77, no. 1: 158–74.

Weber, Max. 1978. *Economy and Society, Vol. 1*. Ed. Guenther Roth and Claus Wittich. Berkeley: University of California Press.

Weffort, Francisco C. 1976. "Clases populares y desarrollo social: Contribución al estudio del Populismo." In Weffort and Quijano, *Populismo, marginalización y dependencia: Ensayos de interpretación sociológica*, 2nd ed. Ciudad Universitaria Rodrigo Facio, Costa Rica: EDUCA.

Weffort, Francisco, and Anibal Quijano. 1976. *Populismo, marginalización y dependencia: Ensayos de interpretación sociológica*, 2nd ed. Ciudad Universitaria Rodrigo Facio, Costa Rica: EDUCA.

Weyland, Kurt. 1996. "Neopopulism and Neoliberalism in Latin America: Unexpected Affinities." *Studies in Comparative International Development* 31, no. 3: 3–31.

———. 1998a. "The Political Fate of Market Reform in Latin America, Africa, and Eastern Europe." *International Studies Quarterly* 42 (December): 645–74.

———. 1998b. "Swallowing the Bitter Pill: Sources of Popular Support for Neoliberal Reform in Latin America." *Comparative Political Studies* 31, no. 5 (October): 539–68.

———. 1999. "Clarifying a Contested Concept: 'Populism' in Latin American Studies." Paper presented at the 95th annual meeting of the American Political Science Association, Atlanta, September 2–5.

Wiles, Peter. 1969. "A Syndrome, not a Doctrine." In Ghita Ionescu and Ernest Gellner, eds., *Populism: Its Meaning and National Characteristics*. N.p.: The Macmillan Company.

Wise, Carol. 1994. "The Politics of Peruvian Economic Reform: Overcoming the Legacies of State-Led Development." *Journal of Interamerican Studies and World Affairs* 36, no. 1:75–126.

World Bank.1993a. *Argentina: From Insolvency to Growth*. Washington, D.C.: World Bank.

———. 1993b. *Argentina's Privatization Program: Experience, Issues, and Lessons*. Washington, D.C.: World Bank.

———. 1995 *Argentina's Poor: A Profile (Report No. 13318–AR)*.

World Values Study Group. 1994. *World Values Survey*, 1981–1984 and 1990–1993 (Computer file). ICPSR version. Ann Arbor, Mich.: Institute for Social Research (producer), 1994; Ann Arbor, Mich.: Interuniversity Consortium for Political and Social Research (distributor).

Worsley, Peter. 1969. "The Concept of Populism." In Ghita Ionescu and Ernest Gellner, eds. *Populism: Its Meaning and National Characteristics*. N.p.: The Macmillan Company.

Zaffaroni, Adriana, and Arturo Armada. 1991. "El movimiento villero entre la negociación y la protesta." *Cambios* 1 (June): 51–64.

Zagorski, Paul W. 1994. "Civil–Military Relations and Argentine Democracy: The Armed Forces under the Menem Government." *Armed Forces and Society* 20 (spring): 423–37.

Zaller, John R. 1992. *The Nature and Origins of Mass Opinion*. New York: Cambridge University Press.

Index

Absolute Liberal Democracy (AL), 186–88, 190

Absolute Results Regime (AR), 193–97, 208

adjustment policies (*ajustes*), 260*n6*; interviewees' views of, 97, 99, 173, 175

Adriana: assets of, 122; child's future, 103; housing, 60, 64, 84–85

Alfonsín, Raúl, 1, 225; and democracy, 147, 184, 197, 200–2, 267*n11*; and military, 38–39, 166; and PJ, 159–60; economy and policies of, 41–43, 45, 47, 138; interviewees' views of, 144–46, 157; public opinion of, 170

Alianza (Alliance for Work, Justice, and Education), 226

Amanda, 96–98; housing of, 60, 65; human assets of, 122–23; on inequality, 107–8; on party reputations, 156–57

Andrés, 117–18; 258*n24*; assets of, 51, 122, 125; views of, 106, 123, 152, 163, 175–76, 183, 187

Angeloz, Eduardo, 157, 160, 172, 266*n44*

Argentina: as case study, 2–3; political history of, 35–39

assets, 121–25

Association of State Workers (ATE), 119–20, 131, 137

Atilio, 117–18; assets of, 122; coping by, 134; housing of, 60, 65; views on democracy, 189; views on Menem, 156; voting by, 164

Betina, 104–5, 158, 261*n3*, 261*n16*; AR pattern views of, 196–98; human assets, 101, 125

blame. *See* responsibility

Bolivia, 47

Boltvinik, Julio, 93, 96, 98

Braden, 151, 263*n13*

Buenos Aires (Federal Capital): city council of,

71, 77, 207; types of housing in, 52–60; shantytown movement in, 69, 75

Buenos Aires (Greater), 43, 47, 54–55, 64, 100, 113

Bulgaria, 232, 235

Bunge y Born, 46, 153, 264*n16*

Carlos, 103, 165, 204–6, 261*n15*, 264*n28*; assets of, 122; coping by 34; expectations of, 65–66, 136–37; housing of, 56, 267*n13*; perceived needs of, 91–92

Carrion, Julio F., 230

casa tomada, 54–57, 62; collective action in, 65, 68–69; compared to other housing types, 58, 63, 84; identity with, 69–70

Castells, Manuel, 75, 77, 81–82

Catholic Church, 5, 36, 49, 143, 156, 178; charity by, 126–27; public opinion about, 172

Catterberg, Edgardo, 198–201; and María Braun, 147

Cecilia, 56, 112, 114–17, 258*n24*, 262*n8*; assets of, 122; coping by, 131–34; expectations of, 136–37

CEPA (Comité Ejecutivo para el Estudio de la Pobreza en la Argentina), 124, 256*n29*

CGT (General Labor Confederation), 42, 220, 224, 225, 229

changas, 122–25, 222. *See also* self-help

charity, 125–27, 130, 133

children: as political interests, 77, 83, 111, 116; educational opportunities for, 100–2; impact of housing on, 58, 62, 65; parents' expectations for, 103–5

Chile, 73, 75, 228

citizens, 17, 142, 243; governance on behalf of, 23–26; political interests of, 17–18, 33, 190–91

citizenship: as basis of democracy, 5–6, 23;
coping and, 238–39; expressive acts of, 217;
quality of, 203–8, 237

civil society, 29, 31, 39. *See also* grassroots, organizations; social movements

class identity: and ideology, 165; and microfocus 111, 177; and partisanship, 97–98,
147–49, 162; and poverty, 89, 145; and
regime legitimation pattern, 208; in Argentina 144–45. *See also* identities; political
parties

class, social: 29, 78, 104, 111–12, 116, 145

Claudia, 165–67, 194–95, 260n9, 265n36

clientelism: and coping, 130; and microfocus,
111; and micro-macro link, 118; housing
movements try to avoid, 69, 74–75, 80, 82,
217; in Montserrat and San Telmo, 127–28;
in political science literature, 29, 33, 67, 73;
interviewees and, 15, 146, 154–55

Cohen, Youssef, 252n5

collective action, 6–7, 33, 178, 221; for housing, 67–86

Communist Party, 161, 204, 206

CONADEP (National Commission on Disappeared Persons), 38

Congress, Argentine, 42, 44, 67, 159, 163, 189,
202, 224

consciousness, 26, 28, 72–83, 111, 165,
217–18. *See also* micro-macro linking

constitution, Argentine, 83, 85, 135, 137, 143,
183

contexts, 2–3, 10, 211–15, 218, 219; and coping with unemployment, 222, 234–35; and
democratic legitimacy, 180–81, 200–1,
208–9; and perception of interests, 10–11,
21, 27–28, 112, 177–79, 219; economic,
137–38; expectations affected by, 135–39,
200–1; needs changed by, 90; in Argentina
in mid-1990s, 224–26; in Eastern Europe,
233–35; in Peru, 230–32; in populism literature, 28–29; political, 32–33

conventillo, 59–60, 65, 102–03, 105–06. *See
also inquilinatos*

Convertibility Law, 46–49, 220, 225

coping, 3, 10, 19, 21, 211–12, 262n7; and citizenship, 203–4, 238–39; and political interests, 213, 217–18; and poverty status, 134;
capacity for, 130, 132, 134, 212, 220, 235;
strategies, 2, 83, 121–36; strategies considered normal, 133, 136–38; strategies in Eastern Europe, 232–33, 269n29; strategies in
Latin America, 228; with low inflation, 222;

with high unemployment, 222–24. *See also
specific strategies:* assets, clientelism, credit,
informal sector, in-kind goods, collective action, resources, self-help

Corrientes, 221

corruption, 39, 172, 202, 209, 265n36, 267n18

credit, 47, 129, 222

crime, 116, 119

De la Rúa, Fernando, 172, 221, 224, 226,
264n17, 265n41

De la Torre, Carlos, 253n26

debt, foreign, 36, 41, 44–45, 162, 216, 227; effect of on expectations, 138; views about,
168, 173, 175, 207

democracy, 1–2, 4, 6–8, 18; attacks on,
165–66; delegative, 159; impact of poverty
on, 180–81; political culture and, 177; populism literature and, 29; legitimacy of,
180–81, 185–202; parties' reputations for,
147; public opinion surveys on, 169–70,
198–200; quality of, 32, 236–39; quality of
in Argentina, 39, 188, 192, 202–3; views on,
76, 149, 167. *See also* democracy, definitions
of

democracy, definitions of: Alfonsín's, 1,
267n11; citizens', 180–85; freedom, 182,
185–86, 209; institutions and rule of law,
183–87, 209; "not-military," 184, 197, 209;
physical well-being, 194; political scientists',
4, 185, 189; popular and participatory,
184–86

Di Tella, Torcuato, 253n26

Diego, 108, 151, 192, 202

Dietz, Henry, 7

discrimination, 14, 76, 97

domestic work, 14, 97

Duffey, John J., 255n23

Duhalde, Eduardo, 255n18

Eastern Europe, 232–35

Easton, David, 251n4

Eckstein, Susan, 19

economic voting literature, 22–28, 32–33, 205,
215–17, 219; compared to other literatures,
28, 30; context missing in, 27; sociotropism
in, 32–33, 82; developments in, 252n13;
U.S./European basis of, 24, 27, 252n9

economy, 18, 23–24; and democratization, 4.
See also economy, Argentina

economy, Argentina, 1, 39–48; military
regime's policies, 40–41; Alfonsín's policies,

41–43; Menem's policies, 43–48; decline in, 34, 137–38; diverse impact of policies of, 10; views about alternative policies, 141

Eduardo, 13–15, 21, 57, 102, 128, 141, 261n15, coping by, 124, 126; views of, about political actors and issues, 154–55, 158, 176, 187, 264n21

education level: and citizens' ideologies, 161; and employment, 268n8; and legitimation pattern, 190, 195, 197; and views in former Soviet Union, 233; as asset, 125; and focus, 112, 117

education: 144, 172–73; in macrofocus, 116, 119; opportunity for, 99–102, 107

Effective Liberal Democracy (EL), 188–92, 197–98, 266n5

elections: and democracy, 183–85; in 1973, 36; in 1983, 1, 38, 163; in 1989, 1, 38, 135–36, 149, 160; in 1991, 166; in 1992, 168, 172, 264n17, 265n41; in 1994, 178, 225; in 1995, 2, 136, 220–221, 225, 267n3; in 1997, 221; in 1999, 226

electoral system, Argentine, 163

elites, 17, 19–20, 29, 30, 35; and democracy, 5, 8, 239; in research literatures 4–5, 32–33

employment: interest in, 77, 83; coping via extra, 123, 130. See also unemployment

envy, 108

Esperanza, 75, 106–7

Evans, Geoffrey and Stephen Whitefield, 235

expectations, 10, 19–21; about alternatives, 178–79, 234; about democracy, 200–1, 236; about future, 101–7; about government responsibilities, 49, 210–11, 237–239; about housing, 65, 86, 135; about inflation (ca. 1992), 96; about military coups, 159; about normal living, 93–94, 136–38, 211–13, 216, 233, 262n15; learned, 136–38

feasibility, 18–19, 21, 33, 213, 217, 251n4

Finifter, Ada, 233

flux, 94–99, 260n5

focus of political thinking: 120–39, 226. See also microfocus, macrofocus, micro-macro linking

Francesca: assets of, 122; housing action by, 70–71, 74–77, 80–83, 85; on democracy, 184, 192; on her children's futures, 103–4; on Perón, 208; views of, 143–44, 150, 260n8

freedom: democracy as, 182, 185, 202; positive, 93–94, 98–99, 107, 212. See also AL, AR, EL, and PD

Freire, Paulo, 73

Frente del Sur, 193

Frente Grande, 44, 225

FREPASO (Frente del País Solidario), 44, 80, 114, 178, 220–21, 225–26

Fujimori, Alberto, 9, 181, 184, 187–88, 195, 228–32

Gabriela, 90, 122, 153, 178, 261n16

Geddes, Barbara, 8–9

Goren, Paul, 23

Graciela, 96, 98–99, 158, 261nn15, 16

grassroots: in political science literature, 29–30, 211; level of analysis, 4–6; organizations, 26–28, 32–33, 114, 137, 217–18; political interests and activities of, 5–7, 17, 20. See also civil society; collective action; expectations; Padelai; social movements

guerrilla movements, 37, 161, 193, 231–32

Guidry, John, 254n33

Haggard, Stephan, and Robert R. Kaufman, 8

Hilda 59, 64, 66–68, 84–85

home ownership, 51–52, 84, 98–99, 130–31

Horacio 151, 195

hotels: 54, 57–59, 257nn8, 10; and collective action, 68–69; compared to other housing types, 58, 60, 63, 84

housing: 14–15, 49, as asset, 125; collective action for, 52, 61, 67–86, 259n33; coping and, 135; dangerous, 15, 57, 65, 258n22; evictions from, 56, 70, 85, 115; government responsibility for, 26, 135; impact on quality of life, 52–62; individual political action for, 66–67; interests, 50–86, 114–15; non-political action for, 64–66; public, 53–54; rental, 53, 64; rights to, 14, 62, 78; shortage, 53–54, 135, type, impact on quality of life, 51–53, 56–63, 84–85; types compared, 58, 60, 63, 84–85, 124. See also specific types of housing

Hungary, 232

Ianni, Octavio, 29, 253n26, 253n27

identities: and interests, 3, 10, 177–78, 211–12, 214, 218–19; and social movements, 72; in microfocus, 111; with housing, 62–63, 69–70. See also class; political parties

ideology, 22, 27, 137, 146–47, 160–61, 163–64, 192

Ignacio, 101, 164, 193

import substitution industrialization (ISI), 4, 28, 35–38, 48

indemnifications, 128, 224

individual-level coping strategies. *See* self-help

industrialization: decline in, 38, 40, 42, 48; growth of, 36

inequality, 17, 99–109, 145, 222, 261nn15, 16; and democracy, 76, 192–93, 203–08, 251n6; levels of, 38, 41, 43, 48

inflation: and support for Menem, 2, 31, 97, 220, 222; as an interest, 2, 25, 216, 227; coping with, 33, 135–36, 138–39, 220, 222, 227; in Argentina, 1, 36, 38, 42–43, 46–49, 96, 113; in Eastern Europe, 232, 234; in Latin America, 41, 227–28; in Peru, 228–32

informal sector, 41–42, 47–49, 123–24, 130, 228, 233

information, 23–27, 215–16, 252nn12, 13, 15, 16, 253n20

in-kind goods, 125–26, 130

inquilinatos, 54, 59–60, 257nn8, 10; compared to other housing, 58, 60, 63, 84; identity with, 69–70

insecurity, 94–99, 119–20, 124, 212–13, 223, 230–235. *See also* security

interests: activities in pursuit of, 7; class-based, 29; conceptualizing, 16–20, 251n4, 252nn5, 7, 10, 16; contexts and, 2, 28, 142–79; in health care, 83, 119, 144, 175; nonmaterial 22, 25, 116, 170, 191–92, 197, 210; defined political, 16; discussed political, 2, 19–22, 33, 65, 210–14; public goods as, 78. *See also* housing; values

International Monetary Fund (IMF), 224–25

interviewees (overall): citizenship status of, 261n2; coping by, 121–27, 129–34; grass-roots action by, 130–31; material conditions of, 49, 51, 54; views about Menem of, 263n10. *See also specific names of relatives*

interviewees and relatives. *See specific names*

interviews, 2–3; analysis of, 246–48; conduct of, 243–46, 251n2; confidentiality in, 244–45; foreigner's advantage in, 246; goals of, 11, 198; selection of persons for, 242–43

IPA (Study of Argentine Poverty), 50–51, 124, 256n29

Jacobo (Cecilia's husband), 103–4; 260n9

Jorge, housing and, 61–63, 70, 74–82, 85; mentioned, 261n16, 112, 117; microfocus of, 13–15, 21

Juan Antonio, 156, 162–63, 168–69, 174, 176, 207, 261n16; on housing stigma, 62; on unemployment, 222; on his children's opportunities, 100, 106–7

judiciary, Argentine, 39, 119

Julio, 137, 151, 164, 168, 216, 261n18; expectations of, 65; housing and quality of life of, 60–61; on democracy, 184–85; on inequality 108–9

Justicialist Party (PJ): 36–38, 149, 183, 220; neighborhood activities of, 127, 263n5; versus Alfonsín, 41–42, 159–60. *See also* Peronism

Kiewiet, D. Roderick, 24

labor market, 40, 119

labor reforms, 202, 223–24

labor unions: in Argentine history, 35, 37–38, 42; and Menem, 44–46, 221, 229; in-kind goods from, 125; and democracy, 8

Lagos, Marta, 8

Latin America, 4, 7–8, 41, 227–28

Latin Barometer, 8, 251n7

Lawton, Jorge, 5

left, the: 78, 137, 193, 254n10; Carlos and, 66, 204–6; views about, 79–80, 160–65, 182. *See also* ideology; Marx

legitimacy: bases of democratic, 7–11, 180–81, 185–202, 208–9, 212, 231, 235; defined, 185–86, 202

Leonardo, 65, 122, 188, 261n16

level of analysis, individual, 6–7, 32

Levine, Daniel, 254n33

liberalism, 16, 23, 182. *See also* neoliberalism

liberation theology, 73

Linz, Juan, 9, 185–86, 202, 209

Luder, Italo, 146, 263n7

luxury, 88–92, 107–8

macrofocus, 13–16, 21, 111–12, 116–18, 133, 142, 213; and citizenship, 236; and identities, 177; in legitimation patterns, 196

Madsen, Douglas and Peter G. Snow, 253n26

Marcela, 122–23, 140–41, 158, 174, 182

marginality, literatures on, 260n4

María José, 34, 122; views of, 91, 140, 165–67, 176, 197–98, 261n16

María, 175–76, 206–7, 265n36; on MODIN, 165–67; on military, 195, 197; on needs and constraints, 91, 106

Martín, 122, 258n24; and housing, 67–68, 70–71, 74–76, 79–83, 85; views of, 100, 162, 176, 189, 261nn15, 16

Marx/Marxism, 16, 29, 136, 160, 193, 204

MAS (*Movimiento al Socialismo*), 113–14, 162, 164, 264n25

Maslow, A. H., 88

material conditions (objective), 20, 29, 49, 99–101; emotional/spiritual deprivations from, 92–94; living with, 33, 88; heterogeneity of, 30–31, 134; not factor in focus, 112, 117

material interests: 16, 25, 30, 33, 48, 84–109, 157; and class, 87–88; and regime legitimation, 2, 196, 198, 208; and social norms, 93–94; as political interests, 13–16, 141, 210–19; compared to "needs," 88–94; conceptualization of, using poverty literature, 93–94; coping with, 135–36; housing as, 82–84. *See also* interests; micro-macro linking; values, nonmaterialist

Matilde, 151, 196–97

McAdam, Doug, and John D. McCarthy and Mayer N. Zald, 6

McGuire, James, 45–46

media: in Argentina, 38–39, 49, 156, 161; and economic voting, 23–26, 32–33, 216, 253n20; and micro-macro linking, 26; and Padelai, 71–72; framing by, 150

Menem, Carlos: 1–2, 9, 38–39, 220–26, 267n10; alternatives to leadership of, 157–60; 170–72; alternatives to policies of, 172–77; and elections (various), 38, 172, 265n41; and military, 38–39, 201; as Peronist, 143, 150–55; as populist, 31–32, 264n20; compared with Fujimori, 229–31; economic policies of, 43–48, 138–40; public opinion polls on, 221; quality of democracy under, 201–3, 269n26; social policies of, 128–29; views about, 114–15, 118, 144, 145–46, 149–57, 202, 263n10; views about policies of, 97, 99, 106, 141, 192–93, 220, 265n35

methods: generalizing from, 226–27, 241–42, 247–48; of this study, 2–4, 13, 32, 181, 206; qualitative, 2–4, 245–48. *See also* interviews

Mexico, 222, 228

microfocus, 13–16, 21, 111–116, 133, 142, 213; and class identity, 177; and contexts, 178; and the left, 165

micro-macro linking: and citizenship, 20,

237–239; by elites, 19–20; causes of, 21, 132–33, 137–38, 164–65; compared to microfocus, 116; defined, 11, 13, 16, 112, 118–20; in Eastern Europe, 232; media and, 24; mentioned, 142, 150, 177, 205, 213; on housing, 81–83, 85; various literatures and, 26–28, 30, 32, 165, 215–19; *See also* consciousness; responsibility of government or state

military, 8; in Argentine history, 35–41, 157, 265n6; and MODIN, 167–70; public opinion about, 169–70, 199–201; as threat to democracy, 201; regime(s), 182, 184, 188, 192–98, 209, 235

Mitnik, Oscar, 99

MODIN (Movement for Dignity and Independence) 165–70, 178, 188, 266n36

MOI (Squatters and Tenants Movement), 65, 68–69, 71–73; views of, 79–80, 117

Mondak, Jeffrey, J., 252n11; and Diana Mutz and Robert Huckfeldt, 23

Mónica, 145–46, 155, 207

Montoya, Silvia, 99

Montserrat, 55, 126–27, 129, 165, 242–43, 257n16; housing in, 59, 64, 69–70

Mora y Araujo, Manuel, xiii, 265n41

Mutz, Diana C., 23–24, 216, 253n22

nationalism, 167, 197

needs, problems with conceptualization of, 88–94

Nelson, Joan, 10, 262n7

Nena, 119–20, 158, 187–88

neoliberalism: interviewees' views about, 31, 106, 151, 176, 192–93, 202; policies, 4, 38, 40–41, 48, 141, 147; populism and, 28–29; public support for, 9–10, 169–70; subsidiarity and, 139–40

Neuquen, 42, 221

nonelites. *See* grassroots, citizens

O'Donnell, Guillermo, 5, 159, 251n3, 269n32

Olivia, 91, 155, 175–76, 183, 207; assets and resources of, 125, 128

Oscar, 112–14, 260n8

Ostiguy, Pierre, 264n19

Oxhorn, Philip, 73, 75, 80–81, 253n26

Pablo, 106, 148, 161, 168, 176, 182, 261n15, assets of, 101, 122, 125

Padelai (Patronato de la Infancia), 55, 61–63,

Padelai (Patronato de la Infancia), *(cont.)*
 90, 259*n36*; activists of, 137, 204, 208,
 217–18, collective action by residents of,
 70–83; Martin and, 67–68
Palacios, Alfredo, 147
participation (political): and democracy
 184–85; and micro-macro linking, 217–18;
 constraints on, 203–6; forms of, 5–7, 17, 20
participation (social). *See* social inclusion
Partido Intransigente (PI), 162–63
Patai, Daphne, 5
Paula, 141, 159, 178, 208, 258*n24*; coping by,
 122, 126
pensions, 42, 49, 172–73; as political interest,
 25, 111, 116, 146, 160, 174; capacity to
 cope with low, 120, 134–35, 214, 221; in
 Eastern Europe, 232
Pepe (Amanda's son), 97, 156–57, 100, 182,
 261*n15*
Perlman, Janice, 260*n4*
Perón, Evita, 36, 151
Perón, Isabel, 37, 200
Perón, Juan Domingo, 36, 128, 147, 161,
 263*n13*; as democrat (per interviewees),
 184, 189, 208; as populist, 31, 219; compared with Menem, 43, 45, 146, 152–54;
 critics' views of, 147; ideology of, 150–53;
 social justice under, 106, 144, 151, 164
Peronism: Amanda's view of, 97–98; as an ideology, 263*n15*; Atilio's view of, 164; discourse and values of, 78, 119, 137; identity
 with, 218; Martin's view of, 79–80; Menem
 and, 150–57; populist appeal of, 219; reputation of, 146–49, 155. *See also* Justicialist
 Party
Peru, 73, 189, 228–32. *See also* Fujimori, Alberto
photography metaphor, xiv, 13–14, 20–21,
 214, 252*n8*
pocketbook: interest in, 22–26, 81, 129; micro-
 macro focus versus, 111, 116, 165; support
 for democracy despite, 199, 235; populism
 literature on, 30. *See also* economic voting
 literature; sociotropism
Poland, 232–35
political culture, 18, 177, 191
political parties: citizens' identities with, 31,
 97–98, 144–49, 229; in-kind goods from,
 127–128; leftist, 160–65; loyalty to, 15, 22,
 152–55, 158; neighborhood activities of, 70,
 263*n5*; social movements and, 75–77, 80–83
political repression, 36–38

political science, 5, 16, 211–12, 185, 189
poor, the: as political actors, 31, 85; attitudes
 toward, 76, 145; concerns expressed for,
 111, 116, 119, 144, 174; fatalism among,
 260*n13*; interests of, 17; rights of, 78
Popular, Justice-based Democracy (PD),
 192–93, 197, 208
populism: EL pattern versus, 191; in Argentina, 3, 31–32, 35, 198; literature on,
 28–33, 67, 218–19, 228, 253*nn24–27*;
 MODIN tries, 166, 170; Peronism as,
 155–56
populists, 216, 218–19, 228–30
Porto, Avelino, 153, 172, 264*n17*,
poverty: Argentine incidence of, 40–43, 47–49,
 222, 256*n28*; conceptualization of, 89–90,
 93–94; Eduardo and Jorge, on their own,
 14–15; heterogeneity of, 210–11; identified
 with housing, 50–51, 70, 97; in U.S., 24;
 line, 97, 259*n1*, 262*n9*; literature on, 7, 88,
 90, 93–94, 132, 262*n16*; measures of, 88–89,
 120–21, 124, 256*n29*; "new" versus "structural," 51, 100, 124, 258*n29*, 260*n10*; politicians' responses to, 172, 221–23; quality of
 democracy and, 203–8; school enrollment
 and, 100
Powers, Denise, and James Cox, 10, 233
priorities, 18, 21, 67, 191, 210–11, 251*n4*
privatizations, 125, 174; in Argentina, 40–41,
 43, 45–46, 255*nn22*, 23; Menem and,
 152–53, 267*n10*
Process of National Reorganization (*Proceso*),
 37, 153. *See also* military regimes; repression
productive revolution, 1, 43, 158, 255*n18*
protests, 220–21, 223
Przeworski, Adam, 8, 234–35
public employees, 98–99, 119–20, 126, 174,
 214; interests of, 25; protests by, 220–22
public opinion polls/surveys in Argentina: on
 confidence in institutions, 39; on corruption, 172; on democracy, 198–200; on Aldo
 Rico, 169–70; on alternatives to Menem
 (1992), 170–72; on Menem, 157, 221; on
 sources of citizens' political attitudes, 144;
 on unemployment, 268*n9*
public opinion polls/surveys, 3–4, 18, 226,
 247, 254*n32*; in Eastern Europe, 235; in U.S.
 on taxes 253*n29*; on Fujimori, 231. *See also*
 public opinion polls/surveys in Argentina
public opinion, 6. *See also* economic voting literature; public opinion polls/surveys

Radical Party: 35–36, 38, 127, 220, 225; interviewees' comments about, 79, 183; reputation of, 147, 158–60, 171–72

Rafael, 124, 194–98, 265n7

Ramón (Hilda's husband), 64, 66, 121

Ranis, Peter, 161, 188, 266n4

Raúl (Gabriela's husband), 90, 153–54, 161–62

regime: distinguished from government, 9, 180–81, 194–96, 198, 201, 231, 235–36. See also legitimacy

relative deprivation: research on, 138

Remmer, Karen, 8–9

repression: political, 36–38

resources, 125–32

responsibility of government or state, 48, 94, 109, 118–20; compared to that of regime, 201; expectations about, 210–214, 216, 237–39; for housing, 66; for unemployment, 25; for welfare and justice, 140–41, 143; in economic voting literature, 23, 215; in macrofocus, 111; obstacles to recognizing, 25–26, 32, 132–33, 136. See also micro-macro linking

Ricardo, 124, 134–35, 261n15

Rico, Aldo, 165–66, 168–70

rights, 25, 78, 83, 85, 93, 99, 116; civil, 39; enforcement of, in Argentina, 38, 207–209

Roberts, Kenneth, 253n28

Rodrigo (Graciela's co-worker), 99

Romania, 235

Rose, Richard and William T. E. Mishler, 235

Rosenthal, Gert, 41

salariazo, 1, 43–44, 47, 158, 221, 255n18. See also wages

Samuel, 101, 106, 151–52, 162–63, 174; housing of, 56, 59

San Telmo, 55–56, 129, 242, 257n16; and Padelai, 62, 76–78, 90; charities in, 126–27; housing in, 59, 69–70; hypothetical newborn in, 102–3, 105–6, 260n12; Menem's visit to, 157; MODIN in, 165, 167; right to live in, 78, 90

Scott, James, 5

security: desire for, 30; home ownership brings, 51–52. See also insecurity

self-help, 14–15; 101–5; 108, 127, 238; feasibility of, 134–36; via grassroots organizations 114, 164; norms about 137, 233

Sen, Amartya, 93–94, 96, 98, 107, 212

shantytowns, 54, 84; compared to other housing, 56, 58, 63, 258n19; housing movement in, 69–70, 75; identity with, 69

Smith, William, 264n16

social exclusion, 66, 90–91, 94, 107–8. See also social inclusion

social inclusion, 93–94, 212–13, 238; and populism, 29–31, 219

social justice: desire for, 65, 140, 174–75, 187–88, 207–8, 214; in macrofocus, 236; in PD and EL patterns, 192–93; Menem's discourse on, 44; Peronist ideal of, 80, 137, 143, 165, 222

social mobility, 25; decline in 34–35, 40–41; populism literature on, 29; Menem's impact on, 106–7. See also San Telmo, hypothetical newborn in

social movements: consciousness-raising by, 72–73, 216–18, 237; literature (mentioned), 6, 22, 111, 136–7; literature (discussed), 26–28, 32–33, 177, 217, 219; non-partisan strategies of, 75–77, 80–83. See also collective action; grassroots organizations; micro-macro linking

social policy, 91, 107, 130–31; food programs, 128–29, 262nn12, 13; Perón's, 36; targeted spending in, 88, 211, 238

sociotropism: as a luxury, 237; compared to microfocus, 111, 115; defined, 22; discussed, 22–28, 230, 252nn12, 13, 15 253nn22, 23; explanations of, 215–17; in interviews 76, 83, 230. See also economic voting literature

solidarity, 127, 137, 143–44

Soña, 106, 182, 261n16

squatters. See casas tomadas; MOI; shanty-towns

state: restructuring of, 44, 119–20, 128

Stepan, Alfred, 9

Stokes, Susan, 10, 73, 80–81, 173, 217, 230

subsidiarity, 3, 19, 140–41, 233

survival, 91–92, 94; civic, 205; different from coping, 262n15

taxes, 160, 175–76; real estate 56, 258n17; U.S. public opinion on, 30

timing: impact on coping capacity, 138–39, 213

Tomás, 119–20, 137, 155–57, 168, 261nn15, 16

Townsend, Peter, 90, 93, 212, 216

trust: across classes, 79–80; of politicians, 76

unemployment, 25, 49, 150; as political inter-
est, 2, 33; capacity to cope with, 128, 227; in
Eastern Europe, 234–35; in 1990s Ar-
gentina, 1–2, 47–48, 220, 222–24, 268n11
Union of the Democratic Center (UCeDé), 46,
151, 166
United Nations Development Program
(UNDP), 5–6, 93–94
United States of America (U.S.), 24–25, 27, 30,
44, 237
Uruguay, 47, 115

values: in Argentine culture, 77–78, 82, 137,
143–44, 176–77; nonmaterialist, 25, 77,
191–92, 197, 209. See also social justice; solidarity

Vicente, 102, 148, 159–60, 174, 183, 261n16
villero, 62, 107
voting: and ideology, 163–64; en blanco, 150,
156; mandatory, 6, 39, 261n3; "sincere,"
163–64, 217

wages: Argentine, 1, 42, 47–49; inequalities in,
107; interviewees on, 150, 160, 166; Latin
American, 41. See coping strategies
Walter, 102, 182, 188, 261n15
Weatherford, M. Stephen, 23, 252n12
Weyland, Kurt, 10, 233, 254n30, 254n31
World Bank, 88, 99, 139–40, 223
World Values Study, 144, 160–61, 241–42,
255n15

Zaller, John, 247, 254n32